DEVELOPING READERS & WRITERS IN THE CONTENT AREAS K-12

SECOND EDITION

DAVID W. MOORE
Arizona State University West

SHARON ARTHUR MOORE
Arizona State University West

PATRICIA M. CUNNINGHAM
Wake Forest University

JAMES W. CUNNINGHAM
University of North Carolina, Chapel Hill

Longman

Developing Readers and Writers in the Content Areas, K–12

Longman, 10 Bank Street, White Plains, N.Y. 10606

Associated companies:
Longman Group Ltd., London
Longman Cheshire Pty., Melbourne
Longman Paul Pty., Auckland
Copp Clark Pitman, Toronto

To our children: **Wendy, Aaron, John, Kevin, and David**

Senior acquisitions editor: Laura McKenna
Development editor: Virginia L. Blanford
Production editor: Linda W. Witzling
Text design adaptation: Jeannette Jacobs
Cover design: Jeannette Jacobs
Text art: Fine Line, Inc.
Photos: Patricia M. Dashiell and John Wedman
Production supervisor: Richard Bretan

Library of Congress Cataloging-in-Publication Data

Developing readers and writers in the content areas / by David W.
    Moore . . . [et al.].—2nd ed.
        p.   cm.
    Includes bibliographical references (p.   ) and index.
    ISBN 0-8013-0467-9
    1. Language arts—Correlation with content subjects.   2. Content
area reading.   I. Moore, David W.
LB1576.D455   1993
428.4′3—dc20   93–19974
                                                                    CIP

4 5 6 7 8 9 10-CRS-979695

CONTENTS

P R E F A C E

Of the many responsibilities that teachers assume, helping students use reading and writing as tools for learning certainly ranks near the top. *Developing Readers and Writers in the Content Areas, K–12* introduces prospective and practicing teachers to this fascinating aspect of education. A special distinction of this book is that it shows how literacy and subject matter instruction can be combined in elementary as well as secondary schools. This distinction is especially valuable because more and more elementary teachers are incorporating literacy instruction with instruction about the world.

Elementary- and secondary-school teachers alike will find this book to be a practical guide. Its engaging prose and numerous examples describe the theory underlying specific teaching practices, which are explained fully. The chapters devoted solely to teachers' journal entries about their content area literacy instruction bring the descriptions to life and show how they fit into the everyday world of the classroom.

Developing Readers and Writers in the Content Areas, K–12 can be used in courses with such titles as Literacy Across the Curriculum and Content Area Reading. Its attention to elementary and secondary teaching concerns makes it appropriate for courses aimed at either audience as well as for courses with a mixture of upper-grade and lower-grade teachers. It is intended for use in undergraduate or postbaccalaureate teacher preparation programs, during staff development activities, and in introductory graduate teacher education courses.

SHARED FEATURES OF THE FIRST AND SECOND EDITIONS

The second edition of *Developing Readers and Writers in the Content Areas, K–12* retains those features of the first edition that our students and colleagues found especially noteworthy. These include:

Integration of Elementary and Secondary Instruction

We chose to address K–12 instruction in this book because learning and teaching processes across the grades are fundamentally similar. We also felt it important to show how literacy and subject matter instruction can be combined even as subject matter becomes more complex and specialized across the grades.

Integration of Reading and Writing

We believe that treating written language as a whole preserves the benefits reading and writing have on each other and on the exploration of subject matter. For this reason, even though separate chapters are devoted to comprehension and writing, each chapter addresses literacy, the combination of reading and writing.

Focus on Basic Learning Processes

Chapter 1 describes nine thinking skills that contribute to learning. The remaining chapters then demonstrate how these processes play out in teachers' instructional methods and students' learning strategies. These processes provide coherence to the numerous suggestions presented in this book.

Thorough Explanations of Key Concepts

We assumed that our audience did not already know what we were presenting, so we sought to develop our concepts clearly and completely. Our goal was to allow ready implementation and adaptation of the teaching practices we presented.

Narrative Accounts of Teaching

Like the first, this second edition contains two parts. Part I includes eight chapters written in expository form; that is, the information is explained in a straightforward, objective fashion. The final four chapters, which make up Part II, follow a nontraditional form for textbooks: They are written in narrative style. Each is a fictional account of how one teacher spends a school year developing readers and writers in the content areas. These narratives are meant to show how teachers juggle the instructional methods presented in Part I. To specify the relation between Parts I and II, we included *locators* in the margins of Part II. Looking up locators in the index will help you find where topics from Part II are explained in Part I.

NEW FEATURES IN THE SECOND EDITION

Scholarship and classroom practices related to content area literacy have changed substantially over the years. In addition, we have realized that some portions of the first edition communicate better than others. To ensure that our readers would keep pace with the field of content area literacy and to improve communication, we included the following in this second edition of *Developing Readers and Writers in the Content Areas, K–12*:

Improved Organization

We shifted the chapters' order of presentation and wrote an entirely new one (Chapter 3, "Learning Independence") to show how teachers move from general to specific concerns. The first three chapters of this edition present a context for content area literacy instruction. The remaining chapters in Part I then present ways to plan daily lessons.

New Chapter: "Learning Independence"

Chapter 3, "Learning Independence," is new to this edition. It describes integrated units, inquiry units, and independent study, specifically addressing issues related to interdisciplinary teaching and student problem solving.

Major Revisions of Original Chapters

Many of the original chapters have been rewritten for accuracy, currency, clarity, and added depth, with many new items placed in the recommended Additional Readings. We completely rewrote and class-tested the chapters on comprehension and writing to facilitate novices' lesson planning. Chapter 2, "Reading Materials," which addresses content area literature, has been revamped to include resources from computer technology, reference works, and multicultural literature.

Expanded Pedagogical Features

New learning aids were placed in Part I of the text to enhance understanding and retention. The following aids are found either at the beginning or the end of each chapter to help you anticipate, review, and elaborate chapter contents:

- *Looking Ahead*, which appears at the beginning of each chapter, presents an overview of that chapter's contents.
- *Key Ideas* are listed at the opening of each chapter, following the Looking Ahead section. They form the main headings for the chapters, indicating the major points within each chapter.
- *Looking Back* summaries occur at the end of each chapter.
- *Add to Your Journal* also appears at the end of each chapter. This learning aid suggests topics to consider and questions to answer when responding to this book in journal form.
- *Additional Readings*, the final section of each chapter, suggests books and articles that amplify the material presented in the chapter.

Along with expanding the learning aids at the beginning and end of the Part I chapters, we interspersed the following learning aids throughout these chapters to promote interaction with the ideas presented:

- *Do It Together* suggests group activities. Small-group collaborative effort can promote learning.
- *Listen/Look and Learn* contains suggestions for checking out chapter contents with students and practicing teachers. It is a reality check for ideas and an opportunity to develop them.
- *Try It Out* encourages application. Learning occurs best when you do something with the ideas you encounter.

Instructor's Manual

The instructor's manual contains many of the extras we use when teaching courses with this text. For each chapter in Part I, the manual contains such features as student projects, questions for essay exams, and transparency masters.

ACKNOWLEDGMENTS

We thank our students and colleagues who have commented on the first and second edition manuscripts of this text. They have sharpened our thinking. We thank the schoolchildren with whom we have worked, especially those in Arizona, Iowa, and North Carolina. They are excellent informants about which literacy tools and teaching methods help them learn about the world. We also thank the following reviewers, whose comments have helped guide this revision:

Diane Barone, University of Nevada, Las Vegas

Janet Bossange, Trinity College

Ruth Davenport, University of Missouri, Columbia

Kris Dixon-Bills, Stephen F. Austin State University

Barbara Edwards, University of North Carolina, Charlotte

Cindy Gillespie, Ball State University

Kathy Hinchman, Syracuse University

Raymond Kimble, University of Scranton

Rosary Lalik, Virginia Polytechnic Institute

Alexandra Leavell, University of North Texas, Denton

Barbara Lewis, University of Alabama, Birmingham

Ruth Loring, Cameron University

Jamie Myers, Pennsylvania State University

Sue Rogers, Averett College

Lynn Smith, Southern Illinois University

Roger Stewart, University of Wyoming

George Strine, Shippensburg University

Diane Truscott, Eastern Montana College

PART I

DEVELOPING READERS AND WRITERS . . .

CHAPTER 1

Content Area Reading and Writing

LOOKING AHEAD

The finest elementary teachers extend their literacy instruction beyond the times set aside specifically for reading and language arts. The finest middle-grade and secondary teachers assume responsibility for supporting their students' literacy efforts when teaching such academic specialties as science, mathematics, social studies, and vocational education. During subject matter study outstanding teachers utilize reading and writing as tools to improve their students' learning of both subject matter and subject-specific literacy strategies. One of the best ways to promote literacy across the curriculum is to capitalize on the thinking processes that underlie reading, writing, and learning. Teachers can plan learning activities that elicit one or more thinking processes when students read and write about subject matter. Such planning must meet the demands of the subject being studied and relate to previous and future lessons.

Content areas are bodies of thought that present ideas about the world or universe in a systematic fashion. Some of the content areas are science, mathematics, and fine arts. Elementary-, middle-, and high-school students acquire an incredible amount of knowledge from studying the content areas. They learn that Confucius was a Chinese philosopher, lizards are reptiles, yeast causes dough to rise, an isosceles triangle has two sides of equal length, and countless other facts. They also discover that basic facts are tied together by subject matter principles. These principles include *interdependence* in social studies, *supply and demand* in economics, *diffusion* in biology and chemistry, and *exponential growth* in mathematics. Such concepts are gained from numerous interactions with multiple sources. This book addresses learning through those interactions that reading and writing in the content areas can provide.

These are the key ideas in this introductory chapter:

1. There are compelling reasons for content area literacy instruction.
2. Reading, writing, and learning require thinking.
3. There are many approaches to content area reading and writing instruction.

THERE ARE COMPELLING REASONS FOR CONTENT AREA LITERACY INSTRUCTION

At this point, you may be wondering about the reason for focusing on literacy in the content areas. "After all," you might think, "shouldn't reading and writing be taught during classes devoted exclusively to those subjects?" If you are a middle- or secondary-school teacher, you also might think that literacy skills should be taught only by elementary teachers: "Shouldn't lower-grade teachers emphasize students' reading and writing so that upper-grade teachers can just present their content?" These reactions are common when people first consider developing readers and writers in the content areas.

There are many reasons for incorporating literacy instruction with subject matter instruction. The reasons we find most compelling are as follows:

1. Reading and writing are tools for learning.
2. Literacy requirements continually increase in school and society.
3. Each mode of expression requires distinct language abilities.
4. Each content area requires distinct language abilities.
5. Readers and writers perform a variety of tasks that require distinct language abilities.
6. Content area teachers can teach content area reading and writing best.

Reading and Writing Are Tools for Learning

Because content area sources and courses consist largely of language, the study of content areas is really the study of language. Postman (1979) presented the case this way:

> Biology is not plants and animals. It is language about plants and animals. History is not events. It is language describing and interpreting events. Astronomy is not planets and stars. It is a way of talking about planets and stars. (p. 165)

Biologists, historians, and astronomers do not work wordlessly; they use language to construct and convey knowledge. Indeed, textbooks, magazine articles, brochures, library books, and other reference materials are important tools for passing on subject matter knowledge and stimulating students to think about the issues of each discipline.

If you still question the importance of literacy as the major learning tool in schooling, think about how many courses you have completed in college without engaging in a quantity of both reading and writing. Because language is such an integral part of every content domain, helping students read and write in a content area is the same as improving their tools for learning in that content area.

Literacy Requirements Continually Increase in School and Society

Literacy requirements increase sharply as students move from elementary to secondary school and as our society moves from an industrial-based to a technical/informational one (Cole, 1990; Resnick, 1987). You will have some

Students integrate reading and writing in order to learn content area information.

students who need only a few suggestions to keep up with these changing requirements and others who need considerable help. Teachers cannot solve all the problems of school and society, but we have the opportunity to assist students at all ability levels in coping with increasing literacy demands.

As students progress through school, they are expected to read more and more expository material. For instance, students read about neighborhood helpers in the primary grades, world geography in the middle grades, and comparative governments in the upper grades. The materials students encounter as they read about these topics becomes increasingly difficult. Figure 1.1 shows excerpts from materials that represent what students might face at successive levels of difficulty. The concepts move from the familiar to the unfamiliar, from the simple to the complex, and from the concrete to the abstract. Upper-grade students often require as much help learning from their more challenging materials as lower-grade students need with their less challenging materials.

Helping students with written language such as that contained in Figure 1.1 is an important teaching role, but what happens when students leave their teachers? What will students do when they have no one to assist them regularly? They must discover how to cope with the continual stream of new, complex ideas in books and other written language they undoubtedly will encounter outside school; they need to learn how to be lifelong learners. To quote a popular aphorism: "Give me a fish and I eat for a day. Teach me to fish and I eat for a lifetime."

Due to the technical/informational changes of our time, graduates require increasingly sophisticated reading and writing abilities. Practically all occupations have been affected by revolutionary changes in technology. Office workers a generation ago relied on manual typewriters, filing cabinets, and single-line telephones; office workers today use word processing programs, computerized databases, computerized multiline telephone systems, fax machines, and electronic mail. Future office workers will need to learn to master technology unheard of today as well as respond to the new demands this will bring. Jobs that call for predictable, simple routines are giving way to work that requires complex problem solving and decision making.

Teaching students how to learn on their own is essential. Students require reading and writing instruction across the curriculum and throughout school because literacy instruction provided during only one part of the day for the first few years of school cannot suffice. Extended subject-specific instruction is needed so that individuals can handle the dramatic changes they will experience in school, in their future workplaces, and in their personal lives.

Each Mode of Expression Requires Distinct Language Abilities

Students need different language abilities to cope with different modes of expression. Two different—yet related—modes of expression are written language and spoken language. Look at any paragraph on this page. We doubt that you have ever heard a spoken conversation in which the words were arranged in a similar way. You have heard people read aloud, but that is just

Basic

Quicksand can swallow a pig, or a human, or even an elephant.

Quicksand often looks like plain wet sand. But it is really a soupy sand with so much water between the grains that you can't stand on it.

If you step into quicksand, you will slowly sink up to your knees. (Mullis & Jenkins, 1990, p. 26)

Intermediate

Have you heard of the National Boxball Association, the Los Angeles boxball team, or Kareem Abdul-Jabbar, the famous boxball player? Or have you ever heard of boxball at all? Well, it is the game that almost was.

Today we call the game basketball, of course, but it almost became known as boxball. (Mullis & Jenkins, 1990, p. 28)

Adept

One of the greatest victories of the Progressive movement has not yet been mentioned. This victory came when women won the right to vote.

The battle for women's suffrage was a long one. Ever since the 1840's, some women had demanded the right to vote. They had hoped to get the vote after the Civil War, but the Fifteenth Amendment gave voting rights only to Black men. A few women ran for President, but they got very few votes. (Mullis & Jenkins, 1990, p. 31)

Advanced

In the years between 1940 and 1960, literature, the arts, and culture in general became increasingly oriented to the many. In an economy of high productivity, deluging millions of people daily with movies, magazines, books, and television programs, American culture achieved a degree of homogeneity never dreamed of before. However, if such cultural homogeneity spelled loss of individuality— which it undoubtedly did—and if mass culture was often produced primarily for profit and only secondarily for aesthetic reasons, nevertheless mass productions of ''art'' made available to millions of people what in previous times had been the privilege only for the aristocratic few. (Mullis & Jenkins, 1990, p. 33)

FIGURE 1.1 Excerpts from Reading Materials at Successive Levels of Difficulty

written language "wired for sound." In conversations, speakers frequently make false starts and use informal and unconventional word choices and grammar. However, when writing, authors typically delete false starts and inappropriate phrases before submitting a finished product; then professional editors polish the text further. Because of these revisions, written language (such as what is on this page) is usually more precise and conventional than spoken language.

Written language is also usually more rigid than speech because it lacks a give-and-take quality. A frown, puzzled expression, or request for clarification on the part of listeners can help speakers tailor their messages to fit their audiences, and listeners often interject their own thoughts and get feedback during a conversation. In this way two or more people jointly articulate one message. Such actions are not ordinarily available to writers and readers. If you do not understand what you are reading, you can reread the words, but you will do so without any helpful feedback from the writer.

Finally, written language is assumptive. Conversations typically occur between people who know one another, and a topic of conversation generally arises after some shared experience, so speakers often know how much knowledge their listeners have about a topic. In contrast, authors do not know exactly who their readers will be, so they cannot fit their messages to the particular needs of each reader. Authors have to assume what their readers already know; sometimes they are correct, and sometimes they are not.

Because of the formal, precise, rigid, and assumptive nature of most written language, students need to do more than simply pronounce words and listen to what they are saying (Olson, 1977). They need special strategies for making sense of the written language about content; these strategies are learned best during the study of content because the material is important to understand for reasons other than just to learn how to read it better.

Two other modes of expression that require distinct strategies are narration and exposition (Spiro & Taylor, 1987). Much literacy instruction for young students is based on simple narrative stories that engage interest and attention at a personal level. The stories contain imaginative literary structures. Notice the emotion of the following sentence:

His life began veering out of control last winter.

If this sentence began a passage, you would be prepared for a story that invited emotional involvement. You would anticipate being drawn into the narrative, participating vicariously in the character's life, and receiving an account of why the person's life was out of control. The episodes that advance the story line would connect in ways that reflect real-life situations.

Unlike narrative stories, expository writing analyzes the world through an objective, often abstract, perspective. Consider the following sentence:

Large bodies of water affect the weather of their nearby regions.

If this sentence began a passage, you would expect a detached, factual presentation to follow. The passage probably would contain facts about water undergoing temperature change more slowly than land, and it would describe how those temperature differences affect the atmosphere. Expository writing tends to hold readers at a neutral, distant level.

Because expository writing is a common mode of expression in most content areas, students need help with it if they are to benefit from the ideas represented in that exposition. As with the special demands of written language in general, subject matter teachers can do much to help students become proficient with expository writing.

Each Content Area Requires Distinct Language Abilities

Different disciplines present distinct perspectives on the world (King & Brownell, 1966). Think how various specialists might perceive a large boulder they encounter during a walk in a meadow: A paleontologist might look for fossils in order to learn about the prehistoric plant and animal life of the area; an anthropologist might look for pictographs to obtain greater insight about ancient cultures; a sculptor might search for the inspiration to compose an original piece; and a metallurgist might analyze the rock to determine what it revealed about the metallic elements in the surrounding area.

To further appreciate differences among the content areas, read the following brief samples of subject matter text:

Cells enclose protoplasm, the substance of life. Protoplasm consists of two parts. The nucleus is the more solid central part, and the cytoplasm is the softer, more liquid part. The bulk of protoplasm is made up of carbon, hydrogen, oxygen, and nitrogen.

In 1215, a group of barons forced King John of England to sign the Magna Carta. The barons wanted to restore their privileges; however, the Magna Carta grounded constitutional government in political institutions for all English-speaking people.

An angle is the union of two rays that do not lie on the same line. When the sum of the measure of two angles is 90°, the angles are complementary; when the sum of the measure is 180°, the angles are supplementary.

The technical terms in these passages—such as *protoplasm, constitutional government*, and *sum*—usually refer to specific subjects. Other terms—such as *cell, ground, angle*, and *ray*—have different meanings in different content areas. In addition, these passages, like the analyses of the boulder in the meadow described above, present diverse perspectives on the world. The science sample describes the structure of a substance, the social studies sample explains the outcome of a human action, and the math sample presents measurements. The first piece explores the world of nature, the second discusses human actions, and the third concerns spatial relations. Students need help learning to manage the distinct literacy demands of the numerous content areas.

Readers and Writers Perform a Variety of Tasks That Require Distinct Language Abilities

Readers and writers perform many types of tasks (Brice-Heath, 1980; Britton, 1978; Mickulecky, 1982). Three general kinds of literacy tasks are experiencing, doing, and learning. We usually read to experience when we read novels, short stories, comics, and other materials that provide a pleasurable escape. Being in the middle of a good book and knowing that several chapters are still to come is surely one of life's basic enjoyments. We usually write to experience when we compose letters to our friends and family, confide in personal diaries and journals, or produce creative pieces. Reading and writing to experience occur whenever we read or write without expecting utilitarian benefits.

Students explore their feelings and reactions to classroom experiences by writing in journals.

We also read and write to do. This general task involves completing procedures that require literacy. Following directions to operate an appliance, order or prepare a meal, or assemble a toy frequently requires reading to do. Completing an application, responding to a memo with one of your own, and filling out a form are examples of both reading and writing to do. On-the-job expectations often require this type of reading and writing.

Reading and writing to learn is the third general literacy task. We gather and store vast amounts of knowledge and ideas from reading and writing both in and out of school. As students progress through school and begin to read books and magazines they select themselves, reading and writing become increasingly powerful tools for their learning about the world.

The three general literacy tasks—experiencing, doing, and learning—tap different abilities. For instance, experiencing a joke is not the same as learning it. All of us have heard a joke, laughed readily, and remembered the experience; but we might have forgotten the details of the joke when we tried to retell it. We experienced the joke superbly but learned it poorly. Furthermore, reading and writing to learn assumes that individuals will encounter unfamiliar concepts. Reading and writing about something with which you are familiar is easier than reading and writing about something with which you are unfamiliar. Your comprehension and retention of a passage about a favorite celebrity probably would exceed what you would learn from a passage about an obscure mathematical theorem. When students encounter unfamiliar concepts to learn and elaborate procedures to perform, they will often benefit from your assistance.

Content Area Teachers Can Teach Content Area Reading and Writing Best

The reasons for content area reading and writing instruction presented so far emphasize the challenges students encounter. Students will meet increasingly challenging materials and tasks as they progress through their school grades and subjects, careers, and personal lives. To be prepared to meet these demands, they require ongoing literacy instruction, and content area teachers can best provide much of it.

Students seem most receptive to receiving help when they need it to accomplish specific assignments. For example, teaching students to take notes about social studies concepts seems most appropriate when they need to understand and remember these concepts for a test. Teaching students how to solve mathematics word problems is done best in math class when they are expected to solve these problems. Students who are taught how to take notes or solve math word problems in a reading or an English class frequently lack motivation and have difficulty transferring what they were taught to other classes.

Content area teachers also have insights into their specialties that reading or English teachers lack. People who want help interpreting tax forms typically go to tax preparers rather than reading teachers. Tax preparers are the logical choice because these individuals know the special vocabulary of taxation, the structure of the materials, and generally what it takes to make sense of the forms. In brief, content area teachers are in the best position to teach students how to read and write in their particular specialties.

DO IT TOGETHER

The preceding section presented six reasons for promoting reading and writing during subject matter study. As a pair or a group, list these reasons and produce personal examples to illustrate each. For instance, how have you used reading and writing as a tool for learning? What experiences have you had with increased literacy requirements? After producing your list, compare it with that of another pair or group. Do you understand each of these six reasons for content area literacy instruction? Did your pair or group think of another reason for content area literacy instruction?

READING, WRITING, AND LEARNING REQUIRE THINKING

Since antiquity, philosophers and learning theorists have attempted to identify the processes of thinking. Countless books and articles have been written on this subject, with countless thinking processes suggested. The nine processes listed below account for a large share of the cognitive activity involved in most reading, writing, and learning. Our selection of these nine was shaped by many influences; sources that we believe to be especially valuable presentations of thinking processes are listed in the Additional Readings at the end of this chapter.

Nine Thinking Processes

Call up	Form an image
Connect	Monitor
Predict	Evaluate
Organize	Apply
Generalize	

Before you read further about the thinking processes that will help your students develop as they read and write about your subject matter, think back to your midteens when you were preparing for your driver's license test. You probably obtained a copy of your state's driving manual and sat down to learn the driving rules, regulations, and suggested operating techniques. As the nine thinking processes are described in this section, think about the processes you went through back then to learn the information in the manual.

Call Up

Most likely, you began learning the rules of the road when you were a child, sitting buckled into your seat belt in the back seat of the family car during trips and outings. You absorbed a lot of information about driving a car in this country. You noticed, subconsciously perhaps, that the driver of the car sits in a particular seat and performs a sequence of activities to make the car start and keep it moving along the road safely and at a desirable speed. You also noticed that certain signs cause a driver to respond in certain ways. You came to know that red means "stop" and green means "go" before you entered kindergarten.

As a teenager studying the driver's manual, you began to *call up* all those insights and bits and pieces of information about driving that you had absorbed over the years. Without that background knowledge and experience to build upon, learning how to drive would have been nearly impossible to accomplish in the relatively short time you took. Calling up what you already knew about road signs, for example, would have allowed you to skim through that section because the information was so familiar. You probably needed to concentrate on just the few unusual signs that you had not yet learned. The point of reminding you of this aspect of your experience with the driving manual is that when confronting any new topic, readers and writers call up what they already know so they can interact with the topic as efficiently as possible.

Connect

Learning also involves having to *connect* information. When you encounter a presentation of ideas organized around a topic with which you already have some experience, you connect the new input with what you already know. You call up previous knowledge and experience and either add to the information there or change the information to accommodate the new data. Connecting information is a matter of relating what is being presented to what is already known. As such, connecting requires calling up but goes beyond it.

Think again about your state driver's manual. You may never have considered that the road signs you had seen over the years were color-coded. You did know, however, that whenever drivers see a stop sign they are required to come to a complete stop at the designated location. What you learned upon reading your manual was that whenever you saw a red sign, no matter what shape it was or what message it contained, your basic thought should be to stop. Do Not Enter, Wrong Way, and No Left Turn signs are all red. While studying your manual, you might have called up your prior knowledge that a red light signals a stop and related that knowledge to the new fact that any red sign means movement is prohibited. Retrieving old information from your mind is calling up; bridging old information with new information is connecting.

Predict

When you first obtained your copy of the manual and began to thumb through it, you were trying to *predict* what it had to teach you as well as what it contained that you already knew. You engaged in this process automatically, without necessarily being aware of it. For instance, you might have thought there would be sections on starting the car and economizing on gas. In reality, however, you probably found practically no information on those topics. Upon seeing in the manual headings about road signs, on the other hand, you probably expected to find information about their shapes and messages, and your examination of the manual verified that prediction.

Like connecting, the predicting process requires that you call up information you already possess. If you had no information to call up, making predictions would be impossible. Again, you can call up without predicting anything; you cannot predict without calling up what you already know. You almost never simply call up information; generally you call up information so that you can do something with it. In the case of predicting, as you opened the driver's manual you anticipated what you might find there. You based those predictions upon any prior knowledge that you could call up about driving and learning to drive.

Predicting involves thinking about what is to come, thus giving you a head start on learning. Predicting also tends to motivate you to get involved with the material. For example, why do movie theaters show previews of coming attractions? This motivates customers to come back to the theater.

Organize

To have made sense of the driver's manual, you needed to *organize* the information presented there. You probably arranged the information according to some type of framework, perhaps according to the headings you found in the manual. Most manuals are divided into chapters with such headings as Parking, Turns, and Licenses. Within each chapter are headings that group the information into related subsets. A chapter on hazardous driving conditions might include such topics as driving at night, driving in adverse weather, and driving under the influence of alcohol and other drugs. Readers and writers who analyze information, grouping it into meaningful categories, go far in making sense of the world.

Generalize

Readers and writers *generalize* when they note similarities. They form a generalization by noting trends, commonalities, or patterns among specifics; they discover the rule or principle that unites various phenomena. For instance, when you read the Right of Way section in the driver's manual, you probably found much information about yielding to oncoming vehicles when turning left, yielding to pedestrians whether or not they are in crosswalks, and yielding to emergency vehicles. After reading these laws, you might have concluded this: "The pattern in all this information about yielding right of way is 'Safety first.' Preventing accidents is the thread common to these laws." Knowing this generalization helped you tie together all the right-of-way laws, which otherwise might have been a meaningless assortment of details to be memorized by rote.

When you read a passage, you might need to infer generalizations on your own or might note the generalizations that the author provides. When you write, you may explicitly state or merely imply your generalizations.

Generalizing and organizing are related thinking processes since the ability to organize ideas into similar groupings underlies most generalizing. Generalizing often consists of labeling or describing what you or someone else has organized into a cluster. Organizing sometimes means placing ideas under headings or descriptions that you or someone else has generalized.

Form an Image

Engaging your senses internally and cognitively as you read and write adds to the learning experience and makes it more memorable. This process often consists of having to *form an image*. Visual images are used most frequently, although other sense "images" certainly come into play. Vicariously seeing, feeling, hearing, smelling, or tasting what is described in print can all help you think deeply and richly about the ideas you are reading or writing about. Of course, imaging subsumes calling up but goes beyond it.

Imagery may have helped you with your driver's manual. Think about the part of the manual that discussed the appropriate distances to maintain between two vehicles in motion. Safe following distances vary according to how fast you are traveling. For instance, at 50 miles per hour a safe following distance is 84 yards. You could easily have forgotten these figures if there had been no way to transform them. Thus, you might have imagined a 100-yard football field and then mentally placed a car at one goal line and your car 84 yards down the field. This visual image would have helped you remember the appropriate distance to keep between two vehicles traveling at 50 miles per hour.

Imagery also may have helped you deal with the information about turning at intersections. You probably studied the abstract diagrams and discussions about turning and visualized particular instances of those procedures. In your mind's eye you might have run a little motion picture of pulling up to a multiple-lane intersection and then executing the appropriate turn.

Monitor

Throughout your study of the driver's manual, you needed to *monitor* how well you were doing with the information. Internally, and probably subconsciously, you asked yourself, "Am I understanding this? Am I getting what I need? Does this make sense?" Part of monitoring is checking internally to determine how well your learning or thinking is progressing.

The other part of monitoring involves repair work. If you sense a problem with what you are trying to learn, then you need to do something about it. If their understanding breaks down, good thinkers stop, identify the source of the difficulty, and try to get over that difficulty. For instance, when you got to the part in your driver's manual about different kinds of licenses, you might have plunged into information about chauffeur's license expirations, the minimum age for driving mopeds, and the cost of instruction permits. Eventually you realized that you were being overwhelmed, so you stopped and thought, "Now, what do I need from this section?" You might have determined that the renewal period and minimum age for a regular operator's license was all that was important, so you selected that particular information for careful study before moving on to the next section. Monitoring your learning by assessing its status and repairing breakdowns is a crucial thinking process.

Evaluate

When you *evaluate*, you judge the author's writing style and the content being presented. Judgments about writing style frequently relate to the clarity of the presentation. Was your driver's manual easy to understand, or did you find it confusing? Was the information explained clearly?

When you evaluate, you also judge the contents of the passage. As you read your driver's manual, you may have encountered a section on safety belts under the heading Equipment. "What's that doing there?" may have been your response. "Are there laws requiring me to wear safety belts in my state? Why should I have to read about them?" As you read on, you might have learned some new information about the value of safety belts and seen why that section was included in the manual.

On the other hand, you may have discovered in the back of your manual a section on recording car expenses. If you had no plans to keep track of your expenses, you might have decided that those pages should not have been included.

Evaluating reading material is important for learning because it is engaging. Readers and writers who decide about the style of writing and the value of information strengthen their grasp of the information. Those who simply accept information without examining it critically are at a disadvantage.

The difference between evaluating and monitoring is clear cut. Whenever you assess the quality of what you are reading or what you have written, you are evaluating. Whenever you assess the quality of your reading or writing process while you are actively engaged in it, you are monitoring.

Apply

The ninth thinking process is *apply.* The reasons you plowed through the driver's manual were so that you could pass the driver's test, obtain a license, and get behind the wheel of a car. When you finally got behind the wheel, you were required to remember all the rules and regulations: how fast to go on various streets under various conditions, who has the right of way in different situations, and what the road signs mean. Applying is adapting what you have learned to anticipated or actual situations.

When you apply knowledge, you select the most appropriate response from all the ones you have acquired. As was noted at the beginning of this chapter, this book is meant to help you teach students to read and write in the content areas. Our goal is to help you plan and actually use (i.e., apply) the thinking processes discussed here in classroom situations.

Thinking Is Complex

Because thinking is a complex phenomenon, you should keep in mind several points about the nine processes presented above. One point is that our labels and descriptions overlap those presented by many other authors. Fostering thinking is a time-honored common goal among educators, and many types of thinking have been discussed. The professional literature about thinking contains such terms as *hypothesizing, speculating, inferring, extrapolating, elaborating, problem solving, synthesizing, analyzing, creating,* and *categorizing. Metacognition* frequently is used to denote a special constellation of thinking processes considered to be above the others. Indeed, our list contains many of the cognitive behaviors presented in the classic Bloom's *Taxonomy of Educational Objectives* (1956). The essential thinking processes presented in this chapter are listed below alongside the ones presented by Bloom and his colleagues. We believe that the nine terms and descriptions of mechanisms presented in this chapter cover the most important types of thinking. Our terms are often synonymous with several others available, and ours share most of the characteristics of the others. Our list provides a solid basis for fostering thinking through content area reading and writing instruction.

Essential Thinking Processes	*Bloom's* Taxonomy of Educational Objectives
Call up	Knowledge
Connect	Comprehension
Predict	Application
Organize	Analysis
Generalize	Synthesis
Form an image	Evaluation
Monitor	
Evaluate	
Apply	

A second point about our essential thinking processes is that presenting them separately implies that each is isolated from the others. And listing them in order, from call up to apply, suggests that thinkers do first one, then another, then a third, and so on, in a prescribed sequence. But these thinking processes do not stand alone and are not used in a rigid order. Instead, each thinker integrates the processes differently according to the demands of each situation. Students might form images and predict upcoming information simultaneously; they might evaluate the first few sentences of what they read or write, organize their thoughts, and continue processing the information. Our point is that students combine thinking processes and emphasize certain ones at different times in order to conceptualize what they are reading or writing about.

Third, students at all grade levels can benefit from assistance with the thinking processes outlined above. To paraphrase Bruner's famous quotation from *The Process of Education* (1977): We begin with the hypothesis that any thinking process can be taught effectively in some intellectually honest form to any child at any stage of development. This principle means that organizing, for example, can be taught in the primary- as well as the high-school grades. Primary-school children might categorize pictures of animals according to those that fly, those that walk, and those that swim; high-school students might classify one-celled life forms according to their kingdom, phylum, class, order, family, genus, and species. Similarly, very young children can learn to evaluate by thinking about a question like, "Did a real boy named Jack climb a beanstalk and meet a giant?" Older students can ponder how well *Lord of the Flies* illustrates basic human nature. In brief, schoolchildren seem to share the same mental processes (Donaldson, 1978). Students from kindergarten through twelfth grade call up, connect, predict, organize, generalize, form an image, monitor, evaluate, and apply with varying degrees of sophistication. This book addresses K–12 reading and writing because of the fundamental similarity of these processes across the various grades.

Fourth, our list provides a solid basis for fostering thinking through content area reading and writing instruction. Knowing about thinking processes allows you to plan good learning experiences. You can continually ask yourself how you can provide opportunities for students to actively call up, connect, predict, and so on. This book explains how to plan activities that engage students in these thinking processes.

Finally, motivation underlies thinking. Students who become involved with ideas and independently seek knowledge and experience have a distinct advantage over unmotivated students. Think about how well your education proceeded when you had an intense desire to know something as opposed to when you were not interested in the subject. Many adolescents who perform poorly in school do amazingly well with the relevant, compelling demands of their driver's manual. Teachers should remember that promoting students' motivation to learn and think is at least as important as developing their thinking processes.

LISTEN/LOOK AND LEARN

Visit a class during a subject matter lesson or tape-record a lesson that you present. Pretend that you are a student during this activity and list the chief thinking processes you would use. Were thinking processes elicited regularly throughout the lesson? Which were most frequent? Which were least frequent? What could be done to elicit the thinking processes that were not elicited?

THERE ARE MANY APPROACHES TO CONTENT AREA READING AND WRITING INSTRUCTION

So far this chapter has presented reasons for content area reading and writing instruction and described thinking processes to be promoted therein. This final section focuses on teaching approaches: How can you present reading, writing, and thinking strategies along with subject matter? How can you teach students to use the nine thinking processes?

This section presents four approaches to the extremely complex but rewarding job of teaching content: functional instruction, fading, personalized inquiry, and collaborative learning. These approaches are general ways to provide students opportunities to interact with ideas.

Functional Instruction

Teachers frequently grapple with the difficult question of *when* to teach specific aspects of reading, writing, and thinking: When should students be taught to organize printed information? When should they be taught to apply what they are encountering in print? When should connections be made between familiar and unfamiliar concepts? Instruction is *functional* when it occurs as needed for students to complete an important task (Moore, 1986). For instance, if a teacher wants students to write essays on a particular topic, then he or she should make sure that each student knows how to produce an essay. If a teacher wants students to take notes, then he or she must make sure that each student knows how to do so. If students are having trouble visualizing a certain concept, then the teacher shows how to form an appropriate image. If students are having trouble with a long word, then the teacher points out the meaningful parts of that word. Functional instruction occurs whenever a teacher presents reading, writing, and thinking strategies as students need them to succeed with subject matter expectations.

Content area reading and writing instruction is isolated, or not functional, when it is divorced from any subject matter that students are expected to learn. To illustrate, a teacher might present lists of random words (e.g., *polyphonic, defoliate, pyrometer*) and explain their prefixes, roots, and suffixes. This instruction would be isolated because the words were selected to demonstrate word parts; they were not related to a topic being studied at the time. A teacher who wants to provide functional instruction on prefixes, roots, and suffixes waits until such items appear in the subject matter. For example, the prefixes *kilo-, milli-,* and *centi-* are presented functionally when taught during a study of the metric system.

Fading

Fading is an approach that answers *how* to deliver reading, writing, and thinking instruction. It calls for a teacher to demonstrate the processes he or she wants students to engage in and then to diminish assistance gradually until the students can perform the processes by themselves. Fading is an essential part of strategy instruction and is a long-term endeavor.

Fading is used extensively when teaching a sport. Imagine that you are an accomplished tennis player and have a friend who would like to learn to play. What would you do? You probably would first focus on a particular aspect of the game, perhaps how to grip the racquet. You would *demonstrate* the correct grip and talk about it at the same time. You might say, "Watch how I grip my racquet. I hold it with one hand and pretend I am shaking hands with the leather. Your grip should be like a firm handshake." The instruction at this demonstration stage involves a teacher performing the task while describing what he or she is doing.

After demonstrating the grip, you would have your friend try it. Not expecting immediate success, you might say, "Now it's your turn. Give it a try, and I'll be here to help you get it right. Believe me, it takes a while to get the hang of this." You would provide feedback right away about the grip your friend produces, pointing out specific things that were right or needed to be improved. You also would encourage your friend to keep trying. This stage of the fading process is called *guided practice*. You oversee the learner's attempts to perform what you have just demonstrated. Keep in mind that some reading and writing processes, like some tennis behaviors, take only

Teachers demonstrate what students are to practice and apply.

brief amounts of time for demonstration and guided practice and others take quite a while.

Finally, after your friend grips the tennis racquet reasonably well, you would have him or her apply the grip to hit some balls. You might have your friend grip the racquet and hit a ball up, down, or against a backboard; you two might hit the ball back and forth; or you might play a set and keep score. Your purpose would be to help your friend apply the grip in actual tennis situations. This is the stage of *independent application*. You provide realistic opportunities for learners to use what has been demonstrated and practiced.

You might never teach anyone how to play tennis, but you might teach students how to take notes from a passage in your content area. To teach note taking through fading, first select a passage that seems within the grasp of your students. Then demonstrate how you would take notes from the passage by actually producing notes and explaining how you decided to write what you did. Next, guide students as they practice note taking. Direct them to a portion of the passage, telling them to write notes about it like you just did. Compare your notes with some of the students' notes and have students compare their notes with one another's. Provide feedback about how they are doing. Eventually, in order to promote application, direct students to record their notes in a notebook and check them occasionally.

Fading moves from demonstration to guided practice to independent application as teachers fade out and students fade in. Teachers show students how to perform a task and then gradually move back so the students can do it on their own. The aim is to develop student independence.

Personalized Inquiry

Another approach that answers *how* to provide content area reading and writing instruction is personalized inquiry. This approach calls for a teacher to set the stage for learning to occur and help as needs arise (Joyce & Weil, 1986). A teacher who follows personalized inquiry plays mainly a supportive, facilitative role in students' learning.

Many people who have learned to play tennis did so with practically no faded, direct instruction. Tennis courts, racquets, balls, and partners were available, and people who wanted to learn to play jumped right in. These people persisted with the game because they found it fascinating, and they figured out much of it through trial and error. They sought help when they faced problems they could not solve ("How do you hit a consistent first serve?"), watched others, and asked questions. Immersing themselves in the game and solving problems as they came up, these individuals took the lead in deciding what they wanted to learn.

There are many ways to use personalized inquiry in the study of the content areas. For example, a teacher designates a topic like the solar system, digestive tract, or constitutional government, and students choose which aspects to investigate. The teacher sets out various materials for students to browse through in their spare time. Library books, magazines, textbooks, encyclopedias, filmstrips, interviews, and field trips are employed. Students discover reading and writing strategies because they are motivated to learn, because they own the topic under investigation.

The personalized inquiry approach to instruction gives students much responsibility. They receive many opportunities to determine for themselves what specific aspect of a topic to study and what reading and writing task they need help performing. Teachers actively work to motivate students and provide resources that answer their questions.

Collaborative Learning

A fourth approach to instruction, collaborative learning, leads students to cooperate in order to learn. It offers systematic practical techniques for students when working together in small groups or in pairs. Collaborative learning is nearly synonymous with cooperative learning; we prefer the term *collaborative* because it signals any plan that facilitates and promotes peer interaction.

Collaborative learning goes beyond simply grouping students and assigning a task to be completed. One key feature of this approach involves individual and group accountability. Students engaged in collaborative learning are accountable for their own learning as well as that of their teammates. Success happens only when everyone on a team achieves a goal. For instance, if students are to learn the meanings of a list of vocabulary terms, individuals work to ensure that they and their partners know the words.

Individuals' performance with the word meanings would be recorded along with the group's performance. Two scores rather than one would be generated.

A second key to collaborative learning is the instruction students receive about how to act in a group. Before collaborative learning procedures were codified, teachers typically grouped students and reminded them to "act right" before presenting a task. Now that collaborative learning structures are explicit, teachers typically have a group demonstrate positive interactions (e.g., clarifying tasks, praising others, encouraging others to participate) so students will do the same when they work together. Teachers specify particular group interactions to be emphasized and comment on the interactions during and after group work. This instruction in group processes seems to enhance group productivity.

Collaborative learning is a specific instructional approach that fits either fading or personalized inquiry. As a part of fading, it is appropriate during the guided practice and independent application stages. To illustrate, a teacher first might show students how to summarize what they read. The students would form collaborative groups for guided practice and later for independent application of their summarizing strategies. Individuals would help one another refine their abilities to get the gist of what they read. If personalized inquiry were being emphasized, students working in small groups could select topics to research, brainstorm what they already knew about the topics, bring together information, and devise formats to share what they learned.

Collaborative learning seems to enhance students' social, emotional, and attitudinal dispositions along with their academic achievement (Slavin, 1990). Students who work together as equals to accomplish something frequently improve their self-esteem, tolerance of racial and ethnic differences, and enjoyment of their classes. Indeed, racial integration was part of the impetus for designing this approach. As American business and manufacturing turn to site-based management and shared decision making, the importance of collaborative learning in the schools is underscored.

LISTEN/LOOK AND LEARN

Observe a subject matter class for one period, keeping in mind the four approaches to content area literacy instruction described here. Note instances of these approaches during the class period. Describe what, if anything, the teacher did relative to functional instruction, fading, personalized inquiry, and collaborative learning.

LOOKING BACK

Developing students' reading, writing, and thinking abilities in the content areas is one of the schools' major responsibilities, and content area teachers can be the most effective agents in accomplishing this goal. Focusing on

Collaborative learning enhances social dispositions and academic achievement.

thinking processes enables teachers to plan and deliver learning activities that enhance content area literacy and content acquisition. Students who call up, connect, organize, and apply, among other processes, go far in bringing active thought to their schooling. Academic experiences that build these processes can be planned within a framework built on functional instruction, fading, personalized inquiry, and/or collaborative learning. These are the key ideas presented in this chapter: (1) There are compelling reasons for content area literacy instruction; (2) reading, writing, and learning require thinking; and (3) there are many approaches to content area reading and writing.

ADD TO YOUR JOURNAL

Think about the three key ideas of this chapter. Use the nine thinking processes to compose a response. You can *organize* the chapter by summarizing or outlining it. You can *connect* the chapter's information with past experiences and report events that are associated with what is presented. You also can *evaluate* the chapter and pass judgment on the writing style and content. What is your opinion of this book so far? Finally, you could begin to *apply* what you have read. How do you plan to use what you have learned so far? What applications do you foresee between what has been discussed in this chapter and your future teaching?

REFERENCES

Brice-Heath, S. (1980). The functions and uses of literacy. *Journal of Communication, 30,* 123–133.

Britton, J. (1978). The functions of writing. In C. Cooper & L. Odell (Eds.), *Research on composing* (pp. 13–28). Urbana, IL: National Council of Teachers of English.

Bruner, J. (1977). *The process of education.* Cambridge, MA: Harvard University Press.

Cole, N. S. (1990). Conceptions of educational achievement. *Educational Researcher, 19*(3), 2–7.

Donaldson, M. (1978). *Children's minds.* New York: W. W. Norton.

Joyce, B., & Weil, M. (1986). *Models of teaching* (3rd ed.). Englewood Cliffs, NJ: Prentice Hall.

King, A., & Brownell, J. (1966). *The curriculum and the disciplines of knowledge.* New York: John Wiley.

Mikulecky, L. (1982). Job literacy: The relationship between school preparation and workplace actuality. *Reading Research Quarterly, 17,* 400–419.

Moore, D. W. (1986). Laura Zirbes and progressive reading instruction. *Elementary School Journal, 86,* 663–672.

Mullis, I. V. S., & Jenkins, L. B. (1990). *The reading report card, 1971–88.* Princeton, NJ: National Assessment of Educational Progress, Educational Testing Service.

Olson, D. B. (1977). From utterance to text: The bias of language in speech and writing. *Harvard Educational Review, 47,* 257–281.

Postman, N. (1979). *Teaching as a conserving activity.* New York: Delacorte.

Resnick, L. (1987). *Education and learning to think.* Washington, DC: National Academy Press.

Slavin, R. E. (1990). *Cooperative learning.* Englewood Cliffs, NJ: Prentice Hall.

Spiro, R. J., & Taylor, B. M. (1987). On investigating children's transition from narrative to expository text: The multidimensional nature of psychological text classification. In R. J. Tierney, P. L. Anders, & J. N. Mitchell (Eds.), *Understanding readers' understanding* (pp. 77–93). Hillsdale, NJ: Erlbaum.

ADDITIONAL READINGS

The following report reviews the professional and research literature devoted to content area reading instruction that was published during the first half of the twentieth century; it presents the thinking of the time that promoted content area reading instruction and describes the issues that continue to confront educators:

Moore, D. W.; Readence, J. E.; & Rickelman, R. (1983). An historical exploration of content area reading instruction. *Reading Research Quarterly, 18,* 419–438.

Many methods textbooks focus on content area reading instruction in secondary schools; the following two are noteworthy:

Readence, J. E.; Bean, T. W.; & Baldwin, R. S. (1989). *Content area reading: An integrated approach* (3rd ed.). Dubuque, IA: Kendall/Hunt.

Vacca, R. T., & Vacca, J. L. (1994). *Content area reading* (4th ed.). Glenview, IL: Scott, Foresman.

The following article presents a rationale for attending to literacy in the content areas that emphasizes the role of reading and writing as tools for learning:

McKenna, M. C., & Robinson, R. D. (1990). Content literacy: A definition and implications. *Journal of Reading, 34,* 184–186.

These are some classic and some modern references that are helpful in specifying the thought processes essential for learning content area information:

Ausubel, D. P. (1968). *Educational psychology: A cognitive view.* New York: Holt, Rinehart & Winston.

Bloom, B. S. (Ed.). (1956). *Taxonomy of educational objectives. Handbook I: Cognitive domain.* New York: McKay.

Bransford, J. (1979). *Human cognition: Learning, understanding, and remembering.* Belmont, CA: Wadsworth.

Collins, C. & Mangieri, J. N. (Eds.). (1992). *Teaching thinking: An agenda for the twenty-first century.* Hillsdale, NJ: Erlbaum.

Dewey, J. (1910). *How we think.* Boston: D. C. Heath.

James, W. (1925). *Talks to teachers on psychology, and to students on some of life's ideals.* London: Longman.

Marzano, R. J. (1991). Language, the language arts, and thinking. In J. Flood, J. M. Jensen, D. Lapp, & J. R. Squire (Eds.), *Handbook of research and teaching the English language arts* (pp. 559–586). New York: Macmillan.

Nickerson, R. S. (1988). On improving thinking through instruction. In E. Z. Rothkopf (Ed.), *Review of research in education* (Vol. 15) (pp. 3–57). Washington, DC: American Educational Research Association.

Segal, J. W.; Chipman, S. F.; & Glaser, R. (Eds.). (1985). *Thinking and learning skills* (Vol. 1). Hillsdale, NJ: Erlbaum.

Smith, F. (1990). *To think.* New York: Teachers College Press.

Stroud, J. B. (1956). *Psychology in education.* New York: Longman, Green.

Swartz, R. J., & Perkins, D. N. (1989). *Teaching thinking: Issues and approaches.* Pacific Grove, CA: Midwest Publications.

Weinstein, C. E., & Mayer, R. E. (1985). The teaching of learning strategies. In M. C. Wittrock (Ed.), *Handbook of research on teaching* (3rd ed.) (pp. 315–327). New York: Macmillan.

Collaborative learning stresses cooperation among students; these sources (as well as Slavin [1990] listed under References) describe the mechanics of beginning and maintaining collaborative learning groups as well as the outcomes to expect:

Johnson, D. W., & Johnson, R. (1987). *Learning together and alone* (2nd ed.). Englewood Cliffs, NJ: Prentice Hall.

Johnson, D. W.; Johnson, R.; & Holubec, E. (1986). *Circles of learning* (rev. ed.). Edina, MN: Interaction Book Co.

Webb, N. M. (1982). Student interaction and learning in small groups. *Review of Educational Research, 52,* 421–445.

C H A P T E R   2
Reading Materials

LOOKING AHEAD

Publishers regularly flood the market with print and nonprint instructional materials. Students deserve access to many of these materials to promote the subject matter and literacy learning required today. Students who regularly use brochures, encyclopedias, periodicals, word processing programs, informational library books, and textbooks have an advantage over those who must rely on a single source of information. These materials can foster advanced thinking as well as positive values in our multicultural society. Having access to various reading materials should be complemented by receiving opportunities to respond to these materials in various ways. Students who produce collages, bring to class representative objects, dramatize scenes, and write and talk about what they are reading have an advantage over those who respond in only one way.

When you tour a new location, you might travel by car using different types of roads. You might use freeways, divided and undivided highways, residential streets, and unpaved trails. These roads serve different functions while allowing you to explore and learn about an area. Similarly, you and your students have access to many paths during subject matter study. For example, when you use print, you might employ library books, magazines, newspapers, computer technology, and textbooks.

Think of traveling through your state via different types of roads. Freeways get you through the territory quickly and efficiently. Freeway planners did not design routes to show off the surroundings or develop people's thinking but to move people through the area with maximum speed. Freeways traverse only a small part of the territory within your state; if you want to get to a special area of interest—such as a small town, a lake, a state park, or a historical site—you most likely would use a freeway for only part of your trip. A freeway might speed your journey to a certain point, but it will rarely take you directly to where you want to go. Even when you arrive at a major city, freeways whisk you around on a perimeter belt loop or shoot you through the city (unless it is rush hour!), revealing only a few outstanding landmarks.

Traditional content area textbooks are like freeways. They may get you through a lot of territory, but they move you so quickly that you are unable to learn close, personal insights about the area. In order genuinely to know an area, you need to get off the freeway and travel the connecting roads. The connecting roads of subject matter study are such print forms as library books, magazines, newspapers, and computer software. These avenues allow you and your students to explore an area thoroughly, make decisions about the side routes you want to take, and obtain personal meanings from your journey. They provide multiple avenues to learning.

This chapter introduces you to content area reading materials. You will find three key ideas:

1. Students deserve a variety of content area reading materials.
2. Many types of content area reading materials are available.
3. Reading-response projects take many forms.

STUDENTS DESERVE A VARIETY OF CONTENT AREA READING MATERIALS

Multiple materials offer students (1) depth of information, (2) motivation to read, (3) distinctive points of view, (4) materials that fit their abilities, (5) a sense of ownership over what they are learning, and (6) opportunities to make decisions and solve problems.

A major reason for providing students access to many reading materials during subject matter study is to deepen their understandings. Reliance on a single source of information can lead to superficial knowledge. Think of how a typical middle-school social studies textbook presents the ancient Greeks. The textbook probably devotes ten to twenty pages to such topics as Greek mythology, government, social order, culture, art, architecture, warfare, and overall influence on modern life. The text most likely gives passing mention to such "landmarks" as Zeus, Aesop, Homer, Plato, and Alexander; to Athens, Sparta, and Macedonia; and to city-states, democracies, and republics. That is quite a lot of ground to cover in only ten pages, but the Roman Empire comes next, and it too has several noteworthy features that must be covered.

But now think of library books and magazine articles on ancient Greece. For instance, *Gods, Men, and Monsters from the Greek Myths* (Gibson, 1982) takes 152 pages to describe only one aspect of ancient Greek life: mythology. This book contains a full account of the exploits of the mythical characters, memorable graphics depicting scenes from the various myths, a chart depicting the relationships and roles of the gods, and an index. Prometheus, Apollo, Jason, Helios, and others come alive in this book. Such a carefully detailed, well-crafted treatment of a topic is not possible in a textbook because textbooks must cover too many topics.

Textbook authors rarely devote much page space to motivating readers because they realize that they have a captive audience once their book is adopted in a classroom. These writers know that adults, not students, select the books. Thus, the composition of textbooks is designed to impress adults who look for extensive coverage of information.

Writers not involved with textbooks, on the other hand, realize that their readers will be working mostly on their own. Writers and publishers know that teachers tend to explain what is presented in textbooks but won't have time to explain the material in most library books. Writers and publishers also know that young readers select and stay only with books that are interesting to read. Therefore, they know that they must present their information in as interesting a way as possible. Such a presentation might include introductory comments, questions, and scenarios that arouse curiosity; vivid images and analogies; explanations of how the information might be used in real-life situations; humor and personalized anecdotes; and print size, graphics, and layout that appeal to the intended audience.

Students also deserve a variety of content area reading materials because such literature can present a distinctive point of view on a topic, whereas textbooks tend to present no specific viewpoint or only a traditional perspective. For instance, *The Roots of Crime* (LeShan, 1981), an adolescent-level book, argues that children who learn to hate themselves frequently grow into lawbreakers. The roots of criminal behavior are said to be found in such problems as child abuse, uncaring families, and unemployment. This argument offers a clear contrast to neutral presentations of crime-related facts and to fervid appeals for strong-armed law and order. Such a contrasting view might interest an otherwise apathetic student.

In *The Accident* (Strasser, 1988), another book for adolescents, teenagers confront their own mortality while reading about the drunk-driving deaths of the book's characters. They deal with such concerns as jumping to conclusions and placing blame without evidence. Norma Klein's *No More Saturday Nights* (1988) helps students understand the implications of becoming an unwed parent and trying to continue an education. An interesting wrinkle on this one is that the parent is a teenage boy who has custody of his child. Readers will empathize as this boy makes the transition to adulthood. Content area materials also can present alternative, interesting points of view on such issues as genetic engineering, UFOs, nuclear power, sex roles, and treatment of the mentally or physically handicapped.

If you took students out on a football field and had them run 100 yards, individuals would finish at different times, and some would enjoy the exercise more than others no matter which place they came in. In fact, the differences among students' running times and feelings about running probably would increase as students got older. The same holds true for reading. When you give your class a reading assignment, you can count on students finishing at different times, with different amounts of understanding and degrees of interest. Thus, a variety of materials is needed to match the variety of students. Incorporating many library books, periodicals, encyclopedias, newspapers, brochures, and other reading materials into the study of subject matter allows students to work with what they can handle.

One finding that has consistently emerged from classroom research is that students who spend time on tasks they can do well learn the most (Cunningham, 1985). Students do best when reading and writing tasks are well within their limits. In addition, students' behavior on a task is related to the task's level of difficulty. Understandably, students tend to avoid frustrating assignments and search for something else to do. Making available a variety of reading materials allows more students to succeed.

Let's face it: Students do not always appreciate teachers telling them what to learn. Sometimes they like to figure things out for themselves. Substituting varied materials for the single all-powerful textbook allows students to read for the purposes that they find satisfying, seeking the answers to their own questions. Instead of reading a chapter because it was assigned, students read a book or an article because it captures their attention. In this way,

Students enjoy opportunities to browse through a variety of reading materials.

students may spend even more time actively engaged in reading and learning. Students who have a choice in what they will read and write about develop a sense of ownership in the assignment. They are willing to go the extra mile because it means something to them.

A final reason why students deserve a variety of content area materials involves opportunities to employ the various thinking processes. Teaching practices centered about a textbook tend to emphasize only information recall. This situation seems due partly to the authoritative tone of textbooks. Textbook language has an all-knowing stance, dispensing information in domineering fashion. Textbooks give an impression of objectivity and validity and appear comprehensive.

Teachers who follow textbook-based instruction typically end up having students read the passage and then providing corrective feedback as students recall the contents. Such instruction inhibits opportunities for students to employ such thinking processes as evaluate, apply, and generalize. On the other hand, multiple materials are more conducive to problem solving and decision making than a single textbook. For instance, teachers who use a variety of materials can have students compare different versions of the same Greek myth or compare Greek myths with those from other cultures. Such activities, which elicit thinking that goes beyond a rote level, help demystify print. They allow students to control what they read by showing that some authors disagree with one another, some present a topic more clearly and completely than others, and some provide inaccurate or biased accounts.

LISTEN/LOOK AND LEARN

Informally interview a teacher who uses multiple reading materials during subject matter study. Ask why he or she uses multiple materials rather than a single text. Compare the reasons you obtain from the interview with the six listed in this section.

MANY TYPES OF CONTENT AREA READING MATERIALS ARE AVAILABLE

We hope that you are by now convinced to provide your students with a variety of reading materials. You should realize the advantages of allowing students to interact with multiple sources of information. This section presents general types of materials students should have access to, describing the major types of content area reading materials that are available: reference materials, periodicals, computer technology, and trade books.

Reference Materials

Students consult reference materials for facts or general background information. These materials typically display information in a straightforward, concise manner. Two types of reference materials are available: compendiums and special-interest publications.

Compendiums, handy collections of fields of information, include encyclopedias, dictionaries, atlases, and yearbooks. Students are frequently intimidated by compendiums, because the information in them is presented differently than the information in other books. Compendiums usually have extremely dense text summarizing a great deal of information in very little space. Nonetheless, some materials are better than others. Some publications contain striking visuals, accurate information, and accessible writing. In one book's presentation of the layers of the atmosphere, an illustration shows the sea, the world's tallest building, an eagle flying, Mt. Everest, and an airborne jumbo jet in order to provide concrete examples of height.

Brochures, pamphlets, and fliers exemplify special-interest references. When studying cities or states, students often obtain colorful promotional literature from chambers of commerce; when investigating occupations, students examine brief publications produced by trade unions, professional organizations, and government agencies. Classrooms stocked with special-interest references have filing cabinets and shelves full of such real-life reading materials as maps, application forms, menus, food labels, legal documents, and telephone books.

While the majority of reference materials is aimed at good readers in the intermediate grades and above, there are some excellent materials for primary-grade students. When searching for reference materials, keep student reading abilities in mind and examine the composition of the materials. Are they well organized? Are examples provided? If the material is too sparse, students will not be informed and may even go away from the material confused because information was missing.

Periodicals

A wide range of published material is available by subscription. Periodicals are excellent content area materials because they are timely and include short, lively, well-illustrated articles on interesting topics. Periodicals can provide students with an introduction to a new subject, pique student interest in a subject not considered interesting, and summarize information after students have done other research. Periodicals from *Ranger Rick's Nature Magazine* to *Popular Mechanics* to *Junior Scholastic* to the community newspaper are available for class or individual subscriptions. Practically every subject area has at least one periodical appropriate for upper-grade students, and general periodicals that report the weekly news and special features exist for all grades. S. Richardson (1991) and D. Stoll (1990) provide extensive lists of magazines for children.

Computer Technology

Education changed when the use of print led to permanent records of oral language and when the printing press resulted in affordable books. Learners depended less on individuals and more on themselves to become educated. Computer technology probably will affect teaching and learning as much as these past technological innovations. Virtually every school district today is attempting to capitalize on what computers have to offer.

Computer technology makes information accessible. Students can search databases and record information with a few keystrokes. They can manipulate what they find through word processing, spreadsheet, and graphing programs. Students can experience phenomena through multimedia presentations that include print but go far beyond the capacity of books. They can access and share information through telecommunicating with students at other sites. The power and versatility of this new technology allows students of all abilities to engage in active collaborative projects. Teachers often work to orchestrate, or facilitate, these projects rather than transmit information through a traditional lecture. Computer technology is a tool for learning that includes at least five major components: personal productivity tools, simulations, multimedia, tutorials, and telecommunications.

PERSONAL PRODUCTIVITY TOOLS   Word processing is perhaps the main personal productivity tool. Even young students can acquire some control of keyboarding to record their thoughts in writing. Most students appreciate word processing for its help with revising text and producing clear printouts. Programs that support word processing include those that help students organize their thoughts, check spelling and grammar, produce bibliographies, and lay out text. Desktop publishing applications coupled with ink-jet or laser printers provide professional-looking products.

Word processing programs and their supports often are integrated with database and spreadsheet applications for storing and manipulating information. For example, students might compare several countries' average temperature and rainfall with their exports to see what relationships exist.

Personal productivity tools have great potential for helping students learn how to find relevant information, think critically, and communicate ideas. These strategies are important for success in school as well as in the workplace. The need to familiarize students with computing tools will increase as more and more occupations require computer literacy.

SIMULATIONS   Simulations allow students to make decisions and see their results. Students who cannot participate in a scientific or historical event firsthand take part in it vicariously through a simulation. Simulations often have gamelike features, with points scored for desirable decisions. For instance, the classic simulation *Oregon Trail* has students reenact part of the westward expansion saga. Players decide what provisions they should set out with; what food rations and travel pace they should follow; and how they should acquire food, cross rivers, and handle adversity. Successful players reach Oregon's Willamette Valley; unsuccessful ones are said to die on the trail. Other popular social studies simulations include *SimCity,* which uses natural disasters to test students' plans for developing a city, and *Gold Rush,* which calls for decisions about how to get from New York to the 1849 California gold fields.

Lunar Greenhouse is a science-oriented simulation that has students control variables affecting the growth of vegetables. They set levels of temperature, light, water, and plant food for different types of crops. Information that is acquired from initial experiments is used to inform decisions about subsequent experiments at increased levels of difficulty.

MULTIMEDIA Videodiscs and CD/ROM (compact disc/read only memory) contain incredible amounts of integrated information in the form of print, graphics, sound, animation, and video. This technology is expensive, but its potential is exciting. Teachers presenting the election process through *The '88 Vote* might show film segments of the seven Democratic nominees' campaign speeches along with the text describing them. Asking students to describe each candidate's appeal to the voters calls for active investigations of the data within the videodisc as well as in the library. Generalizations need to be formed and tested before being accepted.

The *Middle Ages School Kit* combines videos and text to portray thirteenth-century Europe. Daily life, religion, and technology are some of the topics covered in this resource. Students view portions of the disc, read related materials, and respond to what they discover. *Salamandre* presents external and internal detail on fourteen castles for students to compare and contrast.

Multimedia that is organized through a hypercard relates multiple forms of media from various sources. This application might be used to link video-taped speeches by equal-rights activists, texts from pertinent documents, anthems and theme songs, and suggested readings and activities. Students would have access to the sights, sounds, and printed words of this social movement.

TUTORIALS Tutorials, called *electronic worksheets* by many educators, allow students to master specific items of information through drill and practice. They offer the least richness of the computer applications and by themselves do not justify the cost or classroom space of computers; however, many tutorials perform their limited function quite well. For instance, *Swamp Gas* presents an outline map of the United States and is designed to teach the location of the states, state capitals, important cities, and such landmarks as the Grand Canyon and Niagara Falls. This program pictures a space alien hovering over the United States with a mission to visit several locations. It provides locational clues when requested and records the travel time learners take to move the alien to the specified places. Students can play different levels of difficulty that vary according to the number and familiarity of the sites to visit.

Computer technology offers many literacy resources.

Students learning to recall bits of information can benefit from these re-sources. Tutorials frequently are motivating, full of amusing sound effects, visual displays, and gamelike formats. They provide unlimited differently ordered exposures to the same information and give both immediate and delayed feedback. Tutorials provide students with a sense of security while freeing teachers for more creative endeavors.

TELECOMMUNICATIONS Modems attached to computers and programs allowing students to communicate with others across time and space can be a real boon in the content classroom. One program, *Fredmail*, is distributed for a low cost to schools and allows them to make multiple copies at no additional cost for various sites. With nodes set up in locales across the nation, students connect to a node, and a server passes the information on to the desired site. The only charge for connections is for any long-distance calling. Students enjoy communicating with other classrooms or individuals to gain and share information on topics being studied. Higher-cost programs, such as Local Area Networks (LANs), are also available with programs like *Ethernet*.

Wire Service allows students across sites to put together a newspaper focused on a topic of study. If students wanted to distribute a countywide newspaper on a topic of interest, such as local elections or the protection of animals in national forests, having articles from numerous high schools would widen the scope of their project. There is a lot of motivation built into such projects. Students seem to be motivated to access information electronically and write for long-distance readers (Eastman, 1984; Lake, 1986).

Distance education has been used by universities for many years. School districts are now beginning to take advantage of this opportunity for learning as well. Though there have been learning programs for home television viewing for many years ("Sesame Street" and "Reading Rainbow," for example), it is relatively recently that schools and older students have become the target for televised learning through such programs as "Channel One." The daily broadcast of news programming into junior- and senior-high classrooms is an attempt to make the news palatable to and understood by students so that they will not only be currently informed but also become accustomed to accessing their news information from television.

Trade Books

Trade books are intended for sale in general bookstores; they make up a bookseller's trade. Some educators use the terms *trade book* and *library book* as synonyms. Trade books differ from textbooks, technical manuals, reference materials, and the like.

To appreciate the differences between traditional textbooks and well-written trade books, think back to what you learned in this text about the organize and connect thinking processes. Remember that good readers arrange information into categories, and good readers also form associations between what they already know and what a passage contains. Likewise, proficient writers compose passages that are well organized and help readers make connections. A series of studies on improving instructional texts demonstrated that thoughtful rewriting of textbook materials resulted in students recalling more information and enjoying the passages more (Graves et al., 1991). The most effective revisions were well organized and tied interesting familiar information to the topic. They were unlike the textbooks that presented baskets of facts about topics.

Successful authors of trade books for children and adolescents are well aware of the pitfalls of typical textbook writing. Good writers make organizing and connecting seem effortless. Let's consider how writers have organized and connected information for their readers when presenting ancient Greek mythology.

ORGANIZING MATERIAL   A typical middle-school social studies textbook might mention myths in a paragraph on festivals in ancient Greece. The text might point out that Herodotus, the first historian, shared his knowledge through public speaking; that many theaters were dedicated to Dionysius, the god of festivals; and that in these theaters myths were occasionally acted out. The next paragraph might shift to a discussion of the early Greek thinkers: Socrates, Plato, and Aristotle. Such a treatment of mythology is not well organized. The fact that the ancient Greeks retold myths could just as easily have been inserted into the presentation of the Acropolis and the Parthenon. Students thus face a basket of isolated facts that need to be organized into some type of system that the author did not provide.

On the other hand, the writer of a book that might be found in a school library has many opportunities to point out the relationships among ideas. Two books of myths, *The Warrior Goddess: Athena* (Gates, 1972b) and *Lord of the Sky: Zeus* (Gates, 1972a), exemplify solid organization. These books include only the myths that center on each main character, Athena and Zeus. Thus, one personality ties together the numerous stories in each book. Mythology can appear fragmented and disconnected, but Doris Gates, the author of the two books, imposed order by using single main characters as unifying elements. She arranged the information in such a way that her readers did not need to impose an organizational scheme of their own.

CONNECTING MATERIAL   As you know, learners who connect information tie together already learned information with the new information being presented. Learners link what they already know to what they are trying to learn. Writers help readers make connections by reminding their audience of what they already know, then comparing that knowledge with new facts and generalizations.

Textbook writers rarely are able to suggest connections for readers, whereas writers of content area trade books usually have enough space for this. They can call up direct experiences for readers: The concept of untied balloons flying through a room might be compared to jet propulsion in science; families voting on where to go out for dinner could be linked to democracy in social studies; and dividing a chocolate cream pie among friends might be connected to fractions in math.

Michael Gibson, the writer of *Gods, Men, and Monsters from the Greek Myths* (1982), presented a connection for his readers that was quite effective. In one chapter of this book, Hades, the ancient Greek concept of the underworld, is compared to modern notions of Hell. The author points out that Hades, like Hell, was a place for the dead where sinners suffered eternal damnation. However, Gibson explains, Hades differed from Hell because all the dead— good and bad—first traveled to Hades to have their fates decided. Those who had led commendable lives then continued on to an afterlife of great happiness. Young readers who encounter this concept of Hades for the first time will probably have little difficulty understanding and remembering it, thanks to the author's connecting it to a familiar concept.

Content area trade books, which frequently excel at providing organizational patterns and connections along with other features of fine writing, come in a wide range of types for preschool children through adults. The following are the major categories of trade books likely to be found in elementary- and secondary-school libraries: concept books, poetry, fiction, nonfiction narrative, how-to, and biography.

CONCEPT BOOKS We use the term *concept books* somewhat more broadly than those who typically write about literature for schoolchildren. We use two related definitions. The first is the traditional definition of books primarily appropriate for very young children. These books introduce such concepts as size, shape, color, spatial relations, the alphabet, and numeral recognition and number sets. For instance: T. Hoban's *Push, Pull, Empty, Full* (1972) depicts fifteen pairs of opposites: *In* and *out* are represented by a turtle whose head is pulled inside and then extended outside the shell; *whole* and *broken* are represented by two intact eggs and two eggs smashed on the floor. In *Animalia* (Base, 1987) each page contains dozens of lavish pictures of items that begin with that page's letter of the alphabet. Such alphabet books not only help children understand the sound-symbol code of English but also help build children's meaning vocabulary.

The other type of concept books we refer to are those that deal with a single topic or specific subject in expository fashion. These books are written for very young children through adults. Some authorities call these nonfiction informational books. *Glaciers and Ice Caps* (Bramwell, 1986), *Digging Deeper: Investigations into Rocks, Shocks, Quakes, and Other Earthly Matters* (Markle, 1987), *Einstein* (Hunter, 1987), *Danger—Icebergs!* (Gans, 1987), and *The Sun: Our Nearest Star* (Branley, 1988) are examples of nonfiction informational concept books.

POETRY While the use of rhyme and rhythm to teach concepts has much appeal, poetry books are not as readily available as are ones in the other categories. In general, there are fewer poetry books published than those in other genres, and of those published there are a limited number to be used to teach content information. However, poetry can be used as supplements to develop mood, a sense of fun, or lighten the content presentation. A unit on weather would be enhanced with haiku poetry or *Windy Day: Stories and Poems* (Bauer, 1988). Insect study would be more fun with *Bugs: Poems* (Hoberman, 1976). *Tyrannosaurus Was a Beast* (Prelutsky, 1988) and *Dinosaurs* (Hopkins, 1987) are wonderful ways to begin or conclude a unit on those prehistoric beasts.

FICTION There is a whole realm of materials that present facts in the context of a story. For instance, books that follow a story line while presenting extremely valuable information include *Linnea in Monet's Garden* (Bjork, 1987), *Inspector Bodyguard Patrols the Land of U* (Cobb, 1987), *Beyond the Ridge*

(Goble, 1989), and *Shark beneath the Reef* (George, 1989). We would say that a great deal of your knowledge about the climate, language, flora, fauna, and ethnic groups in certain parts of the world came from reading fiction by such authors as James A. Michener.

There are two basic types of fiction suitable for content area classrooms: realistic fiction and historical fiction. Realistic fiction portrays events and people who seem to be involved in the recognizable trials and uncertainties of life. Books such as *I'll Get There, It Better Be Worth the Trip* (Donovan, 1969) and *A Day No Pigs Would Die* (Peck, 1972) are classic statements of young adults' changes from dependent children to independent adults. Many books now are available that deal with such issues as divorce, developing sexuality, mental and physical handicaps, and death and dying. For instance, *Johnny Got His Gun* (Trumbo, 1939) is a compelling piece of antiwar fiction that has a place in an English or a social studies class.

Historical fiction attempts to re-create a believable past. Authors of such works often create fictional characters who interact with people who actually shaped events in history. Through these imagined and real characters, the past can be interpreted. After reading *Across Five Aprils* (Hunt, 1964), *Rifles for Watie* (Keith, 1957), or *Zoar Blue* (Hickman, 1978), students begin to understand much better why the Civil War was so devastating on a personal as well as a national scale.

NONFICTION NARRATIVE   A category of content area trade books that deserves attention is narrative accounts of actual happenings. These nonfiction narratives contain events and dialogue as it is remembered or recorded by the participants. Authors typically maintain a journal of the events if they were participants, or they interview those who actually participated and present a story that documents the events. Classic examples of nonfiction narratives appropriate for secondary students include *Black Like Me* (Griffin, 1977), *The Double Helix* (Watson, 1968), *Hiroshima* (Hersey, 1946), *Never Cry Wolf* (Mowat, 1963), and *The Right Stuff* (Wolfe, 1979).

HOW-TO   How-to books describe a process and explain how to perform such activities as playing chess, conducting science experiments, folding paper artistically, cooking, repairing cars, and making music. This category has somewhat limited usefulness because it applies to only a few content areas. Numerous how-to books exist to support the sciences, mathematics, and vocational skills; however, such books are rare in the social sciences and the humanities.

BIOGRAPHY   Books about people who have made contributions to the content areas are numerous. Biographies are available about people prominent in reform movements, politics, sports, medicine, war, and entertainment, to name only a few fields. Abraham Lincoln, Jim Thorpe, Marie Curie, Anne Frank, and Bill Cosby are only a small sampling of those whose life histories have been written. Young readers often appreciate biographies as they search for heroes and heroines to emulate. Unfortunately, some biographers let their own infatuation with the subject interfere with the honest depiction of a multifaceted human being. Students need to be on the alert for folklore that passes for truth from one book to another. For instance, the story about George Washington and the cherry tree is not substantiated. Some myths are easily spotted; others pass into the general culture as truths. Though more biographies exist for people in the content areas of the arts, humanities, and social sciences, biographies have been written about important figures associated with all major curricular areas.

Instructional Packages and Textbooks

Instructional packages consist of numerous print and nonprint materials centered about particular topics. Educational supply companies offer supplemental readings, workbooks and tests; printed simulations and games (e.g., passing a law through the United States Congress); overhead transparencies, filmstrips, slides, films, and videotapes; records and cassettes; bulletin board materials; and such manipulatives as flash cards, geometric shapes, and puzzles. These materials might be tied to a specific textbook or might stand alone. The amount of text related to these materials varies substantially. For instance, a filmstrip might contain only illustrations, be captioned, or accompany a pamphlet that each student receives. The school-district budget and administrators' and teachers' judgments affect the purchase of instructional packages. However, practically all students have access to a textbook for each subject they are studying.

By now you might be convinced that we are totally opposed to the use of textbooks. This is not so! After all, we wrote the textbook that you currently are reading. Textbooks play a needed role in education: They systematically introduce readers to a body of knowledge; they save teachers time by outlining learning sequences for students; and they specify content beforehand so that teachers know how to plan. Textbooks provide the glue that holds together a wide assortment of facts and generalizations.

We expect you to use textbooks when you teach, but we hope that you will also use trade books and other reading materials. To repeat, multiple materials give students a chance at getting something meaningful from their reading; they meet students halfway. Some of the time you might spend helping students understand their textbooks would be better spent getting other materials into their hands.

Although textbooks are found in practically every classroom, the way teachers use them varies substantially (Alvermann & Moore, 1991; Stodolsky, 1989). Some teachers slavishly cover their texts' contents from front to back, following suggestions from the teacher's manual and piloting students through as many of the activities as possible. Those who teach by the book might have students take turns reading orally and answering the end-of-chapter questions. At the other extreme, some teachers leave textbooks on the classroom shelves or in the closet. These individuals might have students rely only on lectures, audiovisual presentations, and hands-on manipulatives.

Others might incorporate print only from reference materials, periodicals, computer technology, and trade books. Teachers in the middle of these extremes use their textbooks selectively. They guide students through parts of the book that present content appropriately, point out textbook portions that reinforce what was introduced in class, and consult the text as a reference source.

You probably will inherit from your school a class set of textbooks for the subjects you will teach; the way you use these books is something for you to decide. This text is meant to inform your decision by describing ways to incorporate textbooks and all other forms of print into daily classroom instruction.

Multicultural Literature

Multicultural literature is a category that differs from the others in this section because it refers to the content of materials rather than to their form. Multicultural literature is printed matter that reflects the cultural diversity of American society; it recognizes ethnicity, race, religion, age, gender, socioeconomic class, and exceptionality. Reference materials, periodicals, computer technology, trade books, and instructional materials and textbooks might or might not demonstrate multicultural awareness.

Multicultural awareness during subject matter study is part of educators' responses to a pluralist vision of the ideal society. This vision prizes diversity, viewing group membership as an integral and a beneficial part of individuals' identities. The pluralist position holds that various groups in a society should retain their cultural ways so long as all the groups can coexist in peace. Pluralists often present a metaphor of the ideal society as a salad, a vegetable soup, or a mosaic, each of which contains identifiable elements in a harmonious blend.

To create and sustain multicultural awareness, educators need to address such factors as community participation, testing procedures, and school staff attitudes (Banks, 1989b). Including multicultural reading materials during subject matter study is another important step. Students should have access to reading materials whose contents, illustrations, and language accurately and fairly represent diverse groups. One way to accomplish this is to check available textbooks and other forms of print for stereotyping, omissions, distortions, and language bias (Hernandez, 1989). Stereotyping occurs when all individuals in a particular group are depicted as having the same attribute: Are Native Americans characterized as warlike? Are women presented as dependent? Omissions occur when the contributions of particular groups are underrepresented: Are women's roles in westward expansion described? Are scientific discoveries by physically disabled individuals noted?

Texts present distortions when they systematically misrepresent certain groups. For instance, referring to Asian Americans rather than to Japanese or Chinese Americans gives a false impression of uniformity between these two groups. And depicting Native Americans in only historical or ceremonial settings ignores their contemporary status. Finally, language bias happens when subtle, frequently subconscious, choices about words affect the message about certain groups. Are revolutionaries working to overthrow an established government *terrorists* or *freedom fighters*? Did Americans in the 1860s fight a *Civil War* or a *War between the States?* Were African Americans *given* the right to vote, or did they *win* it? Do you receive letters from a *mailman* or a *mailcarrier*?

A good way to integrate multicultural literature into your curriculum is through a *transformation* approach (Banks, 1989a). Those who follow this approach enable students to view the world from the perspective of diverse groups. This approach goes beyond merely adding a list of diverse heroes and holidays to be memorized. For example, rather than have students simply remember what happened to Crispus Attucks during the colonial revolution, have them study this event from the points of view of Anglo revolutionaries, Anglo loyalists, African Americans, Native Americans, the French, and the British. Compare the sympathetic view of the revolution presented in *Johnny Tremain* (Forbes, 1946) with the one presented in *My Brother Sam Is Dead* (Collier & Collier, 1974). When studying the age of discovery, provide *The First Voyage of Christopher Columbus* (Smith, 1992), which maps out the voyage in exceptional detail, along with *The Encounter* (Yolen, 1992), an account of the arrival of Columbus as seen through the eyes of the Tianos people who met him.

Myriad books with multicultural perspectives fit the myriad topics covered in school. Young children studying shelter will see the different types of houses built throughout the United States in *The House I Live In* (Selzer, 1992) and gain perspective on the children who live in them. *Rosa Parks* (Parks, 1992) offers older children a personal account of the events that led this woman in 1955 to refuse to give her bus seat to a white man in Alabama, turning the civil rights movement into a national issue. *Report from Engine Co. 82* (Smith, 1972) describes the emotional as well as the physical side of a firefighter's life.

Transforming your curriculum with multicultural literature allows you to help students understand how diverse groups of people have participated in the formation of U.S. culture and society. It can sensitize members of one group to the heritages of others, resulting in appreciation of their contributions. And it can affirm individuals' particular cultural identities.

DO IT TOGETHER

Form small groups of three or four students each according to academic specialization (e.g., social studies, mathematics, English). If you teach all subjects, select a particular one for this activity. Go on a scavenger hunt to locate and bring to class on a certain date published materials that fit your specialization in each of the categories below. On the day that everything is brought in, share the materials you found. Indicate what is special about their contents, writing style, and potential classroom uses.

Reading Materials Scavenger Hunt List

Reference Materials
  Compendium
  Special-interest publication

Periodical

Computer Technology
  Personal productivity tool
  Simulation
  Multimedia
  Tutorial
  Telecommunication

Trade Books
  Concept book
  Poetry
  Fiction
  Nonfiction narrative
  How-to
  Biography

Instructional Packages and Textbooks

Multicultural Literature

READING-RESPONSE PROJECTS TAKE MANY FORMS

Knowing about materials is a good beginning for teachers who promote literacy during subject matter study, but more is needed. You need to promote the materials so that students will want to read them. Many teachers display posters, book jackets, and other enticements to attract students to materials in the classroom. These displays change as the unit of study changes. In order to inform students about the contents of selected materials and hook them on the idea of reading the books, teachers present book talks. These are sales pitches. Teachers describe the books, often connecting their contents with the unit of study and pointing out their noteworthy parts. Teachers often summarize the beginning of a passage or read a portion of it aloud in a manner similar to priming a pump: They help students get started so the reading flows easily. Information about the author is presented, and similarities between other books are described.

Along with promoting materials, teachers should provide class time for students to read them. One way is to have students read on their own when they finish assigned tasks. Many teachers provide reading opportunities by setting aside a certain time for *sustained silent reading* (SSR). SSR calls for students and teachers to do nothing but read. Students may not work on assignments, and teachers may not grade papers. Instead, students and teachers begin an SSR period by locating reading materials, and then spend a

Secondary students find a range of reading materials engaging.

specific amount of time reading them. If some form of accountability is required, teachers may record the amount of time spent reading rather than books completed or projects submitted.

SSR time frequently is scheduled immediately after breaks in the day, such as lunch or class changes, because it tends to calm young people. Students might remain in their seats during free reading time; however, they also might go in pairs to an attractive designated free reading area. A specific time is set, from five to twenty minutes, and students are held to it.

Developing students' responses to what they read is also crucial. Response to reading takes many forms. It often is spontaneous, such as the short breathing that occurs while reading a particularly gruesome part of a horror story. Children spontaneously respond to stories when they unknowingly structure their play activities according to the latest superhero's dress, actions, voice qualities, and mannerisms. A pair of adults reading the Sunday morning paper respond spontaneously when they interrupt each other to share tidbits of information just encountered.

For reading-response projects readers consciously produce a reaction. Teachers often guide students' reading-response projects. Traditional book reports are a type of this project, although the emphasis on summarizing information in traditional reports rarely seems to engage students.

To use literature effectively during the study of subject matter, teachers need to elicit from students a wide range and depth of thought and feeling about what they are reading. Response activities should lead students to insights about what they have read. Students activate essential thinking processes while participating in meaningful projects. In fact, meaningful projects can lead students to all nine of the thought processes we have described.

Younger students enjoy time to read a good book.

When left alone, students can slip into passive reading habits, barely attending to the print. Books become a sort of mental chewing gum; they feel good for a while but have no long-lasting benefit. Students require opportunities to read freely and experience well-written prose, but they also benefit from sharpening and extending their understanding of what they read by expressing their reactions through various projects.

Perhaps the greatest contribution of response projects is the criteria they provide for students to monitor their comprehension independently. In order to produce some tangible reaction to print, students need to step back mentally and collect their thoughts. If students find portions of their understanding to be unclear, they can reread and rethink the passage that contains the confusing information. Without reading-response projects, students can remain at superficial levels of understanding.

A common reason for having students respond overtly to print is to have them demonstrate that they actually read what they claim to have read. That is, response projects are for purposes of assessment. We would emphasize instructional purposes rather than assessments. Projects should lead students to increased understanding; they should not just allow teachers to assess what was understood.

Reading-response projects take many forms. Students can make visuals, locate or create concrete objects related to passage contents, dramatize events, produce somewhat lengthy written or spoken reactions, maintain a journal of their reactions, and discuss what they read with others. These projects can be done as part of out-of-school or in-school reading, be in response to any single material or set of materials, or be assigned by the teacher or selected by the student. The point is that students' reading-response projects can and should take many forms. These are some forms that we have found to be effective: visuals, concrete objects, and dramatizations.

VISUALS   A picture is worth a thousand words. Students benefit from viewing visuals in order to learn information, and they also benefit from producing visuals in reaction to what they read. If the purpose of a response project is, "Identify three pieces of new information that you learned," the best way to represent the new learning may be visually.

Illustrations. Illustrations and photographs are good substitutes for the real thing. Students often draw pictures, collect photographs, or take their own photographs in order to depict what they encountered in a passage. They may also make posters or bulletin boards. Such visuals graphically depict what words can only suggest. For example, the Grand Canyon, cell division, parts of the body, and geometric figures are natural candidates for illustrated projects.

Time Lines and Murals. The key events of a phenomenon are frequently displayed on a time line. Any number of illustrations, or none at all, may be on a time line. The essential feature is that events are labeled and represented in sequence on a linear chart. Murals are similar to time lines in that they represent a sequence of events; the difference, of course, is that murals consist solely of pictures.

Maps. Representing an area graphically requires careful reading and composing. Students need to decide what locations to represent and then produce that representation. Illustrations can be added to maps for greater detail. Maps can depict locations on many scales. For instance, locations within a building, a neighborhood, a community, a state, a nation, the world, or the universe can be mapped.

Collages. Collages are groups of pictures and various other materials glued to a surface. These artistic compositions generally symbolize a topic. Making a collage of an area of study such as ethnic and racial groups, geographic locations, inventions, or animal groups is a good project for students of all ages.

Homemade Transparencies. Older students can make their own overhead transparencies. Have your students take thin-line, permanent-ink felt-tip markers and either draw or trace pictures on a sheet of acetate. Give the pictures a few minutes to dry and cover them with clear adhesive plastic. If appropriate, cut the pictures apart so they can be reassembled when the report is presented. Homemade transparencies made up of separate parts are especially useful when presenting development, such as the growth of the United States; components, such as the parts of a plant or animal; and processes, such as photosynthesis and weather changes.

CONCRETE OBJECTS   Concrete objects either represent or actually are the phenomenon being studied. Models are concrete representations of objects (such as buildings) and processes (such as radiation). Actual objects, models, and simulations can be displayed in the classroom in order to approximate direct, firsthand experiences. A table of books and concrete objects that students prepared for a unit of study in American history is shown in the photograph below.

Students can buy, borrow, or make concrete objects as part of their projects. For instance, young students reacting to *Frontier Living* might collect objects that represent life on the western frontier in the 1800s. Farm tools, kitchen implements, clothing, and assorted household items can be brought into class to depict aspects of a bygone way of life. Students who read about the formation of islands could fashion a clay-and-water representation of geologic actions. Older students who read about cooking could bring in

Assembling a display of objects and related reading materials is an effective book project.

representative pots, implements, and other devices that are used. Students who read about scientific processes such as evaporation, covalent bonding, and friction cannot bring in the actual "thing," but they can demonstrate the outcomes that result from those intangible forces. Indeed, science fairs, which are traditional parts of many schools' curriculums, are excellent examples of students producing concrete objects.

DRAMATIZATIONS Many students like to stage short skits in reaction to what they have read, simulating certain phenomena through action and dialogue. For example, older students might read Elisabeth Kübler-Ross's *On Death and Dying* (1974) and then present different skits that portray the stages people exhibit when facing their own imminent deaths. Other students might take Studs Terkel's *Working* (1981) and present selected scenes wherein people talk about the emotional side of their jobs and how their jobs affect their whole lives. Young students who read about collecting rocks could go through a series of scenes that illustrate the recommendations for gathering a personal collection.

Another option is for students to break into pairs or small groups and simulate an interview with the author of or a character from the reading. Television talk shows provide a model for the interviewing format. Along this same line, students can form pairs to review what they have read, with one student emphasizing the positive features and the other stressing the negative. Finally, students' dramatically reading selected portions of a text to their classmates or younger students is another form of dramatization.

Readers theater is a way for students to dramatize narratives they have read. It is a method of oral interpretation that provides a relevant purpose for reading orally. You do not need to prepare special scripts for readers theater; have students read right from the passage. Most children who have basic reading proficiencies enjoy reading plays; readers theater allows playlike reading with regular prose.

When you first introduce readers theater, have a small group demonstrate the process. Show how each speaking part is indicated in the text with quotation marks and how the speaker is revealed by the flow of the conversation. The narrator's role of reading all the material outside the quotation marks should be made clear. When first presenting this activity, the narrator might read all the "he said" and "she said" phrases, but this practice should be stopped when the students become adept. Explain that only the key parts of a book and the parts that contain extensive dialogue should be selected for readers theater.

When readers theater groups are formed, have the students first react to the entire passage so they have a good understanding of what they are staging. Then have them identify and practice their parts before reading. Some groups tape-record themselves and submit the recording as their response project, and others perform for the class. Simple props and sound effects frequently are included. Readers theater is quite popular among students, so you might consider setting aside a certain time of the week for these presentations.

TRY IT OUT

Produce a visual, a concrete object collection, or a dramatization in response to this chapter. Share your reading-response project with your class or a small group of classmates.

WRITTEN AND ORAL COMPOSITION   When students compose, they combine pieces to form a whole. Producing visuals, concrete objects, and dramatizations is a kind of composing, although educators typically reserve the term *composition* for written and oral work. Students who write or speak at some length about what they have read are producing compositions.

To stimulate and help structure students' written and spoken compositions, teachers provide prompts. Prompts can be questions ("What was the most important message of what you read?") or directives ("Describe the most important message of what you read"). Prompts also can be distinguished between those that are content-specific and those that are generic. Content-specific prompts refer to specific information in a passage ("How does sunlight help produce oxygen?"); they contain terms from the passage, so they are appropriate for only the specific contents of that passage. On the other hand, generic prompts fit any passage, containing general language ("What did you learn from this passage?") that is appropriate for anything students have read.

An advantage of generic prompts is their applicability to more than one piece of text. For instance, students can learn to ask, "What have I learned?" after each reading, thereby refining their thinking. Such self-questioning is a powerful learning strategy. In addition, teachers can demonstrate how they answer a question such as, "What have I learned?", thereby providing a pattern for students to follow. Generic prompts also allow divergent thinking within a clear structure. Students have a clear focus in mind yet substantial latitude for forming their responses. Finally, applying a few questions to many materials produces a routine for teachers and students. Routines help ensure that students receive the necessary continual exposure to become proficient.

Figure 2.1 contains numerous generic prompts for written and oral compositions. These prompts are meant to elicit students' thinking about the contents of what they read; they can be the core of many reading-response projects. Upcoming chapters on comprehension and writing go further in describing how such prompts can be used during subject matter study. What follows are four specific reading-response formats that structure classroom interactions to capitalize on these prompts: discussions and recitations, book study groups, response guides, and reading journals.

DISCUSSIONS AND RECITATIONS   Discussions and recitations specify two distinct types of classroom communication. Discussions are give-and-take dialogues in which teachers are not necessarily committed to a single correct

Universal Reading-Response Prompts

What will I/you remember about this material?
What ideas did I/you gain from my/your reading?
How did this material help me/you better understand the world?
What is the most important word, sentence, or section?
What materials have I/you read that are similar?
What does this material remind me/you of?
What was I thinking while reading?
What did I/you notice while reading?
What was the author trying to share?
What is the most important message of this material?
How will I/you think differently after reading this material?
What questions did the material leave unanswered?
Why did I/you choose to read this material?

Information for a Best Friend

How could I convince my best friend to read this material?
What would my/your best friend like to know about this material?
Should I/you tell a friend to read this? Why?

Image

What pictures, sounds, and other sensory feelings did I/you experience while reading this material?

Evaluation

What did I/you like best about this material?
What was my/your favorite part of this material?
Should the material receive a literary award? Why?
Is anything missing that should be included? What?
What caused me/you to keep reading?
How far did I/you go before wanting to finish the material?
If I/you rewrote this, what would I/you change?
Is the material unique? Why?
What part of the material was realistic or unrealistic?
Will I/you choose other materials by this author?

Literary Structure

What event begins the story?
What situation in the story reminded me/you of a situation from my/your own life?
What did I/you think was going to happen when ____?
How would I/you have reacted to the situations in the story?
If I/you were ____, what would I/you have done when ____?
If I/you could become a part of the story, at what point would I/you like to enter? What would I/you do?

Characterization

Why did the main character behave as he or she did?
Which characters, if any, did I/you especially like or dislike? Why?
Did any characters change? If so, how?
What did the characters learn?
What advice would I/you give the characters?

FIGURE 2.1 Generic Prompts for Written and Oral Compositions

Emotions

How did ____ feel when ____ happened?
How did I/you feel when reading this material?
What parts made me/you feel the strongest?
Did any part of the material surprise me/you? Why?

Author's Craft

How did the author hold my/your attention?
How did the author signal important information?
How did the author reveal the meanings of difficult or unfamiliar terms?
How did the author organize the material?
How did the author balance illustrations and print?
How did the author develop his or her ideas?

FIGURE 2.1 Continued.

answer, whereas in recitations teachers expect students to produce specific information. Discussions are suited more for problem solving and applying and evaluating concepts; recitations are more conducive to factual learning. Recitations typically contain content-specific prompts that allow students to recall the contents of a text and receive feedback about their performance. Discussions seem to work best with prompts containing generic language. Recitations currently predominate in most U.S. classrooms (Goodlad, 1984), although authorities recommend holding more discussions in order to promote the higher-order thinking that our society requires.

Discussions are open explorations of ideas among teachers and students and among students themselves. Discussants seek to arrive at an answer to a question or a solution to a problem; they do not recite an answer or a solution that has been determined beforehand. Discussions involve students in reacting to what they read and supporting their reactions with facts and ideas from the materials, with the teacher initiating and sustaining students' thoughts and feelings. Ideal patterns of talk move from student to student rather than from teacher to student in Ping-Pong fashion.

To begin a discussion, use an open-ended prompt such as the ones listed in Figure 2.1. These prompts start students talking about what they have read. An important rule is to ask only those questions that you consider to have more than one possibly acceptable answer. If you are committed to a single correct answer, then the students' task becomes one of determining what is in your mind rather than of thinking through the contents of a passage on their own terms.

To keep a discussion going after a student has finished speaking, consider the four moves presented by J. T. Dillon (1988): statements, student questions, signals, and silence. Statements are someone's selected thoughts to what has just been said. You might state your understanding ("As I understand it, you're saying . . ."), describe what you would like to have expanded ("I'm interested in hearing more about . . ."), indicate your state of mind ("I'm confused about . . ."), or relate what has just been said with what has been previously stated ("So you're saying . . . , while ____ is saying . . ."). Interestingly, students respond to statements.

Students' questions often seem to invigorate discussions more than teachers' questions. Your role, then, is to encourage and facilitate such questions. You might state, "This seems to be a good time to know what else we should be asking about," then wait for someone to initiate a new direction in the exchange. Discussion signals are somewhat neutral gestures that indicate you heard what a student said and are ready for someone else to talk. Signals might consist of a comment such as, "All right," "Well said," or "OK." You can nod your head in agreement or lift your hands and eyeballs in wonder. Finally, deliberate teacher silence can go far in encouraging students to speak. Keeping silent for at least three seconds after a prompt by you or after a comment by a student might not seem like much, but it is a clear indication that someone should speak.

BOOK STUDY GROUPS   The photo below shows students in a book study group. One child is sharing the book he has read with members of his group. The children know how to discuss the book because their teacher has demonstrated such discussions several times and has specified the procedures to follow. Those who have not read the book question the reader and react to his ideas in order to develop their subject matter knowledge.

All the children in book study groups frequently select the same book to discuss. They can share their reactions daily, a chapter at a time, or they can wait until all have read the entire book. Members of book study groups often evaluate themselves according to how well their group interacted and how well they learned new knowledge.

Children in a book study group.

Directions: Complete one task that is listed under each literary element.

Character

1. Write to a friend, a member of your family, or an actor or actress a letter that describes how he or she is like a character in your book.
2. Pretend that you are one of the characters in your book. Write a letter to Ann Landers to get her advice on coping with the main problem you faced. Write her response.

Plot

1. Produce a calendar of events that reflects the story line. (The calendar can be divided among hours, days, weeks, months, or years.)
2. Produce a diary that one of the characters might have kept in order to chronicle the events of his or her life.

Setting

1. Pretend that the book is being turned into a one-hour special or a miniseries for television. Describe at least five locations where five different scenes should be filmed.
2. You are responsible for obtaining the props for a stage production of your book. List five props that are essential for the production and justify their use.

Theme

1. Describe at least one insight that the main character gained by the end of the book.
2. Describe how another book that you know makes the same point as the one you read.

FIGURE 2.2   Sample Literary Response Guide for Older Readers

RESPONSE GUIDES   Teachers frequently distribute response guides to help structure students' reactions to what they read. Worksheets and study guides containing content-specific prompts that emphasize factual information are kinds of response guides familiar to many students but should be used sparingly.

Literary response guides contain generic prompts grouped according to such literary elements as character, plot, setting, and theme. Figure 2.2 displays a sample guide for older readers that contains two prompts under each literary element; other prompts certainly might be included. Figure 2.3 shows a sample literary response guide for young readers. Teachers often have students choose the prompts they wish to complete or create ones for themselves.

1. Tell how far you read before you knew for sure that you wanted to finish the book.
2. Describe your favorite part of a chapter or of the entire book.
3. Think of a book that is like the one you just read and explain how the two are alike.
4. Identify the main problem and its solution in the book.
5. Explain why you would or would not choose someone in the book for a friend.

FIGURE 2.3   Sample Literary Response Guide for Younger Readers

1. Tell what you learned from this book.
2. Explain why you would or would not choose to read other books by this author.
3. Describe what information in this book you would like to know more about.
4. Describe what made this book interesting.
5. Explain how you might use what you learned from this book.

FIGURE 2.4   Sample Expository Response Guide

Expository response guides differ from guides for literary materials because expository guides do not refer to story characters or the main problem and solution of the plot. However, many of the items in expository guides could be applied to literary materials. Figure 2.4 shows an expository guide that fits younger as well as older readers.

Generic expository guides such as the one in Figure 2.4 are helpful, but guides containing content-specific language also can be produced. For instance, if a student chooses to produce a written or an oral composition in response to *Megatrends* (Naisbitt, 1982), then the teacher might help him or her decide which questions about the book need to be addressed: Should the student explain the ten new forces transforming modern lives? Should the most important new trend be selected and reasons for the selections described? Should the actual, foreseeable impact of one trend on the student producing the composition be predicted?

Many teachers produce response guides that fit certain types of materials. For instance, a prompt for a biography might be to describe how the individual was influenced by others as well as how he or she exerted an influence on others. If a passage is associated with a movie, you might ask students to describe the differences. After reading a mystery, students might list the clues that led to its solution.

READING JOURNALS   Rather than provide guides for students to follow, many teachers have students maintain journals about what they are reading. Reading journals allow students to express their feelings freely about any aspect of what they are reading, explore new ideas, and ask questions. One teacher who used reading journals with literary materials found that many of her students' comments fell into five broad categories:

(a) *Opinions about plot episodes and characters,*

(b) *Direct expressions of personal engagement ranging from enthusiastic appreciation to placing the book within the framework of the child's life and concerns,*

(c) *Discussion of the author's style, language, and techniques,*

(d) *Reflections on the reading process and on expectations for narrative texts, and*

(e) *Questions about vocabulary, language, or plot. (Wollman-Bonilla, 1989, p. 118)*

A good way to promote students' thinking about what they read is to recommend that they use several of the essential thinking processes described in Chapter 1. Connecting, generalizing, forming an image, evaluating, and applying are powerful processes. Indeed, we discourage too much use of organizing because we tell students that we already know most of the information and want to know what students think.

Teachers often introduce reading journals by presenting an entry or two and describing important features, such as their informality and personal involvement. Students typically write in their journals several times a week. Some teachers have students produce their entries in the form of an informal letter to the teacher. Replying to the students as an aunt or uncle instead of as a teacher-as-examiner goes far in allowing you to express interest in students' insights and strategies and prevents the journals from becoming an exercise no different from assigned writing.

Growth in motivation to read and in confidence are two of the most noticeable outcomes of having students maintain reading journals. Students who write on their own terms about what they are reading and who receive sincere reactions to their entries tend to respond more than they would to assigned factual prompts. At the same time, teachers are able to monitor students' progress in reading and writing when they read the journals. A special feature of journals is that they allow teachers to stay in touch with each individual in class, not just the vocal ones; teachers can maintain a dialogue with the shyest student through reading journals.

LOOKING BACK

When you use multiple reading materials in your classroom, you and your students will benefit greatly. Your teaching and your students' learning is energized. Reading materials vary from computer technology to trade books to periodicals. Students can respond to these materials many ways, too. In this chapter you encountered three key ideas: (1) Students deserve a variety of content area reading materials, (2) many types of content area reading materials are available, and (3) reading-response projects take many forms.

ADD TO YOUR JOURNAL

Think about the role of multiple reading materials in the classes that you will be teaching. How far beyond the text do you intend to go? What types of materials will you use? How do you intend to have the students respond to what they read?

REFERENCES

Professional Publications

Alvermann, D. E., & Moore, D. W. (1991). Secondary school reading. In R. Barr, M. L. Kamil, & P. D. Pearson (Eds.), *Handbook of reading research* (Vol. 2) (pp. 951–983). White Plains, NY: Longman.

Banks, J. A. (1989a). Integrating the curriculum with ethnic content: Approaches and guidelines. In J. A. Banks & C. A. McGee Banks (Eds.), *Multicultural education: Issues and perspectives* (pp. 189–207). Boston: Allyn & Bacon.

Banks, J. A. (1989b). Multicultural education: Characteristics and goals. In J. A. Banks & C. A. McGee Banks (Eds.), *Multicultural education: Issues and perspectives* (pp. 2–26). Boston: Allyn & Bacon.

Cunningham, J. (1985). Three recommendations to improve comprehension teaching. In J. Osborn, P. T. Wilson, & R. C. Anderson (Eds.), *Reading education: Foundations for a literate America* (pp. 255–274). Lexington, MA: Lexington Books.

Dillon, J. T. (1988). *Questioning and teaching: A manual of practice.* New York: Teachers College Press.

Eastman, S. T. (1984, May). Videotext in middle school: Accommodating computers and printouts in learning information processing skills. Paper presented at International Communication Association, San Francisco (ERIC Document Reproduction no. 248 870).

Goodlad, J. I. (1984). *A place called school.* New York: McGraw-Hill.

Graves, M. F., Prenn, M. C., Earle, J., Thompson, M., Johnson, V., & Slater, W. H. (1991). Improving instructional text: Some lessons learned. *Reading Research Quarterly, 26,* 110–122.

Hernandez, H. (1989). *Multicultural education: A teacher's guide to content and process.* Columbus, OH: Merrill.

Huck, C. S., Hepler, S., & Hickman, J. (1987). *Children's literature in the elementary school* (4th ed.). New York: Holt, Rinehart & Winston.

Lake, D. T. (1986). Telecommunications from the classroom. *The Computing Teacher, 13*(7), 43–46.

Richardson, S. K. (1991). *Magazines for children.* Chicago: American Library Association.

Stodolsky, S. S. (1989). Is teaching really by the book? In P. W. Jackson & S. Haroutunian-Gordon (Eds.), *From Socrates to software: The teacher as text and the text as teacher* (Eighty-eighth Yearbook of the National Society for the Study of Education, Pt. 1) (pp. 159–184). Chicago: University of Chicago Press.

Stoll, D. R. (1990). *Magazines for children.* Newark, DE: International Reading Association.

Wollman-Bonilla, J. E. (1989). Reading journals: Invitations to participate in literature. *The Reading Teacher, 43,* 112–120.

Children's and Young Adults' Trade Books

Base, G. (1987). *Animalia.* New York: Abrams.

Bauer, C. F. (1988). *Windy day: Stories and poems.* New York: Lippincott.

Bjork, C. (1987). *Linnea in Monet's garden.* New York: Farrar, Straus & Giroux.

Bramwell, M. (1986). *Glaciers and ice caps.* New York: Franklin Watts.

Branley, F. (1988). *The sun: Our nearest star.* New York: HarperCollins.

Cobb, V. (1987). *Inspector bodyguard patrols the land of U.* New York: Julian Messner.

Collier, J. L., & Collier, C. (1974). *My brother Sam is dead.* New York: Four Winds Press.

Donovan, J. (1969). *I'll get there, it better be worth the trip.* New York: Harper & Row.

Forbes, E. (1946). *Johnny Tremain.* New York: Houghton Mifflin.

Gans, R. (1987). *Danger—icebergs!* New York: HarperCollins.

Gates, D. (1972a). *Lord of the sky: Zeus.* New York: Viking.

Gates, D. (1972b). *The warrior goddess: Athena.* New York: Viking.

George, J. (1989). *Shark beneath the reef.* New York: HarperCollins.

Gibson, M. (1982). *Gods, men, and monsters from the Greek myths.* New York: Schocken.

Goble, P. (1989). *Beyond the ridge*. New York: Bradbury Press.

Griffin, J. H. (1977). *Black like me*. Boston: Houghton Mifflin.

Hersey, J. (1946). *Hiroshima*. New York: Knopf.

Hickman, J. (1978). *Zoar blue*. New York: Macmillan.

Hoban, T. (1972). *Push, pull, empty, full*. New York: Macmillan.

Hoberman, M. A. (1976). *Bugs: Poems*. New York: Viking.

Hopkins, L. B. (1987). *Dinosaurs*. New York: Harcourt Brace Jovanovich.

Hunt, I. (1964). *Across five Aprils*. Chicago: Follett.

Hunter, N. (1987). *Einstein*. New York: Franklin Watts.

Keith, H. (1957). *Rifles for Watie*. New York: Crowell.

Klein, N. (1988). *No more Saturday nights*. New York: Knopf.

Kübler-Ross, E. (1974). *On death and dying*. New York: Macmillan.

LeShan, E. (1981). *The roots of crime*. New York: Scholastic.

Markle, S. (1987). *Digging deeper: Investigations into rocks, shocks, quakes, and other earthly matters*. New York: Lothrop, Lee & Shepherd.

Mowat, F. (1963). *Never cry wolf*. Boston: Little, Brown.

Naisbitt, J. (1982). *Megatrends*. New York: Warner Books.

Parks, R. (1992). *Rosa Parks: Mother to a movement*. New York: Dial.

Peck, R. N. (1972). *A day no pigs would die*. New York: Dell.

Prelutsky, J. (1988). *Tyrannosaurus was a beast*. New York: Greenwillow.

Seltzer, I. (1992). *The house I live in: At home in America*. New York: Macmillan.

Smith, B. (1992). *The first voyage of Columbus*. New York: Viking.

Smith, D. E. (1972). *Report from Engine Co. 82*. New York: McCall Books.

Strasser, T. (1988). *The accident*. New York: Delacorte.

Terkel, S. (1981). *Working*. New York: Simon & Schuster.

Trumbo, D. (1939). *Johnny got his gun*. Philadelphia: Lippincott.

Watson, J. D. (1968). *The double helix*. New York: Atheneum.

Wolfe, T. (1979). *The right stuff*. New York: Farrar, Straus & Giroux.

Yolen, J. (1992). *The encounter*. San Diego, CA: Harcourt Brace Jovanovich.

Computer Software

The '88 Vote
ABC News Interactive
Distributed by Optical Data
30 Technology Drive
Box 4919
Warren, NJ 07060
(800) 524-2481

Gold Rush!
Sierra On-Line, Inc.
P.O. Box 485
Coarsegold, CA 93614
(800) 344-7448

Lunar Greenhouse
Minnesota Educational Computing
  Corporation
6160 Summit Drive North
Minneapolis, MN 55430-4003
(800) 685-MECC

Middle Ages School Kit
PBS Video
Alexandria, VA
(800) 424-7963

Newsroom's Wire Service
Scholastic Software
P.O. Box 7502
2931 E. McCarty Street
Jefferson City, MO 65102
(800) 541-5513

Oregon Trail
Minnesota Educational Computing
  Corporation
6160 Summit Drive North
Minneapolis, MN 55430-4003
(800) 685-MECC

Salamandre
The Voyager Company
1351 Pacific Coast Highway
Santa Monica, CA 90401
(800) 446-2001

SimCity
Broderbund Software
500 Redwood Boulevard
P.O. Box 6121
Novato, CA 94948
(415) 382-4400

ADDITIONAL READINGS

The National Education Association offers a useful introduction to the wide range of print and nonprint instructional materials:

National Educational Association. (1989). *Instructional materials: Selected guidelines and resources.* Washington, DC: Author.

As computer technology becomes a common tool for subject matter study, more and more references suggest ways to use it wisely:

Howie, S. H. (1989). *Reading, writing, and computers: Planning for integration.* Boston: Allyn & Bacon.

Norton, P. (1992). When technology meets the subject-matter disciplines. *Educational Technology, 32*(3,4,5). [This is a three-part series covering different aspects of integrating technology and subject matter.]

Roberts, N., Carter, R. C., Friel, S. N., & Miller, M. S. (1988). *Integrating computers into the elementary and middle school.* Englewood Cliffs, NJ: Prentice Hall.

Several references focus on trade books for the young. The following three textbooks are first-rate. The first text addresses young adults' literature; the next two address children's literature:

Donelson, K. L., & Nielsen, A. P. (1989). *Literature for today's young adults* (3rd ed.). Glenview, IL: Scott, Foresman.

Huck, C. S., Hepler, S., & Hickman, J. (1987). *Children's literature in the elementary school* (4th ed.). New York: Holt, Rinehart & Winston.

Sutherland, Z., Arbuthnot, M. H., & Monson, D. L. (1986). *Children and books* (7th ed.). Glenview, IL: Scott, Foresman.

The article that follows extends reasons and practices for using multiple reading materials:

Moss, B. (1991). Children's nonfiction trade books: A complement to content area texts. *The Reading Teacher, 45,* 26–32.

Scholars are beginning to examine the contents and roles of textbooks; three good collections of this research are as follows:

Altbach, P. G., Kelly, G. P., Petrie, H. G., & Weis, L. (Eds.). (1991). *Textbooks in American society.* Albany: State University of New York Press.

DeCastell, S., Luke, A., & Luke, C. (1989). *Language, authority and criticism: Readings on the school textbook.* London: Falmer.

Venezky, R. L. (1992). Textbooks in school and society. In P. W. Jackson (Ed.), *Handbook of research on curriculum* (pp. 436–461). New York: Macmillan.

The following emphasize the role of reading materials in promoting multi-cultural learning:

DeVillar, R. A., & Faltis, C. J. (1991). *Computers and cultural diversity: Restructuring for school success.* Albany: State University of New York Press. [This is a scholarly, somewhat weighty account of the topic.]

Rasinski, T. V., & Padak, N. D. (1990). Multicultural learning through children's literature. *Language Arts, 67,* 576–580.

The following reports convey what researchers have learned about students' responses to literature:

Beach, R., & Hynds, S. (1991). Research on response to literature. In R. Barr, M. L. Kamil, P. Mosenthal, & P. D. Pearson (Eds.), *Handbook of reading research* (Vol. II) (pp. 453–489). White Plains, NY: Longman.

Martinez, M. G., & Roser, N. L. (1991). Children's responses to literature. In J. Flood, J. M. Jensen, D. Lapp, & J. R. Squire (Eds.), *Handbook of research on teaching the English language arts* (pp. 643–654). New York: Macmillan.

These two articles present valuable suggestions for eliciting students' responses to what they read:

Saul, E. W. (1989). "What did Leo feed the turtle?" and other nonliterary questions. *Language Arts, 66,* 295–303.

Simpson, M. K. (1986). A teacher's gift: Oral reading and the reading response journal. *Journal of Reading, 30,* 45–50.

The following two books offer response guides for children's and young adults' literature; although the guides contain more content-specific questions than we recommend, their lists of related readings and writing activities are good examples of possible reading-response projects:

Somers, A. B., & Worthington, J. E. (1979). *Response guides for teaching children's books.* Urbana, IL: National Council of Teachers of English.

Somers, A. B., & Worthington, J. E. (1984). *Candles and mirrors.* Littleton, CO: Libraries Unlimited.

Conducting discussions of what students have read is not as easy as it might seem; the following suggest ways to conduct productive discussions:

Alvermann, D. E. (1991). The Discussion Web: A graphic aid for learning across the curriculum. *The Reading Teacher, 45,* 92–99.

Alvermann, D. E., Dillon, D. R., & O'Brien, D. G. (1987). *Using discussion to promote reading comprehension.* Newark, DE: International Reading Association.

C H A P T E R 3
Learning Independence

LOOKING AHEAD
Developing students' abilities and predispositions to be lifelong learners is a paramount goal of education. Conducting integrated and inquiry units and providing study strategy instruction are ways to achieve this goal. Teachers conduct integrated units by identifying an organizing center and orchestrating learning activities about that center. Students consolidate subject matter, language arts, interactions with other students, and personal experiences during integrated unit study. Inquiry units emphasize students' personal involvement and in-depth analyses, with them making choices and forming their own generalizations. Study strategy instruction involves, among other things, teaching students how to take notes, question themselves, and organize what they read. Explicit instruction in how to study readily fits integrated and inquiry units.

The ability to name the seven continents and five oceans is a traditional school expectation. However, expectations are changing. Today's students still must name the continents and oceans, but now are expected, for example, to predict the effects that changes in the oceans might have on the land. If students are to fulfill such new requirements, instruction needs to change.

Many educators are responding to these expectations by integrating their instruction, fostering student inquiry, and teaching study strategies. Rather than presenting such topics as oceans one week and continents the next, in isolation from each other, teachers are presenting them together. And rather than only telling students about subject matter, teachers are engaging them in independent subject matter study.

Traditional recitations over isolated bits of information are giving way to learning activities in which students study domains of knowledge independently. Integrated instruction, inquiry learning, and attention to independent study strategies address the complexities of today's world.

This chapter presents three key ideas relative to these approaches:

1. Integrated units combine numerous aspects of instruction.
2. Inquiry units emphasize students' choices and generalizations.
3. Explicit instruction in how to study can occur regularly.

INTEGRATED UNITS COMBINE NUMEROUS ASPECTS OF INSTRUCTION

One of the most important parts of instructional planning involves units (Clark & Peterson, 1986). Teachers generally divide their year or semester into units to produce manageable divisions of schooling and help focus instruction. Instructional units are based on ideas or blocks of subject matter, such as space, body systems, pride, superstitions, occupations, and radiation. They typically last from a few days to a few weeks.

Units are the midpoint in what teachers plan. At one end is course planning, in which teachers lay out goals for an entire semester or year. At the other end is lesson planning, in which they describe daily objectives and activities. By moving from general to specific—by first planning their course, then concentrating on units, then concocting daily lessons—teachers present a series of related experiences and help students consolidate their learning.

Integrated units differ from ordinary units. A unit such as the Civil War would be ordinary if it consisted only of a presentation of details about the causes of the war, the battles, the generals, and the outcomes. During an integrated Civil War unit, students might research trade agreements among the United States and European countries, graph the effect of the cotton gin on cotton production, compare their living conditions with those of plantation owners and slaves, and form small groups to discuss novels set during the war.

Integrated units have a long history, sharing features of many other curricular plans (Vars, 1991). *Interdisciplinary unit, multidisciplinary unit, thematic unit, focus unit, core curriculum, holistic curriculum,* and *cross-curricular study* either mean the same thing or are in the same family of curriculum as integrated units. These plans grew out of a dissatisfaction with schooling that might have students first read a short story, then correct prepared sentences containing inaccurate punctuation, then watch a movie that is not related to the story or any of the sentences, then practice mathematical operations, and finally study the occupational demands of a trade that has no relation to what has been studied earlier. Proponents of integrated instruction share an aversion to fragmented isolated instruction, preferring unified systems and seeing integrated instruction as a way to help individuals cope with personal and practical situations in life. Problems do not come in chunks shaped like the traditional disciplines. Schooling should be integrated because life is integrated.

Integrated units combine four instructional features: subject matter disciplines, language arts, classroom grouping patterns, and students' personal experiences. Different *subject matter disciplines* are merged about an organizing center, an idea or a block of subject matter, when producing integrated units. For instance, language arts, social studies, science, mathematics, and fine arts could be readily merged about the organizing center of tobacco smoking: Students could critique and produce cigarette advertisements for language arts, research legislation for smoke-free areas for social studies, study the physical effects of smoking for science, determine the percentage of full-page magazine ads devoted to cigarettes for mathematics, and produce a musical or visual statement related to smoking for fine arts.

The *language arts* of reading, writing, listening, and speaking also are tapped when producing integrated units. In an integrated unit on smoking, for instance, students might read a great deal about the physical effects of smoking, listen while interviewing knowledgeable people about smoking's effects, and write and speak when consolidating and reporting what they learned. Teachers have numerous opportunities to develop students' written and oral language during integrated subject matter study.

With regard to *classroom grouping patterns*, teachers typically keep students together as a class during certain stages of ordinary units. Whole-class presentations are especially appropriate when introducing new concepts and strategies, having students share background knowledge, and reviewing previously presented ideas. Teachers deliver whole-class presentations throughout units to guide students through important material and to refocus their attention. On the other hand, students work individually to practice and apply what they are learning, to pursue their own goals, and for some assessments. Whole-class and individual patterns of classroom organization are found in most units; however, units become more integrated when students work together in small groups.

Small-group collaborative learning promotes academic and social interactions. Students who work in small groups have a learning advantage over those who work only in large groups or alone. They support one another when practicing and applying what teachers present and when investigating ideas on their own. For example, during a unit on smoking, students could form collaborative groups to brainstorm what they already knew, share the new information they discovered, and help one another produce finished products. A series of no-smoking messages produced by small groups is potentially more effective than ones produced individually. In addition, students who learn to work together on academic tasks in school are learning to cooperate with others outside of school.

Finally, integrated units merge *students' personal experiences* with schooling. Students' worlds often are separated from the academic world, resulting in the perception that school is irrelevant. Integrated units counteract this situation by combining students' personal experiences with the organizing center of the unit. Topics, resources, and learning activities build on students' interests and abilities during integrated units. Since smoking is an issue that young people face daily, it has an intrinsic appeal that such academic topics as propaganda techniques and government controls lack. Moreover, a study of smoking can lead to fundamental issues that students find interesting, such as, "Why does the U.S. government subsidize an industry that presents health risks?" and "Why do people subject themselves to health risks?" Such activities as interviewing and conducting surveys and experiments are other ways to integrate students' experiences with school. They move students from relying on a lifeless textbook to seeking out flesh-and-blood individuals and experiences.

LISTEN/LOOK AND LEARN

Observe a class at least three times and note the students' learning activities. Describe instances where subject matter, language arts, classroom grouping patterns, and personal experiences were integrated. Also describe instances where these instructional features were not integrated but could have been.

Planning Integrated Units

Integrated units bring together subject matter disciplines, language arts, grouping patterns, and individuals' personal experiences when investigating an idea or a block of subject matter. Synthesizing elements such as these is meant to produce a complete and compelling view of the world, enhancing students' concepts, strategies, and attitudes (Jacobs & Borland, 1986). It is meant to help students see the relationships and uses of what they are learning. To plan such integrated units, follow this seven-step procedure:

STEP 1: IDENTIFYING AN ORGANIZING CENTER   An integrated unit has a center—stated perhaps as an idea, a block of subject matter, a theme, a topic, or a problem—that is general enough to allow multiple perspectives and avenues of investigation. Tobacco smoking fits this criterion because many disciplines, language arts, grouping patterns, and personal experiences can be utilized when investigating it. Dinosaurs is an organizing center that occurs in countless primary-grade units of study. Pioneers, weather, and adventure are good candidates for integrated units in the middle grades; radiation, toxic waste, and substance abuse fit upper-grade students' interests. Such topics as patterns, flight, and bridges, which are deliberately ambiguous, referring to physical as well as social phenomena, also have proven effective as organizing centers.

Events and individual books also can be the center of a unit. Historical occurrences and contemporary news happenings are good candidates. Common events that occur in students' daily lives, such as walking home from school, performing daily chores, and finding a job, lead to multiple avenues of study. Teachers often select a single book title as the basis for an integrated unit. For example, as students read *Where the Red Fern Grows*, a story of a boy's experiences with his two hunting dogs, they could explore such issues as hunting, pets, rural life, friendship, and responsibility.

Once an organizing center is identified, place it in a graphic device called a curriculum web, as depicted in Figure 3.1. There is room about the center of the web for more information. To flesh out an integrated unit, you need to identify objectives, resources, instructional procedures, and evaluation procedures. Clarifying these four components requires several steps.

STEP 2: ESTABLISHING GENERAL UNIT OBJECTIVES   During the second step of this procedure, rather than jumping haphazardly into an interesting topic, you (and possibly your students and colleagues) need to decide what students will be expected to learn. Remember that one or two objectives might be added when your students get involved with this unit. The freedom you have in making these decisions will be determined by the curriculum policies of your school and school district. General unit objectives describe the major concepts, strategies, and attitudes students should acquire from participating in the unit.

At first students' learning objectives might consist of key words or phrases. Smoking covers diverse areas, as the web of possible topics shown in Figure 3.2 demonstrates. After considering topics associated with the organizing center, list the possible objectives. Be sure to include students in these steps.

Perhaps you and your students decide that physical effects, advertising techniques, government assistance and controls, and personal beliefs could be the beginnings of formal objectives. They suggest what students should learn about smoking. These ideas then can be developed into more complete statements for your actual unit plan. General objectives for a three-week unit on smoking might be stated as follows:

FIGURE 3.1
The Organizing
Center of a
Curriculum Web

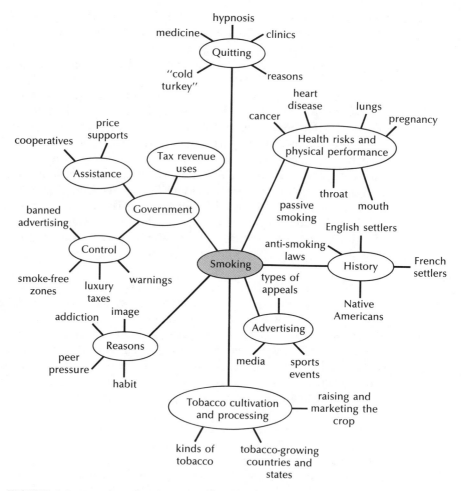

FIGURE 3.2 Brainstormed General Unit Topics

1. To describe the health risks and physical-performance effects of smoking.
2. To identify and evaluate predominant cigarette advertising techniques.
3. To explain reasons for government assistance and control of the tobacco industry.
4. To establish a personal commitment about smoking.

Unit objectives typically are stated in general terms, although their forms may vary. Some educators like to call unit objectives goals and state them in infinitive phrase form such the ones above. Others prefer to call them guiding questions, and state them in question form, such as the following:

1. What are the health risks and physical-performance effects of smoking?

2. What advertising techniques does the cigarette industry rely on? What do I think of them?

3. Why does the U.S. government assist and control the tobacco industry simultaneously?

4. What should I do about smoking?

No matter what form is used, unit objectives are needed to direct teachers' and students' efforts. Journeys are more efficient when the destinations are known beforehand. Objectives indicate the scope of a unit; they show what is to be taught. Record the topics of your general unit objectives at the ends of your webs' strands, as in Figure 3.3.

Once you know your unit objectives, you are ready to decide how to achieve them by identifying instructional resources and procedures.

STEP 3: BRAINSTORMING RESOURCES AND PROCEDURES Brainstorming is a good way to begin identifying resources and procedures for an integrated unit. Freely associate as many ideas as possible; you are producing a rough draft to be revised later.

Generate as many resources and procedures related to the organizing center and unit objectives as you can and write them on a large sheet of paper. Print and nonprint instructional resources are brainstormed during this step. Locate and list specific titles from various types of reading materials: references, periodical articles, computer software, trade books, and textbooks. Also identify such nonprint resources as movies, filmstrips, field trips, and guest speakers. In addition, instructional procedures are brainstormed along with resources during this step: What are some activities you and your students might do? For example, you might decide that creating advertisements for a particular segment of smokers not already targeted by cigarette manufacturers (e.g., senior citizens or urban dwellers) would be a good way to culminate the study of cigarette advertising techniques.

After listing resources and procedures under your unit objectives, code the instructional features. Identify the subject matter discipline(s) and grouping pattern(s) associated with each procedure or objective and indicate which tap

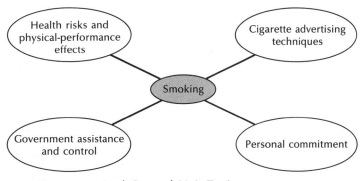

FIGURE 3.3 Revised General Unit Topics

personal experiences. Coding the procedures this way reveals features that are overrepresented or underrepresented. Equal representation is not needed, but each feature should appear at least once in your curriculum web.

Brainstorming produces a rough draft of an integrated unit plan, which you can then refine and organize for eventual implementation.

STEP 4: GATHERING RESOURCES   Once you have decided a unit's objectives and brainstormed resources and procedures, focus your planning. The brainstorming stage of this procedure provides the basis for identifying resources, but now you can intensify the search, making definite decisions and listing the resources on a revised curriculum web.

During this stage seek help from department heads, team leaders, media specialists, experienced teachers, friends, and acquaintances. Preservice and practicing teachers who notify their colleagues about units they are planning often are amazed at what aid they receive. Post notes in conspicuous places and personally contact potential helpers.

Experienced teachers collect resources over time. When a classroom magazine contains a good article about a topic, teachers save that issue. They might maintain picture files for topics they teach. Library books and audiovisual materials are located and requested each year when the appropriate unit of study comes up.

There are many ways to obtain resources for your students without spending any money. You can check materials out of the school or the public library to use in your classroom. While this is a bit time-consuming, the number of books and magazines available makes this method worthwhile. You can also have students produce reading materials for their peers. In only a few years, you will have collected a veritable cornucopia of resources.

Talk with your public librarian as well as your school librarian. Ask them to contact you when they are ready to discard content area books. Typically, books are discarded when they have become too worn for continued use by the public. Sometimes they have even gone through one rebinding process, but that won't matter to you. Look through the books. Is the content useful to you? Are the passages you would like to use in good condition? If so, collect the books, find a razor blade, and slice the passages you want from each book. Using book-binding techniques described in *Children's Literature in the Elementary School* (Huck, Hepler, & Hickman, 1987), create a series of little books, one for each passage you want to use.

Students may be willing to bring their copies of magazines or books to school to share, though they are rarely willing to donate them. A week or two before you begin a unit, request that students who are willing to share related materials bring them to school on the Friday before the unit will begin. This gives you a weekend to go through the available materials and organize them for the students. Remind them to mark their materials with a name before bringing them to school. Also tell them that you cannot guarantee the safety of anything, so if a particular issue of a magazine is a prized one that they could not bear to lose, they ought not to bring it to school.

Two other sources of materials require the expenditure of money, though not yours. Request from your school's parent-teacher organization a specific amount of money for a list of books and magazines that you have compiled. It is often wise to ask for a lot more than you think you will be able to get. If you show that you have a really great need for a large number of special materials, then you are more likely to get at least some of those materials. Another source of supplies is the paperback book clubs that continually send order forms to teachers. Distribute the forms to your students. When they return their order forms and money for books they want, you will discover that your class has earned a number of bonus points you can apply toward the purchase of free books or other content area materials, such as maps or filmstrips.

STEP 5: DESIGNING INSTRUCTIONAL PROCEDURES   At this point you are ready to specify the instructional procedures you and your students will perform. This is the time to design specific teaching techniques and learning activities.

Elementary teachers who are responsible for twenty to thirty students all day long and secondary teachers who encounter this number each class period have a clear need to keep students task-oriented. The concern is that an emphasis on keeping students busy deemphasizes the fulfillment of learning objectives. When you plan instructional procedures, be sure they lead to the objectives that you listed in your curriculum web during step 2.

Instructional procedures should employ a range of activities. Plan for students to participate in whole-class, small-group, learning-pair, and individual efforts that involve reading, writing, listening, and speaking. Ensure that students can relate personal experiences to the objectives and procedures. Consider a wide range of instructional experiences as the means to accomplish your learning objectives.

Instruction has a beginning, a middle, and an end to introduce, develop, and culminate the study of a topic. Plan for instruction that includes the following instructional procedures:

1. *Unit introduction.* Kick off the unit. Motivate students; assess what they already know about the organizing center; call up and connect their previous experiences and prior knowledge; elicit students' desires about what to study; and indicate learning objectives. Teachers schedule at least the first day of the unit for these orientation activities, knowing that additional time can be spent on them if needed.

2. *Development.* Development, which occurs during the middle of the unit, usually takes the most time. Plan to introduce the objectives, explore them, and end the exploration. As during the unit introduction, introduce objectives by motivating, connecting prior knowledge, and indicating expected learning outcomes. Define the

learnings associated with the objectives. Then establish classroom grouping patterns, teach students how to accomplish tasks, guide students through difficult resources, and provide opportunities for applying what has been presented. Allow time for students to explore topics on their own. Monitor students' progress, and reteach when needed.

3. *Unit culmination.* The unit culmination allows students to tie together and celebrate what they have learned. An end-of-unit wrap-up can capitalize on such creative outlets as dramatic productions and visual displays. Students can share what they accomplished with you; with their agemates inside and outside the classroom; and with such adults as parents, teachers, administrators, and community members. Teachers also assess students' learning during this stage. Your assessments can consist of unit tests, project grades, and other formal reviews to supplement ongoing evaluations.

Figure 3.4 shows a curriculum web listing instructional procedures and resources for a unit on smoking. The objectives' procedures are not coded according to introduction, development, and culmination, because these are apparent by the sequence in which the activities are listed. The topics, procedures, and objectives are coded according to their discipline(s) and grouping pattern(s) and whether they involve personal experiences.

STEP 6: PLANNING EVALUATION   Another step in planning integrated units is deciding evaluation techniques. Determinations are needed about how well students fulfilled the unit's learning objectives. These determinations are made through ongoing observations, evaluations of students' daily products and special projects, and test performance. Teachers learn about students when they call up and connect information during unit kick-offs and report on their special projects.

Evaluating students is a complex issue. Some of the decisions that need to be made are as follows:

1. Who will evaluate (only the teacher or the teacher in conjunction with the students)?
2. May students redo work until they achieve a satisfactory evaluation?
3. Will evaluation standards for projects be specified beforehand and distributed to students?
4. What is the balance among daily work, special projects, tests, and effort as means of assessment?
5. How will individual accountability be determined during group interactions?
6. How will late work be treated?
7. How many formal assessments will be recorded?

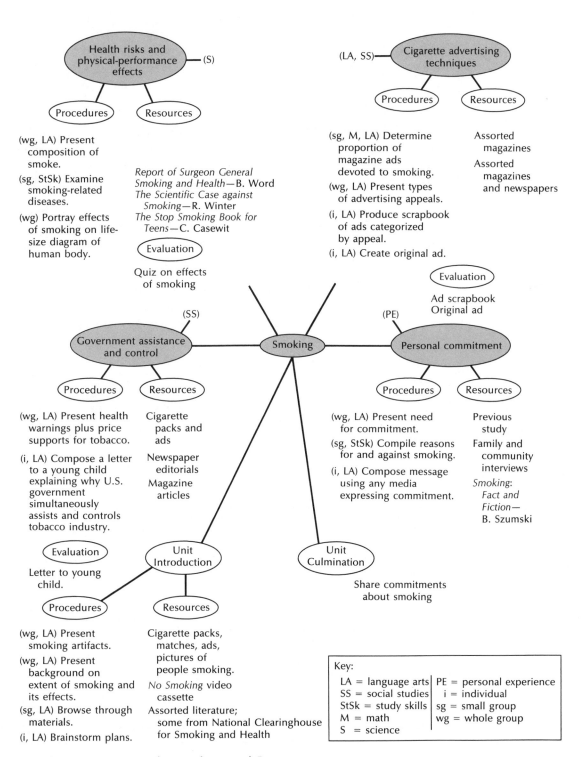

Health risks and physical-performance effects — (S)

Procedures

(wg, LA) Present composition of smoke.

(sg, StSk) Examine smoking-related diseases.

(wg) Portray effects of smoking on life-size diagram of human body.

Resources

Report of Surgeon General Smoking and Health—B. Word
The Scientific Case against Smoking—R. Winter
The Stop Smoking Book for Teens—C. Casewit

Evaluation

Quiz on effects of smoking

(LA, SS) — Cigarette advertising techniques

Procedures

(sg, M, LA) Determine proportion of magazine ads devoted to smoking.

(wg, LA) Present types of advertising appeals.

(i, LA) Produce scrapbook of ads categorized by appeal.

(i, LA) Create original ad.

Resources

Assorted magazines

Assorted magazines and newspapers

Evaluation

Ad scrapbook
Original ad

(SS)

Government assistance and control

Smoking

(PE)

Personal commitment

Procedures

(wg, LA) Present health warnings plus price supports for tobacco.

(i, LA) Compose a letter to a young child explaining why U.S. government simultaneously assists and controls tobacco industry.

Resources

Cigarette packs and ads

Newspaper editorials

Magazine articles

Evaluation

Letter to young child.

Procedures

(wg, LA) Present need for commitment.

(sg, StSk) Compile reasons for and against smoking.

(i, LA) Compose message using any media expressing commitment.

Resources

Previous study

Family and community interviews

Smoking: Fact and Fiction— B. Szumski

Unit Introduction

Unit Culmination

Share commitments about smoking

Procedures

(wg, LA) Present smoking artifacts.

(wg, LA) Present background on extent of smoking and its effects.

(sg, LA) Browse through materials.

(i, LA) Brainstorm plans.

Resources

Cigarette packs, matches, ads, pictures of people smoking.

No Smoking video cassette

Assorted literature; some from National Clearinghouse for Smoking and Health

Key:

LA = language arts	PE = personal experience
SS = social studies	i = individual
StSk = study skills	sg = small group
M = math	wg = whole group
S = science	

FIGURE 3.4 Instructional Procedures and Resources

69

8. What types of tests will be used (criterion- or norm-referenced; multiple choice, fill in the blank, true or false, short answer, or essay)?

9. How will the evaluation be reported (written comments, letter grades, percentages of possible points)?

STEP 7: SCHEDULING UNIT EVENTS   By the time you reach this point in planning an integrated unit, you should have a good idea about students' learning outcomes, resources, instructional procedures, and evaluation procedures. The final step is to design a schedule of events. Decide the sequence of instruction, the order in which instructional procedures will occur.

Figure 3.5 shows a three-week calendar for an integrated unit on smoking. Seeing what is to be done each day helps you evaluate the feasibility of your plans. Teachers often hope to accomplish more than is possible. A daily schedule also helps organize your efforts, informing you about what lessons to plan and helping you monitor the pace of instruction. If your unit turns out to need three months, then you probably need to reduce it. To be sure, your schedule might change once you begin a unit: A school assembly, fire drill, or power outage might disrupt a day's planned procedures; particular

Monday	Tuesday	Wednesday	Thursday	Friday
Introduce unit. Brainstorm understandings, beliefs, and questions.	Continue general introduction. Introduce written commitment task. Demonstrate how to interview.	Introduce health risks. Produce life-size diagrams of human body.	Gather information about diseases. Begin small-group collaboration.	Present guest speaker. Continue gathering information about diseases.
Begin portraying smoking effects on diagram. Introduce government assistance and control.	Gather information about government and smoking. Continue working on diagram.	Finalize portrayals of smoking effects. Give quiz on smoking effects.	Continue gathering information about government and smoking.	Finalize letter explaining government's role in tobacco industry.
Introduce cigarette advertising.	Prepare ad scrapbook.	Produce written commitments. Finalize ad scrapbook.	Finalize written commitments. Finalize original ad.	Culminate unit. Share written commitments.

FIGURE 3.5   Schedule for Unit on Smoking

resources, such as a movie or guest speaker, might not show up as scheduled; and students might accomplish tasks faster or slower than expected. A schedule allows you to plan ahead and accommodate unforeseen events.

Representative Units

The seven-step procedure for planning integrated units might seem intimidating, but your concerns will lessen when you actually begin preparations. One way to reduce any anxiety is to remember that planning is an ongoing repetitive process. Steps 4 and 5 focus on revising original plans, although revisions can be made any time. For instance, the organizing center identified in step 1 might be modified as you design objectives in step 2. Rather than label your center Smoking, you might decide that A Smoke-Free Society by the Year 2000 is a better label. The schedule of events listed in step 7 could lead to changes in the instructional procedures decided earlier.

Teachers often have access to plans produced by others. Previously designed units, district curriculum guides, and commercial teaching materials are good beginnings for your own integrated units. Planning also can be done with students. You can identify an organizing center and have your class brainstorm general unit objectives, resources, and procedures. After an organizing center is defined, student input can be solicited at any time. The organizational structure of middle schools, which emphasizes interdisciplinary faculty teams, lends itself to unit planning with colleagues.

Teachers employ integrated units to various degrees. Some integrate all features of instruction all year long, whereas others present traditional as well as integrated instruction. Elementary teachers often offer traditional instructional routines in spelling and mathematics while integrating language arts, social studies, science, and fine arts. Some units might include all the major disciplines; others might not. Secondary teachers often integrate their instruction in certain classes but not in others. A social studies teacher might collaborate with an English teacher to offer two American studies classes per day yet teach drama in a more traditional manner. And some might integrate instruction for one month and not another.

Figures 3.6 through 3.9 present curriculum webs and schedules for two integrated units: space for the primary grades and Native Americans of the Southwest for the middle grades. These plans further represent what completed integrated unit plans look like, showing finished products rather than what is produced at each step of the planning process.

TRY IT OUT
Plan an integrated unit by forming small groups and following the steps described above. Share your plans with other groups for potential classroom uses.

Unit Introduction

Procedures

(wg, LA) Announce topic and
read several books to students.

(wg, LA) Build bulletin board
of solar system as reading.

(i or sg, LA) Place books, filmstrips, and
activity cards in center.

(wg, LA) Chant poems and sing songs.

(sg, LA, StSk) Select space body
about which to learn and report.

(sg, LA, SS) Begin planning for planetary
bazaar and museum.

Resources

Commander Toad series—J. Yolen
Space Case series—E. Marshall
The Magic School Bus: Lost in the Solar System—J. Cole
If You Were an Astronaut—D. L. Moche
Gravity and the Astronauts—M. Freeman
A Day in Space—S. Lord & J. Epstein
Our Solar System and Beyond—Q. L. Pearce
Amazing Space Facts—D. L. Moche
Songs and poems on space in Scholastic's
Banners: Space learning kit
Space Songs—M. C. Livingston
Filmstrips, space songs record from media center

We know about our Sun, Moon, and other planets through exploration and examination.

Procedures

(wg, LA) Guided viewing and discussion of films
on space exploration

(i) Nighttime viewing of stars with telescopes

(wg, LA) Presentation by head of astronomy club

Resources

The First Space Pioneers and *Lunar Landings*
films from district office
Rockets and Satellites—F. M. Branley
How to Draw Spacecraft—E. Fischel & A. Ganeri
Telescopes borrowed from astronomy club
Guest speaker—Dr. Artis, president of local
astronomy club
Pictures of space exploration equipment

Evaluation

(sg, StSk, LA) Each group selects a kind of tool,
instrument, or machine used for
exploration and examination of space
bodies. Produce a picture and a
description of what it does and what it
has found.

Key:
LA = language arts   M = math
SS = social studies   S = science
StSk = study skills

PE = personal experience

i = individual   wg = whole group
sg = small group

FIGURE 3.6 Primary-Grade Integrated Unit on Space

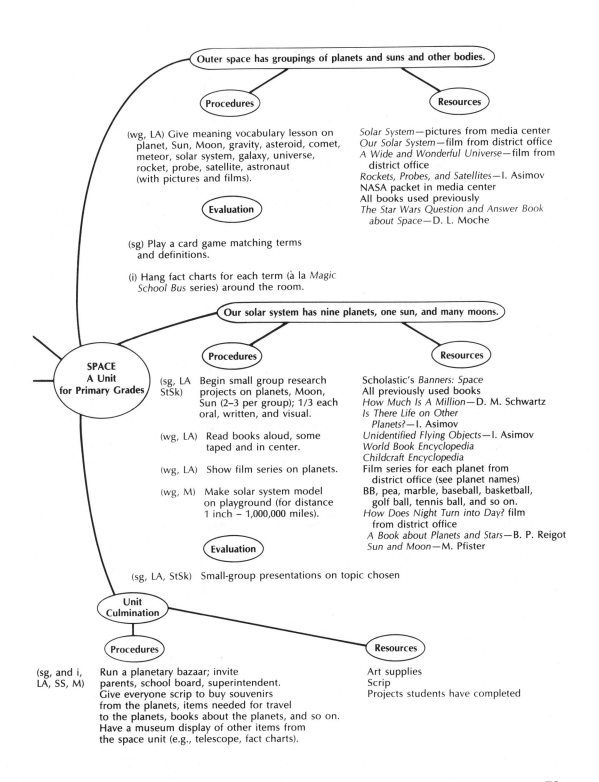

Outer space has groupings of planets and suns and other bodies.

Procedures

(wg, LA) Give meaning vocabulary lesson on planet, Sun, Moon, gravity, asteroid, comet, meteor, solar system, galaxy, universe, rocket, probe, satellite, astronaut (with pictures and films).

Evaluation

(sg) Play a card game matching terms and definitions.

(i) Hang fact charts for each term (à la *Magic School Bus* series) around the room.

Resources

Solar System—pictures from media center
Our Solar System—film from district office
A Wide and Wonderful Universe—film from district office
Rockets, Probes, and Satellites—I. Asimov
NASA packet in media center
All books used previously
The Star Wars Question and Answer Book about Space—D. L. Moche

SPACE A Unit for Primary Grades

Our solar system has nine planets, one sun, and many moons.

Procedures

(sg, LA StSk) Begin small group research projects on planets, Moon, Sun (2–3 per group); 1/3 each oral, written, and visual.

(wg, LA) Read books aloud, some taped and in center.

(wg, LA) Show film series on planets.

(wg, M) Make solar system model on playground (for distance 1 inch – 1,000,000 miles).

Evaluation

(sg, LA, StSk) Small-group presentations on topic chosen

Resources

Scholastic's *Banners: Space*
All previously used books
How Much Is A Million—D. M. Schwartz
Is There Life on Other Planets?—I. Asimov
Unidentified Flying Objects—I. Asimov
World Book Encyclopedia
Childcraft Encyclopedia
Film series for each planet from district office (see planet names)
BB, pea, marble, baseball, basketball, golf ball, tennis ball, and so on.
How Does Night Turn into Day? film from district office
A Book about Planets and Stars—B. P. Reigot
Sun and Moon—M. Pfister

Unit Culmination

Procedures

(sg, and i, LA, SS, M) Run a planetary bazaar; invite parents, school board, superintendent. Give everyone scrip to buy souvenirs from the planets, items needed for travel to the planets, books about the planets, and so on. Have a museum display of other items from the space unit (e.g., telescope, fact charts).

Resources

Art supplies
Scrip
Projects students have completed

Monday	Tuesday	Wednesday	Thursday	Friday
Introduce Space unit. Read books throughout day. Sing songs. Read poems. Introduce science center. Explain planetary bazaar.	Introduce Space unit. Read throughout day. Sing songs. Read poems. Start bulletin board (add to as can).	Introduce Space unit. Read throughout day. Sing songs. Read poems. Choose space body for report.	Meaning vocabulary lesson. Show *Solar System* pictures. Show *Our Solar System* film. Continue reading.	Meaning vocabulary lesson. Show *Solar System* pictures. Show *Wide/Wonderful Universe* film. Continue reading. Play card game to practice terms.
Meaning vocabulary lesson. Show *Solar System* pictures. Use pictures and information in NASA space packet. Continue reading. Construct and hang fact charts.	Show *Sun* film. Read books and parts of encyclopedias. Visual display by small group	Continue to read. Oral report by small group	Continue to read. Written report by small group	Show *Earth* film. Visual display by small group Make solar system model on playground with balls to show distances and proportional sizes.
Show *Moon* film. Oral report by small group Show *How Does Night Turn into Day?* film.	Written report by small group Plan for bazaar and museum.	Visual display by small group Prepare materials for planetary bazaar and museum.	Oral report by small group Prepare materials for planetary bazaar and museum.	Show *Jupiter* film. Written report by small group Prepare materials for planetary bazaar and museum.
Visual display by small group Prepare materials for bazaar and museum.	Oral report by small group Prepare materials for bazaar and museum.	Show *1st Space Pioneers* film. Evening: View stars with telescopes.	Show *Lunar Landings* film. Select tool and so on for research. Make pictures and one-paragraph report of tool.	Culminate unit. Hold planetary bazaar and museum. Guest speaker Display pictures, reports, and so on.

FIGURE 3.7 Schedule for Unit on Space

Young students culminating a Thanksgiving unit.

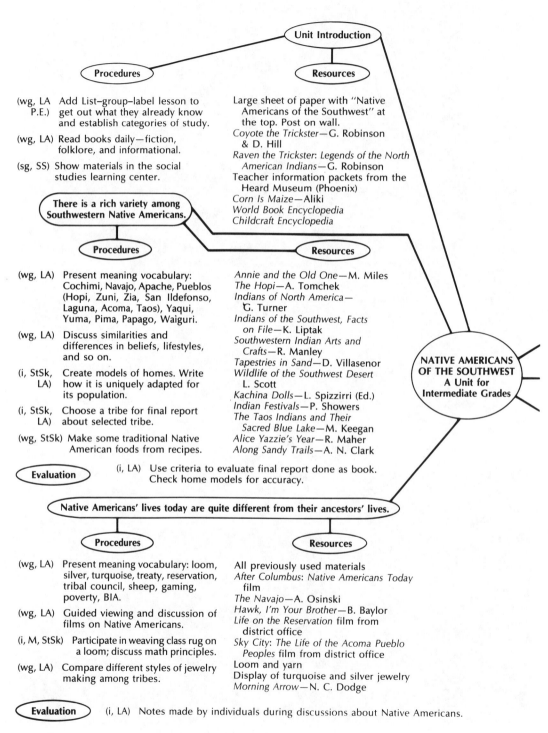

Unit Introduction

Procedures

(wg, LA   Add List–group–label lesson to
P.E.)   get out what they already know
and establish categories of study.

(wg, LA) Read books daily—fiction,
folklore, and informational.

(sg, SS) Show materials in the social
studies learning center.

Resources

Large sheet of paper with "Native
Americans of the Southwest" at
the top. Post on wall.
Coyote the Trickster—G. Robinson
& D. Hill
*Raven the Trickster: Legends of the North
American Indians*—G. Robinson
Teacher information packets from the
Heard Museum (Phoenix)
Corn Is Maize—Aliki
World Book Encyclopedia
Childcraft Encyclopedia

**There is a rich variety among
Southwestern Native Americans.**

Procedures

(wg, LA) Present meaning vocabulary:
Cochimi, Navajo, Apache, Pueblos
(Hopi, Zuni, Zia, San Ildefonso,
Laguna, Acoma, Taos), Yaqui,
Yuma, Pima, Papago, Waiguri.

(wg, LA) Discuss similarities and
differences in beliefs, lifestyles,
and so on.

(i, StSk, Create models of homes. Write
LA) how it is uniquely adapted for
its population.

(i, StSk, Choose a tribe for final report
LA) about selected tribe.

(wg, StSk) Make some traditional Native
American foods from recipes.

Resources

Annie and the Old One—M. Miles
The Hopi—A. Tomchek
Indians of North America—
G. Turner
*Indians of the Southwest, Facts
on File*—K. Liptak
*Southwestern Indian Arts and
Crafts*—R. Manley
Tapestries in Sand—D. Villasenor
Wildlife of the Southwest Desert
L. Scott
Kachina Dolls—L. Spizzirri (Ed.)
Indian Festivals—P. Showers
*The Taos Indians and Their
Sacred Blue Lake*—M. Keegan
Alice Yazzie's Year—R. Maher
Along Sandy Trails—A. N. Clark

Evaluation   (i, LA)   Use criteria to evaluate final report done as book.
Check home models for accuracy.

**NATIVE AMERICANS
OF THE SOUTHWEST
A Unit for
Intermediate Grades**

Native Americans' lives today are quite different from their ancestors' lives.

Procedures

(wg, LA) Present meaning vocabulary: loom,
silver, turquoise, treaty, reservation,
tribal council, sheep, gaming,
poverty, BIA.

(wg, LA) Guided viewing and discussion of
films on Native Americans.

(i, M, StSk) Participate in weaving class rug on
a loom; discuss math principles.

(wg, LA) Compare different styles of jewelry
making among tribes.

Resources

All previously used materials
After Columbus: Native Americans Today
film
The Navajo—A. Osinski
Hawk, I'm Your Brother—B. Baylor
Life on the Reservation film from
district office
*Sky City: The Life of the Acoma Pueblo
Peoples* film from district office
Loom and yarn
Display of turquoise and silver jewelry
Morning Arrow—N. C. Dodge

Evaluation   (i, LA)   Notes made by individuals during discussions about Native Americans.

FIGURE 3.8   Intermediate-Grade Integrated Unit on Native Americans of the Southwest

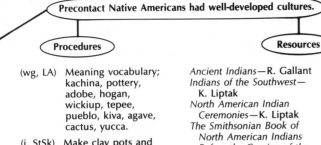

Precontact Native Americans had well-developed cultures.

Procedures

(wg, LA) Meaning vocabulary; kachina, pottery, adobe, hogan, wickiup, tepee, pueblo, kiva, agave, cactus, yucca.

(i, StSk) Make clay pots and decorate with traditional designs.

(Sg, StSk) Wash with yucca root soap.

(i, StSk) Paint with yucca brushes.

(i, StSk) Weave yucca fibers to make a mat.

(wg, arts) Listen to music and learn some dances.

(sg, LA) Compare folktales among tribes.

Resources

Ancient Indians—R. Gallant
Indians of the Southwest—K. Liptak
North American Indian Ceremonies—K. Liptak
The Smithsonian Book of North American Indians Before the Coming of the Europeans—P. Kopper
Sweet Salt—R. F. Locke
Meditations with the Navajo—G. Hausman
Yucca plants
Clay, kiln, and paints
Kids Discover magazine, "America 1492" (Aug./Sept. 1992 issue)
Boy Scout with Indian lore merit badge

At the Center of the World—B. Baker
North American Legends—V. Hamilton
The Trees Stand Shining—H. Jones
Arrow to the Sun—G. McDermott
And It Is Still that Way: Legends Told by Arizona Indian Children—B. Baylor
God on Every Mountain—B. Baylor
A Cry from the Earth: Music of the North American Indians—J. Bierhorst
The Desert Is Theirs—B. Baylor
Moonsong—B. Baylor
Indian Legacy: Native American Influences on World Life and Culture—A. H. Poatgieter
The Indians Knew—T. S. Pine and J. Levine

Evaluation

(i, StSk) Examine projects for accuracy of designs and information.

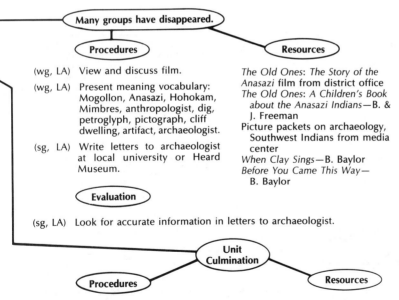

Many groups have disappeared.

Procedures

(wg, LA) View and discuss film.

(wg, LA) Present meaning vocabulary: Mogollon, Anasazi, Hohokam, Mimbres, anthropologist, dig, petroglyph, pictograph, cliff dwelling, artifact, archaeologist.

(sg, LA) Write letters to archaeologist at local university or Heard Museum.

Resources

The Old Ones: The Story of the Anasazi film from district office
The Old Ones: A Children's Book about the Anasazi Indians—B. & J. Freeman
Picture packets on archaeology, Southwest Indians from media center
When Clay Sings—B. Baylor
Before You Came This Way—B. Baylor

Evaluation

(sg, LA) Look for accurate information in letters to archaeologist.

Unit Culmination

Procedures

(wg, LA) Visit Heard Museum for day. Finish books on tribes. Write thank-you letters to guide.

Resources

Tour guide for the Heard (focus on Southwest Indians). Notebooks to record information.

Key:

LA = language arts
SS = social studies
StSk = study skills
M = math
S = science

PE = personal experience

i = individual
sg = small group
wg = whole group

Monday	Tuesday	Wednesday	Thursday	Friday
Introduce unit. Show pictures. Show map. Read passage from informational packet.	Introduce unit. Brainstorm knowledge. Browse and free read.	Introduce unit. Brainstorm knowledge. Share learning objectives. Browse and free read.	Meaning vocabulary: Southwest tribes Emphasize similarities and differences among groups as shown in movie.	Choose a tribe/group to study and report in book form. Begin collecting information from classroom resources.
Meaning vocabulary: Precontact cultures and artifacts Illustrate and plan construction of models of homes and cultural artifacts.	Read folktales aloud. Construct models of homes and cultural artifacts.	Monitor tribe/group reports. Perform traditional dances.	Read folktales aloud. Construct models of homes and cultural artifacts.	Display models of homes. Cook traditional recipes.
Meaning vocabulary: Extinct groups Read folktales aloud.	Compare folktales. Construct cultural artifacts.	Meaning vocabulary: modern and ancient lives Monitor tribe-group reports.	Watch movie and orally compare differences in modern and ancient lives. Plan letter to archaeologist.	Display artifacts (pots, rugs). Cook traditional foods from recipes.
Submit letter to archaeologist.	Plan questions and observations for museum visit.	Monitor tribe-group reports.	Culminate unit. Visit museum.	Culminate unit. Write thank-you letters to museum guide. Share books on tribes.

FIGURE 3.9   Schedule for Unit on Native Americans of the Southwest

INQUIRY UNITS EMPHASIZE STUDENTS' CHOICES AND GENERALIZATIONS

Like integrated units, inquiry units are blocks of instruction smaller than an entire course yet larger than daily lessons. Inquiry units also might combine disciplines, language arts, grouping patterns, and personal experiences, although they do not emphasize such combinations. They stress other aspects of instruction.

Inquiry units are based on the premise that self-discovery leads to the most permanent and transferable learning (Strike, 1975). Proponents of these units believe that the best learning occurs through personal involvement and in-depth analyses. Students who receive just teacher-directed instruction are at risk of learning to perform only on command; inquiry-based instruction promotes independent individual action. Thinking processes, learning strategies, and attitudes are the special instructional focus when students conduct self-controlled inquiries.

The professional literature typically groups inquiry with such educational concepts as discovery, problem solving, research projects, experiential learning, and inductive teaching. These approaches are alternatives to direct didactic teaching. Inquiry units are a somewhat open-ended curriculum plan calling for teachers to take an indirect supportive role in students' learning. Students assume responsibility for planning, conducting, and evaluating their learning efforts. During inquiry units, a teacher acts as a "guide on the side" rather than as a "sage on the stage."

There are two forms of inquiry teaching (Orlich et al., 1990). Some educational writers promote *guided inquiry,* wherein teachers specify learning outcomes, withhold them from students, and subtly direct students toward them. Socratic questioning, which moves students to desired outcomes through a series of leading questions, exemplifies guided inquiry. On the other hand, *unguided inquiry* minimizes the role of teachers in specifying outcomes. In this approach teachers regularly prod students' thinking with open-ended questions, not ones leading to predetermined answers.

Our presentation of inquiry units leans toward unguided inquiry, stressing the importance of students making choices. Teachers emphasize choice when they have students take the lead, or at least actively serve as partners, in their instruction. Rather than make unilateral decisions about learning outcomes and activities, teachers collaborate with students to form mutual decisions. During inquiry units students play a large role in selecting topics for study and choosing procedures to investigate the topics. They might use library materials, but their research extends to interviewing people, writing for information, and conducting experiments. Involving students this way is meant to foster ownership; students sense that what they are learning belongs to them.

Unguided inquiry also stresses the value of students forming their own generalizations. As Chapter 1 explained, students generalize when they form conclusions based on data. They synthesize information to produce a statement about a whole. The difference between teachers presenting generalizations to students and students forming their own is illustrated by the integrated unit plan's treatment of advertising techniques. The plan presented above called for the teacher to describe advertising techniques, have students locate cigarette ads that exemplified each type, then have students produce their own ad. The teacher was to present the generalization, and students were to produce examples. In an inquiry unit, the teacher would ensure that students had access to numerous cigarette ads, then would have students infer the commonalities. The teacher might ask such open-ended questions as these: "What can you say about these advertisements? What do the ads have in common? How are they attempting to convince people to smoke their brands?" The teacher would provide examples and stimulate thinking, and students would produce the generalizations.

When conducting inquiry units, teachers help students form their own generalizations about the world by ensuring that they investigate issues conducive to such thinking. Primary-grade students probably would have trouble reaching a conclusion about why air exists, but they could explain why winds occur. Teachers also foster generalizations by providing students with access to abundant data related to a specific issue. Students can form valid conclusions only when they examine meaningful sets of information. Several cigarette ads would be needed for students to form valid generalizations. Finally, teachers spur students to test and refine their initial generalizations, asking for proof that the statement applies to appropriate situations. If students conclude that cigarette ads emphasize humor, teachers might have them support this conclusion by comparing the number of humorous ads with the number of nonhumorous ones.

Planning Inquiry Units

The steps in planning inquiry units reflect the ones for planning integrated units (presented above), as well as those for planning library research projects (presented in Chapter 6). Care must be taken to generate clear objectives and provide access to abundant rich resources. However, the specific plans teachers produce before conducting inquiry units are limited due to the need for student input. Indeed, inquiry-based teachers find that they make many more decisions when interacting with students than beforehand. The following steps are for planning inquiry units:

STEP 1: IDENTIFYING AN ORGANIZING CENTER   Teachers typically identify the organizing center of inquiry units. As with integrated units, teachers select organizing centers that are general enough to allow multiple perspectives, that students probably will find interesting and relevant, and that come with sufficient resources for a thorough investigation. Smoking would be as appropriate for an inquiry unit as for an integrated unit.

STEP 2: ESTABLISHING GENERAL UNIT OBJECTIVES   Teachers typically make the decision about inquiry units' organizing centers, but students take the lead during the remaining steps. Inquiry-based teachers would ensure that students play a major role in deciding general unit objectives.

To have students select learning objectives, first introduce the organizing center, such as smoking. Teachers might plan to display cigarette packs and advertisements, present statistics on the prevalence of smoking, and elicit students' understandings and beliefs about the topic. The next move is to have students list what they know and do not know about the topic. Have students brainstorm one list of known information and another list of uncertainties and unknown information. If the topic is smoking, students might list smoking-related diseases—such as throat cancer and lung cancer—and

Students brainstorm researchable questions during inquiry units.

ask a question such as, "What other diseases does smoking cause?" General objectives for inquiry units work well when stated in question form.

Plan to spend at least several days producing researchable questions. As noted above, the quality of students' generalizations is related directly to the issues they investigate. Have students work in whole-class, small-group, and individual arrangements to generate and refine questions. In addition, provide resources to inform students' question formation.

STEP 3: FACILITATING STUDENTS' INQUIRIES Once you have a plan for initiating students' inquiries, you need one for facilitating them. As a facilitator, your major role is providing resources and materials. Students require access to quantities of data to form generalizations. Teachers also explain how inquiry progresses. Learners who inquire into practically any topic follow a progression such as the following:

1. Specify the guiding question/problem.
2. Identify preliminary sources of information.
3. Decide on a report format.
4. Collect and examine resources.
5. Create and support generalizations.
6. Share the inquiry.

Planning is needed for whole-class, small-group, and individual meetings to support students as they work through these steps. Teachers often set aside specific times for these grouping arrangements. They introduce the steps of inquiry, guide students through them, and monitor progress, deciding specifically what should be done close to the time of each meeting.

Whole-class activities are good forums for providing background and coherence to individuals' investigations. Teachers often set aside specific times for presentations of subject matter and research procedures, for the class members to reflect on what they are learning through daily journal writing, and for individuals to report what they have accomplished. Whole-class activities provide to inquiry units stability and a sense of order.

Small-group work seems best for practicing what has been presented to the whole class and for exploring ideas. As students become proficient with collaborative group work, they might begin producing joint projects.

Student Name	Question	Preliminary Resources	Report Format	Resources Collected	Generalizations	Inquiry Shared

FIGURE 3.10 Inquiry Unit Checkpoints

Setting aside specific times to confer with individual students as they pursue their investigations allows you to clarify their research questions, propose additional types of data they might seek, suggest resources, react to the generalizations they have produced, and evaluate their progress. Most teachers establish checkpoints for monitoring and supporting the investigations of individual students. Figure 3.10 shows a checklist teachers might use for staying in touch with students.

STEP 4: CULMINATING STUDENTS' INQUIRIES   As with integrated units, in inquiry units teachers make special provisions for culminating students' investigations. This step includes deciding on opportunities for students to cement and celebrate what they have learned. Decisions need to be made about how students will report their efforts: Will their efforts be recorded in a formal report? Will products be written, oral, visual, or a combination of these forms? Will they be presented to the class, to others outside the class, to small groups, or only to the teacher? In addition, decisions about evaluating students' inquiries mirror the ones about integrated unit performance.

Implementing Inquiry Units

A key to successful inquiry units is moving into them gradually. Turning over too much responsibility to underprepared or unprepared students can lead to disorder (Doyle, 1986). Assembling the necessary materials and resources takes time. Students might flounder, behavior problems might erupt, and you might become frustrated. By the same token, turning over too little responsibility also can lead to disorder (McNeil, 1986). Students might become bored with school, feel disenfranchised, and exhibit behavior problems if they always are told what to learn and when to learn it.

Teachers often begin the school year or semester with integrated units and fade gradually into inquiry units. They might make all the instructional decisions for the first integrated unit students pursue, then begin to ask for student input. For instance, teachers might list general unit objectives and have students decide the order in which they want to move through the objectives. Teachers might list several learning activities and have students select which two or three they want to perform. Students might invent their own unit objectives and learning activities to go along with the ones teachers prepare. Students can make more choices and form more of their own generalizations with each succeeding unit.

DO IT TOGETHER
Form small groups of classmates. Share examples of inquiry units that you experienced as either a student or a teacher. Describe the experience and specify its positive and negative features. Explain how your experience might influence your use of inquiry-based teaching.

EXPLICIT INSTRUCTION IN HOW TO STUDY CAN OCCUR REGULARLY

Units of instruction based on integration and on inquiry go far in developing students' independence. Students who examine topics as an integrated whole and direct their own inquiries have the opportunity to discover how to learn. However, setting the stage for discovery is only part of a good instructional program for developing independent learners. Teachers should provide regular explicit instruction in how to study.

The term *study* refers to a conscious effort to learn. Students study when they deliberate over subject matter, working to understand and remember it. Studying is something students do for themselves.

As literacy and learning requirements increase in our complex society and our schools, the need for students to learn how to study increases. Learning how to acquire new ideas and abilities is as important as learning subject matter concepts. As we noted in Chapter 1, individuals need to update themselves continually just to stay abreast of changes in their occupations and personal lives. Developing students who are able and predisposed to be lifelong learners is a paramount goal of education.

DOMAIN OF STUDY

Knowing where to begin study instruction is difficult because the domain of study is huge. Philosophers have commented on study throughout recorded history, and U.S. educators have published voluminous research-based and professional reports about it since the 1920s (Moore, Readence, & Rickelman, 1983). This section describes five central components of learning that fall under the rubric of study: processes, strategies, systems, resource management, and self-regulation. Some components traditionally categorized under study are presented elsewhere in this book: Locating information is in Chapter 6, pages 172 to 176; taking tests is in Chapter 8, pages 244 to 247; and interpreting graphics is covered by the lesson format presented in Chapter 4.

Processes

Processes are the building blocks of study; they are the fundamental elements. The essential thinking processes described in Chapter 1—call up, connect, predict, organize, generalize, form an image, monitor, evaluate, and apply—are study processes. Students are often at a loss when told to "Think about it!"; they require access to one or more of the thinking processes. The processes are the antidote to the passive rote learning achieved by reading something over and over until it is memorized.

Proficient learners sometimes employ processes individually to understand and remember information, as illustrated by our example in Chapter 1 of learning a driving manual's information. However, learners frequently combine processes to form strategies.

Strategies

Proficient learners merge individual study processes into packages called strategies. The following study strategies are used and recommended often:

Defining Learning Expectations
Previewing
Setting a purpose

Questioning
Answering prepared questions
Self-questioning

Organizing Information Graphically
Outline
Time line
Flow chart
Venn diagram
Web
Cause and effect chain

Writing
Study card
Note taking
Summarizing
Learning log
Journal
Essay

Creating Mnemonic Devices
Analogies
Images
Abbreviations
Acronyms
Acrostics
Rhymes
Phrases

Creating Special Word Associations
Meaningful word parts
Idiosyncratic associations
Mnemonic keyword method

Mental Learning
Retelling
Discussing

DEFINING LEARNING EXPECTATIONS   Proficient learners define expectations by clarifying what they intend to learn. They create multistep plans for bringing thought into the learning act. One way of doing this is previewing, when proficient learners look over what they are to learn before examining it closely. They preview printed materials by surveying many sources of information: titles, headings, italic and boldface print, and other typographical aids; illustrations, maps, graphs, and other pictorial aids; introductions, first sentences of paragraphs, summaries, and conclusions; guiding questions, stated objectives, end-of-chapter exercises, and other adjunct aids. Previewing helps learners define learning expectations by establishing what a passage has to offer.

Another aspect of defining learning expectations involves setting a purpose. Learners set purposes when they discern what they should acquire from a passage, lecture, film, or other teaching device. Learners incorporate what they gathered from a preview with their understanding of the learning task to decide what deserves special attention. They attend to their instructors' stated and unstated cues about what they should learn. The age-old tradition of "psyching out" vague instructors to anticipate what should be in a paper or might be on a test exemplifies part of this strategy. When learners set a purpose, they decide what they want to learn and go after it.

QUESTIONING   Students who read and then answer questions about a passage tend to learn more than students who only read the passage. Answering prepared questions often seems like busy work to students, but it can be a potent study strategy. Self-questioning taps learners' creativity. They might pattern their questions after the teacher's, use certain stems (What have I learned about . . .? What should I remember about . . .?), and ask and answer questions of one another in reciprocal fashion.

ORGANIZING INFORMATION GRAPHICALLY   Graphic representations arrange key terms to depict their relationships. Outlines, time lines, Venn diagrams, and webs (which are discussed in Chapter 4, pages 117 to 120) are some formats for graphically organizing concepts. They show how the concepts are organized. A graphic representation of the desert, for example, would consist of terms arranged about such topics as climate, location, plant life, and animal life; it would not be an illustrated scene of coyotes and cactuses.

WRITING   Although such strategies as defining learning expectations and questioning might involve writing, study strategies grouped under this heading typically refer to other techniques. Writing strategies that promote learning progress from simply recording facts to assimilating and reflecting on bodies of knowledge. These strategies activate thinking when learners compose the message; they also provide a record for review and revision.

Study cards usually contain a question or vocabulary term on one side and a corresponding answer or definition on the other. These cards are especially useful for factual learning. Many students would not have passed fact-filled courses without resorting to study cards. Note taking assumes many forms. Learners sometimes copy definitions and key ideas verbatim from a passage, comment in the margins of texts, paraphrase information, or add personal examples. They benefit from rewriting their notes, clarifying and consolidating information from class presentations and readings.

Summarizing involves learners in selecting and condensing important information. They abstract important contents. Learning logs are a variation of class notebooks. Students record information from class presentations, readings, and outside experiences. Students often develop their notes into more lengthy compositions. In addition, they often use learning logs to pose questions and state confusions about what they are learning. Many mathematics teachers have students write—rather than orally ask—questions about their homework in order to clarify the questions. This often leads to independent solutions. Journals emphasize personal reactions to subject matter; students freely associate ideas about what they are learning. Essays that call for integration of subject matter or persuasive writing from a particular point of view are powerful forms of writing, even though they are time-consuming.

CREATING MNEMONIC DEVICES Mnemonic devices—memory aids named after the Greek goddess of memory, Mnemosyne—include several disparate techniques. Analogies stress the similarities between phenomena; for instance, the cell structure of a plant might be compared with the factory structure of an industry. Images become mnemonic devices when they represent abstract concepts; a visual image of mist coming from a block of dry ice might be used to represent the physical process of sublimation, the change of a solid directly into a gas.

Mnemonic devices take such forms as abbreviations (FBI, NAACP, NCAA), acronyms (HOMES for the first letters of the Great Lakes), acrostics ("My very educated mother just served us nine pizzas" for the first letters of the planets in order from the Sun), and rhymes ("In 1492 Columbus sailed the ocean blue"). They also can be phrases that help with meaning ("Hang on tight" for remembering that stalactites are on cave ceilings rather than floors) as well as pronunciation ("It's hot again" indicates the accent to Betatakin, a cliff dwelling in Arizona's Navajo National Monument).

CREATING SPECIAL WORD ASSOCIATIONS A set of mnemonic devices that is large enough and important enough to warrant separate treatment involves individual words. Because understanding and remembering subject matter vocabulary consumes a great deal of students' attention, we present word-study techniques here and in Chapter 7.

Meaningful word parts, or morphemes, are found in derived words with their prefixes, roots, and suffixes. Contractions and compound words also contain these parts. Students often benefit from attending to the meaningful parts of such words as *underground, triangular,* and *immortalize.* Identifying the meaningful parts of words provides control of them and a tool for identifying new words.

Idiosyncratic associations are similar to meaningful word parts, although the word parts are not from our linguistic heritage. Knowing that the princi-*pal* should be your friend and that *lat*itude runs the same way as the equ*at*or represent idiosyncratic associations.

The mnemonic keyword method (Pressley, Levin, & Delaney, 1982) requires first an acoustic link, then a visual one. For instance, to remember that a credenza is a piece of furniture like a buffet or sideboard, the students might recode the word to an acoustic link, such as *dents.* A visual image of someone bumping into and denting the furniture could then be constructed.

MENTAL LEARNING This somewhat amorphous category of study strategies produces no written or visual products (Wade, Trathen, & Schraw, 1990).

It stresses activities to be done either with others as part of a study/discussion group or inside one's own head. Retelling is a way to initiate mental learning. After reading, students individually or in groups recount what has been learned. They focus on specific information, sometimes repeatedly verbalizing or paraphrasing it and sometimes reading it aloud. When uncertainties occur, good learners return to the source to clarify it or make a note to ask the instructor for clarification. Discussing is an open-ended arrangement for students to come together and refine their learning. They might retell particular portions of subject matter, teach it to one another, and ask and answer questions about it.

Mental learning capitalizes on the essential thinking processes. For instance, learners connect known concepts with what they encounter, evaluate the validity and accuracy of the ideas as well as the author's writing style, and apply concepts to their current lives as well as to the future.

Systems

Just as proficient learners incorporate thinking processes into study strategies, they also merge study strategies into systems. Study systems are multi-step plans for bringing thought into the learning act. The classic study system recommended in the literature is SQ3R. Since 1946 it has been presented in many study skills courses; perhaps you were exposed to it. SQ3R consists of the following strategies:

Survey: Preview the material to obtain a general overview of what is to come.

Question: Generate questions from the titles, headings, and subheadings to be answered while reading.

Read: Process the print in order to answer the questions just asked.

Recite: Deliberate over the passage contents, questions, and answers.

Review: Look back over the passage to confirm answers and clarify uncertainties.

Some variations of SQ3R are PQ4R (preview, question, read, reflect, recite, review) (Thomas & Robinson, 1972), OARWET (overview, achieve, write, evaluate, test) (Norman & Norman, 1968), and PORPE (predict, organize, rehearse, practice, evaluate) (Simpson et al., 1988). Reciprocal teaching is a highly acclaimed system that calls for students to predict, clarify, generate questions, and summarize (Palincsar & Brown, 1984).

Study systems share an important characteristic with teachers' unit and lesson plans: They have a beginning, a middle, and an end. Learners' study systems and teachers' instructional frameworks call for the learner to think deliberately about a passage before, during, and after reading. Preparation is done in the prereading, beginning stage; actual reading is done in the middle stage; and follow-up occurs in the postreading stage. Good learners realize this progression when studying with a system.

Resource Management

One of the authors wanted to attend a time management seminar offered during the writing of this book but couldn't find the time. Resource management clearly is easier to talk about than actually to control. You probably will find this to be the case with your students, but we encourage you to continue emphasizing it because of its importance. Students who hear these recommendations over and over eventually might follow them. Principles of resource management related to studying outside of school include the following:

1. *Maintaining a routine.* Establish a consistent time and place to study.
2. *Creating a productive environment.* Establish appropriate levels of noise, light, and temperature. Make sure school supplies are nearby. Have access to food and beverage. Take short breaks.
3. *Completing tasks in an efficient order.* Sequence tasks in an order such as easy to difficult, short to long, interesting to boring, or most favorite to least favorite. Then complete them in the way that is most efficient for you.
4. *Completing tasks on schedule.* Keep up with readings and assignments; do not procrastinate.
5. *Reviewing information at regular intervals.* Conduct frequent short reviews rather than infrequent long ones.
6. *Seeking help when needed.* Contact friends, classmates, or teachers to clarify information. Use tutors or study centers. Initiate study groups or pairs.

Self-regulation

Proficient learners do what it takes to learn, seeking access to processes, strategies, systems, and resources that enhance learning. They also are self-regulated.

Self-regulated learners control their learning actions (Corno, 1986). If deep understanding of a passage were needed, these students might preview it, take notes, and question themselves about it. If mastery of specific facts were the goal, these learners might decide to create mnemonic devices; furthermore, they would know if an abbreviation, acronym, or acrostic was the best type of device for the particular set of facts.

When self-regulated learners read, they sometimes move forward at a medium rate, they sometimes skim, and they sometimes slow down considerably. They are flexible; they change their reading rate according to the demands of the material and their purpose for reading. If the passage is easy and learners want an overview of it, they read rapidly. If the passage is difficult and learners want to master the contents, they read slowly. Good learners monitor themselves as they move through print, focusing on ideas that they know to be important. They often regress to an earlier point in a passage and reread it to fix it in their minds. These learners also focus on confusing ideas. If they are unclear about something, they return and attempt to clarify it. This control of strategies and reading rate is called metacognitive control.

Think of a person skilled in a craft such as plumbing. Good plumbers have many tools and use them selectively to accomplish specific purposes. A plumber might size up a situation, then begin working with a socket wrench. If that tool is not getting the job done, he or she might employ a crescent wrench. When a plumber is at a delicate part of a job, he or she will slow down to be sure to get it right. Students with metacognitive control use learning strategies like skilled craftspeople use tools (Paris & Winograd, 1990). They plan to use strategies appropriate to specific learning tasks, check on how well they are progressing, and make adjustments as needed. They have well-developed flexible repertoires.

Along with having metacognitive control, self-regulated learners are motivated. Students might be full of study strategy knowledge, but it will help only if they are motivated to apply it. Habit and will are as important as content and skill. Self-regulated learners have the predisposition to accomplish academic goals (Borkowski et al., 1990) and persist with tasks even when they become difficult. They engage learning tasks with their full attention, blocking out distractions.

Students with little control of their effort often try to escape learning. They might try to distract teachers or make excuses for their performance. They often create highly charged emotional scenes, acting out verbally and physically or withdrawing sullenly. Feelings of frustration and embarrassment rather than confidence and pride influence their actions.

The affective motivational aspects of self-regulation deserve as much in-

---

Interviewer _____   **Date** _____

Student _____   **Grade** _____

School Subject _____

Note: If students are confused by a question, explain it until they understand. In addition, probe students' responses until they have no more to say about each item.

1. What do you do when you want to learn the information being presented in your (school subject) class? How do you go about understanding and remembering the information you need for this class?

2. How do you prepare for tests in (school subject)?

3. What do you do to understand and remember what you read?

4. How did you learn how to study?

5. When and where do you study?

6. How much reading do you do each week in (school subject)?

FIGURE 3.11   Study Questionnaire

structional attention as metacognitive aspects. The roles of curiosity, persistence, and confidence in learning should not be shortchanged.

LISTEN/LOOK AND LEARN
Interview a few high-achieving and a few low-achieving public school students of the same grade level. You may use the Study Questionnaire presented in Figure 3.11. Describe the similarities and differences between the students' reported approaches to study. Explain how your beliefs about study instruction were affected by interviewing the students.

PRINCIPLES OF INSTRUCTION IN HOW TO STUDY

By now you should be committed to teaching your students how to study. You should know about study processes, strategies, and systems as well as understand resource management and the value of self-regulation.

At this point you probably realize the complexity of studying. Study has many aspects, and many of these rely on higher-order thinking. For instance, such strategies as note taking, self-questioning, and representing information visually cannot be broken down into a fixed sequence of steps that always produce the same results. Long division can be reduced to such a series, but study strategies cannot. Study strategies require countless decisions about the relative importance of information and the relationships among ideas. Knowing which strategy to employ and being motivated to do so add to the intricacies of studying. You can be explicit when you teach students how to study, but do not expect an answer key to help you check students' notes, questions, or visual representations. Their strategies should produce some common outcomes, but students' interpretations will cause these outcomes to vary.

TRY IT OUT
Compare the complexity of long division with that of study strategies. Have two students in your college class compute an answer to an identical long-division problem; then have the same two students take notes on an identical passage. Compare both sets.

Given the complexity of studying, the best teachers can do is explicitly present general guidelines for strategy use, resource management, and self-regulation, then structure regularly occurring situations so students construct systems and habits that work for them. The most common study system seems to be the one students internalize for themselves (Simpson, 1983). This section describes some principles of study strategy instruction.

Presenting Strategies as Needed

As we noted in Chapter 1, reading and writing strategies should be presented when students have the need to know. This practice is known as functional, or content-driven, instruction. Rather than present note taking by itself because a particular textbook calls for it, present note taking when you expect your students to take notes on upcoming subject matter. Rather than present *vapor* as a root word (*vapor*ize, *evapor*ate, *evapor*ation) because it occurs on a worksheet with nineteen other root words, present *vapor* when it comes up during a science unit.

Many upper-grade teachers introduce particular study strategies during the first few weeks of school because they will help students throughout the semester or year. Teachers identify a few preferred strategies or take ones from a school's curriculum guide, then present them to students immediately. If they expect students to keep learning logs throughout a semester, they will demonstrate how to do so at the beginning. If mnemonic devices make especially good sense and are applicable to a subject they are teaching, they will introduce mnemonic devices as soon as possible.

Strategies also can be presented after a semester or school year has gotten under way. Different ways to represent information visually might be presented throughout the year as opportunities and students' needs arise. In social studies time lines might be appropriate during each unit of study, but outlining might be introduced only when students create tables of contents. If students are having special difficulty with a portion of subject matter, then self-questioning might be introduced.

Fading

Once you have decided when to introduce particular study strategies, follow an instructional approach based on fading. As we explained in Chapter 1, fading occurs when teachers show students how to perform a strategy, then gradually move back so students do it on their own. Teachers fade out, and students fade in.

Fading requires planning on your part to make sure it happens. Teachers often lead students through particular learning procedures, never fading out and relinquishing control to students. But think about it: If you always ask the questions, when do students learn to question themselves? If you always present an outline of course topics, when do students learn to outline independently? When teachers always do the questioning and outlining, these procedures are teaching strategies rather than study strategies.

There is no question that teachers should fade out during study strategy instruction, but sometimes teachers can fade too quickly. Sometimes teachers simply tell students to "Take notes on the upcoming material" or "Get ready for a quiz on Friday," with little or no instruction on how to take notes or prepare for a quiz. Teachers sometimes assume students are proficient with these strategies when they are not. Guard against not fading out or fading out too soon. Plan study strategy instruction that balances demonstration, guided practice, and independent application.

DEMONSTRATION   During the demonstration stage, teachers begin as the dominant figure in the class. As Figure 3.12 shows, teachers label and define the desired study strategy by naming it, presenting a general description, and forming analogies whenever possible. Teachers explain the relevance of the strategy by indicating when and why it is useful. They model the strategy by performing the process, explaining it as they go along. Finally, they list prompts for the strategy.

When labeling and describing word-study cards, tell students this:

Today I will present word-study cards to you. These cards are ways to focus on the technical vocabulary of this class. They are like snapshots of individuals rather than a total class picture. Word-study cards contain a vocabulary term on one side and ways to understand the word on the other. Making these cards will help you understand the terms, and reviewing the cards will help you remember them.

To explain the relevance of the strategy, you might say this:

Using these cards is one way to cope with the terrific amount of new terms you'll be encountering here. Knowing this strategy will help you in other situations, like getting a new job or being on a sports team when you suddenly have to learn a lot of specific new ideas.

As you model the strategy, you could say this:

Watch how I produce word-study cards. First, I acquire a stack of index cards. Then I decide which terms to transfer to the cards. I select words in boldface print, ones listed at the end of the passage, and ones that seem important to me.

As you can see, I chose *monarch* as one of the words, so I print it in ink on the front of the card. Then I turn the card over and record information that will help me understand and remember this word. I decide to write a definition, "Ruler. A king or queen"; a sentence containing the term, "Queen Elizabeth is the monarch of England"; and a note on word parts "*mon* = one (*mon*orail)." I could have drawn a

Demonstration

Label and describe the strategy:

Explain the relevance of the strategy:

Model the strategy, thinking through the actions aloud (perform the strategy, explaining what you are doing):

List the strategy's prompts:

Guided Practice

Have students use the strategy; provide feedback:

FIGURE 3.12 Demonstration and Guided Practice Steps for Introducing Study Strategies

picture or produced other examples of *monarch*, but what I have here seems to be enough.

Now I put this word card into my pile to review later. I might simply quiz myself on the meanings, separate known from unknown words, get with someone else and take turns quizzing each other, or group the words into different categories.

Finally, listing prompts consists of specifying as well as possible the procedure you followed. Prompts are general guidelines; they are not rules that always lead to the same outcome. You might tell your students this:

As you saw, I followed the three steps that I posted on the bulletin board:
   1. Identify important terms.
   2. Record one term on one side of a card and memory aids on the other.
   3. Review the cards regularly.
The memory aids you record are the key to this strategy. Remember to use personal experiences, meaningful word parts, and illustrations as much as possible.

GUIDED PRACTICE After demonstrating the study strategy, provide guided practice. Direct students to use the strategy and provide feedback. You might say, "Now it's your turn to produce your own study cards. Work with a partner or on your own. We'll get together as a whole class in fifteen minutes to check on progress." As you work with students, you can probe their understanding of the strategy, praise and encourage their efforts, remind them of missing steps, and suggest improvements.

INDEPENDENT APPLICATION Showing students a strategy and having them practice it several times is a good beginning, but students need to apply the strategy regularly to make it their own. During the independent application stage, teachers plan situations for students to use and refine the strategy; they determine students' grasp of it and reteach what is needed.

Routine attention to study strategies is needed during the independent application stage. Plan your teaching so that your instructional routines incorporate study strategies and students succeed in class when they apply them. Open-notebook quizzes exemplify this type of planning. Regularly provide class time for students individually or in groups to take notes from their readings. Then allow students to use these notes during quizzes. Many teachers collect students' learning logs or journals, comment on them, and record a plus or minus grade depending on the amount of writing students produced. Representing information visually becomes an instructional routine when every Monday you randomly select a student to share what he or she produced for an assigned reading. You ensure that self-questioning leads to success when student-produced questions appear on quizzes.

TRY IT OUT
Select a study strategy and plan an introductory lesson that contains the Demonstration and Guided Practice steps listed in Figure 3.12. Conduct the study strategy lesson with a group of peers or public school students. Evaluate the lesson: Describe what you would keep and what you would change if you were to do it again. Also describe your next steps to follow up this introductory lesson with opportunities for independent application.

Scaffolding

Construction workers use scaffolding to prop up structures and gain access to them as they are being erected; scaffolds are used in various ways until the building can stand on its own. In education, scaffolds are the supports teachers and students use to construct new knowledge. Dialogue among students and their teacher is a central feature of scaffolded instruction (Paris & Winograd, 1990). Students need a nonevaluative setting to verbalize their understandings and beliefs about study strategies so teachers and other students can suggest the right actions at the right times. Scaffolds also can be teaching tools, such as cue cards, or teaching techniques, such as classroom grouping patterns (Rosenshine & Meister, 1992).

When you plan and present study strategy lessons through an approach based on fading, decide what scaffolding is needed. Working closely with your students will help you determine the supports to include, gradually decrease, and eventually remove. Thinking about the following types of scaffolding helps you plan what to fade: prompts, analogies, classroom grouping patterns, reading materials, strategy complexity, and process checks.

PROMPTS   As we described in Chapter 2, prompts stimulate thinking. They are questions or directions that cue learners to the critical features of the strategy. They induce learners to think a certain way.

Like the outcomes of a traditional task analysis, prompts indicate the actions to perform in multistep strategies. The three guidelines for producing study cards presented above exemplify prompts (identify important terms; record one term on one side of a card and memory aids on the other; review the cards regularly).

The five steps of SQ3R (survey, question, read, recite, review) cue readers to the actions they should take during this particular study system. Mathematics teachers usually present a multistep strategy for solving word problems with prompts such as the following:

1. Survey the problem.
2. Determine what is given and what is asked for.
3. Determine what operations to use and when to use them.
4. Estimate the answer.

5. Solve the problem.

6. Determine if the solution is reasonable.

The prompts should be recorded for students' reference. They might be placed on a bulletin board, distributed on cue cards, or copied into students' class notes. You should refer to the prompts frequently at first, then begin to fade this out.

Prompts such as the above do not specify invariant rules; they signal general actions. The survey part of SQ3R, for instance, involves examining many parts of a passage in no particular order. However, despite their generality, prompts are valuable supports that guide learners.

ANALOGIES   Another form of scaffolding to include in study strategy instruction is analogies that compare a study strategy to something vivid. Analogies can motivate students and make strategies concrete and sensible. They are good vehicles for discussions.

Many types of analogies are available. You can compare word-study cards to snapshots, note taking to gold mining or eating digestible bites of food, and representing information visually to sketching a picture or framing a building. Teachers sometimes compare readers to detectives: Both search for clues, form hunches, and support their generalizations.

If you cannot think of an analogy for the strategy you are presenting, ask students for one. Their analogies frequently are more vivid and apt than the ones adults produce.

CLASSROOM GROUPING PATTERNS   Adjusting classroom grouping patterns is a good way to scaffold instruction. Students can develop strategies when participating in whole-class, small-group, learning-pair, and individual configurations. Teachers change classroom grouping patterns to keep their instruction fresh, accommodate the type of lesson they are presenting, and promote dialogue.

Teachers often demonstrate study strategies to a whole class, then begin fading by jointly performing the strategy with students still grouped as a class. After collaborating with students in a whole-class setting, have them perform the strategy in small groups or learning teams. Students who take turns teaching the strategy to one another go far in refining their knowledge of it. Small-group or learning-pair production of questions, visual representations, or mnemonic devices are clear tasks that fit group work nicely. Individuals can perform strategies on their own and then join a group or a partner to share what they produced and receive feedback. Finally, group support can be removed as students work to internalize the strategy on their own.

READING MATERIALS   Ensuring that your instruction offers an appropriate challenge is an important feature of scaffolded instruction. The materials you use when introducing study strategies should present minimal difficulties to your students so they can concentrate on the strategy. We have seen many

Students can learn study strategies while working in groups.

study strategy lessons torpedoed by lengthy difficult reading materials; the students became confused about the material and the strategy.

When you introduce a strategy, one way to ensure appropriate materials is to use ones already studied in class. Return to a passage that your class knows and show how the strategy applies to it. Another way is to locate very easy topic-related materials. Secondary-school English teachers often introduce such literary elements as plot, setting, theme, and symbolism with children's literature. After introducing a strategy with short easy materials, you can begin increasing the length and difficulty of the materials to meet your students' abilities. Once students have a strategy for identifying the plot of *The Three Little Pigs*, they can begin transferring it to *Charlotte's Web* and eventually *War and Peace*.

STRATEGY COMPLEXITY   Another way to control the difficulty of study strategy instruction involves the strategy being taught. Be sure that the prompts are appropriate for your students. If a step in summarizing is "Determine the main idea of the passage," you would need to ask yourself if your students can accomplish this. Perhaps this main idea prompt should be modified to "Determine the topic of the passage."

You can regulate the difficulty of a multistep strategy by presenting each prompt gradually, giving manageable yet meaningful portions a step at a time. Ensure that students can perform the first step before beginning the second. If students are to ask themselves or one another generic questions, be sure that they understand each question and know how to go about answering it.

PROCESS CHECKS   A final way to scaffold instruction involves process checks. Process checks are good ways to keep students in pursuit of study strategies, directing them to maintain what they are learning. Have students take stock of their strategy use at various intervals. When they are preparing to read, ask, "What are some things you might do to learn this information?" At other times simply remind students of strategies: "Remember what you know about forming an image when you read this passage."

Questions such as the following check on students' processing:

Before Reading

How will you remember this?
What can you do learn this?

After Reading

What led you to that conclusion?
Why do you say that?
How did you figure that out?
How did you approach this?

Process questions focus students on how they studied rather than on what they learned. If a student claimed that the Spanish conquistadors were criminals rather than heroes, this would be a product-oriented check: "What did they do that was criminal? Were the French settlers any more criminal or heroic?" This would be a process-oriented check: "Why do you say that? What led you to that conclusion?"

Motivating

Motivation, another instructional principle to tap during study strategy instruction, is a principle of instruction as well as a learning outcome. It is a means to an end, as well as an end in itself. Motivating students to learn in your class can result in students who remain self-regulated, motivated learners throughout their lives.

Teachers affect motivation in part by the tasks they present (Ames & Ames, 1984). In Chapter 8, pages 239 to 243, we present five aspects of learning tasks that are associated with motivation: success, choice, meaningfulness, independence, and involvement. Students exhibit motivation when they succeed, when they have a hand in selecting their activities, when they are engaged in relevant material, when they can do it with little external control, and when they actively manipulate ideas and objects.

We conclude this chapter by tying it back to its beginning and middle sections. Students who are engaged in integrated units and inquiry units have a better chance at motivation than those involved daily in isolated, cold-blooded subject matter lectures. Integrated units and inquiry units provide a good setting for subject matter instruction and for explicit instruction in how to study that students find motivating. Capitalizing on these opportunities can lead to motivated independent learners.

LOOKING BACK

Teachers produce different types of plans to promote students' independence. They plan integrated units that incorporate subject matter, language arts, grouping patterns, and personal experiences about an organizing center. They plan to have students take the lead in inquiry units. And they instruct students in how to study. You encountered three key ideas in this chapter: (1) Integrated units combine numerous aspects of study, (2) inquiry units emphasize students' choices and generalizations, and (3) explicit instruction in how to study can occur regularly.

ADD TO YOUR JOURNAL

Record in your class journal your reactions to this chapter. What integrated units or inquiry units have you experienced? What were their strengths and limitations? What were their similarities and differences? How do you plan on implementing them in your teaching? Also think about instruction in how to study. Which strategies will you emphasize with your students? What instructional routines do you foresee for highlighting study?

REFERENCES

Ames, C., & Ames, R. (1984). Systems of student and teacher motivation: Toward a qualitative definition. *Journal of Educational Psychology, 76,* 535–556.

Borkowski, J. G., Carr, M., Rellinger, E., & Pressley, M. (1990). Self-regulated cognition: Interdependence of metacognition, attribution, and self-esteem. In B. F. Jones & L. Idol (Eds.), *Dimensions of thinking and cognitive instruction* (pp. 53–92). Hillsdale, NJ: Erlbaum.

Clark, C. M., & Peterson, P. L. (1986). Teachers' thought processes. In M. C. Wittrock (Ed.), *Handbook of research on teaching* (3rd ed.) (pp. 255–296). New York: Macmillan.

Corno, L. (1986). The metacognitive control components of self-regulated learning. *Contemporary Educational Psychology, 11,* 333–346.

Devine, T. G. (1991). Studying: Skills, strategies, and systems. In J. Flood, J. M. Jensen, D. Lapp, & J. R. Squire (Eds.), *Handbook of research on teaching the English language arts* (pp. 743–753). New York: Macmillan.

Doyle, W. (1986). Classroom organization and management. In M. C. Wittrock (Ed.), *Handbook of research on teaching* (3rd ed.) (pp. 392–431). New York: Macmillan.

Huck, C. S., Hepler, S., & Hickman, J. (1987). *Children's literature in the elementary school* (4th ed.). New York: Holt, Rinehart & Winston.

Jacobs, H. H., & Borland, J. H. (1986). The interdisciplinary concept model: Theory and practice. *Gifted Child Quarterly, 30,* 159–163.

McNeil, L. (1986). *Contradictions of control.* London: Routledge & Kegan Paul.

Moore, D. W., Readence, J. E., & Rickelman, R. R. (1983). An historical exploration of content area reading instruction. *Reading Research Quarterly, 18,* 419–438.

Norman, M. H., & Norman, E. S. (1968). *Successful reading.* New York: Holt, Rinehart & Winston.

Orlich, D. C., Harder, R. J., Callahan, R. C., Kauchak, D. P., Pendergrass, R. A., Keogh, A. J., & Gibson, H. (1990). *Teaching strategies* (3rd ed.). Lexington, MA: D. C. Heath.

Palincsar, A. S., & Brown, A. L. (1984). Reciprocal teaching of comprehension-fostering and comprehension-monitoring activities. *Cognition and Instruction, 1,* 117–175.

Paris, S. G., & Winograd, P. (1990). How metacognition can promote academic learning and instruction. In B. F. Jones & L. Idol (Eds.), *Dimensions of thinking and cognitive instruction* (pp. 16–51). Hillsdale, NJ: Erlbaum.

Pressley, M., Levin, J. R., & Delaney, H. D. (1982). The mnemonic keyword method. *Review of Educational Research, 52,* 61–91.

Rosenshine, B., & Meister, C. (1992). The use of scaffolds for teaching higher-level cognitive strategies. *Educational Leadership, 50,* 26–33.

Simpson, M. (1983). Recent research on independent learning strategies: Implications for developmental education. (ERIC Document Reproduction Service No. ED 247 528)

Simpson, M. L., Hayes, C. G., Stahl, N., Connor, R. T., & Weaver, D. (1988). An initial validation of a study strategy system. *Journal of Reading Behavior, 20,* 149–180.

Strike, K. (1975). The logic of learning by discovery. *Review of Educational Research, 45,* 461–483.

Thomas, E., & Robinson, H. A. (1972). *Improving reading in every classroom.* Boston: Allyn & Bacon.

Vars, G. F. (1991). Integrated curriculum in historical perspective. *Educational Leadership, 49,* 14–15.

Wade, S. E., Trathen, W., & Schraw, G. (1990). An analysis of spontaneous study strategies. *Reading Research Quarterly, 25,* 147–166.

ADDITIONAL READINGS

Two thorough descriptions of integrated units are found in the following:

Integrating the curriculum. (1991). *Educational Leadership, 49*(2) [Special issue].

Jacobs, H. H. (Ed.). (1989). *Interdisciplinary curriculum: Design and implementation.* Alexandria, VA: Association for Supervision and Curriculum Development.

Secondary-school science teachers might find the integrated teaching of physics presented in this article to be informative:

Lijnse, P. L., Kortland, K., Eijkelhof, H. M. C., Van Gendern, D., & Hooymayers, H. P. (1990). A thematic physics curriculum: A balance between contradictory curriculum forces. *Science Education, 74,* 95–103.

Classroom organization patterns appropriate for different phases of subject matter instruction are explained in the following:

Pardo, L. S., & Raphael, T. E. (1991). Classroom organization for instruction in content areas. *The Reading Teacher, 44,* 556–565.

Many publications emphasize the integration of language arts and subject matter instruction. These are a few examples:

Elementary

Gamberg, R., and others, with Gail Edwards. (1988). *Learning and loving it: Theme studies in the classroom.* Portsmouth, NH: Heinemann.

Thaiss, C. (1986). *Language across the curriculum in the elementary grades.* Urbana, IL: Clearinghouse on Reading and Communication Skills and the National Council of Teachers of English.

Middle School

Atwell, N. (1987). *In the middle: Writing, reading, and learning with adolescents.* Portsmouth, NH: Boynton/Cook.

Rief, L. (1992). *Seeking diversity: Language arts with adolescents.* Portsmouth, NH: Heinemann.

Although the first reference below describes inquiry teaching at the college level, its vivid examples make it appropriate for teachers of all grades. The second is a classic statement of the value of learning through inquiry. The third describes a form of inquiry originally developed for the natural sciences that is usable for all subjects.

Bateman, W. L. (1990). *Open to question.* San Francisco: Jossey-Bass.

Bruner, J. (1977). *The process of education.* Cambridge, MA: Harvard University Press. (Original work published 1960)

Joyce, B. R., & Weil, M. (1986). *Models of teaching* (3rd ed.) (chap. 4). Englewood Cliffs, NJ: Prentice Hall.

These two articles present clear guidelines for inquiry units:

Johannsen, L. R. (1989). Teaching writing: Motivating inquiry. *English Journal, 78*(2), 64–66.

Kleg, M. (1986). Rights in conflict: An inquiry simulation on smoking. *Social Science Record, 25*(2), 30–33.

Thorough descriptions of studying and guides for instruction in how to study are found in the following:

Devine, T. G. (1981). *Teaching study skills: A guide for teachers.* Boston: Allyn & Bacon.

Gall, M. D., Gall, J. P., Jacobsen, D. R., & Bullock, T. L. (1990). *Tools for learning: A guide to teaching study skills.* Alexandria, VA: Association for Supervision and Curriculum Development.

Pressley, M., Johnson, C. J., Symons, S., McGoldrick, J. A., & Kurita, J. (1989). Strategies that improve memory and comprehension of text. *Elementary School Journal, 90,* 3–32.

Self-regulated learning is described fully in the following:

Corno, L. (1987). Teaching and self-regulated learning. In D. C. Berliner & B. V. Rosenshine (Eds.), *Talks to teachers* (pp. 249–266). New York: Random House.

CHAPTER 4
Comprehension

LOOKING AHEAD

Comprehension is thinking while you read, listen, or view. Because comprehension is primarily thinking, you comprehend by bringing to bear some or all of the thinking processes. Teachers can help students think about what they are reading, listening to, or viewing. They can build background knowledge so that students have more information to call up and connect to new information they will encounter when they attempt to comprehend. Teachers also help students to think by having them predict, organize, form an image, or monitor as they read or listen for specific purposes. During and after reading or listening, teachers can help students generalize about, evaluate, and apply information they learned. Teachers support students' thinking by planning and carrying out minilessons in which the purposes are made clear and their fulfillment is ensured by group tasks and feedback.

Think back to your years as an elementary- and secondary-school student. What do you remember about reading your science, social studies, and other content area books? Perhaps you remember a scene like this:

The teacher has everyone open his or her book to the beginning of the chapter. Each student takes a turn reading part of the chapter aloud while everyone else follows along. Some students read well and fluently. Others stumble and miss words, and you think they will never get through. You look ahead instead of following along to figure out what part you might have to read so you can rehearse it before being called on.

After the students take turns reading orally, the teacher spends some time firing questions at different students. The questions almost always have short answers, and if a student does not answer a question right away, the teacher calls on another student to answer. For each question, the teacher continues to call on students until getting the desired answer. Finally, the students are assigned to finish reading the chapter and write answers to the questions at the end of the chapter.

The scene just described exemplifies an ineffective way to use content area books. This chapter will present you with more effective ways.

Most of the time, we take reading comprehension for granted. We read words and automatically understand what we are reading. But comprehension does not always occur automatically. The following passage from a statistics book (Kirk, 1972) shows that comprehension is more than a matter of being able to read each word:

> *Fractional factorial designs have much in common with confounded factorial designs. The latter designs, through the technique of confounding, achieve a reduction in the number of treatment combinations that must be included within a block. A fractional factorial design uses confounding to reduce the number of treatment combinations in the experiment. As is always the case when confounding is used, the reduction is obtained at a price. There is considerable ambiguity in interpreting the outcome of a fractional factorial experiment, since treatments are confounded with interactions. For example, a significant mean square might be attributed to the effects of treatment A or to a BCDE interaction. (p. 256)*

Did you understand what you read? Could you retell it to someone in your own words without looking back at the text? Most people who are not knowledgeable about statistics could not comprehend that paragraph, although to statisticians, the paragraph makes perfect sense. As a teacher, you are knowledgeable in all the content subjects you will teach. Elementary- and secondary-school textbooks almost always make perfect sense to you because you already know a lot about what you are reading. You may feel as if you are learning a whole new set of facts by reading the text, but in fact, you already know much of the information presented, and are simply adding a little new information to the vast amount you already understand. Comprehension is indeed automatic when you are reading about topics for which you have adequate background, know most of the appropriate vocabulary, and know enough to sort out important from trivial information. Many students are seldom in that position when reading content areas.

These are the key ideas in this chapter:

1. Comprehension is thinking and can be increased when teachers support students' comprehension.
2. Planning a comprehension minilesson includes deciding on clear learning purposes, background knowledge, and motivation.
3. Comprehension minilessons guide students through the before, during, and after phases of reading.

4. There are many variations within the comprehension minilesson framework.

5. Students become independent learners when teachers gradually fade their guidance and turn over responsibility to students.

COMPREHENSION IS THINKING AND CAN BE INCREASED WHEN TEACHERS SUPPORT STUDENTS' COMPREHENSION

In Chapter 1, we explained that reading and writing are primarily thinking and discussed nine thinking processes that seem particularly pertinent to reading and writing. Consider these nine thinking processes now and see how your inability to perform them coincides with your lack of comprehension of our intriguing passage explaining fractional factorial designs. You probably cannot call up very much prior knowledge because you do not know (or care) much about fractional factorial designs. Calling up little, you have sparse old knowledge to which you can connect the new information. You cannot predict where the author might be leading you or form an image of the experiments, treatments, or interactions. You find that organizing the ideas in some manner or forming a generalization from the facts given is impossible, as is applying this knowledge to solve any statistical problems you might have. You may, however, have monitored, "I don't know what they are talking about," and evaluated, "This is stupid and irrelevant."

In order to make sense of what we read or listen to, we think along with the author. If we cannot or do not want to think, we stop reading or listening—unless there is a test to follow. Imagine that in order to get through this course, you had to be able to answer the following questions:

1. Why does a fractional factorial design use confounding?
2. What two factors might cause a significant mean square?

Perhaps you could use your knowledge of sentence structure to come up with these answers:

1. To reduce the number of treatment conditions.
2. The effects of treatment A and a BCDE interaction.

If these two questions were on a test, could you memorize the answers? Of course you could. Everyone who has survived several years of high school and college has memorized their way through a course. However, memorization is not comprehension. Comprehension is the ability to think, not just memorize. Comprehension is an active process during which you mentally work on creating meaning from the words you see or hear. In this chapter, you will learn how to support students thinking as they read, listen, or view. Your students will learn to work actively with ideas, not just memorize words.

TRY IT OUT

Find a one- or two-page newspaper or magazine article about a subject in which you are interested. Slowly read the article and try to "get inside your own head" to analyze your thinking processes. It will help to stop once or twice in each paragraph to reflect. Find in the article something that triggered each of several thinking processes for you. Write initials (CU, C, P, FI, O, G, E, A, M) on the article to code where you use certain thinking processes. Summarize in two or three paragraphs which thinking processes you used most and which you used least. Give specific examples (I could smell that football locker room; I thought, "That's a lie!") to show how your comprehension is really a product of your active thinking processes.

Think back to some of the books that you have read. Do you remember any that read like the fractional factorial designs passage? Hopefully, you don't; realistically, you probably do. When text is this hard, you cannot possibly comprehend it, and your only choices are to skip it or—if there is a test—try to memorize it. We call this type of text "too challenging." Most likely, the books you have available will not be this foreign to any of your students.

Most of what you read and listen to is very easy. Recall the scene we described at the beginning of this chapter. Because you have probably experienced the kind of instruction in that scene, your comprehension of our written description was probably immediate, instantaneous, and effortless. You called up classrooms in which this was the modus operandi. Perhaps you even formed an image of the voice, face, and scent of a particular teacher. You probably predicted that there might be a pop quiz on the day after the chapter was assigned. You may have generalized that "this was the way things were in social studies." Perhaps you evaluated: "I hated it. It was so boring." You may even have applied: "I'm not going to teach like that!"

When you read something that is so familiar and well known to you that comprehension seems effortless and automatic, you are probably reading text we would describe as "easy" or "comfortable." The write-up in the sports page of last night's basketball game, which your favorite team won, is probably easy for you to read with good comprehension. Even if you did not see the game, you know all the players, their positions, and the likely moves they would make. The "escape" novel you read last summer was probably comfortable for you to read with understanding. You did not know exactly what would happen to the characters, but you have read many novels with similar characters and plots. If you devoured a series of books as an early adolescent (about Nancy Drew, Star Trek, or Dr. Who), you were increasing your reading speed and fluency by reading lots of easy materials.

Text that is too challenging for us is so unfamiliar and difficult that we never read it unless we are forced to. Text that is easy for us is so familiar and comfortable that we read it whenever we have the time, freedom, and interest in the topic or type of writing. Most books that we use in classrooms, however, are neither too challenging nor too easy for the majority of students; rather, most books are in that range of difficulty we describe as "teachable." Teachable text is text that students will understand better if teachers guide their reading or listening than if they approach it independently. Teachable text is not so difficult that nothing the teacher says or does can help the majority of students understand it or learn from it. It is not so easy or well written that most students can read it and think along with it just as well independently as with the teacher guiding them. In other words, teachable texts are those for which it helps to have a teacher.

When reading teachable text, students often need support to help them access background knowledge they may have but cannot automatically call up or to build prior knowledge they may lack. Students also need support in setting their own purposes, which require them to connect, predict, organize, form an image, generalize, evaluate, or apply. They need help to monitor whether they are meeting their purposes and to learn how to employ fix-up strategies when their comprehension breaks down.

This support takes many different forms but usually involves the teacher in doing some activities with the students before they read or listen, then following up these activities. Before reading, teachers help students build background knowledge and set reading purposes. Background knowledge is accessed or built when students watch films, brainstorm ideas, and engage in discussion and interaction, sharing what they collectively know. Purpose setting includes helping students use pictures and other visuals as clues to the important information, predict what they will learn, and form an opinion prior to reading and then reading to find support for that opinion. After reading, teachers help students see if their reading purposes were met and connect the new information to what they already knew.

Activities in which teachers guide students before and after reading or listening are called comprehension minilessons. Numerous research studies have investigated the effects of a variety of comprehension lesson formats on student learning. The almost unanimous conclusion from this research is that when students are reading something that is not easy for them, their learning is significantly increased when the teacher engages them in some before and after activities that elicit thinking.

DO IT TOGETHER

From a book used in a course in your major or area of expertise and interest, choose a four- to five-page section. Read it once, close the book, and quickly write everything you remember from your reading. Have a friend who has a different major or area of expertise and interest do the same thing with a book section he or she selects.

Once you have separately read and recalled as much as possible from the books you chose, swap books, read the same sections your friend read, close the book, and write everything you can recall.

Compare the results. Did you recall much more from the book you chose than from the one your friend chose? Can you see from the amount recalled that your chosen book was probably easy for you and your friend's book was probably teachable text for you?

The content area you choose to teach is usually one in which you are very interested and about which you have much accumulated knowledge; thus the books you read in that area always seem "remarkably simple." Looking at a book through the eyes of a novice will help convince you that most students require instruction to help them think and learn from reading in various content areas.

PLANNING A COMPREHENSION MINILESSON INCLUDES DECIDING ON CLEAR LEARNING PURPOSES, BACKGROUND KNOWLEDGE, AND MOTIVATION

To increase your students' comprehension and learning, you must make sure that they have enough prerequisite knowledge to make sense of what they are reading, are motivated to try to make sense of it, and know what they should learn. Imagine now that it is the first week of school. You have met your students and have a general idea of their varied abilities. You also have one or more books, a curriculum guide, and other resources that provide you with some teachable text for most of your students. You are looking through the available reading, listening, and viewing materials and have several critical decisions to make. How you make these decisions will affect how much thinking and learning your students do.

Choosing What to Use as Material for Comprehension Minilessons

Time is a teacher's most precious commodity. Using your time well is one of the keys to successful teaching. Books, curriculum guides, and other resources are filled with information, some of which is critical to understanding in your subject area, some of which your students already know, and some of which is trivial, highly technical, or boring. Good teachers are more interested in "uncovering the mysteries and joys of their subject" than in "covering the text." Good teachers know that you cannot teach it all and that if you try, many students will retain very little.

As we discussed in Chapter 2, one of the advantages of having a variety of materials is that the best treatment of a subject for your students can be chosen from several possibilities. Alternative sources of content information can often add clarity and depth to lackluster or even erroneous textbook sections.

As you look through your available resources, rate the various sections, chapters, parts, and so forth, on a three-star scale. The selections to which you give one star are parts or resources that may not be used at all or be used by individual students as they pursue their own interests. Selections that you decide are "interesting, important, but not critical" should be given two stars, and you should have students work with these selections individually or in small groups as time and student needs permit. Those resources and selections that you determine contain critical content area information and concepts should be given three stars. Whatever class time you can devote to helping your students think as they read, listen, and view should be devoted to teaching comprehension minilessons on these three-star selections.

Determining What You Want Everyone to Learn

Once you have determined which part of your books and other resources get the three-star rating and deserve your attention, you are ready to decide what critical concepts you want students to learn from these selections. Try to read or view various selections from the naïve learner's standpoint. Imagine yourself once again as a novice in your subject area. What are the critical, exciting, stimulating, generative ideas that you want your students to take away from their interaction with this selection?

Because you are an expert in this topic, it may all seem simple and important, but some concepts, generalizations, and ideas are surely more critical than others. Many teachers find it helpful to view or read the selection first and then (with the book closed or the video film stopped) list the most important ideas and information. Listing what is critical does not limit students to learning or thinking about only these critical ideas, but it does mean that your students' attention will be focused on the critical concepts, thus greatly increasing the chances that most students will learn them.

Motivating Students to Read

Once you know what you want students to learn from their reading, you must think about why they would want to learn it. The most common problems cited by content area teachers are the inability of students to read well and the "Who cares!" attitude many students bring to reading. You can take care of the first problem by not asking students to read text that is clearly too challenging and by providing content comprehension minilessons so that they are apt to think about what they are reading and not just try to remember all the facts and terms. You also must consider what to do about the second problem.

While many factors affect motivation, the two greatest factors are the expectation of success and interest. Students must feel that they can successfully do what is being asked of them or they won't even try. Many students have experienced failure with reading to learn. When reading is assigned with little background building or purpose setting, students do not know what they are "supposed to get out of it," so they just read and hope they will know whatever it is the teacher asks. Comprehension minilessons in which you provide scaffolding by building background, giving clear purposes, and following these purposes up with group tasks will convince students that they can successfully read in your subject area and, over time, change their expectation of failure.

The interest factor, however, must still be considered. How do you engage students' interest and make them want to read? Mathison (1989) cites five research-based strategies for piquing student interest: using analogies, relating personal anecdotes, disrupting readers' expectations, challenging students to resolve a paradox, and introducing novel or conflicting information. For simplicity's sake, we will combine the last three into one.

Using analogies. In real life, we use analogies to explain new phenomena all the time. We describe a new friend to someone who has never met him by saying something like this: "He looks a little like John Lennon, but taller, and he is always upbeat and fun just like Hank was." We describe a new restaurant by comparing it to a familiar restaurant: "The food is wonderful, a little spicier than Chico's. It has big comfortable chairs and great, leisurely service just like Armando's."

According to Mathison, analogies make "the strange familiar and the familiar strange" (p. 171). When students are presented with analogies, their interest is aroused initially because the first part of the analogy is something with which they are familiar; thus they feel secure that they will be successful. The new information appears more interesting because they become intrigued with how the new, unfamiliar information is similar to and different from what they are familiar and comfortable with.

A social studies teacher might create an analogy between parliamentary and congressional forms of government when the class is studying England, Canada, or Israel. A science teacher might create an analogy between airplane and bird wings when the class is studying birds. An algebra teacher might compare solving an equation with two or more unknowns to how Sherlock Holmes solves mysteries.

Relating personal anecdotes. Aren't you always curious about the personal lives of your teachers? Have you ever been surprised to come across one of your teachers competing in a local marathon or coaching the local soccer team? Don't you enjoy meeting your teachers' spouses and/or children and imagining your teachers as "real people"?

Students are naturally curious about the lives of their teachers. When teachers tell personal stories or anecdotes as lead-ins to reading, student interest is increased because they have a personal context in which to place the new information.

A math teacher might relate a personal anecdote about his or her experience learning how to solve quadratic equations in high school during that unit of Algebra I. While teaching about famous painters, an art teacher might relate a personal anecdote about his or her first visit to an art museum as a child.

Arousing curiosity by disrupting readers' expectations or challenging them with a paradox or conflict. Our past experience with any situation colors what we expect out of similar situations. When our expectations are not met, our attention is caught. When we go to see a movie by a favorite director or read a book by a favorite author, we have expectations about the kind of work we will enjoy. If the director or author has done something dramatically different, we will immediately take notice. We may end up concluding that the change was marvelous and "mind-boggling," or we may hope that this was a temporary aberration and that the person will soon go back to the things we know and love; we do notice when our expectations are not met.

Students bring certain expectations to each content area. Sometimes these expectations are wrong. By noting these expectations before they read and alerting them that the text will not agree with their expectations, we utilize surprise and confusion to heighten student curiosity.

A paradox is an apparent contradiction in which two situations seem like they could not both be true and yet are. Good teachers challenge students to resolve paradoxes by "leading them down the primrose path," then presenting them with some conflicting but equally convincing information. Students then are challenged to read to see how this paradox might be resolved.

A conflict is a disagreement or struggle between two persons or groups. It may also be a struggle of a person or group against some inanimate condition or foe. Readers' curiosity may be aroused by informing them of the conflict so that they will want to find out how it gets resolved.

A health teacher might arouse readers' curiosity by explaining that the "No cholesterol" printed on packages of cookies or potato chips will not protect them from increasing their cholesterol level as a result of eating those foods. A French teacher might arouse readers' curiosity by stating that they will be reading a conversation in French between an advocate and an opponent of nuclear power plants.

Designing a Group Task That Clearly Communicates a Purpose

Once you know what you want students to learn and how you will motivate them to want to read, you must decide on a group task that students will complete together after reading. This task must meet two criteria: Completing the task must result in the students learning what you decided was important; and the task must be clear to the students before they read.

Imagine, for example, that you decided that from a particular science resource, students should be able to list the nine planets, know their relative positions and sizes, and explain their orbits. How would you communicate this clearly? What joint task could the class complete after reading to show that everyone had learned the important information?

There are many possibilities for this. The most traditional is to make up questions. For our example, these are some questions:

1. What are the nine planets?
2. Which planet is the largest?
3. Which planet is about the same size as Earth?
4. Which planet is closest to the Sun?

Of course, there would have to be at least twenty questions to cover all the important information. Students would be told to either answer the questions or prepare to discuss them, which is not a very motivating or intriguing purpose.

What else could you do to communicate your purpose clearly? Imagine that you drew the chart in Figure 4.1 on the chalkboard. Notice that you partially fill in the chart for students, talking as you write about what is needed in each column: "Earth is the sixth-largest planet. Its mean distance from the Sun is 92,960,000 miles. The year is the number of days it takes a planet to orbit the Sun, and the Earth year is 365 days." Now, you point to the second row and have students explain what they will try to figure out about Mars to put in each column. For the third row, you help them to notice that, since you put a "1" in the size column, this has to be the biggest planet. The fourth row must be completed for the planet that is 3,660,000,000 miles from the Sun. The planet that takes 60,188 Earth days to orbit the Sun goes in the fifth row. The last four rows are filled in with the remaining four planets.

This partially filled in chart is one example of a group task that makes the purpose for reading clear and gets at the important information. Depending on what you want students to learn, there is an endless variety of group tasks that will clearly communicate a purpose for reading. You will see many more examples of groups tasks in the section about the different forms comprehension minilessons can take.

Building Background Knowledge

Students vary in the background knowledge they are able to call up about a particular topic. Students who live in Florida or California may know about oceans and oranges; Midwestern students may be more familiar with wheat

Planet Name	Size (1 = biggest)	Distance from Sun (miles)	Earth Days in Year
Earth	6	92,960,000	365
Mars			
	1		
		3,660,000,000	
			60,188

FIGURE 4.1 Planets in Our Solar System

and blizzards. The author of a textbook may have assumed that students can call up certain information that you know your students lack. For instance, a passage on volcanoes may assume that students are aware of the "bubbling" action of heated liquids. Thus, the passage may deal primarily with a volcano's effect on the earth's crust, while failing to explain what forces magma up through it. If students are confused about the initial thrust of the magma, they may not be able to follow the rest of the description of volcanic action. We suspect that you had difficulty understanding the paragraph on statistics at the beginning of this chapter because of your own limited background in fractional factorial designs.

If certain information seems prerequisite to students learning from a text, then you should teach this information directly, before having the students read or listen to the text. If students already know the prerequisite information, this instruction will help them call the information up. Because the initial learning or calling up of relevant information is essential for comprehension, every comprehension lesson should include attention to it.

Wait to choose the background concepts to teach in a particular comprehension lesson until you have chosen the purpose for comprehending. For any selection, there will probably be several background concepts you would want your students to know. But teaching concepts well takes time. In a single minilesson you can teach only one or two concepts. By waiting until the purpose is established, you can identify what background students need to fulfill that purpose.

This teacher is planning a comprehension minilesson.

COMPREHENSION MINILESSONS SUPPORT STUDENTS THROUGH THE BEFORE, DURING, AND AFTER PHASES OF READING

Once planned, a comprehension minilesson is fairly easy to teach. Before students read, you help build motivation and prior knowledge and clarify the group task they will complete after reading. After students read, you lead them to complete the task and help them monitor how well they did. You may also want to be sure they have connected the new information learned from reading with prior knowledge. While it is impossible to set firm guidelines about how much time to spend in each phase, many teachers find that dividing the time available roughly into thirds is a reasonable guideline. With this distribution of time, the before, during, and after reading phases are seen as more or less equally important in determining what students will learn from their guided reading. Younger and less able readers usually do the during reading phase in class and require more time for all three phases; older and more able readers usually do the during reading phase outside of class and require less time for all three phases.

Before Reading (Or Listening or Viewing)

There are three major goals that you want to accomplish before students read, listen, or view: (1) establish the motivation that will make them eager learners; (2) provide the prerequisite knowledge that will enable them to accomplish their purposes; and (3) help them clarify and understand what they are trying to learn. Sometimes these three goals are accomplished through separate activities. Other times, one activity can accomplish all three. In the preceding example about the planets, the teacher was building background knowledge while creating the chart on the board and filling in the entire row related to Earth as well as parts of the other rows. The background concepts included these:

There are nine planets.
They are all different sizes.
They are various distances away from the Sun.
They all orbit the Sun, and it takes different numbers of Earth days for them to orbit. This orbit is called a year.

Partially completing the chart for students makes the task clear, so their success-driven motivation should be high. Some interest is also piqued by the students' guesses before they read. Many students might say (or think), "That must be Jupiter," when the teacher makes clear that the planet for the third row is the largest one. Students are also apt to be intrigued by the idea that a planet could be more than three and a half billion miles from the Sun and that a year on some planet would take 60,188 Earth days.

Since most students have some prior knowledge and considerable interest in the solar system, the talk engaged in as the teacher sets up the partially completed chart might be sufficient for developing both background knowledge and motivation. In this fortunate case, one activity accomplishes all three prereading goals.

Sometimes one minilesson provides the background and motivation for another lesson later on. Students might watch a film on oceans that would build prior knowledge and pique their interest. This film could set the stage for the following day's minilesson, in which they read to find out the main sources of ocean pollution and evaluate the feasibility of some proposed solutions.

How much background building and motivation are required? Generally, the less familiar a topic is to students, the more time and effort you will have to expend building background and motivation.

Perhaps the most important part of the before reading phase of a comprehension minilesson is making clear the students' purpose for reading. What is clear to you as the teacher is often a mystery to your students. Has an English teacher ever told you to read so that you can discuss how the setting of a story or novel affects the plot development? In order to accomplish this purpose you must understand clearly what setting and plot entail, then must clearly perceive the setting, follow the plot, and finally get to the task of thinking about how setting and plot interact. This complex task is further complicated by the jargon—*setting* and *plot*. Many students are confused by such terminology as *setting*, *plot*, *main idea*, and *summary*. When alerting students to the purposes for which you would like them to read, try to avoid unnecessary jargon or make the jargon clear by including examples.

In a situation where the interaction between setting and plot was important, students would be more apt to understand what you wanted them to read for if you drew on the board a diagram such as Figure 4.2.

After displaying the diagram, you could explain to students that the setting changes three times during the story and that certain things happen in the different settings. Students should read so they can fill in the three settings and the major events that happened in each setting. They should also think about how the different times and places affected what did and did not happen.

	Setting (Time and Place)	Plot (What Happened)
Beginning of story		
Middle of story		
End of story		

How did the setting at different points in the story effect what happened?

FIGURE 4.2 Plot/Setting Diagram

In this example, you have clarified the purpose by making a little chart on the board and explained what is meant by the jargon, *setting* and *plot*. You have also written the chart and the question on the board so that as students are reading, they can look up and think about what they can contribute to the group task of filling in the chart and discussing the question.

Purposes for reading, listening, or viewing vary tremendously: Some are very specific and target particular learning; others give the students an opportunity to determine what they want to know or how they will respond to the content they are attempting to comprehend. To whatever extent you are limiting or focusing what they are to gain from their reading, listening, or viewing, you must clearly communicate that sense of purpose to them before they begin.

When students have the necessary motivation and prior knowledge and know their purpose for reading, they are ready to move into the next phase.

Reading (Or Listening or Viewing)

Now the students go to work and read, listen, or view to fulfill their purposes. Often students read silently, but the reading can take other forms. Students can be paired and read the passage together, with each one taking a page or a paragraph. As they read, you may notice their eyes going up to the board as they come upon some piece of information they want to include. During the first few comprehension minilessons, you may need to interrupt the reading after just a few minutes and point to the purpose on the board to remind students of it.

Sometimes the reading phase finds the teacher reading and the students listening. If you have only one copy of a newspaper or magazine article containing information that you want to share with students, this is a perfect opportunity to do a listening comprehension lesson. For young children and some older remedial readers, their comprehension ability is greater than their ability to figure out the words. In this case, you may want to read something to them so that their limited word identification ability does not hinder their ability to learn and think about important content area information.

Some minilessons may find the teacher and the students watching and listening to a film, video, or speaker. Because thinking underlies reading, listening, and viewing comprehension, the same plan is appropriate for all three information-gathering avenues.

After Reading (Or Listening or Viewing)

If you have set a clear purpose, what happens after comprehending is obvious: Students contribute their ideas and as a group complete the task you set for them.

As students contribute to completing the task, the teacher should try as much as possible to be nonjudgmental and record what students suggest. If there is disagreement, the teacher should resist the temptation to "be the

A teacher recording the responses of students during a group task.

expert" and write both responses with question marks next to them. When teachers resist the temptation to make corrections during the group comprehension task, it helps students become more responsible for their own learning.

During the initial task completion, it is generally best not to let students have their books open or look back but rather to record all the relevant ideas they have and just mark with blanks or question marks what students are unsure of or have conflicting opinions about.

Once students have done as much as they can, give them a chance to reopen their books and check or seek support for those parts of the class response that are in question. (If this were a listening or viewing activity, you would reread or reshow the parts needed to clear up the confusion; fill in the gaps; or provide clues to the inferences, generalizations, or conclusions required by the task.) As students tell you what to revise or add, have them read part of the text aloud and explain how this information or statement helps to resolve the disagreement. Again, the teacher should remain a guide and not assume the expert role. If there is some misinformation or misunderstanding that students cannot resolve, help them clarify what needs fixing and why. Guide them to see what they have read as the source and you as their guide to understanding rather than you as the expert with the "right answer." Students will work harder if they know they are really responsible for finding information and thinking about what it means.

Finally, ask the group if what they have come up with represents what most of the members believe to be their best thinking. Spend a few minutes talking about what they did and how they did it. For the setting-plot purpose discussed above, you might say something like this:

> Today you did a great job of charting the time and place and the major events. You could then see the relationship between the setting and the plot. Often in books and movies, the setting affects the plot. If we think about the time and place in which things happen, we can see how this occurs.

In the planet example, your purpose was for them to learn some basic facts about the planets. Once you established that the planet chart the group completed was as accurate and complete as possible, you might point out how much more they knew and how efficiently they had recorded it on the chart. If this information was information you wanted everyone to learn, you might have them copy the chart into a science notebook so that they would have clear, concise notes to study.

The after reading phase is critical to both the development of students' content knowledge and their reading strategies. As the students help complete the task, they connect new knowledge to old. As they are guided to revisit parts of the texts to resolve disagreement or fill in gaps, they learn not only how to monitor their comprehension but also some fix-up strategies to use when comprehension fails.

THERE ARE MANY VARIATIONS WITHIN THE COMPREHENSION MINILESSON FRAMEWORK

Now that you understand the general events comprising the before, during, and after reading phases of a comprehension minilesson, we want to expand your vision by presenting a variety of possibilities. This variety in the specific ways a comprehension minilesson can proceed allows you to teach minilessons that provide variety and are appropriate for a wide range of reading passages, instructional goals, and types of students.

Minilessons Using Graphic Organizers

You already have two examples of minilessons using graphic organizers. Both the planet chart and the setting-and-plot chart were graphic organizers. Graphic organizers are visual diagrams that help us see the relationships among concepts. There are many kinds, and you can create your own variations. Figures 4.3 to 4.8 show popular graphic organizers in various stages of completion by students.

If the relationships depicted by the graphic organizers in these figures is obvious, you can see how clearly graphic organizers communicate purposes to students and how well they help students see important relationships in the information they are reading. On the semantic feature matrix, students indicate with a plus or minus which qualities are possessed by various Amer-

Famous Americans in Four Poems

Qualities (+/−)	Abraham Lincoln	Georgia O'Keeffe	Martin Luther King, Jr.	Betsy Ross
proud				
controversial				
artistic				
political				
———				
———				
———				
———				

FIGURE 4.3 Semantic Feature Matrix

Human and Animal Communication

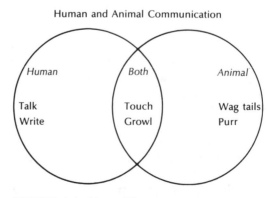

FIGURE 4.4 Venn Diagram

World War II

Sept. 1, 1939 Sept. 3, 1939 June 22, 1940 Dec. 11, 1941 Sept. 3, 1943 June 6, 1944 May 7, 1945

Germany
invades
Poland

FIGURE 4.5 Time Line

icans depicted in poetry. On the Venn diagram, students compare and contrast how animals and humans communicate. These graphic organizers are helpful in comparing and contrasting members of a particular group.

The time line is an excellent device to use when sequence is important. Here, students fill in the important event that occurred on each date. A variation is to give students a time line of events and have them fill in the dates. If you want more details, draw two lines under each event line and have students fill in two details about each event.

Both the whale web and the Yukon outline help students organize information when they are to learn a variety of information about one big topic. Most students find it easier to web ideas than to outline them because when they outline, they often get lost in the trivia of upper- and lowercase letters and indentation. The partially completed outline allows students to concentrate on the information and the relationships because the skeleton and a few pieces of information are included.

Notice in the cause and effect chain that some causes have multiple effects, some effects have multiple causes, and an effect often becomes a cause of another effect. These diagrams help students sort through the complex relationships that comprise much of the information they need to understand in the real world.

Of course, these figures are just a sampling of graphic organizers to spur your thinking about how to help students see important relationships by considering how you would depict those relationships graphically. When you determine that students need to learn some facts and their compare-contrast relationships, time/order relationships, topic/subtopic relationships, or causal relationships, a graphic organizer is often your most efficient group task.

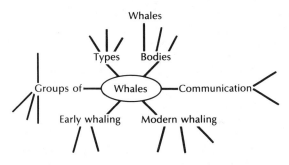

FIGURE 4.6 Web

The Yukon
A. Geography
    1.
    2.
    3.
    4.
B. Economy
    1. Fishing
       a.
       b.
    2. _____
       a. lynx
       b.
       c.
    3. Manufacturing
       a.
       b.
       c.
    4. _____
       a. gold
       b.
       c.
       d.
       e.
C. Government
    1. Canadian
       a.
       b.
       c.
    2. Territorial
       a.
       b.

FIGURE 4.7 Outline

TRY IT OUT

Find a book that you might use in your teaching. Select a five- to ten-page section that you would consider important enough to teach a comprehension minilesson on. Consider the important facts and relationships. Construct a graphic organizer that your students could complete as a group task. Include enough of the pieces so that students would clearly understand what information goes where.

Minilessons Using Prediction

Organizing information is one of the thinking processes we utilize to learn information; predicting is another. We are predicting whether a particular book will interest us when we peruse the title, author name(s), and cover

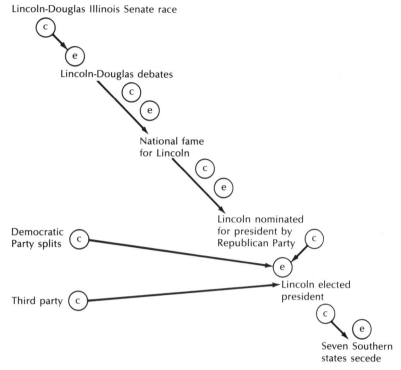

FIGURE 4.8 Cause and effect chain

illustration. We are predicting when we thumb through a magazine, looking at the pictures before we start to read. We are predicting when we read a heading such as "Are We Once Again Headed into Recession?" and assume that the author will give us reasons to believe we are or are not. Across the years of reading instruction, various ways of having students make predictions have been devised. We will discuss three with some unique practical features: a prediction guide, KWL, and DRTA.

A prediction guide is a list of statements or key words, some of which are true and some of which are false. The students are presented with the statements or key words and guess which are true and which are false. They then read to check their predictions. Below is a prediction guide used before students read about the life of Babe Ruth. What are your guesses?

Babe Ruth

1. Orphan
2. Good kid
3. Only child
4. Irish
5. German
6. Over six feet tall
7. Right-handed
8. Pitcher
9. Catcher
10. New York Yankee
11. Still living

How did you do? Do you have some guesses about which you are quite sure and others for which you do not have a clue? Do you want to know the answers? Of course you do, and you therefore see the power of prediction as a motivating device. Students who have made some guesses want to read to "see if they were right." Students who guess about some statements before reading are nearly always motivated to read and be clear about their purposes for reading.

One of the most flexible and popular ways of organizing a comprehension minilesson based on student predictions is a KWL (Carr & Ogle, 1987; Ogle, 1986). The letters stand for what we *know*, what we *want* to find out, and what we have *learned*. Imagine that the class is about to read about Washington, D.C. The teacher might begin by finding Washington, D.C., on a map and asking which students have been there. A chart such as the following would then be started:

WASHINGTON, D.C.

What We Know	*What We Want to Find Out*	*What We Learned*

The teacher then has the students brainstorm what they know about Washington, D.C., and writes the facts in the first column. When the students have brainstormed all their prior knowledge, the chart might look like this:

WASHINGTON, D.C.

What We Know	*What We Want to Find Out*	*What We Learned*
Capital		
White House		
President lives there		
Lots of drugs		
Azaleas in spring		
Cold in winter		
Near Virginia		
Near Maryland		

Next, the teacher would direct the students' attention to the second column and ask them what they would like to find out about Washington, D.C. Their questions would be listed in the second column:

WASHINGTON, D.C.

What We Know	What We Want to Find Out	What We Learned
Capital	How old is it?	
White House	How big is the White House?	
President lives there	What else is in D.C.?	
Lots of drugs	Where is the FBI?	
Azaleas in spring	What kind of government does D.C. have?	
Cold in winter	Why is it not a state?	
Near Virgina	How many people live there?	
Near Maryland	What do the people do who aren't in the government?	

Once the questions are listed, students read to see which of their questions was answered and find other interesting "tidbits" they think are important.

After reading, the teacher begins by seeing which of the questions were answered, then leads students to add other interesting facts. This information is recorded in the third column. All class members are encouraged to contribute, and no one looks back at the book until all initial responses are shared. Disputed or unclear information is noted with question marks.

When all the initial recalls are recorded, students go back to the text to clarify, prove, or fill in gaps. The teacher leads the students to read the relevant part aloud and explain their thinking. When the information on the chart is complete and accurate, the teacher points out how much was learned and how efficiently the chart helped to record it. Inevitably, there will be questions that were not answered in the reading, and a natural follow-up is to help the students use additional resources to locate the answers.

A Directed Reading Thinking Activity—DRTA (Stauffer, 1969)—is a way of getting students to predict what they will learn. In a DRTA, the teacher usually leads the students to make predictions, read portions of the text, stop and make more predictions, read some more, and so on until the text is finished. Predictions are written on the board, checked when confirmed, and erased when not confirmed. How many times the students stop and make predictions depends on the length of what they are reading and their maturity. Here is an imaginary script for a modified DRTA on a science section about sound:

TEACHER: Today we are going to begin learning about sound. What do you think we might learn?

The teacher waits for students to respond, then writes these responses on the board:

What sound is.

How you hear.

What different kinds of sounds there are.

Where sounds come from.

TEACHER: Let's open our books now and see if we can predict anything else we might learn just by looking at the visuals.

The teacher directs students' attention to several pictures, a chart, and a diagram. Students add predictions, which the teacher writes on the board:

Sound travels in waves.

You make sounds with guitars.

Your ears let you hear sounds.

Sounds are measured in decibels.

Bats can hear sounds.

The teacher reads all the predictions aloud and ask students to read the first three pages to see which predictions are true. Students do so. They read a part of the text to prove each prediction, then the teacher puts a checkmark next to that prediction. The teacher asks if there are more predictions students would like to add before finishing the sections. After students make suggestions, the teacher writes this:

Soft sounds have decibels.

Loud sounds have really big decibels.

Pitch is how high or low the sound is.

Students finish reading the section on sound, then tell which predictions should be checked because they are true and which should be erased because they either are not true or were not mentioned.

This section has presented three formats for minilessons in which students make predictions about what they will read. Prediction guides, KWLs, and DRTAs differ in how much input the teacher and students have into the predictions. All three, however, motivate students to think about what they know and might find out and then to read with clear purposes.

Minilessons That Lead Students to Generalize, Evaluate, Form an Image, and Apply

This book began by describing the nine thinking processes most directly involved in reading and writing. This chapter began with the idea that comprehension is thinking and can be greatly increased. The thinking processes calling up, connecting, and monitoring are constant players in the comprehension process. Calling up occurs as background knowledge is accessed and built prior to reading. Connecting occurs whenever new knowledge is connected to old. Monitoring occurs during reading as well as after reading as students regulate their learning.

Other thinking processes are used depending on the particular minilesson. It is obvious that minilessons in which students complete a graphic organizer involve organizing and minilessons that use prediction involve predicting. What may not be so obvious is that other thinking processes—generalizing, evaluating, forming an image, and applying—are often included.

After completing the Venn diagram on human and animal communication (Figure 4.4), the teacher may lead the students to conclude that "there are many similarities between humans and animals," a generalization based on the data students have put into the graphic organizer.

Students who learned about whales and organized the information into a web (Figure 4.6) might take a stand on whether whales should be hunted. This discussion would involve the thinking process of evaluating.

After students complete the World War II time line (Figure 4.5), teachers may lead them to talk about the events and imagine what it would have been like fighting those battles on either side. This discussion would involve the students in forming images of the events they had just organized.

Applying what you have learned to your current and future life can also occur in some of the comprehension minilessons described. After learning about the Yukon or Washington, D.C., students could be asked if they would like to live there.

In addition to discussions that have generalizing, evaluating, imaging, and applying as extensions of the basic lessons, you can conduct minilessons in which these thinking processes are the primary ones. Here are some group tasks, the completion of which requires students to generalize, evaluate, form an image, or apply.

GENERALIZING Generalizing occurs whenever we take some specific pieces of information and conclude something about them. We generalize when we look at a chart showing London's average monthly rainfall and conclude this: "It must rain almost every day!" Often a generalization is a main idea or summary statement. We read about the economies of various Latin American countries and conclude this: "The vast majority of the people there live below the U.S. poverty level."

When you decide that the major thing you want students to do is draw some conclusions or form some big ideas about what they are reading, you will want your group task to lead them to generalize as they read. There are many tasks that accomplish the purpose. We will describe two: GIST and Sustained Summary Writing.

In GIST, the group task is to write a summary in twenty words or less. The teacher explains that the "gist" of something is the main idea and that sometimes we do not need to remember all the details but read just to get the gist of the material. The teacher draws twenty word-size blanks on the chalkboard or on a transparency and explains to the students that, after reading, they will try to write a sentence or two of no more than twenty words that captures the gist of what they have read.

The students read a short section—no more than three paragraphs—then work with the teacher to record the gist of what they have read. Students take turns telling the teacher part of what to write. In no case will the teacher write a twenty-first word. Students must revise what they want the teacher to write so that it will fit into the twenty blanks. The discussion challenges students to distill what is really important. This is an example of a gist statement a class might produce:

Tropical	rain	forests	are	lush
forests	near	the	equator	that
are	hot	and	get	a
lot	of	rain.		

Next, the teacher tells them to read the following section and says that they must now incorporate the information from both the first section and the second in just twenty words. Students groan but usually rise to the challenge of trying to compact twice the amount of information into the same limited set of words. This is an example of the revised gist statement, including information from both sections:

Tropical	rain	forests	are	hot,
rainy,	and	important	because	of
the	many	species	of	plants
and	animals	that	live	there.

It is possible that the teacher might then have the students read a third short section and attempt to incorporate its information into the GIST statement. (No more than three sections should be used with this challenging task.) This is an example:

Tropical	rain	forests	lower	the
carbon	dioxide	in	the	air
and	provide	new	medicines	and
products.	They	must	be	protected.

During this process, students learn how to ignore the details and just get down to the core of what they are reading. Of course, you can expect your average students to be less able to contribute as more sections are read. As a result, it is a good idea to delay calling on the ablest students until the going gets difficult. That way most students will be able to make a contribution at some point during the GIST process.

Sustained Summary Writing is similar to GIST, but students read a longer passage and are given a limited time (three to five minutes) to write the most important information they remember. When the time is up, students share their summaries as the teacher records on the board the major ideas. These ideas are then included in a group summary dictated by the class and written by the teacher.

EVALUATING   You will remember from Chapter 1 that the thinking processes are not separate and distinct. Often generalizing is quickly followed by evaluating. After generalizing that it rains almost every day in London, you

Advantages	Disadvantages

Which way would you vote if you were a senator?

FIGURE 4.9   Raising Taxes to Reduce the Deficit

might decide this: "I wouldn't want to live in a place like that!" After generalizing that most people in South America live below the U.S. poverty line, you might decide this: "That's awful!" When we want students to decide how they feel about something, we must come up with a group task that requires them to make judgments and form opinions. Figure 4.9 is a graphic organizer that has students not only organize but also evaluate.

Here is another group task that involves evaluating:

Decide if you think our country's involvement in the Persian Gulf War was the right thing to do or did more harm than good. Come up with defensible reasons for your position.

There are many other purposes you can use: Students can prepare to debate. They can draft letters to officials. They can hold mock elections and referendums. The critical words in a group task requiring evaluating are *you* and *decide*. Students must understand that they are to weigh the evidence and consider the ideas but that what you ultimately want is their opinion.

FORMING AN IMAGE   Forming an image is using the senses to learn. It involves imagining something, seeing it, and putting yourself there. When we want students to form an image, we must move away from the two-dimensional world of the chalkboard into the real world. Here are some suitable tasks:

Draw, paint, or sculpt a pioneer.

Create a diorama of a scene from pioneer days.

Pick or create a piece of music that evokes Switzerland.

Create a skit or play in which you act out a confrontation between the president and Congress.

Imagine that two pioneers were transported to the twentieth century. Decide what kind of food each would most prefer. What kind of car would each drive? Which baseball team would each root for?

APPLYING   Finally, we want students to apply what they read to their own lives. Here the key words are use and do. Students apply when they read to figure out how to do an experiment or make a kite or fix a faucet. When the group task for a minilesson is something students are actually going to do, you do not have to worry about motivation.

It is not always possible to actually have the students apply. Since we are all dreamers, however, you can use tasks that call for applying to help students think about how they might realize some of their dreams. Students apply when they read a *Consumer Reports* article in order to choose which CD player is the best buy or read about certain countries and plan an ideal trip.

This section has contained numerous examples of comprehension tasks you can use to clarify students' purpose for reading. If you pick and choose from these to match what you determine is most important, you will not only help students learn more from their reading but also ensure variety in your mini-lessons and provide students many ways to think about what they read.

DO IT TOGETHER

Work with three or four others to plan a comprehension minilesson, but do not share what you come up with until everyone is finished. All group members should have the same piece of text. Working separately, list what you would like students to learn from reading this. Then come up with a group task that will make clear students' purpose for reading. Finally, decide what prerequisite knowledge you must build and how you will motivate students to want to read. Get back together and share your comprehension minilessons. Did you find some variety? Did people differ in what they thought students should learn, and thus were the group tasks different? All comprehension lessons require students to call up, connect, and monitor. Decide as a group which of your minilessons also required organizing, predicting, forming an image, generalizing, applying, or evaluating.

STUDENTS BECOME INDEPENDENT LEARNERS WHEN TEACHERS GRADUALLY FADE THEIR GUIDANCE AND TURN OVER RESPONSIBILITY TO STUDENTS

The major goal of all teachers is students becoming independent learners. So far in this chapter, we have stressed teacher support and guidance, because in content classrooms in which students are left to "sink or swim," many sink. In other classrooms, teachers keep students afloat by teaching the content without ever having students read, and, while students do learn some information, they never learn how to read content area materials. They do not sink, but they still do not swim.

We hope that as we near the end of this chapter, you will be looking at your books and other learning resources and your students and seeing the potential for a happier marriage between the two. We hope you will teach a variety of comprehension minilessons that will help all your students succeed in learning how to think about what they read. When you arrive at this point, however, we want you to think once again about the "sink-or-swim" mentality. Your students can swim but only with you alongside, coaching them on, telling them what strokes to use and when they have arrived at their destination. Now is the time to begin to fade your guidance and move them toward independence. This chapter ends with a discussion of two strategies you can use for moving your students toward independence: study guides and fading.

Study Guides

Study guides are generally lists of questions that guide students' reading. They have been used for years and, while well-intentioned, can easily become monotonous "busywork" that students do not view as very helpful. On the other hand, study guides can help teachers move students toward independence and clarify reading purposes.

The most useful and "nonboring" study guides we have come across are the point-of-view reading guide and the interactive reading guide. The point-of-view reading guide (see Figure 4.10) engages the reader by making that reader and his or her reactions the central focus of the questions. The guide invites students to become one of the participants in what is being described and asks for the reader's thoughts about and reactions to the events. Notice the liberal use of the words *you* and *your*. No doubt, you can see that many of the questions on a point-of-view study guide require students to evaluate.

The distinctive feature of the interactive reading guide (see Figure 4.11) is the interaction it ensures among students. The circle symbols at the top indicate which activities are to be done by individuals, pairs, small groups,

America After 1941
America's Huge War Needs

1. As a worker in a U.S. defense plant, tell what effect the War Production Board has had on you, your coworkers, and the soldiers overseas.

Americans Go Back To Work

2. As one of the leaders in a national labor union, what is your reaction to the need for war supplies?
3. As a farmer, tell how your life has changed from the Depression days to the present days of wartime.

Opportunities for Blacks

As a black person from the South:
4. Tell why you and others moved to the northeast and midwest sections of the U.S.
5. Describe the effect of Hitler's racist doctrine on your situation at home.
6. Tell why Executive Order 8802 was important to you.

FIGURE 4.10 Point-of-View Guide (U.S. history—secondary level). SOURCE: Wood, Lapp, & Flood (1992). Reprinted with permission of Karen Wood and the International Reading Association.

Interaction codes:

○ = Individual

⊘ = Pairs

⊛ = Group

◯ = Whole class

⊛ 1. In your group, write down everything you can think of relative to the topics listed below on Japan. Your group's association will then be shared with the class.

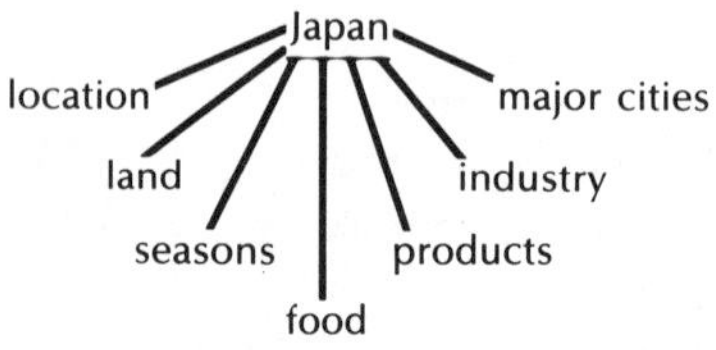

Japan
location — land — seasons — food — products — industry — major cities

⊘ 2. Read page 156 and jot down 5 things about the topography of Japan. Share this information with your partner.

◯ 3. Read to remember all you can about the "Seasons of Japan." The associations of the class will then be written on the board for discussion.

⊘ 4. a. Take turns "whisper reading" the three sections under "Feeding the People of Japan." After each section, retell, with the aid of your partner, the information in your own words.

b. What have you learned about the following?
terraces, paddies, thresh, other crops, fisheries

⊛ 5. Put two pencils together and allow each person in the group to try eating with chopsticks. Discuss your experiences with the group.

⊘ 6. With your partner, use your prior knowledge to predict whether the following statements are true or or false *before* reading the section on "Industrialized Japan." Return to these statements *after* reading to see if you've changed your view. In all cases, be sure to explain your answers. You do not have to agree with your partner.

a. Japan does not produce its own raw materials but instead gets them from other countries.

b. Japan is one of the top 10 shipbuilding countries.

c. Japan makes more cars than the U.S.

d. Silk used to be produced by silkworms but now it is a manmade fiber.

e. Silkworms eat mulberry leaves.

f. The thread from a single cocoon is 600 feet long.

○
⊛ 7. After reading, write down 3 new things you learned about the following topics. Compare these responses with those of your group.
Other industries of Japan
Old and new ways of living

⊘
⊛ 8. Read the section on "Cities of Japan." Each group member is to choose a city, show its location on the map in the textbook, and report on some facts about it.

◯ 9. Return to the major topics introduced in the first activity. Skim over your chapter reading guide responses with these topics in mind. Next, be ready to contribute, along with the class, anything you have learned about these topics.

FIGURE 4.11 Interactive Reading Guide (Social Studies—Intermediate Level).
SOURCE: Wood, Lapp, & Flood (1992). Reprinted with permission of Karen Wood and the International Reading Association.

130

and the whole class. As you look through the guide, notice that students have clear purposes for reading and that the actual reading is often done alone or with partners taking turns whisper reading. Small groups often provide the after reading task completion and feedback part of a comprehension lesson. The whole class gets together at certain points to brainstorm and discuss what is being learned.

Study guides such as these can serve as a bridge between teacher-directed minilessons and student-centered independent learning.

LISTEN/LOOK AND LEARN

Interview two teachers who use study guides and two students who have used study guides. If possible, look at the study guides and compare them with the two samples here. How do the teachers feel about the study guides? Is this different from how the students feel? What kinds of activities are included on the study guides? Do questions require a variety of thinking processes? Do the study guides provide some activities that can be done with a partner or small group? Summarize what you learned, including the benefits and pitfalls of using study guides. Then apply this to your own teaching: What will be the place of study guides in your instruction? What kinds of study guides will you use?

Fading

Fading is a process of gradually decreasing the amount of guidance you give and letting students take on more of the responsibility. You will know when to fade your guidance as you observe the success your students are experiencing. One of the ways you fade is to move from the specific purposes that are usable with only one piece of text to more generic purposes that can be used with many pieces of text.

Imagine, for example, that you have used many webs in class. Your students have gotten good at reading to find information for the various spokes of the web. Suddenly you remember that partially completed webs will not mysteriously appear when students need them; if they leave your classroom forever dependent on you to create the web, they will not be able to use this valuable strategy independently. Consequently, it is now time to fade your guidance. In fact, the next time you think a web will make a good group task, have the students create it.

Tell students that webbing is a wonderfully efficient way to organize topic/subtopic information and that they can create their own webs. On the board or an overhead transparency, write the topic in a circle and draw several lines pointing out from it. Have the students do the same on their own paper. Give students a few minutes to preview the text section you have selected and have them use the headings and visuals to create spokes of the web. Let several students come to the board and draw their web skeleton. Lead the students to understand that there is no magical number of spokes to include and that different labels for the spokes are equally good. Help them see that as long as the spokes contain main topics, the web will help them organize what they read.

Have students read and write details on the spokes of their own webs. After their reading, put students in groups of four or five to compare webs. Encourage them to accept diverse webs but also to add to their own webs information that the group sharing convinces them they need. Help students view webbing as a note-taking strategy that they can use independently.

Once students complete webs independently, discuss the other graphic organizers and move students toward independence in these. Use the same procedure to help them choose the categories for a chart or semantic feature matrix, the main topics for an outline, the important dates for a time line, or the entries for a cause and effect chain. Then have them read and independently complete their own organizers, which they can compare with others' in a small group.

When you have your students independently webbing, charting, outlining, and so on, your task is nearly complete. One more little piece of teacher fading is needed. Your students will not always have you there to decide how to organize the text information graphically, so let them decide. Have them preview the text and decide how best to organize the information. Let different students or groups organize the data as they think best, then share their work with the class. When students can preview something they are

Students construct time lines in order to display information they have gathered.

about to read, decide what kind of graphic organizer would most efficiently and clearly depict the important relationships, and create the graphic organizer, they are becoming independent learners.

This same kind of fading of teacher guidance and content-specific purposes can be applied to the other comprehension formats. Students who have been engaged in KWLs and DRTAs can learn that before they read they call up what they already know and try to predict what questions the text might answer or what they might learn. They can preview the text and use the headings and visuals to make these predictions. After reading, they should ask, "What do I know now that I didn't know before I read?" and "Have I learned what I wanted to learn?" Students who have been involved in creating GIST statements and summary paragraphs can learn to do this for themselves. Students can learn that it helps you understand, enjoy, and remember if you imagine yourself transported into the book. They can learn to ask themselves the evaluate question, "What do I think about this?" and the apply question, "What can I do with this information?"

Fading is not difficult to do, but it is sometimes difficult to remember to do it. Just when your minilessons are going well and your students are succeeding with your support, you must remember that some day they may have to do these tasks on their own.

LOOKING BACK

Most of what we choose to read is on topics for which we have a great deal of background knowledge, thus motivation is usually quite high. When we read this easy (for us) material, comprehension seems to occur effortlessly and automatically as we process the words. In content area classrooms, however, students often read materials for which they have little prior knowledge and motivation. It is when students are reading this teachable text that comprehension minilessons are needed. In this chapter, you learned the why and how of supporting students' comprehension and some strategies for weaning them off this support. These are the five key ideas: (1) Comprehension is thinking and can be increased when teachers support students' comprehension; (2) planning a comprehension minilesson includes deciding on clear learning purposes, background knowledge, and motivation; (3) comprehension minilessons guide students through the before, during, and after phases of reading; (4) there are many variations within the comprehension minilesson framework; and (5) students become independent learners when teachers gradually fade their guidance and turn over responsibility to students.

ADD TO YOUR JOURNAL

Reflect on this chapter's key ideas: Do you see why students need support as they read unfamiliar text? Does the procedure for planning comprehension minilessons make sense? Can you imagine yourself guiding students through the before, during, and after phases of reading, listening, or viewing? Do you see that within the basic framework there are almost endless variations? Do some of these variations seem more applicable to your content area and your purposes for reading? Finally, what do you think about study guides and fading as ways to make students more independent learners? Describe your reactions to each of the five key ideas and generalize about the role of comprehension minilessons and independence in your classroom. What do you believe will be most useful to you?

REFERENCES

Carr, E., & Ogle, D. (1987). KWL plus: A strategy for comprehension and summarization. *Journal of Reading, 30,* 626–631.

Kirk, R. E. (1972). Classification of ANOVA designs. In R. E. Kirk (Ed.), *Statistical issues: A reader for the behavioral sciences.* Belmont, CA: Wadsworth.

Mathison, C. (1989). Activating student interest in content area reading. *Journal of Reading, 33,* 170–176.

Ogle, D. (1986). K-W-L: A teaching model that develops active reading of expository text. *The Reading Teacher, 39,* 564–570.

Stauffer, R. G. (1969). *Directing reading maturity as a cognitive process.* New York: Harper & Row.

Wood, K. D., Lapp, D., & Flood, J. (1992). *Guiding readers through text: A review of study guides.* Newark, DE: International Reading Association.

ADDITIONAL READINGS

More examples of graphic organizers and ways to use them can be found in these two sources:

Peresich, M. L., Meadows, J. D., & Sinatra, R. (1990). Content area cognitive mapping for reading and writing proficiency. *Journal of Reading, 33,* 424–432.

Pittelman, S. D., Heimlich, J. E., Berglund, R. L., & French, M. P. (1991). *Semantic feature analysis: Classroom applications.* Newark, DE: International Reading Association.

The importance of purpose in reading comprehension and how various strategies help students set purposes is the focus of this article:

Blanton, W. E., Wood, K. D., & Moorman, G. B. (1990). The role of purpose in reading instruction. *The Reading Teacher, 43,* 486–493.

In this article you will learn how to write previews for short stories; previews are study guides, tailormade for short stories:

Graves, M. F., Penn, M. C., & Cooke, C. L. (1985). The coming attraction: Previewing short stories. *Journal of Reading, 25,* 594–598.

This book contains a wealth of ideas and variations for the before reading phase of a content comprehension lesson:

Moore, D. W., Readence, J. E., & Rickelman, R. J. (1989). *Prereading activities for content area reading and learning* (2nd ed.). Newark, DE: International Reading Association.

The following summarize the research on the theory and teaching of reading comprehension:

Orsanu, J. (Ed.) (1986). *Reading comprehension: From research to practice.* Hillsdale, NJ: Erlbaum.

Pearson, P. D., & Fielding, L. (1991). Comprehension instruction. In R. Barr, M. D. Kamil, P. B. Mosenthal, & P. D. Pearson (Eds.), *Handbook of reading research* (Vol. II) (pp. 815–860). White Plains, NY: Longman.

C H A P T E R 5

Writing

LOOKING AHEAD

Writing is thinking you do with a pen, pencil, or word processor. Because writing is primarily thinking, you use some or all of the thinking processes as you write. Students who write about what they are learning are engaged in thinking. In order to write, students call up what they know and even seek out more information or clarifications. They show the connections they have made. They organize information in new ways. They share their images, generalizations, and opinions. Writing is an application of new knowledge. As people write, they monitor what they know, what they think, and how well they are communicating. Teachers support students' thinking by planning and carrying out minilessons in which the writing tasks are made clear and the fulfillment of these purposes is ensured by group sharing and feedback.

As you no doubt understand by now, learning requires thinking, and thinking usually begins with calling up past experiences. In this chapter, you will learn how to use writing to help students learn. In order to learn about writing, you must think about writing. Your past experiences with writing will be the starting point for your thinking and learning. To determine where your past writing experiences have gotten you, complete this writing attitude self-appraisal. Place yourself on a 1 to 10 scale between these polar statements:

I really hate to write.

| 1 | 2 | 3 | 4 | 5 |

I really like to write.

| 6 | 7 | 8 | 9 | 10 |

I write only when I have to.

| 1 | 2 | 3 | 4 | 5 |

I write for my own pleasure.

| 6 | 7 | 8 | 9 | 10 |

All of my school writing was for a paper or test.

| 1 | 2 | 3 | 4 | 5 |

All of my school writing was to help me express my thoughts.

| 6 | 7 | 8 | 9 | 10 |

All school writing was graded.

| 1 | 2 | 3 | 4 | 5 |

No school writing was graded.

| 6 | 7 | 8 | 9 | 10 |

Most students are terrible writers.

| 1 | 2 | 3 | 4 | 5 |

Most students are wonderful writers.

| 6 | 7 | 8 | 9 | 10 |

Writing should not be used because students cannot do it.

| 1 | 2 | 3 | 4 | 5 |

Writing should be used in every class so that students get better at it.

| 6 | 7 | 8 | 9 | 10 |

In a content class, all writing should be graded for both content and mechanics.

| 1 | 2 | 3 | 4 | 5 |

In a content class, writing should not be graded.

| 6 | 7 | 8 | 9 | 10 |

Now look at your ratings and see where your past experiences with writing have led you. If you rated yourself a perfect 10 on every statement, you have an incredibly positive view of yourself as a writer, others as writers, and the potential of writing as a tool for learning in your classroom. If you rated yourself 1 on every statement, writing for you as an individual and as a teacher is going to be quite a challenge!

Most teachers rate themselves someplace between 1 and 10, often on the low side. Writing for most of us is not something we feel particularly good at, not something we choose to do, and not something we see as a tool that can help students learn the content we need to teach. Consequently, both research and classroom observation confirm that not much writing happens and that the writing that does happen is often for a test or paper. Writing in most classrooms is not a road to learning but an assessment of what has been learned.

In this chapter, we hope to convince you to use writing in your classroom because it is not "one more thing you have to do" but rather an often-overlooked and readily available resource for helping your students think and learn more. We know, however, that your past experiences with writing, your attitudes toward yourself as a writer, and your confidence that students can and will write may be less than positive. If your past experiences have left you with negative attitudes, we ask you to read and think with an open mind and reconsider the potential writing holds for you and your students.

These are the key ideas in this chapter:

1. Because writing requires thinking, content learning can be increased when teachers support students' writing.

2. Planning a writing minilesson includes deciding on clear writing tasks, background knowledge, and motivation.

3. Writing minilessons guide students through the before, during, and after phases of writing.

4. There are many variations within the writing minilesson framework.

5. Students become independent learners when teachers gradually fade their guidance and turn over responsibility to students.

BECAUSE WRITING REQUIRES THINKING, CONTENT LEARNING CAN BE INCREASED WHEN TEACHERS SUPPORT STUDENTS' WRITING

Writing is best defined as "thinking made external." When we write, we "put down our thoughts" and discover new thoughts. Writing, like reading, has before, during, and after phases. Thinking pervades all these writing phases. If you come upon someone who is sitting with a pen in hand or fingertips poised over the keyboard and staring at the blank page or screen, you might ask, "What are you doing?" The person will often respond, "I'm *thinking*."

Continuing to observe, you will see the person eventually move into the writing phase, but the writing is not nonstop. If you are rude enough to interrupt during one of these pauses and ask, "What are you doing?" the writer will probably again respond, "I'm *thinking*."

Eventually, the writer will finish the writing, or more accurately finish the first draft. The writer may put the writing away for a while or ask someone to "take a look at this and tell me what you think."

Later the writer will return to the writing to revise and edit it. Words will be changed and paragraphs added, moved, or deleted. Again, the writer will pause from time to time during this after writing phase; if you ask the writer what he or she is doing, you will likely get the familiar response, "I'm *thinking*!"

We offer this common scenario as proof that writing is at its essence thinking (even the most naïve writer knows this). Because writing is thinking and learning requires thinking, students who write as they are learning think more and thus learn more.

In addition to being thinking (or perhaps because writing is thinking), writing is hard. It is complex. There are many things to think about all at the same time:

What do I want to say?

How can I say it so that people will believe it?

How can I say it so that people will be motivated to read it?

Who are the people whom I want to read it? What do they already know, think, and believe about this subject?

In addition to these major issues, there are a host of smaller, but still important issues:

How can I begin writing in a way that sets up my ideas and grabs the reader's attention?

Which words best communicate these feelings and thoughts?

What examples can the reader relate to?

Do I need to clarify here or include more detailed information?

How can I end it?

What would be a good title?

As if these grand and less grand issues are not enough, there are all the minor details. Sometimes, these are taken care of during the after writing phase, but often writers think about them as they write. These are some examples:

Should I begin a new paragraph here?

Do I capitalize *state* when it refers to North Carolina?

What is the correct spelling of *Beijing*?

Does the comma go inside or outside the quotation marks?

We have not included this sampling to discourage you. We included it to convince you that students need instruction, guidance, support, encouragement, and acceptance if they are going to be able and willing participants in writing.

They need instruction because often they do not actually know how to write (the form) what you want them to write (the message). They need guidance to help them decide what an appropriate form or audience might be. They need support because once they get started, they may not be able to finish writing completely on their own. They need encouragement because writing is hard and often frustrating. They need acceptance because they cannot produce a perfect (or even near-perfect) paper and need to know that you are looking for the expression of their "best thinking."

In this chapter, we give you suggestions for what students might write; for how you can guide, support, and encourage that writing; and for how you can help them become more independent in their writing and learning. As you think about how you can use writing to increase thinking and learning in your classroom, we would like you to consider our content writing guidelines:

1. Because writing is difficult, most students will write more willingly and learn more if they write several short pieces than if they write one long piece.

2. Because it is impossible to write about what you do not know much about, writing should be on topics about which students are learning.

3. Because writers often find they do not know enough, they should be encouraged to read and use other sources of information as they write.

4. Because everyone likes variety, students should write in many different forms, for different purposes, and for different audiences.

5. Because much thinking occurs during the prewriting and writing phases, most of what students write should not have to be revised and turned into a final draft.

6. Because students learn more content and become better writers when they share what they have written, small-group sharing should be the most common after writing activity.

7. Because all published writing requires editing, students should get help from other students and/or the teacher when they need to produce a displayable final draft.

8. Because red marks on writing discourage writers, no red (or any other color) marks should be put on papers.

9. Because the purpose of writing in a content class is to have students think about what they are learning, most writing should not be graded. (If students will not write unless it counts for the grade, everyone who makes a good effort should be given points for engaging in the thinking process.)

10. Because writing and sharing writing involve risk, teachers should show themselves willing to take those risks by occasionally writing and sharing what they have written.

DO IT TOGETHER

The ten guiding principles for content area writing are controversial. Not everyone will agree with them. Many people believe, for example, that every piece of writing should be graded for both mechanics and content because students may get "sloppy" and never learn to write well. The flip side of this argument is that student resistance to writing is directly related to their awareness that they do not write perfectly and their certainty that they cannot "make the grade." Discuss each of these ten guiding principles with two or three colleagues. Decide which ones you can accept and which you cannot. After the group discussion, work by yourself to write guidelines that you can follow.

PLANNING A WRITING MINILESSON INCLUDES DECIDING ON CLEAR WRITING TASKS, BACKGROUND KNOWLEDGE, AND MOTIVATION

In the last chapter, we discussed that to plan a comprehension minilesson, you must decide on clear learning purposes and decide what background knowledge and motivation students would need to achieve these purposes. When planning a writing minilesson, you follow similar steps:

Deciding What You Want Them to Think About as They Write

Once you become convinced that the main purpose for writing in a content area classroom is to get students thinking about content topics, then you must decide about what you want them to think. For every topic, there is a host of possibilities. Imagine that you are teaching about twins and the incredible similarities that exist between identical twins separated at birth (Holden, 1990). Here are some issues about which you might want your students to think:

1. What genetic traits do twins share?
2. What are the advantages and disadvantages of having a twin?
3. What personality traits seem to be most and least accounted for by heredity?
4. How does research on twins help us understand the heredity-versus-environment issue?
5. Should the findings of research on twins influence your decision about whom to marry?
6. How are you similar to and different from members of your own family?
7. What is there about being a twin that makes someone less likely to become famous?
8. How are twins portrayed in literature?

There are many different issues and questions about which you might want students to think. In doing so, they will use different thinking processes. Almost all writing tasks require students to call up what they know and connect new information. Likewise, students must monitor what they know and are communicating as they write. Students' use of the other thinking processes will depend on what you want them to focus on and the writing task you set for them.

Designing a Writing Task That Will Stimulate Them to Think About What You Want Them to Think About

In the previous chapter, we noted that once you decide what you want students to learn, you should design a task that will focus their attention. When writing, once you know what you want students to think about, you design a writing task that focuses their attention. A writing task has four major components: topic, form, audience, and role.

TOPIC The topic is both the "what?" and the "what for?" of writing: the content and the intent. The topic chosen can include what the students will write about and the purpose the writer should attempt to accomplish during writing. In a content class, the topic is selected so that students focus their thinking. If you want students to think about what genetic traits twins share, for example, your topic might be this:

Describe a restaurant meeting between you and your identical twin, who was separated from you at birth twenty years ago, including details about what each of you is wearing; what each of you orders; what pictures of family, friends, pets, and houses you share; and how each of you reacts when the food served is not what you ordered.

The topic can be very broad, but the best writing topics are narrowed so that the writer knows how to focus attention. By assigning topics with specific content, teachers often narrow the topic to help students know better how to plan their writing.

Teachers sometimes narrow the content of a writing task by specifying the approach the writer is to take. There are five general approaches writers can take:

Compare and/or contrast.
Give the sequence.
Make a list.
Relate cause(s) and effect(s).
State the solution to a problem.

Another way teachers sometimes narrow the topic is specifying the intent or aim of the writing. Here are some possible intents for writing:

Describing
Explaining
Expressing feelings
Narrating
Persuading

FORM   Form is the "how" of writing. How are students going to write about the topic? Are they going to write a poem, a story, an essay, or a newspaper article? Writers use a variety of forms, and their choice of form is related to their topic. For example, your writing on the sample topic above might take the form of a play, a letter, a short story, or even a comic strip.

Specifying the form of a passage usually includes specifying its length. Knowing the approximate length of their writing helps students understand how much information to include. Imagine that you are assigning a paper describing the metric system. Do you expect the paper to be one page or five pages long? A one-page paper would leave space for few examples, but a five-page paper would need many examples. Assigning approximate lengths for writing helps clarify the depth of discussion you expect to find in the writing. Often, the teacher will have more success by setting a maximum length than a minimum one. For students to have to meet the demands of the topic within a constraining length, they will have to plan carefully before writing.

Much school writing is limited to a few forms—paragraphs, stories, letters, poems, and reports. Actual writing, however, contains countless forms. In the real world, people write lists, journal entries, and directions. The list below gives just a sampling of some writing forms to get you thinking about the possibilities for writing forms:

A Sampling of Some Writing Forms

ads	encyclopedia entries	obituaries
allegories	epitaphs	observational notes
announcements	essays	plays
autobiographies	fables	poems
biographies	grocery lists	position papers
book jackets	interviews	questionnaires
book reviews	journals	recipes
brochures	lab reports	reports
campaign speeches	letters	résumés
character sketches	lists	reviews
comic strips	magazine articles	scenarios
commercials	memoirs	scripts
contracts	memos	song lyrics
debates	mysteries	stories
diaries	myths	summaries
directions	newspaper articles	
editorials	newspaper columns	

AUDIENCE Imagine this vignette:

It was a dark and foggy night, and you were driving home from class. You did not stop at a Stop sign that had only recently been installed at a familiar intersection. Fortunately, there were no other cars in the intersection, so you got through safely. Unfortunately, a police officer was parked along the curb ahead. You were given a ticket for running the Stop sign.

Now imagine that you are going to write a letter about this sad incident to a seven-year-old cousin, your best friend, your father (in whose name the car is registered), and the judge who will decide on your fine. The topic and form will be the same for all the letters, but the audience for each is quite different. Think about how the four letters would be different.

Audience, one of the "who's" of writing, refers to the person or persons who might read your writing. Sometimes the audience is real. For example, students write pieces to be read by their classmates, students in other classes, younger children, pen pals, parents, school personnel, newspaper readers, and public officials. Sometimes the audience cannot really read the piece, but the writer writes as if the audience could. For example, letters are written to Abraham Lincoln; descriptions of life as it is today are put into time capsules for some possible readers, years or even decades in the future.

Often, writers write for themselves. People keep diaries and journals; make lists, schedules, and notes; and write to clarify their own thinking rather than to communicate that thinking to others.

In schools, the most common audience is the teacher, probably the hardest audience for whom to write. Students who know that their teacher will be the only reader often leave important data unstated because they know that the teacher already knows the information.

Having a real audience other than the teacher has been shown to improve greatly the quality of student writing. Students write more clearly and use more examples when they know that someone who really needs the information is going to read it. Whenever possible, students should write for a variety of audiences, including themselves, their classmates, and other people in the real world. Before students begin to write, they should be clear about who will be the audience for that piece of writing.

Returning to our twins example, the students could write to a friend, to the mother who gave the twins up for adoption, to the person who arranged the meeting after twenty years, or to an audience of magazine readers.

ROLE The other "who" of writing is the role you take as a writer or the perspective you take. Often we write from our own perspective so that we do not think about our role; sometimes we write from different perspectives. Assuming different roles helps students write clear, interesting writing.

Students could write to Abraham Lincoln, and thus Lincoln would be the audience; or they could write what they think Abraham Lincoln would say in a speech today, and thus they assume the role of Lincoln. For actors, getting into the part, believing they are whom they are portraying, is crucial for believable acting. For writers, assuming different roles helps them write more vividly.

Returning one more time to our twins example, students could write from the role of either twin, the role of the restaurant waiter, or even the role of a nosy eavesdropper at the next table.

A writing task thus has four components:

Topic—What are you writing about and for what aim?

Form—How will you write about the topic? How long will your writing be?

Audience—For whom are you writing?

Role—Who seems to be doing the writing?

RAFT (Holston & Santa, 1985) is a mnemonic device for remembering the four components.

When teachers design a writing task for a content area class, they most commonly think about the topic first and then what form, audience, and role would help students think about that topic. Sometimes, however, you may wish to focus students' attention on a particular form or audience. Form would be the component getting the most attention if the minilesson purpose were to learn to write a poem, a mathematical word problem, a first-person historical account, or a lab report. Role or audience would be the focus if you were helping students learn about Lincoln by writing to him or assuming his role.

When planning a writing task, you first decide about what the writing is going to get the students thinking. This can be a topic, a form, an audience, or a role. Once you have done so, you make decisions about the other three components so that they will support the emphasis on the other component by not being too new or difficult.

Writing tasks have these four components, but you do not have to specify all four. Sometimes you may want to decide on the topic and form but let students choose their audience and role; other times you may want to specify the topic and audience and let students decide on the form.

Considering the four possible components of a writing task in light of what you want students to think about while writing guides your thinking as you plan writing tasks. It is important to remember, however, that planning effective writing tasks cannot be done mechanically. In addition to being systematic about planning a writing task, a teacher also needs a sense of what students like and can do. This is really the "art part" of writing mini-lesson planning. You can develop this by actually planning and teaching writing minilessons. Mixing experience with a knowledge of the four components of a writing task will eventually lead you to the professional skill of constructing writing tasks that really accomplish what you want them to.

Here are some examples of writing tasks that get students to think about the twins issues:

1. *Think about*: What genetic traits do twins share?
Task: Write a two- to three-page scenario to be shared with your classmates describing this scene: Imagine that you had an identical twin who was separated from you at birth. You meet twenty years later at a restaurant. What kind of clothes are each of you wearing? What kind of food do you order? What is shown in the pictures (family, friends, pets, houses) you share? When the waiter brings the wrong food order, how do each of you react?

2. *Think about:* What are the advantages and disadvantages of having a twin?
Task: Locate a twin to interview about the advantages and disadvantages of being a twin. Write a one-page magazine article summarizing your interview, which will be compiled with others into a special class magazine on twins.

3. *Think about:* What personality traits seem to be most and least accounted for by heredity?
Task: First, describe your major personality characteristics. Then compare and contrast your major personality characteristics with those of family members or ancestors. Finally, explain which of your major personality characteristics you believe to be most attributable to heredity. You will share your description and conclusions with classmates.

4. *Think about:* How does research on twins help us understand the heredity-versus-environment issue?

Task: Imagine that you are a scientist who is thinking about how you might use twins in research to shed light on the heredity-versus-environment issue. You are talking on the phone to a scientist from another country and seeking advice on how to proceed. Write what each of you might say in this conversation. Remember that international calls are very expensive, so limit your conversation to five minutes.

5. *Think about:* Should the findings of research on twins influence your decision about whom to marry?

Task: Write a thirty-second public-service TV commercial in which you try to convince teens and young adult singles to consider the personality traits of their boyfriend's or girlfriend's family when making a decision to marry.

6. *Think about:* How are you similar to and different from members of your own family?

Task: Write to a pen pal a letter in which you describe yourself and your family and tell about how you are similar to and different from each other member.

7. *Think about:* What is there about being a twin that makes someone less likely to become famous?

Task: You are a freelance writer working on an article entitled, "History's Missing Famous Twins," for submission to a popular magazine. Describe how small is the number of famous people who are twins when they are compared with their actual numbers in the population. Speculate on why twins might be less likely than nontwins to become famous.

8. *Think about:* How are twins portrayed in literature?

Task: Think about the stories and books you have read in which twins were major characters. Were they realistically portrayed, given what you have learned about twins? Write for a literary publication an essay in which you compare twins' portrayal in literature with what you have learned about twins.

TRY IT OUT

Read the writing tasks and decide what the topic, form, audience, and role is for each. For example, for the first writing task, the topic was a restaurant meeting with an identical twin who had been separated at birth, the form was a scenario, the audience was classmates, and the role was yourself. For the second task, the topic was the advantages and disadvantages of being a twin, the form was a magazine article, the audience was class magazine readers, and the role was you as an interviewer. (Remember that not all of these must be specified in every writing task. The third task, for example, does not specify the form.) Choose two of the tasks and change one or more of the components (topic, form, audience, or role) to create a new writing task. Be sure, however, that your new writing task is still getting students to think.

Building Background Knowledge and Motivation

Once you know what you want students to think about and what writing task they will perform, you can decide what background knowledge and motivation you need to build to enable them to carry out the task. Building background knowledge for writing is no different from building background knowledge for reading. Ask yourself what students need to know to complete the task, then think about how most efficiently to build that knowledge. Consider providing direct and visual experience when needed and possible and trying to help students make connections with things they already know. Often a reading or listening comprehension minilesson becomes the source of background knowledge for writing. Sometimes writing and sharing writing is a way of building background knowledge for reading. Sometimes students are required to do independent library research or reading as a means of building their own background knowledge for the content of their writing.

Background knowledge for writing usually includes content related to the topic but may also include how to write the form. Students cannot successfully write a letter, an essay, or a TV commercial if they do not know the way in which this particular form is written. Modeling of the form and/or examples may be required.

Building motivation for writing shares some traits with building motivation for reading. Students are motivated to write when teachers use analogies; share personal anecdotes; or present a puzzle, a problem, or an apparent contradiction. We also suggest you focus more of your attention on the thinking in which students engage and less on the writing product.

Helping Students Plan What They Will Write

Once you have built background knowledge for the task, presented the task, and helped students do any required research, are they ready to write? Not quite. Their writing will be better if they plan what they are going to say. This is the point at which students prepare outlines or webs, jot down words or reasons or names of people or places they may include, discuss with others what they want to say, develop a working title, or compose a final sentence.

You should help students plan before they begin writing. Have them engage in some class activity that will involve them in the planning. If research is involved, help them organize their findings into a writing plan before they begin their paper. One caution: Because writing is a discovery process, do not insist that students follow their plan too closely, even though there will obviously be some relationship between the plan and the paper.

WRITING MINILESSONS GUIDE STUDENTS THROUGH THE BEFORE, DURING, AND AFTER PHASES OF WRITING

Like a good comprehension minilesson, a good writing minilesson is fairly easy to teach once it has been well planned. Before students write, build their motivation and background knowledge, make clear the writing task they will complete, and help them plan. After students write, lead them to share what they have written and/or give feedback on how well they have completed the task. If what they wrote is to be shared with someone outside the classroom, they should be helped to revise their first draft. Here is an example of a minilesson based on the following topic and task from our twins unit:

Think about: What personality traits seem to be most and least accounted for by heredity?

Task: First, describe your major personality characteristics. Then compare and contrast your major personality characteristics with those of family members or ancestors. Finally, explain which of your major personality characteristics you believe to be most attributable to heredity. You will share your description and conclusions with classmates.

Before Writing

Assume that this writing task is being done in the middle of a unit on twins. Students have already learned about how research with identical twins who were separated at birth is providing insight into the heredity-versus-environment issue. They know that scientists at the University of Minnesota Center for Twin and Adoption Research have found amazing similarities between identical twins who were separated at birth.

Since the writing task for this minilesson requires students to think about which personality traits seem to be more or less accounted for by heredity, specific background knowledge building for this task requires that they know what personality traits are and which ones are believed to be most influenced by heredity. Present them with data from the Minnesota Twin Studies, which indicate that leadership, cheerfulness, optimism, imaginativeness, stress vulnerability, and risk avoidance are strongly influenced by heredity. Other traits—such as ability to establish emotional intimacy and the propensity to be sensible and rational—appear to be less influenced by heredity.

Write these traits on the board in two columns under these headings: Personality Traits Most Influenced by Heredity and Personality Traits Less Influenced by Heredity. Next, have the class brainstorm other personality traits, such as these: hot-tempered, impatient, cooperative, laid-back, high-strung, nervous, and cautious.

Write these traits on the board also but not under either heading, then explain that some personality traits seem to be more influenced by heredity than others but we do not know which. Students will write a self-description in which they compare their personality traits with those of their family members and try to conclude—based on their own family experiences—which traits they seem to share with other family members. Remind them that because they have shared the same environment with many of these family members, the traits they share are probably attributable to both heredity and environment; however, it will be interesting to think about from where their personality characteristics come.

Then suggest that the paper should be about two pages long and that they can first describe themselves and then compare themselves to other family members or that they can concentrate on one personality trait, then another, and so on as they go along. Finally, tell them that after writing, they will read their self-descriptions to others in a small group and that the group will see if any conclusions can be drawn about shared personality traits based on that group's self-descriptions. Each group's information will then be compiled, and the class will decide if they can draw any generalizations from the separate experiences of all the class members.

Writing

Now the students write. They are motivated because the topic, themselves, is of universal interest. They are also motivated because they know that small-group sharing will be what happens after they write. Background knowledge comes from what they have learned about the heredity-versus-environment issue and about personality traits combined with the firsthand knowledge they have of themselves and their families. The first two parts of their task, to describe their own personalities and compare them to those of other family members, are clear and easy to do for most students. Make sure that students have enough time to write but not so much time that they will not stay on task.

After Writing

Put the students in groups of three or four and give them about twenty minutes to share their writing. When all students in the group have had a chance to read what they wrote, the group lists all the different personality traits discussed in all the papers and tries to classify them as more or less attributable to heredity. The whole class then reconvenes, you record the small-group decisions on the board, and you lead the class to see if there is any agreement across the groups.

LISTEN/LOOK AND LEARN
Visit a classroom to observe a writing minilesson or watch a videotaped writing minilesson. Summarize what you saw during each phase of writing. Evaluate the minilesson based on what you have learned so far in this chapter. What worked? What might the teacher have done differently?

THERE ARE MANY VARIATIONS WITHIN THE WRITING MINILESSON FRAMEWORK

We hope that you now have a good idea of how writing promotes thinking; how you plan a writing task; and what the before, during, and after phases of a writing minilesson might look like. Of course, each writing minilesson is unique because background knowledge and motivation demands before writing differ and ways to organize for sharing and feedback after writing are numerous. In this section, we suggest some of the possibilities for the three phases of a writing minilesson.

Before Writing Variations

The before writing phase is sometimes called prewriting. In the South, some people call it "fixing to write." D. Kirby and T. Liner (1981) call it "getting it together." There are various ways that teachers help students get ready to write. We have already talked about the importance of providing adequate background knowledge and motivation. Background knowledge is often built through such activities as these:

brainstorming	webbing	charting	outlining
reading	listening	viewing	discussing
role-playing	researching	interviewing	drawing

Sometimes these activities for building background knowledge are done with the teacher directing the whole class, but small groups using the above activities allow for much more participation of each student.

Motivation to write is related to background knowledge because writing is hard enough when you know a lot and just about impossible when you do not know much. As you learn information, you not only have "something to say" but also become more interested in the topic. Students who are engaged in reading, researching, and brainstorming are sometimes overheard to make comments such as, "Hmmm, this is really interesting" and "Wow! I didn't know that!"

Motivation is also related to the writing task. Contrast these two writing tasks in terms of their motivation potential:

Task: Write three paragraphs summarizing what you have learned about personality characteristics and heredity from the twin research.

Task: First, describe your major personality characteristics. Then compare and contrast your major personality characteristics with family members or ancestors. Finally, explain which of your major personality characteristics you believe are most attributable to heredity. You will share your description and conclusions with classmates.

Both tasks require the writer to think about the relationship between personality and heredity, but which would you be more motivated to write? Most people would choose the second topic because it involves applying what is

This teacher is building background knowledge.

learned rather than just recalling. Often, we use writing to "find out what students know." Writers, on the other hand, usually write to "tell what they think." Writing tasks communicating that students' thinking is what you are interested in will result in more motivated writers.

Finally, motivation is related to what students believe will be done with what they write. Variations in what you can do with students' writing will be discussed in the after writing variations section, but student motivation to write will be increased if you let them know beforehand what will be done with it. Consider how motivated students would be given the following after writing possibilities:

Your paper will be graded for both content and mechanics, and points will be deducted for each misspelled word.

Your paper will be graded, and you will rewrite it and turn it in again.

Tomorrow each person will stand and read his or her paper to the whole class.

You will work with a classmate to revise your first draft before turning it in for a grade.

You will read your paper to a small group and then compile the best ideas from all group members.

This writing is just for you. I will read it to see what you think and give you a point for good effort, but I will not grade it.

Once students have sufficient background knowledge and motivation to write, you must make sure that they understand the task. If students do not understand how to write a particular form, you will have to teach it. Students cannot write a lab report, TV commercial, or brochure if they do not know the form.

The most efficient way to teach students the form is usually demonstration. Using the overhead projector, a science teacher can write up the lab report while thinking aloud. As students watch and listen, the teacher talks about what it is important to include where and does the actual writing. It is helpful if the teacher makes some mistakes and false starts. These can then be fixed either immediately or when the teacher demonstrates how to reread the whole thing before turning it in.

This teacher demonstration is called *modeling* and has been shown to be an effective and straightforward way of teaching. Teacher modeling is more effective than just presenting students with an already completed model because when students watch teachers write and listen as teachers think aloud, they learn *how* the product is produced.

Already done models are, however, another way of showing students forms. These already done models are quicker than teacher modeling and are best used when students need just a quick review or a reminder of a form with which they are familiar. Showing students a letter or brochure and pointing out the salient features that all letters or brochures share may suffice to enable them to produce the desired form. Whenever possible, these already done models should be student-produced models, and you should provide several models. Multiple models help students find their own writing style and make it clear that there is never just one right way to write. Students are more motivated if they see something similar done by last year's class. Some students are even challenged to excel as they respond to last year's models with a "We can do it better!" attitude.

All or any combination of activities can go on during the before writing phase. Prewriting sometimes takes two minutes, sometimes two days. This prewriting time does not take away from content learning, however, because most of it involves students thinking about the content they are learning.

During Writing Variations

If prewriting is "getting it together," writing is "getting it down." What happens during the writing phase ought to be fairly obvious. Still, there are some questions teachers must think about and some decisions they must make. The first major decision is whether students will write alone or communally.

Writing is usually conceived of as an individual activity, but in the real world many excellent pieces of writing (this textbook, for example) are group written. You learned in Chapter 1 that students achieve much and enjoy learning when it is arranged in some kind of cooperative learning format. This is also true of writing. When you want students to write communally, you have available a variety of classroom grouping patterns.

Students record their thoughts in the during writing phase.

Students might work in a group of three or four with one person recording the ideas of the entire group. This communal writing seems to work best if everyone contributes ideas and one student acts as scribe and produces a first draft and reads it to the group. All group members can suggest ways to make the writing better and clearer. Alternately, students might work with a partner and switch the roles of thinker and writer.

For a lengthy piece, students might divide up the sections (as we did with the first draft of this book). They would first plan which part each would write and set some guidelines about content to be covered and writing style to be used. Each person would then write his or her part to which everyone in the group would respond. The group would work together producing a draft to which they all had contributed.

Another decision you must make is what students are going to write about and what they will use to do so. Do not assume that all writing must be done with a pencil or pen and a sheet of notebook paper. Variety here is important, too. Students are sometimes motivated to write when they are given an index card and asked to write a brief description. Somehow the small index card is less intimidating than a huge piece of notebook paper. Students can write with nonpermanent markers on transparencies that can then be projected and shared with the class. Students can write with markers on discarded roles of wallpaper, with chalk on sections of the chalkboard, or with colored pens on stationery.

If you are lucky or resourceful, students can write using computers. Those who have regular access to computers for word processing are more willing to write, write more, revise more, and feel more confident in their writing. Writing on a computer frees you from many of the first-draft mechanical, spelling, and formatting concerns because you can fix your writing without copying it over. Many word processing programs have spelling and grammar checkers that actually make editing an entertaining process (relatively speaking). As computers become more available in classrooms, we envision a future in which writers and teachers will find it easier to focus on the ideas and the thinking and let the computer take care of some details.

Elementary-school teachers who want to use computers to help children write should get a copy of *From Scribblers to Scribes: Young Writers Use the Computer* (Katzer & Crnkovich, 1991). It is clear that these authors are real teachers who have worked out most of the nitty-gritty details for using computers with children. The book not only contains lots of easy-to-follow sample lesson plans and suggestions for scheduling and organizing, but also has a whole chapter on using computers with "challenged learners," which includes at-risk students as well as students with visual and physical impairments.

In addition to a normal word processing program that allows the students to write, edit, check spelling, and so forth, there are some writing programs that support writing in specific ways. Some of these help students organize their reports, while others provide basic report structures or writing frames. A whole generation of desktop publishing software allows students to create professional-looking newsletters, reports, and announcements. Other software can produce charts, maps, and graphs. A few programs allow students to scan pictures and place them in their reports. There are artwork files that allow students to select illustrations, logos, and other visuals to spice up stories, news reports, or announcements.

Here is just a sampling of some of the best programs we have seen for using the computer to support writing in content areas. Given the pace of development, by the time this book is out all these will probably be replaced by better and newer programs. We include this list more to illustrate the kind of writing support computers can offer students than as specific recommendations of software. Find the newest software that perform these (and yet unimagined) functions:

- *Print Shop* (Broderbund): This program allows students to produce cards, invitations, posters, and so on with professional-quality layout and graphics.
- *Pow! Zap! Ker-Plunk!* (Author, Queue): This program is a comic-book maker that includes clip art, speech bubbles, and comic-book backgrounds. It enables students to produce books, cards, mobiles, and puppets.
- *Story Starters: Social Studies* and *Story Starters: Science* (Pelican, Author): These programs include clip art and background related to science and social studies topics. Students can use the art and background to produce professional-looking books about U.S. history as well as animals, plants, weather, the solar system, and other science topics.
- *Thinking Networks for Reading and Writing* (Think Network): Students learn about topics, then learn to use skeleton map outlines to create text structured in a variety of ways.
- *Children's Writing & Publishing Center* (The Learning Co.): This is a simple desktop publishing program allowing students to create newsletters, stories, reports, and so on. It includes 150 pictures and the ability to import graphics from other sources.

Finally, you must decide what you are going to do while the students write. Some teachers conduct "miniconferences" with students, stopping for a minute at each desk to say some encouraging words and perhaps make a suggestion. While this seems often to work very well, some students find that this teacher input during first-draft writing hinders their concentration and interrupts their flow of ideas; it also seems to tempt some students to become or remain overly dependent on the teacher.

Some teachers circulate and spell problem words. While students seem to appreciate this support, it is probably not a good idea in the long run. Classroom observation shows that when teachers circulate and respond to raised hands by spelling words, students write much less than they would if left to spell words as best they can. Some students will just wait until the teacher spells their word and spend more time waiting than writing.

Spelling, of course, is a concern for writers and teachers, but it seems best to underemphasize it during first-draft writing. Students should be encouraged to brainstorm lists of words, use a dictionary (if they know how and want to), and write words as best they can. Some teachers encourage students to leave blanks for letters about which they are uncertain or put an asterisk in the margin where they think their spelling is probably wrong.

The procedure just described sounds easier than it is. Because students are afraid of misspelling words, teachers feel a natural tendency to want to help.

But, students will write longer drafts and use more sophisticated words if they are freed up from real or perceived "perfect spelling" demands on their first-draft writing. Students should learn that perfect spelling is not required for them to share their work with a small group and that when their writing is to be publicly displayed or graded, they will be given time and help to fix the spelling.

Fixing spelling, and many more substantive "fixings," is what some teachers do while students produce their first drafts. In some classrooms, teachers work with individuals or small groups who are revising an already completed first draft while the rest of the students are writing their first drafts. These writing conferences are usually conducted quietly in a corner of the room so that the writers are not disturbed.

Perhaps the best thing you could do while students are writing is write a piece yourself. Students rarely watch adults write, and thus they often see writing as something adults "make students do." By writing as the students write and then sharing what you have written, you provide an often-absent model of an adult in the act of writing. If you do write, show your mistakes, cross some things out, and mark some words for a later spelling check. Students need proof that writing is complex and that perfect first-draft writing is not possible; you have the perfect opportunity to present them with a first-hand example of nonperfection.

After Writing Variations

The possibilities here range from doing nothing to sharing the writing by reading it aloud to revising, editing, and publishing it. Let's consider the doing-nothing option first. If your major purpose for having students write is to promote their thinking about content, you may have accomplished that goal with the thinking engaged in by the students before and during writing. In this case, you would simply check to see that the writing was indeed done and that a sufficient effort was made.

The problem with the doing-nothing response is that students do not get any feedback on how well they performed. This feedback can be provided by you, by the person who wrote the piece, or by classmates. You can assess how well each student has done and make some notes on the writing about what the student might have misunderstood or might need to clarify. You can have a short conference with each student and give feedback in this setting. Some teachers use a writing scale to give students feedback about how well they have completed the writing task. A writing scale is a short set of questions, rules, or criteria that guide students' evaluation of their own or others' writing. A writing scale may focus students' attention on the form at the sentence level:

Does every sentence begin with a capital letter?

Does every sentence end with a period, a question mark, or an exclamation point?

Does every question end with a question mark?

Is every sentence a complete sentence?

Or it can focus on the form at the text level:

Does the paper clearly take one and only one position?

Are there at least two different reasons given in support for the position taken?

Is each reason explained and supported?

Is there an introduction that previews the content and raises reader interest?

Is there a conclusion to the paper?

Or it can focus on the meaning:

Does the paper give a clear and accurate definition of anxiety?

Does the paper give a clear and accurate definition of fear?

Does the paper state at least two different and accurate commonalities between anxiety and fear?

Does the paper make at least two different and accurate distinctions between anxiety and fear?

It is possible that a particular writing scale will include questions, rules, or criteria on both form at a variety of levels and meaning so that every student has something new that he or she is ready to learn. The essential factor with writing scales is that the students are taught how to use the scale to correct their own writing.

A second way to help students learn how to improve their writing is to let them assess their own writing. Again, a writing scale would be used, and each student would determine how well he or she had done.

Perhaps the easiest and most effective way to provide feedback is to let students share what they have written with their classmates, which can be done in pairs or small groups. When students are sharing their writing, it is helpful to have a purpose for that sharing. In the example minilesson concerning self-descriptions of personality characteristics described in the previous section, students shared their individual pieces in order to see if there was consensus within the group about which traits might be more influenced by heredity.

Pairs of students could use the scale to help each other assess how well their writing accomplished the task. In this case, you would probably want to let each student "pick a friend" for a partner since constructive criticism is accepted better from a friend.

When the first-draft writing is to be revised, edited, polished, and displayed in some way, the after writing phase becomes more extended and more complex. (If you have used Kirby and Liner's terms "getting it together" and "getting it down" to help students conceptualize the after and during writing phases, you might want to tell them that now they are engaged in "getting it right.") Here again, students could work with a partner, a small group, or the teacher to do the revising and editing process. This help needs to address both the message contained in the writing and the mechanics. The message should be dealt with first, then attention should focus on mechanics. B. Lyons (1981) suggests that PQP—praise, question, polish—is a nifty mnemonic to help students remember how to help one another.

Each writer should read his or her paper aloud to a willing listener or listeners (teacher, partner, or small group). When the writer finishes reading, the writer elicits *praise* by asking something like this: "What did you like about it?" The listener or listeners then provide some positive comments:

"You really learned a lot by interviewing two sets of twins."

"Your reasons for why twins might not become famous really made sense to me."

"Your conversation with the other scientist sounded like a real phone conversation, and you had some good ideas for using twins in research."

Next, the writer should elicit *questions* by asking, "Do you have any questions?" or "Was there anything you didn't understand?" These are sample responses:

"I didn't understand if the twins finally thought it was better or not to have been born twins."

"You lost me in the middle part."

"How would you find the twins for your research?"

Finally, the writer should ask the listeners to help *polish* the paper. The writer might ask, "Can you think of ways to make the writing more interesting, informative, or compelling?" Using the comments, the writer has some concrete things to do in order to revise the message of the piece.

The next step is editing for mechanics, with which students and teachers can help. The most important thing for everyone to remember is that "perfect writing just doesn't exist." Even textbooks such as this one (which has been revised and edited by all four authors and an editor from the publishing company) will still contain some errors when published. (Everyone, however, wants their writing to be perfect, so if you find errors in this textbook, please jot them down and send them to the publisher so that we can correct them on the next printing.) The goal of editing is to produce a finished product of which the writer can be proud. How perfect that needs to be depends on the age and ability of the students and the expectations of the audience who will read the final copy.

Editing may also be done by students following a writing scale while rereading their papers. Once students have practiced proofreading and correcting their writing several times using a similar writing scale, they begin to internalize the standards implicit in the scale. Eventually, this process will even result in fewer first-draft errors.

A writer getting editing help from a teacher.

Once the writer has had help revising the message and editing for mechanics, the piece should be recopied, retyped, or reprinted on the computer. This finished product should then be displayed or published, since the reason for revising and editing first drafts is to make them more readable for a new reader.

The final after writing variation has to do with grading. As we suggested early in this chapter, this is a very controversial issue, but it is one on which you must take a stand. Some teachers grade every piece of writing for both content and mechanics because they believe that students will not improve their writing if it is not graded. Other teachers do not assign any "quality grades" but give students points for good effort. Other teachers give points for good effort for all first-draft writing and grade only those pieces that students have had ample opportunity and help to revise and edit. For writing, the grading issue is complex, and you must make decisions based on what you believe will best motivate your students. Whatever you decide,

A writer getting editing help from a friend.

make your grading policy clear to students so that they know for what they will be held accountable.

TRY IT OUT

Plan a writing minilesson. Make a sheet like the one in Figure 5.1 and fill in what you will do during each phase.

Before writing:
  What I want students to think about:
  The task:
    Topic:
    Form:
    Audience:
    Role:
  Background knowledge motivation:
  Individual planning activity:
During writing:
  Write alone or communally:
  Write on what and with what:
  What I will do while students write:
After writing:
  Feedback given by me, themselves, classmates: How?
  Revising and editing:
  Grading:
FIGURE 5.1 Planning a Writing Minilesson

STUDENTS BECOME INDEPENDENT LEARNERS WHEN TEACHERS GRADUALLY FADE THEIR GUIDANCE AND TURN OVER RESPONSIBILITY TO STUDENTS

Just as with comprehension, our ultimate goal is to have students become independent in using writing as a road to thinking and learning. Teachers who are concerned about independence gradually fade the amount of their guidance and have students keep content journals.

Fading

To produce independent writers, teachers need to fade out their guidance and support. In our discussion of fading in the previous chapter, we stressed gradually turning over responsibility for building background knowledge and purpose setting to the students. This same type of gradual release of responsibility can help students learn to use writing as a way to focus their thinking.

Once students understand that a writing task has four components—topic, form, audience, and role—they should be given some responsibility for deciding on appropriate writing tasks. Returning to our twins example, you may decide that students should think about the advantages and disadvantages of being a twin. This topic might be given to the students, then the students might decide what would be an appropriate form, audience, and role. Here your responsibility is not to specify but rather to lead students to consider the possibilities. Questions such as the following help students begin to make the kinds of decisions real writers make:

In what different forms might your ideas about the advantages and disadvantages of being a twin best be described?

For whom are you going to write this? Will you write it for adults, twins, or parents expecting twins? All kinds of people might read this, but a good writer often has a specific reader in mind; picturing this audience helps the writer to write clearly and use appropriate examples.

What role will you take on as the writer? Will you be a twin? Will you be two twins, each with a different opinion? Will you be an anonymous observer?

Questions such as these help students become independent in deciding how their writing can be most effective. Once students have a writing task in mind, they need to think about their own background knowledge and what additional knowledge they might need. Again teachers help by making suggestions:

What do you need to know?

How could you find out more about twins?

Do you know any twins?

Would it help to interview some twins?

Where could you find some more information about how twins feel about being twins?

If you were a twin, how would you feel?

Teachers can also fade the guidance given in the after writing phase. Students can learn to read their own papers asking themselves questions such as these:

What do I like best about what I wrote?

What is not clear? How can I make it clearer?

Do I need some more examples?

Will the reader be interested in reading it?

Students can learn to use a writing scale for editing and dictionaries for spelling help. Editing, however, is not something real writers do totally independently, so students should be given continued help to produce polished final drafts. Good teachers encourage students by constantly reminding them that even the best and most famous writers need good editors.

Content Journals

We hope that you have been keeping the journal suggested at the end of each chapter. This is just one example of a content journal. A content journal is a place for students to record their personal insights, questions, confusions, disagreements, and frustrations about what is being learned. Journal writing is primarily writing students do for themselves; it helps them sort out what they think about what they are learning.

Content journals may have a great deal of structure or very little. When there is little structure, students choose what to write about. One student might write a diary-style account of what went on in school, while another might write a letter to the teacher, complete with visuals, explaining his or her reaction to what is being studied. When students have control over the specific content they are writing about, the journals are said to have low structure.

With high-structure content journals, the teacher requires students to react to specific ideas they are exploring in class. Students may be asked to explore some controversial issue associated with the content. For instance, if westward expansion were the unit of study in American history, students might be asked to record their impressions of the similarities between nineteenth-century movement by U.S. citizens into Texas and twentieth-century movement by Mexican citizens into Texas. Students could be asked to call up impressions they had before beginning the class and compare them to their current impressions. They might be asked to summarize chapters or articles they are reading. The structure is high because the teacher assigns the writing task; students have little say about what they are to write. It seems useful for the teacher to use high-structure journals initially, identifying specific questions for the students to address. Students can then be faded from high-structure to low-structure content journals.

Typically, students should be expected to write in their journals from five to ten minutes each day. Most teachers using journals allow in-class time for writing some of the entries. With all content journal entries, students are required to date and list the time for each entry, which makes it easier for the teacher to refer to specific pieces of writing. A table of contents also is maintained. When class time is given for journal writing, all students must write for the entire period. If they cannot think of anything to write, they should be asked to discuss in writing why they are having trouble writing about this topic, switching over to information about the topic whenever they are able. Students should be told not to be unnecessarily concerned with spelling or other mechanical factors. They should just try to get their ideas flowing.

Many teachers have students produce journals that combine high and low structure. This calls for students to keep translation writing tasks and totally personal entries together. Additionally, visuals can be maintained in the same place. Such teachers help students produce a combination scrapbook-notebook-diary that becomes a valuable momento of each student's school year.

Journals are collected several times a term in order to make sure that students have been regularly writing, and in order to determine whether students are learning course content and reacting thoughtfully to the ideas they are encountering. While reading the journals, the teacher writes comments to the students, creating a written dialogue, about how well students are learning the course material and how clearly they express what they have learned. Students' attitudes and efforts regarding journal writing seem to be directly related to the frequency and quality of a teacher's comments in the journals. Weekly reactions are ideal, although biweekly and triweekly input is generally more feasible. Grades can be assigned for keeping the journal if the teacher so desires.

LISTEN/LOOK AND LEARN

Find two teachers from the subject or grade you want to teach. Interview them about the writing their students do: How often do students write? Do students write in the different content areas? What kinds of writing tasks do they give students? What kinds of after writing activities do they provide? What do they do about grading what students write? Summarize what you find from your interviews and compare that data with what you read in this chapter. When you find differences between what you learned in this chapter and what you learned from your interviews, explain why you think these differences exist. Apply all this to your own teaching. What would someone find out if they interviewed you on this same topic?

LOOKING BACK

Writing is hard and not something many view as a tool for learning and thinking. Consequently, not much writing occurs in content area classrooms, and the writing that does occur is usually viewed as a way of assessing what was learned rather than as a learning tool. In this chapter, you learned why and how writing should play a role in your classroom and five key ideas about writing in content-area classrooms: (1) Because writing requires thinking, content learning can be increased when teachers support students' writing; (2) planning a writing minilesson includes deciding on clear writing tasks, background knowledge, and motivation; (3) writing minilessons guide students through the before, during, and after phases of writing; (4) there are many variations within the writing minilesson framework; and (5) students become independent learners when teachers gradually fade their guidance and turn over responsibility to students.

ADD TO YOUR JOURNAL

Reflect upon the five key ideas presented in this chapter and decide what you think. Do you see ways that writing can help your students think and learn in your content area? Does the procedure for planning a writing minilesson make sense to you? Do you agree that some writing tasks are more motivating than others and that helping students think about role and audience as well as topic and form can help them focus their writing? Can you imagine yourself guiding students through the before, during, and after phases of writing minilessons? Can you apply the variations to writing tasks you think would work best for you? Finally, what do you think about fading and content journals as ways to make students more independent learners? Describe your reactions to the five key ideas and generalize about the role of writing in your classroom. What and how large a role do you see for writing in your classroom?

REFERENCES

Holden, C. (1990). Double features. In *The 1990 World Book year book* (pp. 140–153). Chicago: World Book.

Holston, V., & Santa, C. (1985). A method of writing across the curriculum that works. *Journal of Reading, 28*, 456–457.

Katzer, S., & Crnkovich, C. A. (1991). *From scribblers to scribes: Young writers use the computer*. Englewood, CO: Teacher Ideas Press.

Kirby, D., & Liner, T. (1981). *Inside out: Developmental strategies for teaching writing*. Portsmouth, NH: Boynton/Cook.

Lyons, B. (1981). The PQP method of responding to writing. *English Journal, 70*, 42–43.

ADDITIONAL READINGS

These books suggest many practical ways to integrate writing into all areas of the elementary curriculum:

Atwell, N. (Ed.). (1990). *Coming to know: Writing to learn in the intermediate grades*. Portsmouth, NH: Heinemann.

Heller, M. F. (1991). *Reading-writing connections: From theory to practice*. White Plains, NY: Longman.

Kirby, D., Liner, T., & Vinz, R. (1981). *Inside out: Developmental strategies for teaching writing*. Portsmouth, NH: Boynton/Cook.

This book is already a classic on writing across the middle-school curriculum:

Atwell, N. (1987). *In the middle: Writing, reading and learning with adolescents*. Portsmouth, NH: Boynton/Cook.

This book is a practical description of how to use journals in different secondary content areas:

Fulwiler, T. (Ed.). (1987). *The journal book*. Portsmouth, NH: Boynton/Cook.

This book includes case studies of seven high-school English, science, social studies, and home economics teachers as they implemented various writing activities in their classrooms; the different writing activities used and the analysis of how they promoted thinking are insightful and thought-provoking:

Langer, J. A., & Applebee, A. N. (1987). *How writing shapes thinking: A study of teaching and learning*. Urbana, IL: National Council of Teachers of English.

This book summarizes the reasearch on writing, particularly the use of inquiry and writing:

Hillocks, George, Jr. (1986). *Research on written composition: New directions for teaching*. Urbana, IL: National Council of Teachers of English and ERIC/RCS.

This summarizes the research on the relationships between reading and writing and the benefits to students of connecting the two:

Tierney, R. J., & Shanahan, T. (1991). Research on the reading-writing relationship: Interactions, transactions, and outcomes. In R. Barr, M. D. Kamil, P. B. Mosenthal, & P. D. Pearson, (Eds.), *Handbook of reading research* (Vol. II) (pp. 246–280). White Plains, NY: Longman.

Most of the chapters in this book are devoted to specific content areas (art, German, math, and so forth), although a few cover such general topics as content journals and what students say about writing to learn:

Gere, A. R. (Ed.). (1985). *Roots in the sawdust: Writing to learn across the disciplines*. Urbana, IL: National Council of Teachers of English.

C H A P T E R 6

Student Research

LOOKING AHEAD

The guidelines in this chapter on developing student researchers should lead students to conduct personalized inquiry. As you know, personalized inquiry calls for teachers to assume a facilitative role, with students at the center of the process. Students, not teachers, are responsible for asking questions and for locating, organizing, and reporting information.

Four essential components of the research process are identifying a question, locating information, organizing information, and reporting the information. Each of these components will be dealt with separately in this chapter; however, as in writing, the components of research interact with one another. The researcher has a question and locates information, causing him or her to return to the question and refine it further. While organizing information, the researcher discovers that additional data are needed, so he or she returns to the references and locates more.

In fact, research skills can be considered a special class of writing skills. Researchers plan, draft, and revise; they have an audience, a topic, a form, and a role in mind; they follow models of finished products; they generate and organize information. The primary difference between the writing process and the research process, as we present it in this chapter, lies in the planning stage. Conducting research implies the need to discover new knowledge before sharing it. Writing activities frequently emphasize articulating what students already know; research activities emphasize learning new things so as to articulate them later.

This chapter on student research also is closely related to the section on inquiry units in Chapter 3. This chapter extends some of the ideas presented earlier on facilitating students' inquiries and presents new information. It contains numerous specific suggestions for helping students direct their investigations about the world.

Parents have learned to fear this announcement by their schoolchildren: "I have a report due Wednesday. I have to do Brazil." Parents typically go through much stress and strain helping their children produce the report. Likewise, teachers often have great difficulty leading each student through the stages of research projects, and students have even greater difficulty completing such projects independently. Therefore, pupils go home with a general topic on which to report, and their parents help them limit the topic, find the resources for research, and put a report together in a reasonably organized fashion. That is, the parents who themselves produced acceptable reports provide such guidance, while other parents cannot help their children produce acceptable reports. Thus, students are often limited to their parents' level of school performance.

Classroom teachers, having few resources and little training in this area, are frequently unsure of how to teach research skills. Additionally, our society seems to have an instinctive awe of anything that smacks of research. Both teachers and students need to demystify "research," learning to define it as merely answering interesting questions. Skilled researchers become curious about some process or trend, so they set out to answer questions about their topic logically and systematically. Student researchers should generate interesting questions so that they, too, can answer questions in a logical and systematic fashion. Children who are told to "do Brazil" probably have little interest and few questions, an attitude that works against becoming an independent researcher.

We see three major benefits of developing student researchers: heightened student interest, improved evaluative thinking, and greater student independence. When students are actively engaged in collecting and sharing information, they have far more interest in the topic than if they are simply passive listeners. Students who are motivated to generate questions, suggest places to hunt for information, find that information, and share their findings typically learn more than students who merely carry out directions from the teacher. These students are building background knowledge about a topic, and generally, the more one knows about a topic, the greater interest one has in it. Interested students typically are better learners than uninterested ones.

Second, in the past, teachers have tended to focus so exclusively on a textbook as the sole source of information that students have little opportunity or motivation to evaluate the materials they read. It is difficult for students to judge the content and writing style of a text when that is the only material they read. Developing student researchers allows pupils to identify a wide range of information sources—visual, oral, and written—and learn to use them well. They also learn how to reconcile contradictory information and how to identify complementary facts. It is very difficult to teach such evaluative reading skills using only a single text.

Finally, a major goal of schooling is to help students become independent learners who not only know how to read and write but also actively desire to do so. When students are taught a process for generating questions that they genuinely want to answer and are then taught a strategy for answering those questions, they begin to see reading and writing as useful and enjoyable activities, not just as required assignments. The processes that students have been taught should help them to search for answers to the other questions they will encounter throughout their lifetimes.

In this chapter we describe methods that will help you develop strategies for your students so they not only can locate information and share it easily but also will develop an interest in doing so. Helping students become independent inquirers and seekers of knowledge is one of our tasks as teachers. Part of helping them develop such an inquiring nature is making automatic the processes that researchers go through in obtaining and sharing their

Research projects motivate students to evaluate and synthesize information.

findings. The more excited they are about sharing what they have learned, the more likely they are to engage in systematic inquiry independently. Keep as one of your goals developing an excitement about learning, and research processes will be learned much more easily.

These are the key ideas in this chapter:

1. Students can learn to ask researchable questions.
2. Students need to know how to locate sources and information within sources.
3. There are a number of ways to organize information.
4. Students can share information learned through research in a variety of ways.
5. Students become independent researchers when teachers gradually fade their guidance and turn over responsibility to students.

DO IT TOGETHER

As a group or pair, think back to the research projects you completed in elementary and secondary school. Which projects were your favorites? Why? Which were your least favorite? Why? What problems did you encounter in identifying a researchable question, locating information, organizing information, and sharing what you learned? Each group or pair should briefly summarize their discussion for the rest of the class.

STUDENTS CAN LEARN TO ASK RESEARCHABLE QUESTIONS

All students have questions. No one ever has to teach a four-year-old to ask a question. Why then do students have problems asking questions in school? Much of the difficulty in helping students develop research questions stems from their lack of interest in the topic being studied and from their lack of knowledge about it. In order to ask a good question, we have to be aware of the gaps in our knowledge, to know what we do not know. Indeed, problem finding might be an even more complex activity than problem solving. A critical aspect of helping students identify questions, then, is the promotion of students' interest and knowledge about a particular topic.

To begin planning research lessons, the teacher should examine the year's units of study for every subject area and sort these units into three groups: high interest (such as dinosaurs for young children or death for older ones); medium interest (such as explorers in the New World or propaganda techniques); and low interest (such as Brazil or forms of government). High-interest topics of study are especially appropriate for research because students are inclined to be more thorough and are better able to sustain their interest through difficulties with these topics. Some medium-interest topics can be developed into high-interest ones. Since students cannot do reports on all aspects of the curriculum, teachers should simply not assign reports on topics in which student interest is low. Assuming then that students have at least moderate levels of interest and background for a topic, the following four strategies are appropriate for helping students identify specific research questions: *WH* Questions, Poster Questions, What You Know and What You Don't Know, and Question Box.

WH *Questions*

Teachers should provide students with the *WH* Questions: who, what, when, where, why, and how. The teacher sets the unit to be studied—oceans, for example—and then helps students frame questions by attaching *wh* words to the subject of the unit. Thus, students ask questions such as, "Who were the first people to explore the Atlantic Ocean?" "What dangers do oceans present to people?" "When was the Pacific Ocean named?" "Where is the deepest part of an ocean?" "Why is the ocean salty?" and "How do oil companies drill in the ocean floor?"

Poster *Questions*

For Poster Questions, a topic is listed on a sheet of chart paper, an overhead transparency, or the chalkboard, so that students can brainstorm questions with the teacher. The questions are posted and inspected by the students,

Children discuss Poster Questions in order to evaluate what has been learned and generate additional areas of investigation.

who then go off to do their reading on the topic. The reading need not consist only of trying to find answers to the posted questions. Indeed, the purpose for reading may be to try to generate additional questions or areas of research. After about a week of independent reading, students look again at the posted questions and compare the answers they have gathered. They then inspect the original questions, modify them, and go off again to find additional resources.

What You Know and What You Don't Know

What You Know and What You Don't Know is another good strategy to build motivation, with the added advantage of helping students call up what they already know. As with poster questions, a topic is given. Students are asked what they think they know about the topic. All information is put down, whether accurate or not. Students then sort the bits of related information into groups and display the data in a web.

Once the known information is displayed, unknown information becomes much more readily apparent. For each area of information, students then list What We Know and What We Don't Know. For instance, if the topic is the human circulatory system, students might develop a category for diseases. Anemia, leukemia, and hemophelia might be listed. Questions then can be generated about other blood- and heart-related diseases, as well as on the nature and treatment of each disease. Under What We Don't Know students might list "What other circulatory diseases are there?" "What causes each circulatory system disease?" and "What cures each circulatory system disease?" Groups of students then take questions, searching for information that validates what is already listed and adding new information.

Question Box

Question Box involves placing a box for questions where it is readily available to students at all times. The teacher encourages students to write down questions that occur to them. Students might ask questions such as, "Why is the sky blue?" "What is France like?" "Why do the number of degrees in the angles of a triangle always equal 180?" or "Why is oxygen necessary for combustion?" Once or twice a week some questions are taken out of the box, and the teacher models putting the question into a form that can be answered. For example, "What is France like?" could be recast as "How is the geography of France different from that of the United States?" or "What do U.S. tourists notice most frequently when they visit France?" As can be seen with this example, the teacher rewrites the pupil's personalized query into a number of focused questions that can be answered through research. When teachers demonstrate how to limit broad, unfocused questions, students become better able to formulate good questions themselves. As with the other strategies presented in this book, fading from teacher modeling to student independence is the goal of this technique.

Modeling researchable question asking is only a part of the Question Box teaching strategy. Once questions have been focused, the teacher and students brainstorm places where students might find the needed information. Students are encouraged to list specific types of books and magazines as well as to mention resource people whom they might contact. For the question, "Why is the sky blue?" students might list the titles of science magazines, their science book, the school principal, the encyclopedia, the almanac, and TV weather forecasters. After a list is compiled, pupils are encouraged to search the library to find more science books to add to the list. Once this large list has been compiled, students are ready to set out to find the answer. Meanwhile, a classroom chart with the question at the top can list the answers that students predicted before beginning the search, as well as what was found during and after the search.

TRY IT OUT

This chapter has described four teaching strategies to help students identify researchable questions. Select one of those strategies to try out with students in a content area that you are interested in teaching. Find out from the teacher what strategies they may already have been taught and which one the teacher suggests teaching. Reflect later on how well the students learned and what you would need to do next. How would you modify your lesson if you taught it again? Remember that students rarely master a skill with only one introduction.

Maintaining the Focus of Research

A word of caution: Students who are seeking information frequently lose their focus. They can become so involved with the tangential information that they are led far astray of their original question. One way to help students remain focused is to have them carry a folder with the question written on the front so that they can frequently refer to it. Students should be told that the only information to be put into that folder is information related to the particular question. It is a good idea, however, to give students another folder labeled Miscellaneous or Other into which they can put all of the other bits of interesting information that they accumulate. The second folder may become the basis for another piece of research.

STUDENTS NEED TO KNOW HOW TO LOCATE SOURCES AND INFORMATION WITHIN SOURCES

Once students have identified a specific question, they need to locate information to answer it. They must learn to efficiently locate appropriate sources and the necessary information therein. One way that teachers can help students in this task is to have students use *key words*.

First, tell students that key words are the keys that open the storehouses of information: textbooks, encyclopedias, library references, and people. Second, tell students that key words help to organize ideas. "If you are going to the store for milk, Kool-Aid, orange juice, root beer, and diet cola," you might say, "What word could you use to describe all those items?" Discuss students' responses, such as *beverages* and *drinks,* in order to demonstrate how different words can be used to organize the five items. Point out that a few key words lead to many specifics. Finally, once students grasp the concept of key words, teach them how to use key words when researching single texts, multiple written sources, and oral interviews.

Single Texts

Three key word teaching strategies appropriate for single textbooks are presented here: Key Word Guess, Key Word Questions, and Key Word Scavenger Hunt. These lessons can be taught using content area textbooks.

KEY WORD GUESS   Key Word Guess is begun by writing questions about the unit. Possible key words that might lead to the desired answer then are written underneath the question. The following is a Key Word Guess that fourth-graders created:

Where did Native Americans live?

| Indians | homes | states |
| teepees | countries | climate |

Who were Native American leaders?

chiefs	Sitting Bull	Chief Joseph
Crazy Horse	medicine men	shaman
Indians	leaders	

What did Native Americans eat?

cooking	hunting	farming
gatherers	food	survival
Indians	basic needs	

It is clear that not all of the above key words would easily lead to the information being sought; however, that is also true of the key word lists that adult researchers generate. Adults list the most likely candidates for key words and check them out. While checking, they alter the list of key words to make it better focused for the question. Recently, in trying to locate articles about oral language use, we came up with the following list of key words to check in the *Education Index: oral language, oral communication,* and *talking.* While searching for articles under these phrases, the index directed us to yet another term, *conversation.* The altered list, with *talking* dropped and *conversation* added, yielded several appropriate articles. Student researchers can likewise alter their key word lists.

After students list their key word guesses, they go to the index in their textbooks to see what can be found. In the example above, the class decided that *Indians* would be a good key word for all of the questions.

After a few sessions with Key Word Guess, it is useful to change the strategy a bit in order to help the students apply what they are learning and gain independence. In the variation, students turn to major headings in their text's table of contents and make up a question for one of them. These questions are given to their classmates, who then guess at key words that might help locate the needed information.

KEY WORD QUESTIONS   With Key Word Questions, the teacher groups related words, lists them on a transparency or the board, and asks students to come up with appropriate questions. As you can tell, Key Word Questions is the obverse of Key Word Guess. An example of grouped key words and students' guesses for appropriate questions is as follows:

Indians   pots   open fire
seeds   meat   woven baskets
  How did Native Americans cook their food?
  What kinds of foods did Native Americans eat?

Indian leaders   Chief Joseph   Squanto
Sequoyah   chief   ruler
  Who were some Native American leaders?
  Who were some peaceful Native American leaders?

It is clear that the grouped key words lead into a wide range of possible questions. In order to promote independence, have students look at the table of contents and the index in their textbooks to find a heading with related words and phrases. The students then list the words and have other students generate key word questions from their list.

KEY WORD SCAVENGER HUNT   Key Word Scavenger Hunt is a third strategy. This strategy emphasizes actual searches through materials using key words. Students are first led through a practice exercise as a whole class to learn through modeling how to find answers to various questions. They then work in small groups to answer questions from a Key Word Scavenger Hunt list. Following are some practice items we have used:

1. A word used in New England for *factory* is *mill*. How many kinds of mills does your textbook tell about?

2. What does *adobe* mean?

3. What is a nuclear reactor? What key words could you use to find information?

4. Look at the key word *Dallas* in your text's index. Then find the listing "Dallas, early history of, 263–264." Write a question whose answer you think you might find in those pages. Do not try to answer the question.

As you can see, some of the questions can be answered by turning to the index only, whereas others require the student to look in the textbook. After practice answering the questions above, students generally are ready to find the answers to some real questions generated within their small groups.

Multiple Written Sources

Locating information in textbooks is only part of being a researcher. Library books and magazines also provide enormous amounts of information. Indeed, a library card catalog can yield a surprising number of references, as can an index such as the *Readers' Guide to Periodical Literature*. If students turn to the heading "Indians" in the *Readers' Guide*, they will discover an enormous number of articles on the topic. To help students gain access to the information contained in these references, teachers must help students apply their understanding of key words to the specific format of each reference work. Teachers can easily connect the process of looking for key words in a textbook index to that of using key words when searching an encyclopedia or a computerized data base.

As for the other strategies we have described, we recommend that you fade your instruction. Demonstrate what students need to do, give them some practice exercises, then launch them into real inquiries. Most teachers find their school librarians extremely helpful in introducing students to specific sources; the teacher needs to provide the guided practice and independent application to follow up the initial demonstration.

Interviews

So far, we have emphasized locating information in written sources. Conducting oral interviews also is a worthwhile way for student researchers to gain access to information.

Young students should begin interviews with familiar, friendly sources. Family members, school personnel, and peers are appropriate candidates for interviews at the early grades. Secondary students can begin interviewing unfamiliar people who are expert in students' research topics. Once a person has agreed to be interviewed, many teachers send the person a brief letter outlining the nature of the students' projects and a description of how the information will be used. Such a letter is especially helpful if the interview is to be tape-recorded.

Interviews work most efficiently when the researcher has specific questions written in a set order. If students are investigating schools of the past, asking the interviewee to "Tell me about your school days" may not be very productive. Instead, the students should be prepared to ask questions about teachers, fellow students, lessons, tests, discipline, and so on. These words might be jotted down at first and then developed into complete questions before interviewing a subject. Questions should be specific, but not so narrow that they can be answered with a "yes" or "no." Asking source people follow-up questions such as, "Can you tell me more about that?" or "What else do you remember?" is a useful way of getting more complete information.

Tape-recording the interview is a good way to maintain a record of what was said, with taking notes during the interview also recommended. After leaving the interviewee, students should write down what they learned. This summary might be shared with the interviewee in order to check for accuracy and elicit additional pertinent information.

Interviewing is an important component of research.

Before sending students out to conduct interviews, teachers frequently demonstrate the procedure by interviewing a guest in the classroom. Students also may want to practice interviewing one another before going outside the classroom.

TRY IT OUT

This chapter has described three teaching strategies to help students locate pertinent information. Select one of those strategies to try out with students in a content area you are interested in teaching. Find out from the teacher what strategies they may already have been taught and which one the teacher suggests teaching. Reflect later on how well the students learned and what you would need to do next. How would you modify your lesson if you taught it again?

THERE ARE A NUMBER OF WAYS TO ORGANIZE INFORMATION

Organizing information is perhaps the most difficult task facing student researchers. They must learn to record only the information that answers their specific question. Students frequently pull out all the information they find because they consider everything to be of equal importance ("If it's not important, then why was it written there?"). Teachers must show students how to be selective.

Students must also be taught how to categorize information according to various aspects of their question. Young students who are seeking answers to "What do bears eat?" soon discover that information is available about the eating habits of different types of bears, at different times of the year, and at different ages and locations. Older students looking at how people measure time soon discover the great complexity with which scientists have addressed this issue. Organizing information is a complex skill. Producing notes, categorizing information, and citing information are three aspects of this phase of the research process, all three of which teachers must demonstrate and explain.

Producing Notes

In order to help students attend selectively to the information that answers their questions, we recommend regular comprehension lessons as described in Chapter 4. Reading for specific purposes is a dominant feature of those lessons, as well as a central feature of research. Producing notes about what one reads is a logical extension of reading for specific purposes; students producing notes record both the targeted information and their initial reactions to it.

We like to distinguish note taking from note making because we see different skills being used in the two. Note taking implies that the reader mainly lifts information from a source, using phrases from the passage itself. Making notes may also involve jotting down exact wordings, but it should also include personal examples, questions, and related information from other sources. The notemaker is not only taking from the source but also evaluating the information. When you make notes you are far more likely to learn the material than when you merely take notes, because in making notes you are consciously connecting the new to the known. You are also monitoring more information when you make notes because you need to be aware of how much you know in order to add personal examples or raise questions about the material.

A partial outline is a good tool for introducing students to notes. Teachers give students a partially completed outline or diagram of the content of a reading selection and demonstrate how to complete it. After a few such lessons, teachers provide students guided practice for completing a partial outline on their own. Figure 6.1 shows a partial outline of this chapter.

By filling out this outline as you read, your attention is drawn to the chapter's major ideas, to the relationships among the major ideas, and to the relationships among major and minor ideas. Notice that because you are provided with the outline skeleton, your attention does not have to focus on the trivia of making an outline ("Do I need an uppercase or lowercase *a*?"). Because you are given a fixed number of slots to be filled in, you can easily

Chapter 6: Student Research

I. Students can learn to ask researchable questions.
A. *WH* Questions
B.
C.
D.
E. Maintaining the focus of research

II. Students need to know how to locate sources and information within sources.
A.
  1. Key Word Guess
  2. Key Word Questions
  3. Key Word Scavenger Hunt
B. Multiple written sources
C. Interviews

III.
A.
B.
C. Data charts
D. Webs
E. Citing information
F. Another look at planning

IV. Students can share information learned through research in a variety of ways.
A. Written sharing
B.
C.

V.

FIGURE 6.1   Partial Outline

determine how many ideas to list and what the relationship among them should be. A partial outline helps you to focus on selecting the important information from a text. The amount of information provided in the outline and the amount of instruction you need to provide will vary with the sophistication of the students and with time as you fade yourself out of the picture.

Categorizing Information

As the notes accumulate in a research project, students need to categorize what they find. It is not efficient to write bits of information on separate file cards or sheets of paper and organize them later. It is far better to establish the categories of facts and to group facts into the categories as the research progresses. In that way, students can see which categories are lacking information, and whether new information corroborates or contradicts earlier findings. Students using this method may also see the need for establishing new categories or revising old ones. Three ways to establish research categories are using question cards, data charts, and webs.

QUESTION CARDS   A simple technique for maintaining category identities is to use question cards. Students list questions to be answered on note cards or on paper, one question per card or sheet. Whenever pertinent information is located, students write notes underneath the question. Later on, students group the information on each card or sheet according to its various aspects. This grouping becomes the outline to answer that particular question. Figure

What is the economy in Connecticut based on?
- wealthy state (1, P.2)
- "The Gold Coast" near New York City (1, P.2)
- 1st industries began because of embargo in time of Napoleon (1, P.16)
- Agriculture: tobacco wrappers and binders for cigars, poultry big (1, p.28)
- Industrialization began during the early 19TH century (3, P.84)
- The Insurance State (4, P.69)
- home office to many major insurance companies (4, P.70)
- State economy: manufacturing, commerce, agriculture, minerals, tourism (5, P.111)
- almost no mining, timber, or commercial fishing (5, P.116)
- most people get income from manufacturing & commerce (5, P.120)
- many historical sites to visit (1, P.2,4, P.73-75 5, P.139)

FIGURE 6.2   Unorganized Question Card

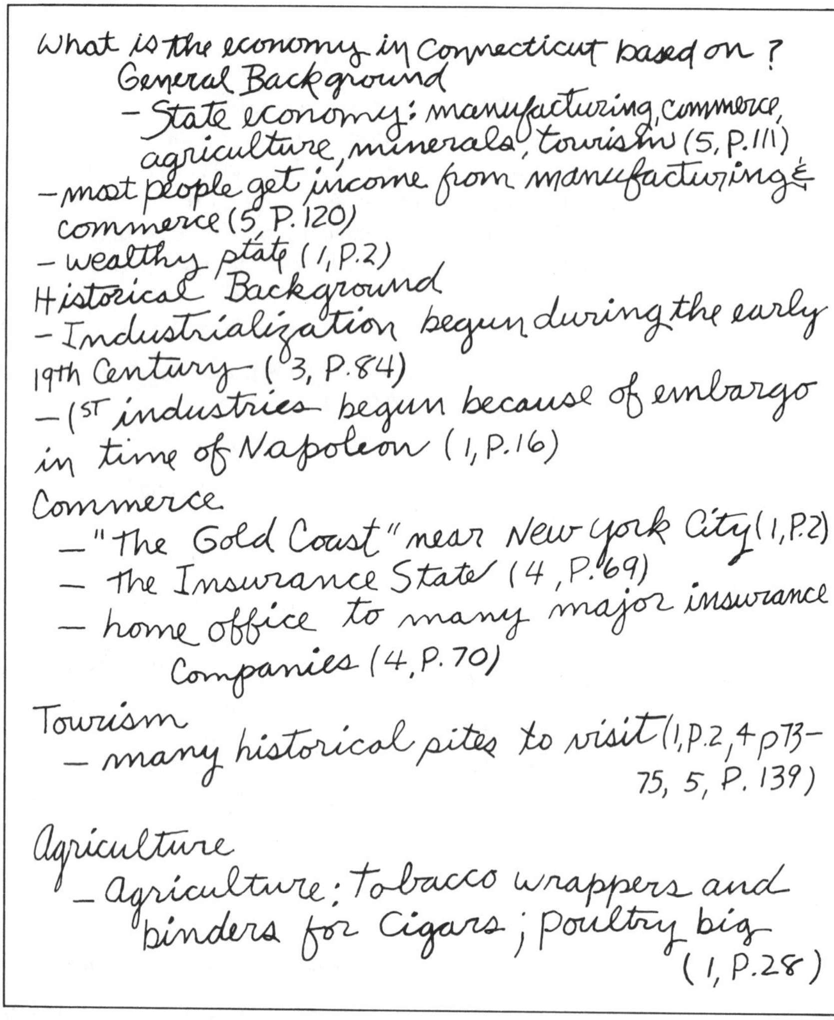

What is the economy in Connecticut based on?
General Background
  - State economy: manufacturing, commerce, agriculture, minerals, tourism (5, P.111)
- most people get income from manufacturing & commerce (5, P. 120)
- wealthy state (1, P.2)
Historical Background
- Industrialization begun during the early 19th Century (3, P.84)
- 1st industries begun because of embargo in time of Napoleon (1, P.16)

Commerce
  - "The Gold Coast" near New York City (1, P.2)
  - The Insurance State (4, P.69)
  - home office to many major insurance companies (4, P. 70)

Tourism
  - many historical sites to visit (1, P.2, 4 p 73-75, 5, P. 139)

Agriculture
  - Agriculture: tobacco wrappers and binders for cigars; poultry big (1, P.28)

FIGURE 6.3 Organized Question Card

6.2 is an example of a student's question card for a study of Connecticut, and Figure 6.3 shows how the information about that state was organized into categories.

DATA CHARTS G. McKenzie (1979) describes data charts as a tool to help students organize content information. He suggests making a grid on paper, with the research questions listed across the top and the resources to be used listed along the side. Each box of the grid then contains the source's information related to the question. Sparsely worded notes are used in order to conserve space and encourage students to use their own words when writing the report. If a particular source provides no information about one of the

Sources	What was his life like?	What themes did he pursue?	What was his influence?
Smith & Jones			
Brown			
Linn			

FIGURE 6.4   Data Chart for Ernest Hemingway Report

questions, an *X* is placed in that square. Figure 6.4 shows a data chart for investigating the career of Ernest Hemingway.

When introducing data charts, we have found that it is helpful to have a large sheet of paper posted in the room or to use a transparency on an overhead projector. Students must be shown how to record information in the proper location of the chart. Students should also be sent out to locate other sources to add to the left column.

Another type of data chart lists questions across the top of a chart and aspects of the questions down the side. For example, if the topic is Wild Animals, the questions across the top might be "What does the animal eat," "Where does the animal live," and "What dangers does the animal face?" Down the side, rather than listing sources, several different wild animals such as tiger, leopard, and lion are listed. Figure 6.5 is an example of this type of data chart.

Data charts are useful for ordering information, and they also help students evaluate what they have gathered. For example, students might be directed to the Wild Animals chart and asked to decide which animal ate the widest variety of food, lived in the most unusual habitat, or faced the greatest dangers.

WEBS   A web is a very flexible outline that graphically depicts the relationships of the parts to the whole and to one another. Teaching students how to use a traditional outline is much easier if they have already been organizing information through webbing. Figure 6.6 is a web of the history of Connecticut produced by a middle-school student. In the middle of a web is the topic

Animals	What does the animal eat?	Where does the animal live?	What dangers does the animal face?
Tiger			
Leopard			
Lion			

FIGURE 6.5 Data Chart for Wild Animals Report

being researched, and radiating out from the center are the subtopics stated either as questions or as words and phrases. Pieces of information about the subtopics are listed around the subtopics, though not necessarily in any specific order.

A web is a good way to depict information that students produce during sessions of What You Know and What You Don't Know, and that students eventually gather. When you introduce webs to students, you might begin by using a topic that they are about to begin in a unit of study. Put that topic in the middle and list questions around it. Next, have students tell what they know or think they know about the topic and you list that information next to the questions. Students then find more information from their sources, return to the web, and revise it in light of the new information. The initial web gives you a good idea of what your students already knew about the topic, with the final web a good basis for a unit review.

Citing Information

An important point to convey to students is the need to record their sources accurately. Accurate records are necessary both for others to check the information and for the students themselves to return to, if necessary. The simplest way to record sources is to make a numbered list of all sources by title and date, including all visual, oral, and written sources. As shown in Figure 6.6, when students find something they want to use they can jot down the information, placing the appropriate identification number after the information, and including a page number if using a written source.

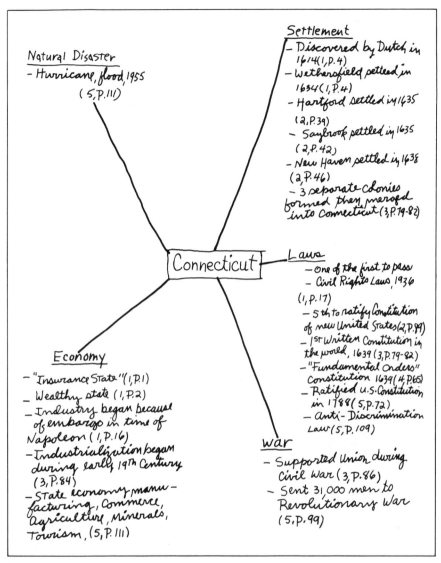

Natural Disaster
- Hurricane, flood, 1955
  (5, P. 111)

Settlement
- Discovered by Dutch in 1614 (1, P.4)
- Wethersfield settled in 1634 (1, P.4)
- Hartford settled in 1635 (2, P.39)
- Saybrook settled in 1635 (2, P.42)
- New Haven settled in 1638 (2, P.46)
- 3 separate colonies formed they merged into Connecticut (3, P.79-82)

Connecticut

Laws
- One of the first to pass
- Civil Rights Laws, 1936 (1, P.17)
- 5th to ratify Constitution of new United States (2, P.99)
- 1st Written Constitution in the world, 1639 (3, P.79-82)
- "Fundamental Orders" Constitution 1639 (4, P.65)
- Ratified U.S. Constitution in 1788 (5, P.72)
- Anti-Discrimination Law (5, P.109)

Economy
- "Insurance State" (1, P.1)
- Wealthy state (1, P.2)
- Industry began because of embargo in time of Napoleon (1, P.16)
- Industrialization began during early 19th Century (3, P.84)
- State economy manufacturing, Commerce, Agriculture, Minerals, Tourism, (5, P.111)

War
- Supported Union during Civil War (3, P.86)
- Sent 31,000 men to Revolutionary War (5, P.99)

FIGURE 6.6   Web for Connecticut Report

Another Look at Planning

The initial steps in teaching research (identifying researchable questions, locating information, and organizing the information) differ only slightly from the planning steps for writing minilessons presented in Chapter 5. The main difference is that planning a research report places great emphasis on locating and organizing new information. The final step of the research process—reporting information—encompasses the drafting and revising stages of the writing process that were detailed in Chapter 5.

TRY IT OUT

This chapter has described a number of ways to help students organize information. Select one of those strategies you have never tried and use it throughout one of your own research ventures. Think about any problems you had applying the strategy and what you might have to do to make it easier for students to learn.

STUDENTS CAN SHARE INFORMATION LEARNED THROUGH RESEARCH IN A VARIETY OF WAYS

Student researchers at all levels benefit from sharing with others what has been learned. Such sharing deepens the understanding both of those who did not conduct the research and of those who did.

Student researchers generally feel compelled to share all the material that they garnered during their searches. They want credit for all the information that they worked so hard to obtain and frequently have difficulty paring down the information to that which directly answers their questions. Such reporting results in undesirably long pieces. Inform your students that expert researchers generally know more than they include in their reports and that students should likewise not try to include every bit of information they gather.

Reporting sometimes is done in an informal, casual manner. Students are assembled after spending time conducting their research in order to share what they have learned in impromptu fashion. If the class spent time in the library investigating customs of dress, then a discussion about those customs might ensue; if students were sent home with the task of asking available adults how they came to their current occupation, then the findings can be informally shared the next day.

As we discussed in Chapter 2, students should have several options for how to respond to what they read. They might produce visuals, such as maps or homemade transparencies; they might produce or collect realia, as is done in most science fair projects; or they might dramatize scenes. However, if research findings are to be reported in a more formal manner, then teachers and students should decide on a set of specifications (e.g., how long the report is to be; who the audience is; how many visuals, if any, are to be included; how citations are to be listed), and students frame the sharing of their information accordingly.

Transferring information and sharing information are two important techniques for students to learn. Transferring information involves moving what has been gathered from sources into a final written, oral, or visual product. Sharing information involves preparing a clear, organized method from which others can learn, a method that is appropriate to the information and audience. Following is a discussion of the three ways (written, oral, and visual) to transfer and share information according to a somewhat formal set of specifications.

Written Sharing

Students must be taught how to transfer information from their question cards, data charts, or webs into written report form. Question cards lend themselves most easily to long reports, as students group all the pieces of information listed under each question into even smaller categories. Show students how to transfer each piece of information under one question onto a small strip of paper and then to arrange those strips physically into categories. Each question might include two, three, or more categories. Students might glue or tape the strips of information onto another sheet of paper with the question at the top to create a reorganized version of the original question sheet.

After this reorganization, show students how to turn each question into a topic sentence for a paragraph or section in a manner similar to that used with one-paragraph essays. For example, the question "What are the main industries in Connecticut?" might be recast into the topic sentence "Connecticut has five main industries." The bits of information beneath the question on the question card then become the supporting details for the topic sentence.

Reporting the information gathered onto a data chart is even more straightforward. For example, the data chart in Figure 6.4 can be the basis for a five-paragraph essay. The first paragraph is the introduction, which prepares people for the upcoming questions (e.g.,"Three aspects of Hemingway's life seem to have been very important"). It may also tell why the topic is important (e.g., "Ernest Hemingway was one of the most influential and well known American authors of the twentieth century"). The second through fourth paragraphs address the three questions, turned into topic sentences, along the top of the data chart (e.g., "Hemingway had a vigorous life style," "Hemingway focused on five primary themes in his writing," and "Hemingway influenced a generation of writers"). The fifth paragraph is a summary of important findings. A data chart works especially well for short reports.

Turning a web into a written report follows a similar pattern. Show students how to arrange the details for each subtopic according to the desired order of presentation. Subtopic headings become topic sentences, and the bits of information become the supporting details. Be prepared to demonstrate this method of organization more than once, providing sufficient guidance when students practice it.

Once information has been organized, students draft and revise their written reports following the guidelines presented in Chapter 5. Reports can be improved by having students go through the revising step of the writing process. Peer response groups work especially well; since each student has been trying to write a similar type of paper, he or she brings to the group the same knowledge of the paper's form.

At the beginning of the year in elementary school, where teachers have inexperienced students, a structured approach to sharing reports is frequently useful. For a unit on domestic animals, for example, the class would generate a series of basic questions. Questions might include these: "How does this animal help us?" "Where does it live?" "What does it eat?" and "What does it look like?" Each child selects a different domestic animal from a group students have previously called up and writes a web about the animal. When it is time to produce the written report, the children decide how many paragraphs each report should have, as well as the order of each paragraph. They might also talk about what the introductory and concluding paragraphs should include. Each student then goes off to write a short report on his or her domestic animal, using illustrations if possible. These individual reports are revised through writing conferences with the teacher and peer editing groups, and the revised reports are bound into a classroom book on domestic animals.

Students frequently prepare constructions or artistic presentations for a report, such as scale models of the Parthenon, the Globe Theater, or the solar system. Consider leaving the objects on display around the room for a few weeks, letting written explanations serve as the means of sharing.

In secondary school, be sure to balance the reports that are due in each class. If you teach two class sections of the same course, require a batch of reports to be done at staggered times during the semester, rather than assigning everything for the final week of the term. Maintaining such a balance

Webs provide a basis for writing well-organized reports.

allows you to spend more time helping students prepare their reports and gives you more time to react thoughtfully to the final products.

Oral Sharing

Transferring information for oral reports is slightly different from the procedures for written reports. Students giving oral reports must rely on note cards or some other type of reminder to help keep the order of presentation straight. Key words and apt phrases should be recorded so that students can glance at them to maintain their flow of speech. For instance, a student reporting on Connecticut might have made the following list: "Industries . . . manufacturing . . . defense products . . . ship building at Groton . . . transportation equipment . . . electrical machinery." Such telegraphic writing clearly differs from the form of a written report.

A good aid for students giving oral reports is to support their talks with visuals and realia. Props allow speakers to maintain focus by discussing the aspects illustrated by each prop.

Oral reports allow immediate questioning, prompting researchers to give additional information about what they have learned. Thus, teachers should allow time for questions after an oral report.

One possibility to save class time during oral reports is for only some students actually to report to the whole class. The others can tape-record their presentations and place them with explanatory material in the classroom or school library for others to hear on their own time. One advantage of this technique is that no matter how well done the reports are, listening to thirty oral reports in a few days is bound to be boring, whereas listening to ten over several days can still be interesting.

Another time-saving device is putting students into teams to prepare a panel presentation. Each panel member could be responsible for researching an aspect of the topic. Some teachers station students with reports to give at separate locations throughout the classroom, and then have various groups of listeners rotate among the presenters. This strategy forces the presenters to repeat themselves, but repetition can be beneficial and the class routine has been varied a bit.

Visual Displays

Chapter 2 enumerates a wide range of book projects: visuals, concrete objects, models, and dramatizations. Students enjoy creating illustrations, time lines, murals, maps, collages, homemade transparencies, and models. They enjoy, too, being able to collect objects and arrange them for others. These can all be used as the basis for visual displays to share information learned. To help these projects meet the communication expectations teachers have for research reports, you could follow some of the guidelines given for science fair projects.

Projects need to be highly visual, self-descriptive, focused, and succinct.

Communicating this to students means explaining that the display ought to be appealing, eye-catching, neat, and interesting. The question being investigated and shared ought to be clear to anyone looking at the display. The entire project ought to be contained within a relatively small space (since no classroom is ever large enough). The research topic being shared should be an interesting one to investigate and of a scope that is neither too large nor too picayune for the students' research capabilities.

Visual displays could be incorporated as part of an oral or a written sharing, too. For evaluation purposes, students should decide, however, which of the three types of sharing is carrying the bulk of the information. Visual displays should have a minimum of oral or written information.

LISTEN/LOOK AND LEARN
Briefly describe to a teacher each of the three ways to share information: written reports, oral reports, and visual displays. Ask the teacher which ones he or she has used and why. Ask the teacher to describe strengths and limitations of each of the sharing formats used. Would the teacher try any of the others you have described? Which one(s) and why?

STUDENTS BECOME INDEPENDENT RESEARCHERS WHEN TEACHERS GRADUALLY FADE THEIR GUIDANCE AND TURN OVER RESPONSIBILITY TO STUDENTS

As we suggested in Chapter 1, you develop student independence as you first demonstrate what you expect students to do, fade out your assistance as your students practice the task with your help, and finally provide opportunities for independent application. Such fading applies to developing student researchers, also. You should model how to identify questions, locate information, organize information, and report information. Students as a whole class can observe the demonstrations, then perform the tasks in small groups with continued teacher guidance; finally, students should embark on their own investigations with minimal teacher intervention. Such fading should occur throughout the school year.

In the elementary grades, teachers might walk the whole class through the entire research process. Teachers should show students how to investigate and report a subject, with teacher and students jointly producing a finished product. Later in the year, when a different unit is being studied, teachers can remind students of the processes they used before. For the second unit to be researched. students might work in small groups rather than with the whole class. As students develop research skills, they are able to carry out the research task more and more independently.

E. T. Cudd and L. Roberts (1989) describe a helpful strategy for beginning researchers, paragraph frames, which are created for students to complete with expository information. Paragraph frames are a variation of the cloze procedure, allowing students to create an organized piece of written text while learning how paragraphs are structured. Students are faded from being given a topic sentence and concluding sentence, with transition words and phrases to fill in the details, to having to complete a written paragraph without teacher-imposed structure. Figures 6.7, 6.8, and 6.9 show examples of various paragraph frames.

At the secondary level, teachers should refine students' research skills. If students are already adept at locating information through an index, teachers might teach them to use a card catalog or computerized data base. Practically all students at the upper grade levels benefit from attention to their notemaking skills. Secondary teachers also must remind students of the skills they learned in earlier grades.

In our experience, most students who copy their reports from another source do so out of ignorance and desperation. They are unaware of any other system for generating a written report. Several techniques can help prevent copying in your classroom. Taking students through the steps described in this chapter will model the research process for them. You might further want to require checkpoints to see what progress is being made. These checks should not be presented as punitive; rather, make it clear that all students need your feedback about how successfully they are dealing with

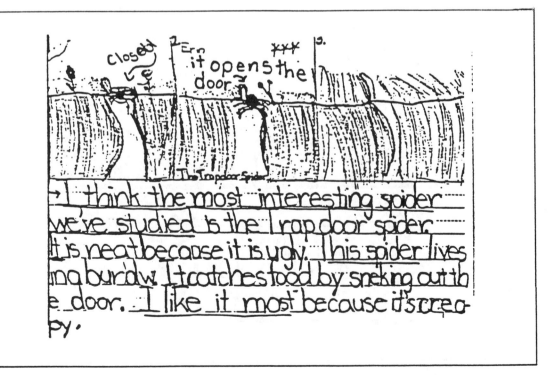

FIGURE 6.7 Paragraph Frame (Erik, Grade 1). SOURCE: Cudd & Roberts (1989). Reprinted with permission of Evelyn T. Cudd and the International Reading Association.

Before a frog is grown, it goes through many changes. First, the mother frog _____
_____.

Next, _____.

Then, _____.

Finally, _____.

Now they _____
_____.

Before a frog is grown, it goes through many stages. First, the mother frog lays the eggs. Next, the eggs hatch and turn into tadpoles. Then slowly the tadpoles legs begin to grow. Finally, the tadpole turns into a frog. Now and then they have to go into the water to keep their skin moist.

Stage No. 1.   Stage No. 2.

Stage No. 3.   Stage No. 4.   Extraordinary!

FIGURE 6.8 Paragraph Frame (Elena, Grade 2). SOURCE: Cudd & Roberts (1989). Reprinted with permission of Evelyn T. Cudd and the International Reading Association.

FIGURE 6.9 Paragraph Frame (Chris, Grade 1). SOURCE: Cudd & Roberts (1989). Reprinted with permission of Evelyn T. Cudd and the International Reading Association.

the various stages of a report. Thus if a student is organizing information on a data chart, you need to check whether key words are being used, whether a variety of sources has been located, and whether sources are being identified with page numbers. Such checking, by the way, also helps teachers prevent student procrastination.

You might also make all initial reports oral or visual to prevent copying, with students not permitted to read reports but only to use notes. Most students are unable to memorize a long selection from the encyclopedia, so they must use their own words. When you praise their ability to speak from notes, you raise their confidence in their ability to write their own reports.

Some students who are well aware that copying is wrong and know of alternative ways to prepare reports still persist in plagiarizing information. Unfortunately, many of them are capable students who have been rewarded through the years for their plagiarism by receiving good grades from teachers. How many students have the ability to write as well as the author of a science trade book? As long as more emphasis is placed on the product of the research, rather than on learning the process well, such copying will continue to be a problem. Typically, we can assume that a good grasp of the process will result in a good product. However, we have all known students who were very good at finding information, but whose verbal skills prevented them from sharing it in a clear manner. By the same token, many good students admit to moving effortlessly through school, doing little work, but presenting their material so well that they get good grades.

In your classroom, you might grade students at each step of the research process. Thus, students need to produce good questions, locate valuable sources, and produce and organize effective notes before they get to exercise their drafting and revising skills. Remember that your main concern is teaching the process of finding and sharing information on a topic; the final product, the report, only reflects students' proficiencies with that process.

Evaluating student reports is never easy. You may want to begin thinking now about how you will explain your criteria to students. Figure 6.10 contains a scoring criteria for middle-school written reports on Traditions, a social studies unit on long-standing customs and practices related to events such as holidays, eating, and courtship. The checklist contains three

REPORT ON TRADITIONS
SCORING CRITERIA

Student:

Content

At least three traditions are described fully.	10	8	6	4	2
Unfamiliar traditions are compared with familiar ones.	10	8	6	4	2
Contexts of the traditions are complete.	10	8	6	4	2
Values of the traditions are complete.	10	8	6	4	2

Mechanics

Organization There are a clear beginning, middle, and end. Major and minor points are distinguishable.	10	8	6	4	2
Creativity Vivid language is used in imaginative, effective ways. The paper grabs the reader's attention.	10	8	6	4	2
Sentence structure Sentences are consistently well formed. Run-on sentences and sentence fragments do not appear.	5	4	3	2	1
Punctuation, spelling, and capitalization All ending punctuation is correct. Internal punctuation (especially commas) is appropriate. All words are spelled correctly. Appropriate words are capitalized.	5	4	3	2	1
Neatness Writing is legible. Margins are appropriate. Paper is clean. Any illustrations are clear.	5	4	3	2	1

Location of Information

Sufficient number	10	8	6	4	2
Varied	5	4	3	2	1
Credible	5	4	3	2	1
Focus on the topic	5	4	3	2	1

FIGURE 6.10   Research Report Scoring Criteria

sections—content, mechanics, and location of information; some items are worth a maximum of ten points and some a maximum of five. We believe it is a good idea to give students a copy of the checklist you will be using to evaluate each of their efforts. This allows students to see how you weigh the different aspects of the assignment. Allow room on the list for your comments and for their comments back to you for each evaluation area. Be specific with your comments. If you write nothing or only innocuous comments, such as "good job," evaluations are largely ignored, whereas more specific comments receive attention.

Distribute checklists such as in Figure 6.10 when your students begin their reports. This practice helps them concentrate on desired outcomes, and the outcomes can be stated in general terms (e.g., "Describe the traditions fully"). Students typically appreciate knowing their teachers' expectations and also knowing that the expectations leave room for student decision making. Furthermore, producing such checklists beforehand takes time during the planning stage of instruction, but it saves time when you help students with their projects and when you evaluate their final products. The number and type of scoring criteria, their values, and the format of the list depends on your expectations and your students' sophistication.

LOOKING BACK

Learning the research process is more important than producing a polished report; otherwise, teachers could be satisfied with students who submitted reports purchased from commercial services. Therefore, help your students develop the excitement and eagerness to answer questions that will carry them through the more mundane aspects of this process; in this way research becomes something they look forward to rather than dread. We have described five key ideas in this chapter to help you better teach the research process: (1) Students can learn to ask researchable questions, (2) students need to know how to locate sources and information within sources, (3) there are a number of ways to organize information, (4) students can share information learned through research in a variety of ways, and (5) students become independent researchers when teachers gradually fade their guidance and turn over responsibility to students.

ADD TO YOUR JOURNAL

Have you ever been involved in any research procedures similar to the ones presented here? Compare the way you generated research questions in elementary and secondary school with the procedures described here. Do you consider yourself an independent researcher? Why? What can you apply from your own background to your future classroom? What kinds of research experiences will you give your students? Why? How often will your students be engaged in research activities? Why?

REFERENCES

Cudd, E. T., & Roberts, L. (1989). Using writing to enhance content area learning in the primary grades. *The Reading Teacher, 42,* 392–404.

McKenzie, G. (1979). Data charts: A crutch for helping students organize reports. *Language Arts, 56,* 784–788.

ADDITIONAL READINGS

The following sources provide especially useful information about helping students research topics and report what was learned; the first set addresses elementary students, but many of the techniques apply to secondary students as well:

Beach, J. D. (1983). Teaching students to write informational reports. *The Elementary School Journal, 84,* 213–220.

Cudd, E. T. (1989). Research and report writing in the elementary grades. *The Reading Teacher, 43,* 268–269.

Graves, D. (1989). *Investigate nonfiction.* Portsmouth, NH: Heinemann.

Hennings, D. G. (1982). A writing approach to reading comprehension: Schema theory in action. *Language Arts, 59,* 8–17.

Jacobs, S. E. (1984). Investigative writing: Practices and principles. *Language Arts, 61,* 356–363.

Tchudi, S. N. (1987). *The younger learner's handbook.* New York: Scribner's.

The information in the following sources focuses on secondary students, but many of the techniques also apply to elementary students:

Another look at the research paper. (1987). *English Journal, 76*(7), 49–60. [This citation is for three articles contained in the *English Journal* as part of a Focus section.]

Larson, R., Hecker, B., & Norem, J. (1985). Student experience with research projects: Pains, enjoyment and success. *High School Journal, 69,* 61–69.

Schumm, J. S., & Radenich, M. C. (1984). Readers'/writers' workshop: An antidote for term paper terror. *Journal of Reading, 28,* 13–19.

The role of collaborative learning in research projects is described in these two articles:

Davey, B. (1987). Team for success: Guided practice in study skills through cooperative research reports. *Journal of Reading, 30,* 701–705.

Wyatt, F. (1988). Rethinking the research project through cooperative learning. *Middle School Journal, 20*(1), 6–7.

Identifying researchable questions is a valuable skill that deserves considerable emphasis; helping students learn how to isolate a problem is an intricate process, as the following reference makes clear:

Getzels, J. W., & Csikszentmihalyi, M. (1975). From problem solving to problem finding. In I. A. Taylor & J. W. Getzels (Eds.), *Perspectives in creativity.* Chicago: Aldine.

C H A P T E R 7

Meaning Vocabulary

LOOKING AHEAD

Reading and writing are important tools for learning and thinking about content. To a great extent, the language one reads or writes depends on words to convey clear and precise messages. Knowing the appropriate meanings for the words used to communicate ideas in a content subject is essential for learning that subject. Even in classrooms in which little time is spent reading and writing, talking and listening are omnipresent. These modes, too, rely on a knowledge of word meanings. Much of what students learn in a content area is knowledge specific to that area. Unfortunately, many students have not encountered the critical vocabulary for each content area through their general world experience or acquired it through previous schooling. All content area teachers are responsibile for teaching the meaning vocabulary essential to communicating about their subject. Part of what it means to know biology, geometry, economics, and so forth is to be able to read, write, listen, and speak using the content area terminology.

Words are used to communicate ideas. You are able to follow an idea only when you can associate the meanings with the given words. When you read words for which you have meanings, comprehension seems natural and effortless. When you read words for which you lack meanings, your comprehension is impaired. Consider some examples:

The avuncular man scratched his philtrum.

She painted all but her lunules.

These are simple sentences. You have a general idea that a "certain" man scratched "something that belonged to him" and that the woman painted all but some specific "things." Because you probably lack meanings for some key words, however, your comprehension is impaired. If you looked for a dictionary definition of *avuncular*, you found that it meant "acting like an uncle." Depending on your experiences with uncles, you conjured up a meaning for the unfamiliar word *avuncular*. You also discovered that you have both a *philtrum* (groove in the middle of the upper lip, below the nose) and *lunules* (moon-shaped white areas at the base of the fingernails that at one time were fashionable to leave white while painting the rest of the nails).

Notice that you did not lack meanings for the three words in this example. But you were unable to connect the meanings with the words. For example, you are very familiar with the groove in the middle of your upper lip, but you may not have known that it was called a philtrum. You lacked not the meaning itself but a knowledge of the word to help you call up that meaning.

Consider another example:

The pharmacist needed lupulin and lupulone.

Again, you know that the pharmacist needed two "things." But which two things? When you look up *lupulin*, you discover that it is the glandular hairs of the hop. Lupulone is a white or yellow crystalline solid. These meanings are not very informative because you probably do not know what the meanings mean. In this example, you lack not only the word but also the meaning. Dictionaries are very helpful when we have a meaning but not the word for it, but dictionaries have limited usefulness when we lack both the meaning and the word.

As you consider how to teach word meanings, you constantly must keep in mind the distinction between words and meanings. If the word to be taught is one for which students already have the meaning and lack only the word, the teaching task is relatively simple. If, as is more common, students lack both the meaning and the word, the task is more difficult. Before considering how to teach students to develop meanings for words and words for meanings, it is important to understand what it means to know a word and how words are learned.

These are the key ideas in this chapter:

1. Words are learned through direct and visual experience and by making connections.

2. Content teachers must decide which words to teach.

3. There is great variety in the strategies content teachers use to teach vocabulary.

4. Once new words are taught, students need practice with these words.

5. Students can become independent learners of words.

WORDS ARE LEARNED THROUGH DIRECT AND VISUAL EXPERIENCE AND BY MAKING CONNECTIONS

What Do We Know When We Know a Word?

L. Burmeister (1978) suggests that knowing a word is like knowing a person. Asking "How many words do you know?" is like asking "How many people do you know?" If we ask the latter question, you will probably look askance at us and not respond, thinking that we could not be serious. If we persist, however, you might answer with a question of your own: "What do you mean by *know*?" "What do you mean by *know*?" is the dilemma that has confounded educators and researchers who have attempted to study the acquisition of vocabulary. The difficulty of defining *know* is one reason, after many decades of research, there is still no definitive answer to other questions, such as "How large is the vocabulary of the average high-school student?"

There are many people whom you know only by name. There are also many words for which you have the name but whose meaning remains vague. *Truffles* is a word known to many people, but perhaps the whole extent of your meaning for *truffles* consists of "I think you eat them." Our meanings for the word *potatoes*, on the other hand, could fill pages. Such meanings not only would include factual or literal meanings such as "the root of a plant" and "eaten in many forms—baked, mashed, french fried," but also would include some judgments. Some people's meanings for *potatoes* include such ideas as "fattening" and "greasy." Thus, we see that "knowing" a word is complicated by the fact that words have not only literal, factual meanings upon which almost everyone can agree, but also personal, evaluative meanings that vary from person to person. Literal meanings are generally found in the dictionary and are referred to as *denotations*. Evaluative meanings are referred to as *connotations*. Returning to our analogy between words and people, we see that the mention of a person's name also calls to mind both connotations and denotations. Richard Nixon, for example, was born in 1913, was a Republican, and was the thirty-seventh president of the United States. These are all denotations for *Nixon*. If you saw Nixon's name and thought "crook" or "beleaguered," then you produced connotative meanings for *Richard Nixon*.

Recognizing that words have connotations as well as denotations is an important part of vocabulary instruction. We want students not only to understand what they read but also to evaluate it. When we say that we want our students to develop their *evaluative* thinking process, we often mean that we want them to have a sense of the connotative meanings of words.

Just as most names stand for many different people, some of whom are related and some of whom are not, most words stand for many different meanings, some related, some not. Look up *root*, for example, and you will find many meanings. Plant roots, tooth roots, root words, and square roots all share a common concept, the idea of a basic part, often hidden, from which other parts, usually visible, emerge and grow. The related meanings of a word may be compared to related people who share the same name. Such people often share a family resemblance—physical (red hair, big bones) or behavioral (mannerisms, gestures, idiosyncrasies of speech). In some families, these resemblances are striking. In others, only the most astute observer would be able to detect family resemblances. So it is with words. The relationship among the many meanings for some words is apparent to everyone; other words reveal their kinship only to philologists. Thus most students need a teacher's help to perceive the family resemblances among words.

Now let us consider the meaning *root* has when we say, "She rooted for the Demon Deacons." This meaning may at one time have had some relationship to other meanings for *root*, but this relationship is no longer apparent. Thinking of these other meanings would hinder rather than help the reader trying to make sense of the sentence: "Does it mean she looked for the Demon Deacons under the ground?" Students must learn that while words may have related meanings, not all meanings of a word are related. The *bear* in the forest does not *bear* fruit. Coat *checkers* in restaurants might wear *checkered* jackets and play *checkers* during off-hours. Words with a large number of distinctive meanings are termed *multimeaning* words. The context in which we read a word allows us to determine its appropriate meaning.

Finally, in considering how many words students know and how well they know the words' meanings, we must broaden our understanding of what words are. When we are teaching students to understand what they read in content area subjects and to write clearly in those subjects, we must be concerned with some terms not usually considered words. A few examples should illustrate this point:

In an ANOVA design, the df is the number of items free to vary until the last item is set.

$AB = CD$.

N.Z. is ESE of Australia.

The president of ASCAP is a member of CORE.

Phrases, symbols, abbreviations, initials, and acronyms all occur in the material students read in content areas. While these terms are not technically "words," they are entities for which meaning must be built, and teachers should remember to teach meanings for any symbols that students will need to understand in order to read and write effectively.

A content teacher who is concerned about student vocabulary should keep in mind that meanings for words are not an either/or situation. Depth of word meaning and flexibility in choosing appropriate meanings for multi-meaning words are important considerations. Furthermore, meaning must be developed not only for words but also for those symbols and abbreviations that stand for words.

How We Learn Words

Learning a word is like learning a person's name. Learning the word's meaning is like learning about the person's interests, personality, and background. Keeping the person's name attached to your image of that person ("I'll never forget old 'what's-her-name' ") is like keeping a word attached to a meaning ("Hand me that whatchamacallit"). You get to know meanings and their words in much the same way that you get to know people and their names.

Think of a person whom you know very well. Try to recall how you learned all the things you know about him or her. You may be able to remember particular instances in which you learned specific bits of information. Perhaps you recall learning that your friend was allergic to chocolate on the evening of the day you spent making chocolate mousse. You may recall learning that he or she had an identical twin after jovially greeting the look-alike on a busy street. For the most part, however, you probably do not remember how you learned all the things you know about your friend. You do realize that you got to know this person during many different encounters in various contexts over an extended period. Now, when did you learn this person's name? You may have learned the name the first time you were introduced—or perhaps you had several casual encounters first. Even if you heard the name when you were introduced, you may have forgotten the name but remembered a lot about the person. As time passes, you are continually adding to your understanding of the type of person your friend is. Your friend's name comes to represent your constantly expanding sense of what sort of person he or she is.

How does this apply to words and their meanings? Imagine that you are a child at a museum and see a giant telescope. You ask your friend, "What's that huge thing?" "It's a telescope," she responds. "Oh, really! How does it work?" Your friend may explain how a telescope works. At this point you have a little bit of meaning for *telescope*, as well as the word that labels that meaning. The next time you see a telescope, you will remember that you saw one before and perhaps some of what your friend told you. You may or may not remember the name *telescope*. Imagine, however, that you become an avid astronomer as a teenager. You will use various types of telescopes, read about them, and perhaps build or modify one. Soon your meaning for the word *telescope* will be an enormous network of ideas. You probably will not remember where all the meanings came from because they grew out of many different encounters, but one day, as a famous astronomer, you may reflect, "When I was eight, I had to ask someone what a telescope was!"

Most of the people whose names you know are people with whom you have interacted over a period of time. You have had firsthand, direct experience with them. Many of the words for which you have meanings are also words with which you have had direct experience. If you have actually seen a tiger in the wild or at a zoo, your meaning for the word *tiger* is based on direct experience. If you have run a marathon or played tennis or basketball, your meanings for these words are based on direct experience. When you experienced fear, love, or sorrow, your meanings for these words became based on that experience.

However, you have not directly interacted with all the people whose names you know, nor with all the meanings whose words you know. You know a lot about Ronald Reagan, Elizabeth Taylor, and George Washington, with whom you have probably not had firsthand experience. But you probably have seen them in pictures or films or on television. You "know" these persons through visual experience. The meanings for some of the words you know are also based on visual rather than direct experience. You know what pole-vaulting is because you have seen it done, even though you may never have actually done it. There are places you have never visited but have seen pictures of; thus you have meanings for words such as *Jerusalem* and *Andes*.

Finally, you know some people whom you have neither met nor seen. These real or fictional people are ones you have read about in novels or historical literature. While you have never met these people, you use the knowledge gained from all the people you have met to understand the unknown people about whom you are reading. So it is with words. Imagine that you are reading this passage about the game of cricket:

The batsmen were merciless against the bowlers. The bowlers placed their men in slips and covers. But to no avail. The batsmen hit one four after another along with an occasional six. Not once did a ball look like it would hit their stumps or be caught. (Tierney & Pearson, 1981, p. 56)

Now, imagine that you have never played cricket nor seen it played, but you call up what you do know to help you build meanings for the word *cricket* and other words in the passage. "Baseball is a lot like cricket," you might think. "The bowlers must be like pitchers. The batsmen are obviously the batters. Maybe the stumps are bases." You use what you know to predict meanings for words. In situations where you build meanings for words without any direct or visual experience with what the word represents, you still draw on your direct and visual experience, but you do so through comparisons: "It is like this known thing in these ways—but different in these ways." We refer to this way of learning as *learning by connection*.

TRY IT OUT

Words and meanings, like names and people, are learned through direct experience, visual experience, and connection. List three people and three word meanings you have learned through direct experience—people and meanings with whom you have actually interacted. Then list three people and three word meanings you have acquired through visual experience—people and meanings you have not actually met or experienced but whom you feel you know through the power of the visual media.

Finally, list three people and three words that you have learned by connection. These people and words were learned by calling up your direct and visual experience in similar situations and connecting those experiences to the new names or words to build meaning.

CONTENT TEACHERS MUST DECIDE WHICH WORDS TO TEACH

Imagine that you have a friend moving into town and want to introduce him to some people. Which people would you choose? You surely cannot introduce him to all the people in your community. You do not even know them all. First, you think about the people you know, considering which of these your friend would like or need to meet. You draw up a list. Carl and Carol are on the list because they share skiing and guitar interests with your friend. You put Juan and Suzanne on the list because, like your friend, they are accountants and might help your friend make some professional connections. Once you have made your list, you arrange the all-important first meeting. A party is planned to which you invite all the potential friends as well as the Boyds, the only people besides you whom your friend already knows. In addition to the party, at which initial introductions are made, you plan several smaller events. Lunches, football games, and bridge foursomes are all opportunities for your friend to get to know these new people better. After several months, your friend continues to interact with some of the people to whom you introduced him, without your arranging the get-togethers. He also hears about some people you know whom you had not thought he might want to know, so he asks you to introduce him or arrange a way for him to make their acquaintance.

You can decide which words to teach your students in much the same way that you would decide which people to introduce a newcomer to. The content area is the new community. There are many more words in this new community than anyone could possibly come to know immediately, so you select the words that the new learner might like to know because they are so interesting. You also select some words that the new learner needs to know if he or she is going to "get around" successfully in this new community. You sit down and make a list of these new words, then plan get-togethers in which students are introduced to the words. After initial encounters, students continue to learn more about the words as they read and hear them in a variety of contexts. As students become more familiar with the new content, they might preview the materials to be read and suggest words they would like to get to know. You can then either arrange encounters for your students or suggest ways your students might independently get to know these words.

Thus, in selecting words to teach, teachers of content areas should follow these commonsense rules:

1. Consider the unit you are trying to teach and list all the key words. Key words are words that unlock the meaning of a passage. Be sure to include multimeaning words, such as *root*, for which the students might know a meaning that is not appropriate. Do not include words that are already known by most students. If your unit is on plants, *plants* would be a key word but would not need to be taught to most students. You would include such known words in your teaching activities, just as you invite known people in the new community to the party, but you would not spend valuable time building meaning for them.

2. The list you come up with by selecting unfamiliar key words will probably be too long. Determining how many words to teach is a difficult task, but research seems to indicate that ten new words per week per class is the outside limit of what we can expect students to learn. Ten words per week may not sound like much, but consider that it means 360 new words per year. Furthermore, if a student is studying five subjects and each subject includes 10 new words each week, that would add up to 1,800 new words per year—a considerable increase in vocabulary.

   To pare your list, first select the words that are important not only to the unit of study but also to the whole understanding of the content area. The word *cell* in a science unit on plants should be kept because it is crucial not only to understanding plants but also to the whole study of biology. Likewise, the word *angle* is crucial to the whole study of geometry. In addition to words crucial to the whole discipline, keep on your list words that occur repeatedly in the unit of study, and that are crucial to understanding it. A word appearing only once is probably less important than a word that occurs frequently throughout the unit.

3. Finally, include words that will be of particular interest to your students, even if such words are not crucial to the discipline or unit of study.

TRY IT OUT

Select a unit of study you might teach to a group of students. Consider what you want them to learn. Preview films, filmstrips, videos, and other teaching aids you might use. Read the text chapters and other sources students might read. As you think, preview, and read, list all the key words. Be on the lookout for multimeaning words. These are hard to spot because when we know the appropriate meaning, we often forget that there are other, more common meanings.

Once you have listed your key words, cut the list to a reasonable number (no more than ten per week) following the guidelines given. Assume your unit will last three weeks and cut your list of words to teach down to thirty. Choose two words for which typical students have meaning but do not know the words and two words for which typical students have little or no meaning.

THERE IS GREAT VARIETY IN THE STRATEGIES CONTENT TEACHERS USE TO TEACH VOCABULARY

Because we learn new words in a variety of ways, there is great variety in the strategies teachers can use to introduce and teach important words. How we teach something should parallel how something is learned. Since we remember best the things that we do, direct experience with the concept represented by the word is the most powerful and lasting way to teach. Providing this real experience, however, is not always possible, and thus we often look to the next best thing, visual representations. Finally, we can teach new words by helping students see the relationships between new concepts and already known concepts. This section presents a variety of teaching strategies to help students build meanings for words by providing direct and visual experiences and by helping them make connections between new words and known words.

The Real Thing

The Real Thing is exactly what it sounds like. You want the students to develop a meaning for a word, so you put them in direct contact with the thing that the word represents. Field trips are often good ways to show students the real thing. If you have ever taken a field trip to a state capitol to watch the legislative process, your teacher was providing you with real experience for a number of words: *capitol, legislature, gavel, quorum, debate, adjourn.* Field trips are one of the best ways of providing students with direct experience on which to base meaning for new words, but they are expensive and time-consuming, and often the things you need to show students are not available at a reasonable distance from the school.

When you cannot take the students to the real thing, the next best option is to bring something to the students. Learners at all levels learn something best when they have actually seen it, touched it, smelled it, listened to it, or even tasted it. Sometimes the actual subject of study could never be available for students to interact with, but a model could. Models of the human heart, a pyramid, or a DNA molecule, while differing in size and other features from the real thing, are still three-dimensional representations that can be

Stitchery provides direct experience during a unit on colonial life.

explored by the senses. For our purposes, we will consider such models as "real things."

Teachers sometimes think that they can provide students with direct experience only when the word for which they are building meaning represents an actual "thing." That is simply not true. You can provide students real experience with verbs like *cringe, catapult,* and *pontificate* by demonstrating these actions, then letting students act them out. You provide students with real experience with such concepts as *assembly line* and *electoral process* by simulations in which each student takes part as the class manufactures something assembly-line style or participates in a mock election. Because of time and other constraints, not all meanings can be developed through this method. But the time and effort involved in providing the real thing must be weighed against the depth and the permanence of the learning and excitement that this method generates.

During field trips and classroom events, such as special guest talks or simulations, the meanings for many words are being developed. Consequently, preparation and follow-up are required. In order to make the most of providing the real thing, follow these guidelines:

1. Help students figure out what they already know as a group about the trip to be taken or the classroom event. Conduct a What Do You Know? discussion in which you make a list of what students know, based on their responses to questions such as the following: "What things will we probably see happening when we visit the legislature?" "What do you think Dr. Horsey will tell us about what a veterinarian does?" "How do you think an assembly line works?"

2. Help students figure out what they would like to know and prepare a list of questions to be sure to try to answer. You may want different students to write down or be responsible for certain questions to make sure they all get answered.

3. Make a list of all the words for which you want to develop meanings. Have students write down these words. As you see and hear things that develop meanings for these words, be sure the students understand how to match words with meanings. You may want students to make notes next to the word, or at least check off each word as meaning for it is developed. Younger children can each be responsible for a word or two.

4. As soon as possible, have a discussion in which the answer to each student question is discussed. If some questions are not fully or satisfactorily answered, this is an excellent time to have students turn to resource books to get more information.

5. Discuss what students saw happening for each of the words. Formulate definitions that are based in this experience, rather than in dictionary style. For example, "The *quorum* was when they called the roll and saw that there were enough senators there. The quorum had to be at least two-thirds of the senators." You may want to write these experience-derived definitions on a piece of chart paper or have students write them in their notebooks.

Skits

Skits are actually a special version of the real thing. Because they require special preparation, we have chosen to give them a separate name and discuss them separately. A skit is a short drama. Generally, the teacher writes a short description of the skit, including the number of actors needed, a sentence containing the word whose meaning is to be acted out, a short description of what the actors should try to get across, and questions the actors should ask the audience after completing the skit.

Here is an example of a skit lesson plan to teach the word *controversy* and its meaning:

Example sentence: All parties had something to say in the *controversy* about whether athletes deserve special privileges.

Skit: (Actors needed: 3) Two students are standing in the cafeteria line when the star football player goes to the head of the line, gets his plate filled with specially prepared food, and takes his tray over to the "athletes' table." "I just don't think it's right," says the first student. "Athletes in this school get all kinds of special treatment." "Well," says the second student, "I don't see what the controversy is all about. Athletes are special people. They need more and better food. After all, they earn their special privileges." The two students continue to discuss the pros and cons of the controversy while the football player eats his lunch, oblivious to the discussion.

Two students complete a skit for the new word *conciliation*.

Questions to ask audience: What did *controversy* mean in our skit? Have you ever been involved in a controversy?

The teacher prepares for the lesson by writing out a skit card similar to that shown above and giving the card to the actors so that they have time to prepare. A teacher might have a skit day and divide the whole class into teams of two to four members, giving each team a skit card and allowing five minutes for each team to prepare. As each group of actors comes up, one of them writes the target word on the board and pronounces it. They then do their skit, trying to sneak in the target word as often as possible. If the actors have done a good job, the watchers should be able to answer the question, "What did the word mean in our skit?" The second question, "Have you ever . . . ?" is intended to help the watchers access any experience they might have had with the target word, and to attach the word to the experiences.

Skits are especially valuable when you are trying to teach an unfamiliar meaning for a multimeaning word. Most students know what *fog* is, but many do not know what it means to be *in a fog*. A skit in which this use of the word *fog* was demonstrated would help students to learn the new meaning.

Skits are strategies for building meaning because watching the skit provides the watchers with visual experience of a concept. For students who have not had the experience represented by a particular word, the skit is the basis of their new understanding. Other students may have experienced controversies but did not know the word that stood for what they had experienced. These students did not actually need the experience of the skit, but only needed the appropriate meaning to be accessed and attached to the new word. For these students, the question, "Have you ever . . . ?" helps them find the appropriate experience to connect with the new word. Classes always contain a wide variation of ability and experiences. Thus, our original breakdown—words for which students need the meaning developed, and words that are themselves new—is a little simpler to describe in theory than in reality. As a general rule, if you cannot decide whether most of your students are familiar with a word's meaning, go ahead and build meaning for that word. Then your activity will build meaning for those who need it, while offering additional review and practice for others.

A Picture Is Worth a Thousand Words

Visuals provide us with "the next best thing to being there." All of us have numerous words for meanings that we have not experienced directly but have developed through movies, television, still photographs, paintings, diagrams, or maps. Imagine trying to explain the Grand Canyon to someone who has never seen it. Describe with words the color teal, what fencing looks like, or life at the bottom of the ocean. Your words are meaningful only to those who have seen what the word represents.

This teacher is using a picture to build meaning for words.

Fortunately, we are surrounded by visual stimuli. Television programs offer great possibilities for content teachers. Most school system media centers contain many videos, films, filmstrips, and other visual aids that suffer from underuse. As you consider how to build meaning for words, ask yourself, "Where could I find a picture of this?" Often, the answer is as close as your textbook.

When you have your list of words for which you must build meaning, look at the textbooks and other books you have available. Note page numbers where various concepts are portrayed visually. You can introduce these concepts by writing the word on the board, pronouncing it and having students pronounce it with you, and directing their attention to the appropriate text visual.

In addition to visuals found in books, look for appropriate prints, slides, and filmstrips. Filmstrips, especially, often are an overlooked source; although most teachers think of showing filmstrips only as a whole, they often contain several frames that vividly portray the concept you want to develop. In this case, you should show these frames only. Use filmstrip titles to save yourself time. If you are looking for a picture of a camel, a filmstrip called "The Desert" is probably a good place to start.

Finally, consider films and videotapes. While you might want to show just a portion of a film or tape to develop meaning for one word, you might also want to show the whole thing to develop many new words and meanings. In that case, follow the guidelines given above for field trips and classroom events. Students who have listed what they know and which questions they want answered and who have been alerted to words for whose meanings they're looking will get more than just enjoyment (or boredom!) out of watching a film. When you have many concepts to develop, you will probably want to show the film more than once. The second time, consider stopping the film at points where it answers questions or develops meanings. Record answers and definitions on a chart or have students record them in their notebooks. After pausing for students to think and record, resume the film.

In the case of visuals, if one is good, two are twice as good. Remember that a meaning is not a matter of "one time—now you've got it." Your meaning for mountains is not based on having seen just one picture of one mountain. If your students see several visuals, the depth of their meaning for the word will be much greater than if they see only one. In addition to broadening their concepts, each visual provides review of the meaning represented by the word.

Scavenger Hunts

Have you ever had firsthand experience with a scavenger hunt? Have you actually gone to gather assorted items, competing to be the team that found the most in a limited time? If you have not, perhaps you have had visual experience of watching others go on one. Scavenger hunts are fun because they develop both competition and a sense of team spirit. For a scavenger hunt that helps your students build word meanings by collecting real things and pictures, follow these steps:

1. Make a list of the items for which you want students to scavenge. Include anything for which students might be able to find a real object, model, or picture, but make sure to include items represented by those words for which you need to build meaning. Be sure to add some well-known, easy-to-collect items so that some of the finds will be easy and immediately satisfying. Here is a list used for a scavenger hunt before beginning a unit on the desert:

sand	woodpecker	cactus	vulture
skunk	dune	fox	kangaroo rat
mesquite	dates	oasis	nomads
roadrunner	coyote	yucca	arid

2. Divide your class into teams of three or four. Ask students to share experiences with scavenger hunts. If necessary, explain how scavenger hunts work. Be sure students understand that they must bring in objects and pictures by a certain date and that each team should keep secret which items were collected and from where the items came.

3. Give each team your list. Tell the team that they get two points for each object or model and one point for each picture. Pictures include drawings and tracings (you may want to make tracing paper available). Only one object and one picture can be counted for each word. Let the team choose a leader or appoint one yourself. Have the leader read the list and lead the group in a discussion of who thinks they can find what and where. Set a date for students to bring objects and pictures to school. One week is a reasonable amount of time. Do not allow objects and pictures to be displayed before the due date.

4. Allow the teams to meet briefly once or twice more to check things off their lists and see what is still needed. Be sure to promote an atmosphere of secrecy and suspense. If students protest that "No one could find a . . . ," assure them that "No one could possibly get objects or pictures for everything. The goal is to collect as much as you can." This will generally result in some students making sure that they have a picture, if not an object, for everything, just to prove you wrong.

5. On the culminating day, let teams meet to go over their findings and tally up their points. Double-check the teams' figures. Count drawings and tracings only when they actually represent the thing and are not merely "thrown together." The winner is the team with the most points. Reward the winners by allowing them to display the findings. Cards on which each word is printed might be attached to a bulletin board and all the pictures representing that object arranged

in collage fashion around the word. Objects that are not alive, dangerous, or valuable can be labeled and placed on a table near the bulletin board. Be sure to include the names of all the winners next to the display.

Scavenger hunts are fun and, more importantly, involve students in the preparation for the unit. These hunts are best done a week or two before you actually begin the unit for which the objects are being collected. That way, by the time you are ready to explore the topic with your students, they already have a lot of information about and interest in the subject. In addition to learning what the words on the list mean, students often pick up incidental information as they peruse magazines looking for pictures or talk to people whom they hope will have objects to loan. In one class where Mexico was the scavenger hunt topic, a student had an uncle in California who had been to Mexico often. He called his uncle, who sent a box containing many of the objects on the list as well as some other objects. In addition, the uncle wrote a long letter describing Mexico and comparing it to the United States, and he sent along many photos he had taken. A scavenger hunt on the weather once included the word *meteorologist*. A student who lived next door to the local television meteorologist brought the woman along as one of the "objects." The meteorologist, of course, brought many of the objects on the list as well as other weather-related paraphernalia and talked to the class about forecasting the weather. You can imagine how interested the students in those two classes became in their units! While these two instances are somewhat unusual, students do become good at digging up objects and pictures. They develop some sense of ownership in the unit to be studied and generally begin the unit with more enthusiasm.

One final benefit of scavenger hunts is the ratio of teacher work to student work. For a scavenger hunt, the teacher makes the list, forms the teams, arranges for them to meet a few times, and checks their tallies of the points. The students do the rest—including the often onerous and neglected task of making a bulletin board.

Analogizing

Analogizing is the process of making up an analogy, or connection, to help students develop a concept for a word that you cannot represent with first-hand or visual experience. You think of something students know that is like the unknown thing you wish to teach them. The idea that cricket is a lot like baseball is an analogy. (*Analogy* is sometimes used narrowly to denote statements such as "Summer is to hot as ____ is to cold"; we use the word in a broader sense.)

To analogize something, you first think of something your students are apt to know that is like the thing they do not know. It is very important that students be familiar with the concept being used to teach the unknown concept. Telling you that cricket is a lot like rounders is not helpful if you do not know rounders either. Once you have decided which analogy to make, consider the similarities and differences between the familiar and unfamiliar concepts.

To present the analogy to the students, first ask them what they know about the familiar concept. Highlight the relevant traits, adding to the information they give you as necessary. Next, tell them that this familiar concept is a lot like another, unfamiliar concept and point out the similarities. Finally, tell students how the new concept is different from their known concept. Here is an analogizing example from social studies:

Imagine that you want to teach the students about taxation without representation and its relationship to the Revolutionary War. You decide to analogize this concept with the idea of belonging to a club to which you have to pay dues. You do not mind paying the dues, even though the club founders meet each year and decide how the dues are to be spent. After a while, it occurs to some club members who are not founders that since the dues are partly theirs, they should have some say in how the dues are spent. The founding members will have no part of this and insist that the power to spend dues is theirs, as is written in the club's bylaws. Once you have gotten from students what they know about clubs and dues, you may have to interject the notion that founding members could have control of the dues since this may not be in the experience of most students. Then, explain that taxation is like dues and that representation, in this case, means the power to decide how something is spent. A difference that should be pointed out is that you as a club member always have the right to quit the club and stop paying dues. When the colonists quit and stopped paying taxes, a war ensued.

Remember When?

Remember When? is a simple two-step strategy that requires no preparation and can be used whenever you discover that students do not know what a word means, but suspect that they have experienced the meaning that the word represents. The first step is for you to recall an experience you had with the word. Then ask students to recall an experience they have had and put the new word with the old experience. Here is a scenario of this method for the word *squeamish*. The assumption is that everyone has felt squeamish about something but may not have the word to describe that feeling.

TEACHER: (Writes *squeamish* on the board.) Many years ago, I was teaching first grade for the first time. I loved it and everything about it—well, almost everything! One day, as the little angels were getting their lunch, Veronica Baines started to reach for her tray and then quickly pulled away. "I can't eat from that tray," she exclaimed. "It has peas on it!" "Well, you don't have to eat the peas if you don't like them," I responded. "Just leave them on your tray." "But I can't even be near peas or I get sick," she protested. "Don't be ridiculous," I ordered as I handed her the tray. "But you don't know what you're doing," she began and then she threw up all over the tray, the peas, and me! Whenever I think of that day, I get a squeamish feeling in my stomach—and I can't stand the sight of peas! In fact, sometimes I get squeamish just hearing about people throwing up. If you teach first graders and you are squeamish about people throwing up, you are going to have some squeamish days! Are any of you squeamish about anything? What are you squeamish about? When do you feel squeamish? (Let children share experiences with squeamish. Be sure to use the word *squeamish* to describe how they feel.)

STUDENT: I hate when my little brother throws up. My mother always gets mad because when he gets sick, half the time she has to clean up after both of us and I'm not really sick. I just feel like throwing up when he does.

TEACHER: So you get squeamish just like I do when people throw up. Are there other things people feel squeamish about besides throwing up? Does anyone get squeamish about anything else?

STUDENT: I can't stand the sight of blood—especially mine.

STUDENT: Snakes, worms, and other creepy, crawly things.

STUDENT: Liver! (Other students agree and pretend to be sick.)

TEACHER: (Decides this is a good time to end the discussion since they all seem to know what *squeamish* means.) Today we have talked about many different things that make us feel squeamish. As you read today, you will notice the word *squeamish* in your story (points to the word on the board and has pupils pronounce it). After you read, we will talk about what made the main character in today's story squeamish.

The only trick to this method is having an interesting experience with the word that you can relate to your class. If you do not have an interesting experience, make one up and tell it as a story.

Capsule Vocabulary

Capsule Vocabulary (Crist, 1975) is a strategy in which students listen to, speak, write, and read words related to a particular topic. These topically related words (using approximately six works best) are presented one at a time by the teacher, who writes each word on the board, briefly tells the students of an experience with the word, and lets students share their own experiences. The first part of the lesson is similar to Remember When?, except that many topic-related words are introduced. In addition to words for which students have meaning but not the word, include some words already well known to students and perhaps some for which you have already built meaning in previous lessons. After all the words have been introduced and all the experiences shared by teacher and students, have each student copy the words from the board onto a sheet of paper. Pair the students and give each pair a limited time (three to five minutes) to try to use the words in a conversation about the topic. Students should check off the words as they are able to sneak them into the conversation. (Use a timer or appoint an official clock-watcher to announce when the time is up.) Finally, have students write a paragraph about the topic in which they use as many of the capsule words as possible. (This step can be eliminated for kindergartners or first-graders.) Form children into groups of four or five and let them share their paragraphs. Then collect the paragraphs and select several to read to the entire class.

Context Power

Often the surrounding words, or *context*, help us access known meaning and put it with a new word. Do you know what a jingo is? Imagine that you are reading and come across the unknown word *jingo* in this context:

All he ever talked about was war. His country was the best country, and anyone who disagreed should be ready to fight in battle. He was really quite a jingo!

You could now infer that a jingo must be a militaristic person ready to defend his or her country (or have someone else defend it) at the drop of a hat. The word *jingo* may have been unfamiliar, but if you have had experience with nationalistic, militaristic people, the meaning was not. The context helped you associate your old meaning with a new word. Context is a valuable tool for associating meaning with words, because once you learn how to use context, you can do so independently without a teacher's help. Many students, however, do not make use of context. They do not know that the surrounding words often give clues to an unfamiliar word and sometimes do not understand how our language gives these clues.

To prepare for a lesson in which you teach students to use context clues, select some words for which students have the meaning but not the word and use them in a few sentences that give clues to their meaning. It is best to use the actual context from the book when that context makes the meaning clear. There is a variety of context clues, and you should try to use all the common types so that students become familiar with them. Common types of context clues include explanatory sentences, as in the *jingo* example above; synonyms ("mean, cruel, and truculent"); antonyms ("Some things are easy, others are arduous."); similes and metaphors ("as fervid as a stove"); and appositives ("the pandowdy, a pudding made with apples"). Once you have chosen the words and written the sentences with their context clues, the steps of the lesson are as follows:

1. Write the words on the board without the context clues. Pronounce each word and have students pronounce it with you. Have students write down a meaning for each word. If there are more than two words, let each student pick two or assign two words to each student. If students actually know a meaning, they can write it down. If they do not know the meaning, they should make something up. They can also make something up if they know the meaning but want to fool everyone. Once everyone has written something down for two words, call on volunteers to tell you what they have written.

Ask them to give their answers as if they are absolutely convinced that they are right. Often students will make up a definition that sounds like the word. For the word *manticore*, for example, students have made such guesses as these: the pit of the manti fruit, a manicure for an apple, and the heart of a mantelope! The guesses are fun, but more importantly, they help students see that they don't know the meaning for the word. Often when a word's context helps us to access meaning, we grasp the meaning so quickly that we think we knew the word all along. Students will see how helpful context is only if they realize that they did not know the word until they saw it in context.

2. Display the word in its context. Then have students guess a second time what the word might mean. Emphasize that context only gives us clues to words, and sometimes these clues can lead us astray. Our ideas about what a word means when we see it in context should be considered tentative. Our context-based guesses, however, are more likely to be right than the guesses we make without any context.

3. As students guess what words mean based on context, have them explain how the context clues helped. Do not settle for "*It* said so." Students who do not understand how context clues are contained in language do not see what is obvious to those of us who do know how our language system gives clues. Through your questions, get students to explain the obvious: "*Mean* and *cruel* mean almost the same, so *truculent* probably does, too." "Stoves are hot; if something is as fervid as a stove, it must be hot, too." "The commas around 'a pudding made with apples' tell you that it is the same as pandowdy."

4. As each word is guessed from context and the reasoning behind the guess is explained, have a volunteer look up the word in the dictionary and read the appropriate definition to the class. This reinforces the notion that minimal context gives only clues, not certain answers, and it models for students using the dictionary to check hunches and gain more precise information.

5. Have students apply the context strategy by finding some unfamiliar words in their books and deriving meanings from the book context.

Multimeaning Luck

Multimeaning Luck is a particular type of context activity in which you want students to use the context to choose the appropriate meaning for a multi-meaning word. Imagine that for a unit on plants you want to teach students the plant-related meanings of the words *plants*, *roots*, *cells*, and *stems*. Prepare for the lesson by writing down each word, with one plant-related and one non-plant-related definition next to each word. Overhead transparencies work best for this lesson, but you can also write the words on the board. On the bottom of the transparency or on a part of the board you can cover temporarily, write one sentence for each word. Be sure to include in these sentences both related and unrelated definitions, as students will have to guess which definition your sentence uses. If you use only related definitions, they will easily figure out the system.

Begin the lesson by displaying the words and their two definitions:

Plants	1. living things including trees and grass
	2. factories for manufacturing things
Roots	1. words from which other words are made
	2. underground parts of plants
Cells	1. parts of jails where prisoners sleep
	2. microscopic structures that make up plants
Stems	1. stalks of plants
	2. makes headway against, as in "stems the tide"

As you read each word and its two definitions, have each student write the word and a "1" or "2" to indicate a guess of which definition you have used in the covered sentences. Be sure to tell students that doing well on this part of the lesson is simply a matter of luck. You may want to tell students this is a way to find out how their luck is running today.

When all students have made their guesses, display the sentences one at a time. Have students give themselves five points for every lucky guess and deduct five points for every unlucky guess. The person with the most points is the lucky person for the day. Once lucky and unlucky persons have been applauded or commiserated with, tell the class that they will be reading and talking about plants today and have volunteers point out the four plant-related definitions.

Are you curious as to how you did with your guesses? If so, you will see one of the advantages of this method. Once you have made a guess, you want to know how you did. You care about which definitions the sentences used. Here they are:

The plants are shut down because of the strike.

The storm was so violent it pulled the tree from the ground by its roots.

Prisons have terrible problems because of overcrowded cells.

Some stems are edible.

Give yourself five points for every lucky guess and subtract five for every unlucky guess. Are you having a lucky day? Did you pick only the plant-related definitions even though we told you to include others?

Morpheme Power

Many of you remember being taught to figure out a word's meaning by examining the word for familiar parts. Prefixes, suffixes, and roots can be helpful as we try to determine the meaning of an unfamiliar word. However, caution must be used when teaching students about these meaningful word parts. Students are often turned off to vocabulary instruction by being taught obscure Latin and Greek derivatives that have few examples in common use today and by meeting a word with a known part that has no relationship to other words with that known part. In order to identify word parts that are appropriate to teach, use the Five Test. Imagine that one of your new words is *malnutrition*. You wonder if helping students see that the prefix *mal-*, meaning "bad or evil," will help them remember the meaning for *malnutrition* and will be useful in figuring out other words they meet. If you are using the Five Test, you will alert students to the meaning of a word part only when you can think of five other common words in which this word part has the same meaning. Can you think of five other words? Do not run to your dictionary. If you cannot think of five, the part with this meaning cannot be very common. Did you think of *malpractice, malice, malignant, malfunction,* and *malcontent* or similar words? If so, the prefix *mal-* passes the Five Test. Once you determine that your word part is worth teaching, use this procedure:

1. Write on the board two familiar words containing the word part and have students tell what the words mean. Most students know that doctors are sued for malpractice when it is alleged they have done something wrong and that a malignant tumor is a bad or cancerous one.

2. Underline the word part and point out to students its common meaning in the two familiar words.

3. On the board, write in a sentence the word you wish to teach. Underline the word and pronounce it for students. Ask students to use their knowledge of the word part to try to figure out the meaning of the word. "If *mal-* means something like 'bad,' *malnutrition* must be bad or 'not good' nutrition." Have the word read in the sentence to see if the meaning makes sense. You may want a volunteer to find the word in the dictionary and check the dictionary definition since morphemes, like context, give clues but are not always completely reliable.

4. Write at least one example of a word students know in which the word part does not have the meaning just taught. *Mallet* and *mallard* are unrelated to the "evil" meaning of *mal-*. Tell them the following: "This method won't work all the time and you shouldn't expect it to, but if your derived definition works in the context of the sentence, you have a good probability of being right."

ONCE NEW WORDS ARE TAUGHT, STUDENTS NEED PRACTICE WITH THESE WORDS

The teaching strategies suggested so far are all good ways to introduce a word, but a good introduction to a word, like a good introduction to a person, is only the beginning. More encounters with the word and its meaning are generally needed before a student can really use a word. You have already built some review into your vocabulary teaching by the way in which you selected the words. By choosing both words that were important to the whole unit, and words that were important to the whole discipline, you assured that students would be hearing, reading, speaking, and writing these words in many different contexts as the unit and year continued. You can also preview words by using them in lessons intended to introduce other words. If you introduced some words, say, through a filmstrip or scavenger hunt, you might also include them in a Context Power lesson or Multimeaning Luck activity.

Word Sort

Organizing and classifying words so that relationships among words can be seen is the goal of a Word Sort. A Word Sort activity requires students to categorize words. In open sort activities, the way of sorting words is not given ahead of time. Rather, students are given words to write on cards and told to group the words together in some way. Then they discuss the different ways they grouped the words and the reasons behind their groupings.

In closed Word Sorts, students are told how to group the words. You might say, "Sort the words according to whether they are important places, people, or discoveries" or "Group the animals according to whether they are mammals, fish, reptiles, or birds."

A student sorts cards by looking for the words with the same root.

Word Books

Many teachers like to have students make Word Books—vocabulary notebooks in which to record the words they are learning. Students may use a notebook or sheets of paper stapled together and decorated with an interesting cover. Words are then usually entered according to their first letter, but in the sequence in which they are introduced, alphabetical by first letter only. Depending on the age of the children and the type of word being studied, different information can be included with each word. Many teachers like children to write a personal example for each word (*"Frigid* is a February day when the thermometer hits 20°F.") as well as a definitional sentence (*"Frigid* means very, very cold."). Although children may consult the dictionary for help, it is best not to let them copy dictionary definitions, since this requires little thought or understanding. In addition to the example and definitional sentence, other information may be included when it is helpful. A phonetic respelling may help students remember the spelling of irregular words. Sometimes, a common opposite is helpful in remembering the word. If the word has a common prefix, root, or suffix that will jog students' memory of its meaning, this can be noted. For some words, pictures, diagrams, or cartoons are helpful reminders.

Word Wall

You should provide as much additional review as your students seem to need and as you have time for. A Word Wall is an excellent device to ensure that the key words are kept in the front of all your minds. Although a Word Wall lends itself to many good review strategies, it should actually be started when you introduce your first words, and you add to it each time new words are introduced. Many teachers reserve one bulletin board for words printed on colored construction paper or large index cards. The space above the chalkboard is another possibility. A Word Wall can be placed above the chalkboard in a primary classroom. With older students, teachers often write new words on a large sheet of butcher paper and have the students write them on a Word Wall page of their notebook.

Regardless of how you display the words, the important principle is that words should be added gradually and remain easily visible to all students. Once you have your Word Wall started, many *sponge activities* are possible. A sponge activity "wipes up spilled minutes." Such an activity can be done with little or no preparation, taking as little time as thirty seconds or as much as ten minutes. Two minutes at the end of a class or when lunch is delayed can be spent having students make up sentences, leaving a blank where a Word Wall word fits. The student who makes up the sentence then calls on a volunteer to repeat the sentence filling in the missing word. That student then gets to make up a sentence for another student. Students may likewise define a word and then call on a volunteer to tell which word was defined.

A Word Wall in a primary classroom is displayed above the chalkboard.

The remainder of the activities in this section can be used with any list of words, including Word Wall words.

Be a Mind Reader

For the class to play Be a Mind Reader, the teacher thinks of one of the wall words and writes it on a slip of paper that is not shown to the students. Students number sheets of scrap paper from one to five. The teacher gives clues, the first of which is always, "It's one of the words on our wall." Successive clues narrow the choices until, by clue number five, everyone should have the correct word. Students write next to each number what they think the word is. If a subsequent clue forces them to change their minds, they write something different. If a subsequent clue does not contradict what they have, they write the same word again. Imagine that the Word Wall contains the names of all fifty states. Here are the mind reader clues and what a student might have guessed for each clue:

FIRST CLUE: "It's one of the states," which is the same as saying, "It's one of the words on the wall!" Students moan good-naturedly. One student writes a guess:

    1. North Carolina

SECOND CLUE: "It has a coast." The student, realizing that North Carolina has a coast, writes:

    2. North Carolina

THIRD CLUE: "The coast is on the Pacific Ocean." The student groans and writes:
>   3. California

FOURTH CLUE: "It does not border Canada." Student writes:
>   4. California

FIFTH CLUE: "Its capital is Sacramento." Student triumphantly writes:
>   5. California

The teacher then has students indicate if they have written *California* next to number five. Let us hope that all hands are raised. Now the teacher asks, "Let's see who read my mind. Keep your hand up if you have *California* next to number four . . . number three . . . number two . . . number one." The teacher then unfolds the slip of paper on which *California* is written to prove that the teacher did not trick the students by changing his or her mind in midstream.

Be a Mind Reader is a review activity that students love. Often, someone gets the word on the first clue and that student is always amazed by his or her good luck. Once the students catch on to the game, let them take turns thinking of the word and giving the clues.

Twenty Questions

1. Establish the subject area and select one word.
2. Have students ask questions that can be answered only by "yes" or "no." (The questions should progress from general to specific, e.g., "Is it an animal?" "Is it four-legged?" "Is it domestic?" "Is it a cat?")
3. If the word is discovered within twenty or fewer questions, points might be given based on how many questions were asked.

Charades

1. Divide the class into small groups of four or five.
2. Choose a vocabulary word from a Word Wall or content area vocabulary list.
3. Present a word to the first person in the first group.
4. Have the first person act out the word using such devices as "sounds like," "rhymes with," or "first syllable."
5. Keep track of time until the correct response is given, with a maximum time of about 120 seconds to guess the word.
6. A round consists of one person from each group acting out a word. Terminate the game at the end of any complete round.
7. The winner is the team with the lowest cumulative time.

OPTIONAL PROCEDURE: Have one student go to the front and act out a word for the whole class. The student who guesses the word gets to be the next one to act out a word.

Password

1. Divide the class into two teams. Use the Word Wall or another list of words.
2. Two people from each team come forward. One person from each pair is the listener and one is the cluegiver.
3. Select one word and show it to each cluegiver.
4. Flip a coin to see which team gives the first clue. (Clues may be only one word; guesses may be only one word.)
5. Cluegivers alternate giving clues until the word is guessed or until six total clues are given.
6. Scoring consists of the first clue equaling six points, the second clue equaling five points, and so on. (Option: If neither team guesses the word, ask the class. The first student to recognize the word gets one point for his or her team.)
7. The cluegiver returns to his or her seat, and the listener becomes the cluegiver. The next person from each team becomes the listener.

OPTIONAL PROCEDURES:

1. First person on each team is the cluegiver.
2. Clues are given alternately by each team.
3. The cluegiver offers a clue to the second person on his or her team, the third person, and so on until a total of six clues have been given. The cluegiver remains constant or the person guessing the word becomes the new cluegiver.

Visual Password

1. Divide the class into two teams. Each team faces a chalkboard, preferably on opposing walls.
2. Write vocabulary words on slips of paper and select one word.
3. Call one member of each team to your desk and show the selected word to the two team members.
4. Participants go to their chalkboard and draw pictures to reveal the word to their team.
5. The first team to recognize the word through the picture gets one point.
6. Options for team responses:
   a. Team members call out answers.
   b. Student illustrator calls on team members.
   c. Teacher calls on team members alternately.

Review Sentences

1. List key vocabulary on the chalkboard or on chart paper or use wall words.

2. The teacher calls for sentences containing at least two words from the list to be dictated about the passages.

3. Information may be contributed in any order; sequence of dictated sentences need not be in the same order as original presentation of information.

4. Example words:

evaporate	fog
condense	moisture
water vapor	rises
invisible	clouds

Possible dictated sentences:

As water *condenses*, it turns into *fog*.

Clouds are formed by *evaporating* water.

Heat causes water to change from a liquid into an *invisible* gas called *water vapor*.

5. After the dictation of the sentences, the students turn to their texts or notes to check the accuracy of the statements.

6. Inconsistencies and errors are corrected, and important missing information is added.

7. This information may be organized and stored in students' notebooks for future use, if desired.

DO IT TOGETHER

In a small group or pair preparing to teach the same content subject, discuss the meaning vocabulary teaching and practice strategies described in the last two sections. Choose three of each type of strategy that your group or pair would be most likely to use with students during content instruction. Have someone in the group or pair take down a one-sentence rationale for choosing each of the six. Compare your list and rationales with other groups or pairs who have engaged in the same activity. Did different groups or pairs pick different strategies for different reasons? Is a variety of meaning vocabulary strategies called for?

STUDENTS CAN BECOME
INDEPENDENT LEARNERS OF WORDS

So far, this chapter has stressed teacher-directed vocabulary instruction. The teacher selects words. The teacher finds films and filmstrips. The teacher creates context sentences. Some of you may have wondered why the teacher seemed to be doing all the students' work. Be assured that we believe students should work also. Indeed, as the year goes on, at every grade level, in every subject area, students should be assuming more of the responsibility for their own learning. But you cannot start out simply hoping that students will learn something; you must teach in such a way that by the end of the year, more of them can direct their own learning. Here are some suggestions for helping students become independent learners of words:

Let Students Select the Words to Be Learned

M. R. Haggard (1982) suggests a vocabulary self-collection strategy in which students preview materials to be read with the purpose of listing two words they consider important and relatively unknown. Help students to define *important* as occurring many times in the material to be read. Help them also to consider whether the word is unknown not by their ability or inability to pronounce it but by their "I wonder what that word means" reaction. The list of words that students suggest should be modified by the teacher to fit the criteria for choosing which words to teach offered earlier in this chapter. Of course, the teacher should add words not suggested by students if these words are crucial to the discipline or the unit.

Let Students Plan a Lesson to Teach the Words

After the teacher has directed the students' lessons, students should know that we can build meanings for words by providing direct experience, visual experience, or an analogy. Students can work individually or in pairs to prepare their lessons, which might include bringing in the real thing or a model; finding a picture, including films, filmstrips, and slides; creating a skit for a word; and creating an analogy. Students will, of course, need some initial help with this work, but as time goes on, they should become more independent. As students teach their lessons, the teacher should remind them that they can perform some of these activities whenever they meet a word for which they do not have meaning. "Where could I find a picture? I wonder if there is one in my text" and "Is this like anything I already know?" are models for how students should think when faced with an unknown, important word.

Move Students toward Independence in the Lessons You Teach

For example, in analogizing, the teacher presents an analogy. That strategy can be modified so that instead of presenting an analogy, the teacher asks students to think of one as they read. "Today, you will be reading about circuits and how electrons move only through a complete circuit. As you read, try to think of how open and closed circuits are a lot like something you already know. When you have finished, we will share all our ideas for what circuits are like." When students finish reading, the teacher should accept all reasonable analogies, helping students to state how their analogies are similar to and different from the new concept. As the teacher, you can of course share your own analogy with students, but be sure not to give them the idea that there is only one right analogy.

This process of moving students toward independence can be applied to all teaching strategies. For example, in Context Power, students guess word meanings first without, then with, context sentences. To move students toward independence, ask them to use the context provided in the textbook rather than sentences you write. In that case, students would guess without context, then be directed to a specific part of a page that contains the new word. Students figuring out meanings from the context in their books are moving toward greater independence. Ultimately, students could be alerted to several words before they begin reading, and then asked to use the text's context clues to figure out meanings. After completing the reading, various students could suggest meanings, and show where and how the text gave them clues.

Teach Students How Best to Use a Dictionary

As you began this chapter on vocabulary, did you expect to find a chapter full of dictionary activities? That expectation is reasonable when you consider the experience you have probably had with vocabulary activities throughout your schooling. The most common vocabulary activity in classrooms at all levels is to assign students to look up words and write their definitions. This frustrating practice is like expecting that you could get to know some new people by looking them up in *Who's Who* and writing down their distinguishing characteristics. Such an activity is helpful only if you already know something about the people and want to find out more. In the same way, dictionaries are wonderful resources for adding to or clarifying a word's meaning.

Students need to see how real people use the dictionary. Real people do not look up lists of words and write definitions that they memorize for a test. Real people consult a dictionary when they cannot figure out the meaning of a word they encounter in their reading. They look up a word they know a little about when they meet it in a new context and need some clarification or elaboration on its meaning. Sometimes a dictionary is used in the real world to check the spelling of a word needed in writing.

All teachers should keep a dictionary handy and model its real use. When students meet a new word and ask the teacher what it means, the teacher may respond with a little information and then say, "I don't really know exactly what that means. Let's look it up and find out." As described in the Context Power lesson, teachers can have children use the dictionary to check or flesh out a meaning derived from context. When teachers are at the board recording a brainstormed list or some other student-generated responses, they can model how to check the spelling of a word of which you are unsure. Showing students that you, the teacher, see the dictionary as the natural tool to discover and clarify meanings and check spelling will go a long way toward making them independent vocabulary learners.

LISTEN/LOOK AND LEARN

Interview three of your friends about their vocabulary remembrances: Do they remember looking the words up and writing the definitions? How did this affect how they felt about the dictionary? Do they use a dictionary now and how do they use it? Ask them also if they remember teachers that let the class choose the important words and let students plan lessons to teach the words. What did they think of these activities? If they never experienced this, ask them to decide if they thought these types of experiences would have made them more independent word acquirers.

LOOKING BACK

Having a thorough knowledge of the key words is essential to learning in any content area. The vocabulary of each content area is specific to that area and not apt to occur in normal conversation, recreational reading, or television viewing. All content area teachers must teach the vocabulary essential to communicating about their subject. These are the key ideas you explored in this chapter: (1) Words are learned through direct and visual experience and by making connections; (2) content teachers must decide which words to teach; (3) there is great variety in the strategies content teachers use to teach vocabulary; (4) once new words are taught, students need practice with these words; and (5) students can become independent learners of words.

ADD TO YOUR JOURNAL

Reflect upon the five key ideas in this chapter and decide what you think: Do you remember learning words through direct and visual experience? Can you think of words for which you have had no experience and which you learned by connecting them to known words? Do you remember teachers who worked hard to provide you with direct experiences? Do you remember taking field trips? Engaging in simulations? Building models? Do you remember teachers who used films and videos effectively? Can you think of ways in which teachers tried to develop abstract concepts by creating analogies to real situations? Think about the teaching and practice strategies described. Which ones could you most easily use in your content area? Remember that even subjects involving more "doing" than reading and writing depend on words to communicate ideas. Vocabulary development is critical to learning in every content area. Which teaching and practice strategies do you think would be most helpful in your content area? Finally, think about independence. Students will not always have you there to ferret out the critical words and devise nifty ways to learn them. What will you do to make your students independent word learners?

REFERENCES

Burmeister, L. (1978). *Reading strategies for middle and secondary school teachers* (2nd ed.). Reading, MA: Addison Wesley.

Crist, B. I. (1975). One capsule a week—a painless remedy for vocabulary ills. *Journal of Reading, 19,* 147–149.

Haggard, M. R. (1982). The vocabulary self-collection strategy: An active approach to word learning. *Journal of Reading, 26,* 203–207.

Tierney, R. J., & Pearson, P. D. (1981). Learning to learn from text: A framework for improving classroom practice. In E. K. Dishner, T. W. Bean, & J. E. Readence (Eds.), *Reading in the content areas.* Dubuque, IA: Kendall/Hunt.

ADDITIONAL READINGS

Approaches to developing vocabulary in general with a special chapter for content area vocabulary can be found in this book:

Johnson, D. D., & Pearson, P. D. (1984). *Teaching reading vocabulary.* New York: Holt, Rinehart & Winston.

Many activities for categorizing and word sorts can be found in the following article:

Gillet, J. W., & Kita, M. J. (1979). Words, kids and categories. *The Reading Teacher, 32,* 538–542.

Research on the use of analogy to develop unfamiliar concepts in a health textbook are reported in the following article; the methods described are applicable to any content area:

Vosniadou, S., & Ortony, A. (1982). The influence of analogy in children's acquisition of new information from text: An exploratory study. In J. Niles (Ed.), *Searches for meaning in reading/language processing and instruction* (Thirty-First Yearbook of the National Reading Conference) (pp. 71–79). Rochester, NY: National Reading Conference.

Practical approaches to vocabulary instruction that could be used in any content area are included in the following articles:

Blachowicz, C. L. (1985). Vocabulary development and reading: From research to instruction. *The Reading Teacher, 38,* 876–881.

Carr, E. M. (1985). The vocabulary overview guide: A metacognitive strategy to improve vocabulary comprehension and retention. *Journal of Reading, 28,* 684–689.

Marzano, R. J. (1984). A cluster approach to vocabulary instruction: A new direction from the research literature. *The Reading Teacher, 37,* 168–173.

Some good syntheses of research on meaning vocabulary instruction and learning include the following:

Baumann, J. F., & Kameenui, E. J. (1991). Research on vocabulary instruction: Ode to Voltaire. In J. Flood, J. M. Jensen, D. Lapp, & J. R. Squire (Eds.), *Handbook of research on teaching the English language arts* (pp. 604–632). New York: Macmillan.

Beck, I., & McKeown, M. (1991). Conditions of vocabulary acquisition. In R. Barr, M. L. Kamil, P. B. Mosenthal, & P. D. Pearson (Eds.), *Handbook of reading research* (Vol. 2) (pp. 789–814). White Plains, NY: Longman.

Graves, M. (1986). Vocabulary learning and instruction. In E. Z. Rothkopf (Ed.), *Review of research in education* (Vol. 13) (pp. 49–90). Washington, DC: American Educational Research Association.

Klesius, J. P., & Searls, E. F. (1990). A meta-analysis of recent research in meaning vocabulary instruction. *Journal of Research and Development in Education, 23*, 226–235.

CHAPTER 8

Issues in Content Area Organization and Instruction

LOOKING AHEAD

Teachers deal with many issues as they plan and carry out daily instruction with large numbers of diverse students. When planning lessons that involve reading, teachers estimate how well their students' reading proficiencies match the reading materials. Since students' attitudes affect learning so dramatically, teachers also think about how to ensure good levels of motivation. Student work is assessed and often graded in order to plan for the future and make progress reports. Some subjects emphasize physical activities over literacy, but even in these activity-oriented courses, teachers make connections whenever possible because they realize how important it is for their students to read and write well and that reading and writing help students think better about whatever they are learning. And teachers constantly work to find the time to accomplish all that they desire. The issues of finding readable materials, boosting student motivation, assessing and grading, striking a balance between activity and literacy, and finding the time to do it all are not easy to resolve. Beginning teachers and veteran teachers alike constantly struggle with them. There are no quick simple solutions to these problems, but this chapter will present the best partial solutions used by a variety of successful teachers.

The previous chapters have presented a variety of approaches and strategies for achieving higher levels of literacy and content learning for all students. Teachers at all grades and in all subject areas recognize their obligation to help promote more sophisticated levels of reading, writing, and learning. Most teachers would like to integrate reading and writing activities into their content area instruction, but there are some difficult issues to be resolved.

The key ideas in this chapter are partial solutions to the most difficult and commonly voiced issues:

1. How can I tell if reading materials are appropriate for my students?
2. How can I motivate my students to read and write?
3. How can I fairly assess what my students are learning and give appropriate grades?
4. What is the place of reading and writing in an activity course?
5. Where can I find the time to teach everything everyone wants me to teach?

HOW CAN I TELL IF READING MATERIALS ARE APPROPRIATE FOR MY STUDENTS?

Knowing if reading materials are appropriate for your students helps you decide what to select for classroom use. You make these decisions when serving on textbook adoption committees, purchasing nontextbook materials, and choosing from materials already in school stockrooms. However, due to limited budgets and available materials, teachers frequently have little choice about what to use, so they go with what they have. Even in this situation, knowing how appropriate reading materials are for students is still important because it helps you decide how much support to provide. In this first section, you will find three methods for determining the appropriateness of reading materials: readability formulas, evaluation checklists, and tryouts. Most teachers use these three in combination with one another.

Readability Formulas

Most textbooks have a teacher's edition with a number that is supposed to represent the book's level of readability. If, for example, a text has a readability level of 5.6, that means it is predicted to be appropriate for students in the fifth grade, sixth month of school. If the readability level ranges from 8.0 to 9.0, that means the various sections of the book range from eighth- to ninth-grade level in difficulty—at least in theory. There are many problems with readability estimates and with reliably estimating the difficulty of a text.

All commonly used readability formulas are based on two factors: sentence difficulty and word difficulty. *Sentence difficulty* typically is determined by the average number of words in a sentence. Long sentences usually are considered more difficult to follow than short sentences. *Word difficulty* is harder to define. Various formulas measure the incidence of long words, assuming that long words are more difficult to read. If someone were applying a readability formula to this textbook, for example, they would select several passages, determine the average sentence length and number of difficult words, consult a formula, and produce a number to be called the readability level.

There are several problems with this apparently scientific approach. First, the formulas take into account only two of the characteristics that make texts difficult. The number, quality, and appropriateness of the visuals can make a text more or less readable, as can the organization of the passages and the connections that are made between students' experiences and new information. Clear content-related headings and good transitions are also important. Introductory and review activities that help students to determine key information and monitor how well they are learning are important text characteristics commonly ignored by readability formulas.

In addition to these text variables, there is the more important reader variable. No readability formula can take into account what level of prior knowledge, interest, or motivation readers bring with them to the text. Imagine that a book on U.S. history has a readability level of 8.0 and is used by average eighth-graders in Williamsburg, Virginia, and Sydney, Australia. The superior knowledge, interest, and motivation of the Williamsburg eighth-graders would make them much more able to benefit from the text than the Australians, most of whom probably would lack prior knowledge, interest, and motivation to study U.S. history.

Yet another variable that formulas do not consider is you, the teacher. Remember that you have control over which sections to use and which to skip, what kind of preparation you will do before reading, how long a segment you will assign, and what kind of follow-up you will do after reading. Your instruction can do much to make a text more or less readable.

Readability formulas have one final problem when they are applied to school textbooks. Because writers of textbooks know that they must achieve a certain readability for a book that is designated for a certain grade, writers compose with the variables of sentence difficulty and word difficulty constantly in mind. The finished writing is checked against a readability formula, and if the score is too high, long sentences are made into short ones and long words are replaced by short words. As an illustration, note the difference between the following two examples:

> Furthermore, the finished writing is checked against a readability
> formula, and if the score is too high, long sentences are made into short
> ones and long words are replaced by short words.

Then the writing is checked with a readability formula. Sometimes the score is too high. Long sentences are made into short ones. Short words are used for long words.

Both the first long sentence and the rewritten four sentences contain essentially the same information. If the readability formula were applied, the four sentences would be rated as much easier to read. But are they? Most people would find them harder to read. In the four short sentences, the reader has to infer that the score being too high results in the long sentences and words being adjusted. In the long sentence, this inference is cued by the word *if*. While most readers can make that inference, doing so takes more attention. Numerous short sentences and vague little words (*that*, *these*, *things*) may actually make comprehension more difficult. Defenders of readability formulas would respond to this criticism by stating rightly that readability formulas were meant to measure the difficulty of "naturally occurring text" and were never intended to be used as a guide to rewrite material. Unfortunately, because most states demand that all textbooks meet the readability requirements for a given grade level, that is the way readability formulas are currently being used.

Another problem with readability formulas is that they are applied to text segments, averaged together, and then said to characterize the entire text. Think how this would affect a literature anthology if a readability formula were run on it. Segments by Ernest Hemingway and James Joyce would be considered at the same level of difficulty, although most readers would find reading Joyce considerably harder than reading Hemingway. The difficulty of most books varies from chapter to chapter—and from section to section—so teachers need to examine the specific portions of texts that they intend to use rather than rely on an overall score for a book or collection of reading passages.

Figure 8.1 includes the popular Fry Readability Graph (Fry, 1977). Knowing the strengths and limitations of these formulas, examine this formula and use it only with the caution all such formulas require.

Evaluation Checklists

Evaluation checklists are another way to estimate the match between readers and texts. Checklists go beyond the word difficulty and sentence difficulty assessments of readability formulas to such aspects as the effectiveness of introductions and the depth of explanations offered for a topic. Checklists can go into these complex aspects of a text because they rely on individuals' judgments. Unlike the objective procedures of readability formulas, checklists call for you to examine material and assign a subjective—but informed— rating. Checklists pinpoint aspects of a text, and you judge whether these are strengths or limitations. As you evaluate a text with a checklist, note the positive and negative features and continually ask yourself how much sup-

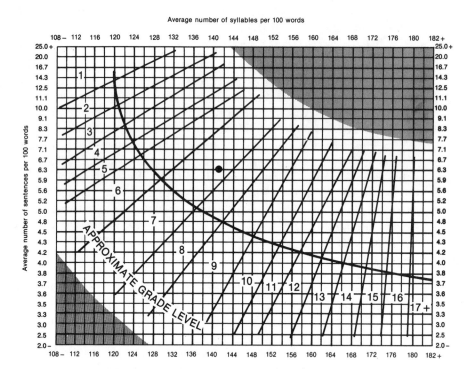

Average number of syllables per 100 words

Expanded Directions for Working Readability Graph

1. Randomly select three (3) sample passages and count out exactly 100 words each, beginning with the beginning of a sentence. Do count proper nouns, initializations, and numerals.

2. Count the number of sentences in the hundred words, estimating length of the fraction of the last sentence to the nearest one-tenth.

3. Count the total number of syllables in the 100-word passage. If you don't have a hand counter available, an easy way is to simply put a mark above every syllable over one in each word, then when you get to the end of the passage, count the number of marks and add 100. Small calculators can also be used as counters by pushing numeral 1 then push the + sign for each word or syllable.

4. Enter graph with *average* sentence length and *average* number of syllables; plot dot where the two lines intersect. Area where dot is plotted will give you the approximate grade level.

5. If a great deal of variability is found in syllable count or sentence count, putting more samples into the average is desirable.

6. A word is defined as a group of symbols with a space on either side; thus, *1945,* is one word.

7. A syllable is defined as a phonetic syllable. Generally, there are as many syllables as vowel sounds. For example, *stopped* is one syllable and *wanted* is two syllables. When counting syllables for numerals and initializations, count one syllable for each symbol. For example, *1945* is four syllables.

FIGURE 8.1 Fry Readability Graph. SOURCE: Fry (1977). Reproduction permitted—no copyright.

port your students would probably require to read and learn from that text well.

Figure 8.2 contains a textbook evaluation checklist that we have found to be useful. To be sure, other lists are available, although none has been demonstrated to be superior (Moore & Murphy, 1987). The checklist presented here is one tool to help you select appropriate materials and identify appropriate parts of a text for use with your students. As you study it, ask yourself what you might add, modify, or delete. Perhaps the best advice about developing and using checklists is for teachers to examine what is available and produce one that reflects their own judgments about what makes reading materials appropriate for students.

Tryouts

A third way to determine if materials are appropriate for your students is to conduct a tryout, during which, as the name implies, you try out the material with your students. Think of it as a pretest. You want to see how well your students can do with a particular passage before providing any supporting instruction. To conduct a tryout, first select a portion of a text that contains some of the most important information, one that students should be able to complete in a single class period. Then decide what you would want your students to learn from their reading and what task you can have students complete to demonstrate their understanding and learning. These steps are identical to some of the steps in planning a comprehension minilesson. However, unlike comprehension minilessons, tryouts do not call for you to prepare students for the reading task by motivating them and building their background knowledge. You simply present the task and see how well students perform on their own.

Students' performance during a tryout provides you with insight about the match among their reading abilities, the materials, and the reading task. A rough rule of thumb for assessing performance is that a score around 90 percent with the task means the students are *independent* with the material; it is so familiar and comfortable that students can easily understand and remember it on their own. Students do not need your help with these materials; they can learn the important information independently. A score around 75 percent indicates *instructional* level. With comprehension minilessons, students at this level can readily learn the information and think about the important ideas. The materials are teachable. Students who score around 50 percent or less probably are on *frustration* level with these materials; simply put, these materials quite likely are beyond their grasp, regardless of how much help and support you offer. Frustration level materials typically require more prior knowledge and reading ability than you can provide your students in a reasonable time.

A word of caution: When determining whether materials are appropriate for students, remember that one text is rarely at the same level of difficulty for all students. The ability and prior knowledge of individuals vary consider-

Title _____

Author(s) _____

Publisher _____ Copyright date _____

School district's intended audience _____

Directions: Rate the text according to each item below using a five-point scale, with 5 being high and 1 being low. Compare the text to an ideal instead of known materials.

After rating each item, decide how much you would need to guide students through the material in order to compensate for its shortcomings. Finally, form a holistic rating of the overall value of the text.

Very Desirable—"I would love to teach with this text!"

Desirable—"With a little support on my part, this text could be quite useful."

Fair—"I could get by with this text, but I would keep hoping for a better one."

Undesirable—"I would have to spend a great deal of time and energy making up for the shortcomings of the few parts of this text I might use."

Very Undesirable—"I would not even hand out this text to my students!"

Adjunct Aids

____ 1. The text contains a detailed table of contents, index, and glossary.

____ 2. Objectives, introductions, graphic overviews, and summaries occur at appropriate intervals and indicate major ideas.

____ 3. Headings, subheadings, and italic and boldfaced words occur at appropriate intervals and indicate major ideas.

____ 4. Graphic aids such as illustrations, maps, and tables occur on the same page as the discussion or at least the facing page. These graphics clarify major ideas presented in the text; they do not introduce new ideas or simply decorate the page.

____ 5. Review, extension, and application activities such as questions, suggested readings, and projects occur at appropriate intervals. They relate directly to the major ideas and elicit a wide range of thinking.

Conceptual Density

____ 6. The chapters emphasize fundamental concepts or principles; they are more then encyclopedic collections of related information. Facts are presented to develop the explicitly stated concepts or principles.

____ 7. Explanations of new ideas include memorable analogies, clear references to previously presented information, and concrete examples. The explanations consist of more then dull dictionary-type wording.

____ 8. The amount of technical vocabulary on each page is appropriate for the intended audience.

Motivation

____ 9. The text includes introductory comments, questions, and scenarios to arouse curiosity about the upcoming contents.

____ 10. The text explains how learners might use the information in real-life situations.

____ 11. The text cover, print size, graphics, and layout are appealing to the intended audience.

FIGURE 8.2 Textbook Evaluation Checklist

Organization

____ 12. The chapters could be outlined easily. The paragraphs and sections move forward in a logical manner.

____ 13. The text explicitly signals how information is arranged. Topic paragraphs and sentences include such statements as, "There are three reasons for this outcome" and "The following presents the key events."

Special Concerns

____ 14. The text fits the course objectives.

____ 15. Groups of people are presented authentically. There is no bias.

____ 16. A teacher's manual provides helpful suggestions for presenting the textual information.

FIGURE 8.2   Continued.

ably. A text that is independent for one student will be frustrating for another. Given this situation, teachers usually seek materials that are teachable for the majority of their students. Accommodations for students at the extremes then are achieved through techniques described earlier, such as writing activities, alternative reading materials, research projects, and collaborative group work.

TRY IT OUT

This section has presented three ways to tell if reading materials are appropriate for students. Select a commonly used text in your subject and apply to it the Fry Readability Graph and our textbook evaluation checklist. In addition, conduct a tryout of the text with a group of students. Summarize the strengths and limitations of the text and decide whether you would use it.

HOW CAN I MOTIVATE MY STUDENTS TO READ AND WRITE?

Motivating students is one of the most difficult tasks for teachers. While all humans seem to be born curious and eager to learn, this curiosity often does not last once they are in school. Many of the activities and strategies suggested in this book help with motivation.

Students care more when their prior knowledge is called up and developed so that they can connect what they already know to what they are reading. Students care more when there are a variety of whole-class, small-group, and individual learning opportunities. They care more when they know that they can make a satisfactory grade if they put forth their best daily effort. Consider as well the following suggestions:

Ensure Success

Think of something at which you are not successful. How motivated are you to engage in this activity? If you are not a very good cook or runner or singer, you probably do not engage in these activities very often, and when forced to participate, you are probably not the most enthusiastic participant. In fact, you may even display a "Who cares?" attitude. Now imagine that someone must teach you to do something that you are not good at, such as cooking. The cooking teacher is probably a good and enthusiastic cook. If the good cook is also a good teacher, he or she will turn you into a decent cook and even have you liking cooking better. Some "can't fail" recipes will be tried first, for which you will be given much guidance and encouragement. When you burn something or forget the sugar, your teacher will proclaim, "No one's perfect," and tell a story about a real disaster made by an expert cook when he or she was just learning.

Thus, if your students appear unmotivated, we prescribe a steady diet of success, teacher enthusiasm, and an attitude of "no one's perfect." Once students experience some success, they generally decide that schooling is not so bad. Once they start to like school, they will care more and learn more. Indeed, developing and maintaining students' expectations for success is one of the best ways to bring about motivation (Good & Brophy, 1991). When students see that success can be achieved, they will more likely put forth the effort. For motivation and learning to occur, teachers should assign tasks that students can accomplish with reasonable effort and provide thorough instruction so that students know what to do and how to do it.

Allow Student Choice

Another way to enhance motivation is to provide students with choices. You may not give a four-year-old a choice of whether or not to take a bath, but you may give a choice of when to take that bath. "Do you want to take your bath now or in twenty minutes?" is used in many households. Young children typically respond, "Twenty minutes!" and in twenty minutes they take their baths without complaint. Students like to schedule their own time. You may require some tasks, but allow your students to decide the order in which to complete them; or you might allow students to choose which assignments from a given list they wish to complete. Given two possible writing assignments, students could pick the one they are most interested in completing. Given ten vocabulary words, students could select their own way of presenting the words' meanings. All of us want to control our lives. The statement attributed to Winston Churchill aptly sums up how many students feel: "I have always enjoyed learning, but I have not always enjoyed being taught." Letting students make choices within parameters set by the teacher is a nice balance of authority and an effective motivational device.

Emphasize Meaningful Activities

Often after students have read, teachers ask a series of quick questions about the facts to make sure the students have understood the reading. These rapid-fire, low-level questions are termed *popcorn questions* because of the rapidity with which one follows another. These questions, like popcorn, also tend to be lightweight and go out to students randomly. Although popcorn questions can be stimulating for some, a steady diet of them soon leads to the belief that school is simply a place to memorize facts and give them back on demand. Many students tire of this situation and retreat.

Meaningful activities are relevant to students' lives, engaging them at a personal rather than an abstract academic level. Information and strategies are learned because they are seen as being useful now rather than only in some unforeseen future. For instance, meaningless letter writing occurs when students practice the forms of friendly and business letters only to receive a grade; meaningful letter writing occurs when students actually mail what they have written and expect a response. Students who write to pen pals, sports figures, and letter-to-the-editor newspaper columns are engaged in meaningful writing activities.

Not only do meaningful activities provide for immediate personal application, but also they tend to call for holistic finished products. In the case of meaningful letter writing, students complete an entire letter to be mailed rather than working on isolated salutations, introductions, and so forth. Meaningful tasks give students a sense of closure, a sense that what they have completed has integrity in its own right.

Develop Student Independence

Students require independent reading and writing proficiencies if they are to be lifelong learners. They also require independence if they are to be motivated in the classroom. Most students eventually tire of attending to teachers' directions for every move they make and often become apathetic or antagonistic. Successful veteran teachers explicitly teach classroom routines, study strategies, and the like early in the year and fade out their guidance as the year goes on. If you visit their classes late in the year, you will see happy, motivated independent learners and classrooms that seem to run themselves. Many beginning teachers wonder when they will get classes full of these independent students. The truth, of course, is that the classrooms were created by a lot of teacher persistence and effort early in the year. All of the chapters in this book provide guidelines for helping students develop independent reading, writing, and study habits. In addition to becoming more independent, these students have a higher level of academic motivation.

Get Everyone Actively Involved

Sometimes we are not motivated because we refuse to get involved, but if we are forced to get involved, we may find ourselves getting caught up in the activity. Imagine that you are teaching a group of first-graders a lesson on living and nonliving things. You have taught the differences; now you want to show some pictures so they can decide whether each picture represents a living or nonliving thing. You could simply call on volunteers. But then only

Students can actively respond in collaborative learning groups.

one child at a time would be responding, with many children uninvolved and not attending. To make this an activity in which all are involved, have each draw a picture of himself or herself on one side of a piece of drawing paper and a picture of a book on the other side. Then as you display each of your pictures, say "Ready, set, show," and have the children show the picture of themselves if they believe the object is living (like them), the picture of their book if they believe the object is nonliving (like the book). Teachers of young children often use yes/no cards for such activities. Another variation is the smile/frown activity. The teacher says, "I am going to try to name living things. If I do name a living thing, smile at me. But if I make a mistake and name a nonliving thing, frown at me!"

For older students, writing is a good active response technique. Imagine that you want to review the major aspects of communicable diseases. You could ask, "Who remembers something we learned about communicable diseases?" You would probably get some hands, but most teachers complain that the same hands are always raised. Do the ones whose hands are not raised not know or simply not care to participate? Three to a Customer is a review activity that gets everyone involved. The teacher asks everyone to take out a sheet of scrap paper and write three things they remember about communicable diseases. After giving students about two minutes to do so, the teacher goes around the room having each student tell one of the things written down. If all of a student's items have been mentioned, that student simply says, "Pass." When there are several passes in a row, the teacher asks if anyone has something written down that has not been mentioned yet. Students like having something no one else thought of. The teacher might then collect the papers and assign points for good effort.

Many other formats for such active written responses are possible. To call up prior knowledge about Shakespeare, you might give students three minutes to write down as many of his plays or characters as they can. Before introducing some new geometric shapes, you might write the names of the shapes on the board and let the students see how many of the shapes they can draw.

Be sure to acknowledge the right answers in these activities, rather than focusing on the wrong answers. Say, "Good, most of you are frowning because a table is not a living thing," and let students share the answers they wrote down that they think are right. If a student does volunteer a wrong answer, indicate that the answer was not right but was a "good try." ("*Our Town* is a play, but Shakespeare didn't write it." "That's close, but a trapezoid has to have two parallel sides and two nonparallel sides.") Active responses help students form the habit of thinking and participating. And once they begin participating, they might become more interested in class.

LISTEN/LOOK AND LEARN

Sit in on about three class meetings of a content area class at any grade level. Observe what is occurring and talk with the teacher and selected students to determine the conditions and teaching techniques that motivate students to read and write. Compare your results with the information presented in this section.

HOW CAN I FAIRLY ASSESS WHAT THEY ARE LEARNING AND GIVE APPROPRIATE GRADES?

Of all the difficult issues teachers face, assessing and grading are perhaps the most troublesome. Grading is an extremely difficult part of teaching because of the differences in student ability. If students came to us with exactly the same amount of prior knowledge and learning ability, we could expect them all to gain exactly the same amount from our good instruction. But students start at different places, with different amounts of ability. How do we grade fairly? Should the student who knows almost nothing about social studies and whose learning ability is limited fail the subject if a good effort is made? Should the student who knows a lot about social studies and is very bright and advantaged get an A even if that student need put forth only minimal effort to do so? These are not easy questions to answer, but teachers must come up with a grading system, one that will encourage rather than discourage students from learning. Following are some guidelines to consider in designing a grading system that encourages all students to work and learn.

Make Sure That Essential Learning Activities Count toward the Grade

Teachers typically assign grades derived from three types of schoolwork: daily work, projects, and tests. One way to motivate students to effort in the classroom is to regularly monitor daily work. If students work in groups, give each cooperative group member a point when the group completes the assignment. If a writing assignment is made, give those who complete it on time a point before assessing the content and mechanics of each piece. Generally give points for tasks completed on time and with good effort. By combining good instruction that focuses on concepts of varying degrees of difficulty with rewards for completing assignments acceptably, you go a long way toward motivating your students to work with you.

Students who regularly succeed with their schoolwork demonstrate the best progress. Thus, students must be successful at their tasks if they are to continue to work and learn. To guarantee success to students of all different levels of achievement, define success as good effort.

Have Some Projects That Allow Hard Workers and Talented Students to Excel

Assigning projects allows students to go beyond linear thinking to creativity. Of course, any student who does a satisfactory project should get the number of points designated for "satisfactory." But those who go beyond the minimum requirement should get more points. Giving everyone equal credit for a good effort for daily work rewards students for a normal, good effort. Grading projects according to their quality allows those who can and will work hard to feel their efforts are appreciated.

Make Tests as Fair as Possible for All Students

Tests are the hardest element of a grading system. Some teachers, particularly at lower grade levels, do not give tests. But many teachers feel the need for some "objective" measure of learning, and many school systems demand that teachers have test grades for students. How do you produce tests that don't penalize students who began your unit with little prior knowledge and who have limited learning skills?

As a general guideline, 80 to 90 percent of material tested should have been thoroughly taught and reviewed during class. Include on your tests information taught in comprehension and writing minilessons as well as information taught through lecture and demonstration. Those students who worked with you on a daily basis—even if their ability is limited—should be able to answer 80 to 90 percent of such a test correctly. The other 10 to 20 percent of the test may include material that was assigned but not thoroughly taught. This is, of course, a compromise position. Some teachers believe it is unfair to students with limited ability to test anything not thoroughly taught in classes. Unfortunately, if you try to test only what was thoroughly taught and reviewed, and you taught and reviewed it well, everyone in class should get an A. Most schools will not permit this, and your more able students will not be motivated to learn from assignments. Other teachers believe that everyone should learn everything—both what was taught and what was assigned. Following this system, many students who worked with you on a daily basis but who cannot learn from assignments done independently will fail the test. And if they always fail tests, they will not continue to work with you on a daily basis. Since success on a daily basis is such an important determinant of content learning, a grading system that does not assure success is bound to create students who learn little.

Make Sure Tests Test Content, Not Reading and Writing Ability

While we want students to develop reading and writing abilities as they are learning content, we do not want the lack of their abilities to mask what they have learned. Imagine a student who is a very poor reader and a very poor writer but who has worked hard in class, listened well, contributed to group discussions, and done everything else you could possibly want a good student to do. Now, imagine that student taking your test, 80 to 90 percent of which is material that was taught and reviewed in class. The student knows the information but, because of limited reading and writing abilities, cannot answer the questions and fails the test. As time goes on, these good students cease being good students. Why bother to listen and try if you learn the important information and fail the test anyway? For such students, consider the following possibilities:

Read the test to everyone. This may seem a little foolish to older students, but you can generally get by with it if you ask, "How many of you have ever gotten a question wrong on a test just because you read it wrong?" Most students will nod and groan as they remember this experience. Next explain, "When we take a test, we are sometimes anxious and when we get anxious, we can read things wrong. I am going to read the test to you to minimize that possibility."

Let students choose whether they would rather read the test to themselves or have it read to them. Say, "When I give a test, I really want to know how much you have learned. I don't want you to get something wrong because you misread it. Some people prefer to read the test to them- selves. Others like to have the test read to them. If you want to read the test to yourself, go to this side of the room. If you want the test read aloud, go to the other side." Then you, an aide, or a student volunteer can read the test in a low voice to those who so choose.

When students write, correct their answers for content only. Mechanics such as punctuation, capitalization, usage, and handwriting should not be allowed to detract from what a student has learned.

Teach Test-taking Skills

Figure 8.3 contains a list of test-taking strategies that are appropriate for middle-grade and older students. The strategies are best presented following an actual test. Return the papers to your students and direct their attention to specific test items as you explain each strategy. Demonstrate how you would perform each strategy. Point out the questions you think most difficult and explain that you would mark them and return to them later. As with all teaching, fade out your instruction by reminding students of the strategies before the next several tests and then gradually omitting mention of the strategies as your students become proficient with them.

Include Portfolio Assessments

Artists deposit samples of their work in portfolios for assessment purposes. These collections of work samples help artists and those interested in their work to determine their current level of attainment and the progress they have made. Teachers and students can also benefit from portfolio assess- ments. Portfolios are working folders, frequently kept in expandable files, that contain such items as student work selected by the student as well as the teacher, teachers' observational notes, students' notes about their own progress, and notes produced collaboratively by the student and teacher (Valencia, 1990; Valencia, McGinley, & Pearson, 1990). The variety of student work that is stored is immense, although caution must be used to ensure that the quantity is limited. Student work to be stored in a portfolio can consist of daily work, homework, tests, and projects. Good teachers, in preparation for parent conferences, have often produced folders of student work. In portfolio

General Strategies

1. Survey the test. Estimate its difficulty and plan your time for each section.
2. Underline the important words in each question. Be especially alert for closed terms such as *always, never,* and *most.*
3. Be sure to answer every required question (unless there is a penalty for guessing).
4. Do not spend too much time on any one question.

Strategies for Objective Tests

1. Answer the easy questions first. Mark the ones you skip and go back to them when you are ready. Remember that information contained in later items can help you answer previous items.
2. Look for the most correct answer when two items seem to be similar.
3. Narrow multiple-choice items to two, then make your choice when you are not sure of an answer.
4. Rephrasing questions and answering questions in your head before inspecting the choices frequently helps.
5. Change your answers only if you misunderstood the question the first time or if you are absolutely sure that your first response was wrong.
6. False items on true or false tests usually contain one essential word that converts the item into an overstatement, an understatement, or a misstatement.

Strategies for Essay Tests

1. Briefly outline all answers before writing. Jot down key terms and then add to those terms while working on your answers.
2. Include only information that you believe is correct.
3. Plan your time for each question and stick to that schedule.
4. Include topic sentences and supporting details in each paragraph.
5. Proofread your writing.

FIGURE 8.3   Test-Taking Strategies

assessment, however, students help decide some of what goes into their portfolios. They thus learn the important skill of self-evaluation.

The value of a portfolio approach is that what is graded comes mainly from what is produced on an everyday basis. It is a somewhat systematic way to make daily work count more than periodic, contrived tests that may distort students' overall level of functioning.

DO IT TOGETHER

Form small groups and decide how the grading policy in the class you currently are taking compares with the one described in this section. What would you recommend changing? What would you recommend keeping?

WHAT IS THE PLACE OF READING
AND WRITING IN AN ACTIVITY COURSE?

Examine these two lists of courses:

List A	*List B*
Economics	Art
English	French
Geography	Mathematics
History	Music
Physical science	Physical education

How are the two lists different? Many people would describe the set of courses in List A as "textbook" courses and those in List B as "activity" courses. This means that, as they are usually taught, the courses in List B have students participating in one or more subject-related activities and reading or writing very little. In art, students usually draw, paint, sculpt, or study pieces of art. In the beginning year of foreign language study, students usually engage in speaking and listening to conversation or completing grammar exercises. In mathematics, students usually study algorithms, theorems, and postulates; work computational problems; or produce proofs. In music, students usually sing, play a musical instrument, or listen to music. In physical education, students usually engage in a sport, game, or physical exercise.

In contrast, the courses in List A have more academic content to be delivered through lecture, discussion, and note taking as well as through reading the course text and library books. Students taking the subjects in List A often write reports and answer essay questions on tests.

After making the distinction between "textbook" and "activity" courses, some people conclude that "activity" courses are and should be essentially devoid of student reading or writing. Many people, however, would examine Lists A and B and see another distinction. They would see the courses in List B as "talent" courses. In other words, they would remember either the difficulty or the ease they tended to have with some of those courses and attribute it to the lack or presence of innate or natural ability. Why is it that people usually consider themselves naturally good at music, art, sports, math, and the like but attribute their learning of history, English, geography, and the like more to hard work and study strategies? While we may have trouble reading or writing to learn, we still realize that we can expend more time and use better learning strategies to improve our learning. With activity courses, we seem either to learn them or to be at a loss about what to do.

You see, all the List A and List B courses have strengths and weaknesses. List A subjects are strong in that they can be learned through effort and studying; List B subjects are weak in that the rich get richer and the poor get poorer. List B subjects, however, are strong in that they are more interesting and learnable for students with a broad range of reading and writing abilities; List A subjects are weak in that they require a certain sophistication with literacy and study strategies before they can be learned well.

While they cannot and should not be taught exactly alike, List A courses should be taught with more activities than is typical and List B courses should be taught with more reading and writing than is typical. These changes would mean that students in courses with academic content would participate more in such activities as simulations, reading narratives, watching movies, doing experiments, taking field trips, and using interactive video and educational software. Students in activity courses would think more about why and how they do activities and how one would apply them in other contexts to solve problems. When people read and write about what they are learning, whether content or activity, it helps them contextualize their learning. However abstract and pure a concept is presented, it came from somewhere and relates to other concepts. Reading and writing help students learn this history and these relationships. Writing and reading cause students to connect, predict, organize, form an image, monitor, generalize, and evaluate in ways they may not otherwise do.

Many of the content teaching strategies we discussed in the first seven chapters would help students in activity courses become more introspective and communicative about what they are learning. Teachers of activity courses can teach meaning vocabulary well so that their students can read, write, listen, and speak intelligently about issues, problems, and applications. Art students, for example, benefit from writing about technique as a means of deciding what they really believe.

Literacy in an activity class.

Teachers of activity courses can seek out content area literature that would help contextualize for students what might otherwise be a trivial exercise. An article, for example, that shows how surveying uses geometry and trigonometry to measure natural land areas, including hills and lakes, can help students learn those subjects better, especially if they lack a natural interest and ability in those courses.

Teachers of activity courses can use book and research projects to broaden their students' understanding of the history and varied applications of the activities they are learning. Music students benefit from researching the uses of music in advertising and marketing, worship, and entertainment.

Teachers of activity courses can use content journals to help their students become self-monitoring about their learning as well as to provide feedback to the teacher. French students, for example, could write in English about their learning of French to assist both them and their teacher to facilitate their acquisition of conversational French.

It also seems that neither List A's nor List B's courses typically prepare students for the real world of work. Because of the lack of activities, List A's courses rarely have an application for anyone who is not a scholar by profession. Because of the lack of reading and writing, List B's courses do not prepare people for today's business, military, artistic, and government organizations.

The hierarchical nature of today's organizations breeds more reports and memoranda and thereby increases the proportion of time a person spends communicating with others through reading and writing, even when one was hired as an accountant, an engineer, a record producer, a music director for an orchestra, or a professor in an art department.

If you see the courses you teach or will teach as strictly content courses, you can balance the information you present with opportunities to apply it in real or vicarious activities. If you see the courses you teach or will teach as strictly activity courses, you can balance the activities you model, guide, and evaluate with opportunities to think about these activities and communicate aspects about them to others.

LISTEN/LOOK AND LEARN

Visit classes in two different content areas, one a class in which reading and writing are traditionally expected and one a class that is more activity-oriented. Observe the students and decide if both classes could learn some things from the other class's approach. Could the "textbook" class do with some more active learning? Were there missed opportunities for quick and helpful reading and writing activities in the activity class?

WHERE CAN I FIND THE TIME TO TEACH EVERYTHING EVERYONE WANTS ME TO TEACH?

No teacher has enough time to do everything he or she wants to do. Therefore you must set priorities. You set priorities by deciding what is most important and making sure that you use your in-class time to accomplish that. You set priorities by assigning less important material and skipping relatively unimportant material altogether.

But you have still more decisions to make: How much time each week can you spend in activities that teach content through reading and writing? How much time can you spend increasing student vocabulary? Finally, which teaching strategies appeal most to you? Teachers, being human, have individual preferences and styles in their teaching as in all other facets of their lives. Some of our teaching strategies for improving reading and writing will seem very "do-able" to you and others will fall into the "I just can't see myself doing that" category. Once you know what content you will stress and how much time you can give to the various literacy goals, choose strategies that particularly appeal to you to reach these goals.

One warning is in order for anyone trying a new teaching strategy: Do not expect great success the first time. It takes a while to get things into a workable routine. This is one reason the first year of teaching is so hectic. Why, when doing something you have never done before with students who have never done it before, would you expect everything to go smoothly? We recommend the rule of "Three strikes and you're out." Try each strategy three times with the same group. During the three trials observe your students' behavior and learning and your own comfort. Then decide if the strategy is one that you want to continue. Be aware that some teaching strategies require a higher energy level and more teacher involvement than others. As you decide which strategies to use and how often, consider your own physical and psychological needs. No one can perform on center stage for six hours every day. Try to stagger the teaching strategies that demand high teacher intensity with those that are less demanding. Balance new strategies with more comfortable familiar ones.

Teaching is a lot like cooking. We often get in a rut of fixing the same recipes week after week. Sometimes we continue to fix recipes even when we are tired of eating them. We have other recipes; we may even have a little box of ones to try someday. But new recipes require more preparation as we make the shopping list, more thought as we prepare them, and more risk. We worry "What if it flops?" "What if everyone hates it?" Trying one new recipe every so often is a compromise that does not demand too much of the cook but holds the promise of better meals to come.

LOOKING BACK

Teaching is at the same time one of the most fulfilling and one of the most frustrating jobs in the world. Watching students catch on, get excited, accomplish something they did not think they could, or discover a talent they did not know they had is what keeps good teachers coming back. The frustration comes from some of the issues discussed in this chapter. There are no "quick fixes" for the problems discussed, but there are some partial solutions. The key ideas in this chapter are partial solutions to some critical issues: (1) How can I tell if reading materials are appropriate for my students? (2) How can I motivate my students to read and write? (3) How can I fairly assess what they are learning and give appropriate grades? (4) What is the place of reading and writing in an activity course? and (5) Where can I find the time to teach everything everyone wants me to teach?

ADD TO YOUR JOURNAL

Reflect upon the five key issues and the partial solutions offered in this chapter and decide what you think: What other solutions have you seen teachers use to resolve these difficult issues? What solutions would you like to try? Which issue impinges most directly on your teaching and which issue is really not an issue for you? Finally, come up with two or three other issues not discussed in this chapter. What partial solutions can you think of to help resolve your own issues?

REFERENCES

Fry, E. (1977). Fry's Readability Graph: Clarifications, validity, and extension to level 17. *Journal of Reading, 21*, 242–252.

Good, T. L., & Brophy, J. E. (1991). *Looking in classrooms* (5th ed.). New York: Harper-Collins.

Moore, D. W., & Murphy, A. G. (1987). Selection of materials. In D. E. Alvermann, D. W. Moore, & M. W. Conley (Eds.), *Research within reach: Secondary school reading* (pp. 94–108). Newark, DE: International Reading Association.

Valencia, S. (1990). A portfolio approach to classroom reading assessment: The whys, whats, and hows. *The Reading Teacher, 43*, 338–340.

Valencia, S. W., McGinley, W., & Pearson, P. D. (1990). Assessing reading and writing. In G. Duffy (Ed.), *Reading in the middle school* (2nd ed.) (pp. 124–153). Newark, DE: International Reading Association.

ADDITIONAL READINGS

These are three somewhat detailed presentations of how to evaluate textbooks:

Tulley, M. A., & Farr, R. (1990). Textbook evaluation and selection. In D. E. Elliott & A. Woodward (Eds.), *Textbooks and schooling in the United States* (Eighty-ninth Yearbook of the National Society for the Study of Education, Pt. 1) (pp. 162–177). Chicago: National Society for the Study of Education.

Tyson-Bernstein, H. (1988). *A conspiracy of good intentions*. Washington, DC: Council for Basic Education.

Zakaluk, B. L., & Samuels, S. J. (1988). *Readability: Its past, present, and future*. Newark, DE: International Reading Association.

Clear descriptions of research findings relative to motivation can be found in the following syntheses:

Ames, R., & Ames, C. (1991). Motivation and effective teaching. In L. Idol & B. F. Jones (Eds.). *Educational values and cognitive instruction: Implications for reform* (pp. 247–271). Hillsdale, NJ: Erlbaum.

Brophy, J. (1987). Synthesis of research on strategies for motivating students to learn. *Educational Leadership, 45,* 40–48.

The first reference presents numerous practical suggestions for grading students' performance in reading and writing; the second reviews research on the impact of classroom grading practices:

Collins, C. (1989). Grading practices that increase teacher effectiveness. *Clearing House, 63,* 167–169.

Crooks, T. J. (1988). The impact of classroom evaluation practices on students. *Review of Educational Research, 58,* 438–481.

Performance assessments are becoming common in schools; these are good references on this methodology:

Belanoff, P., & Dickson, M. (Eds.). (1991). *Portfolios: Process and product.* Portsmouth, NH: Boynton/Cook.

Tierney, R. J., Carter, M. A., & Desai, L. E. (1991). *Portfolio assessment in the reading-writing classroom.* Norwood, MA: Christopher-Gordon.

Using performance assessment. (1992). *Educational Leadership, 49*(8) [Special issue].

The second half of this research review describes classroom conditions that reward control of students and the curriculum; teachers need to cope with these conditions when implementing meaningful, student-centered instruction:

Alvermann D. E., & Moore, D. W. (1991). Secondary school reading. In R. Barr, M. L. Kamil, P. Mosenthal, & P. D. Pearson (Eds.), *Handbook of reading research* (vol. 2) (pp. 951–983). White Plains, NY: Longman.

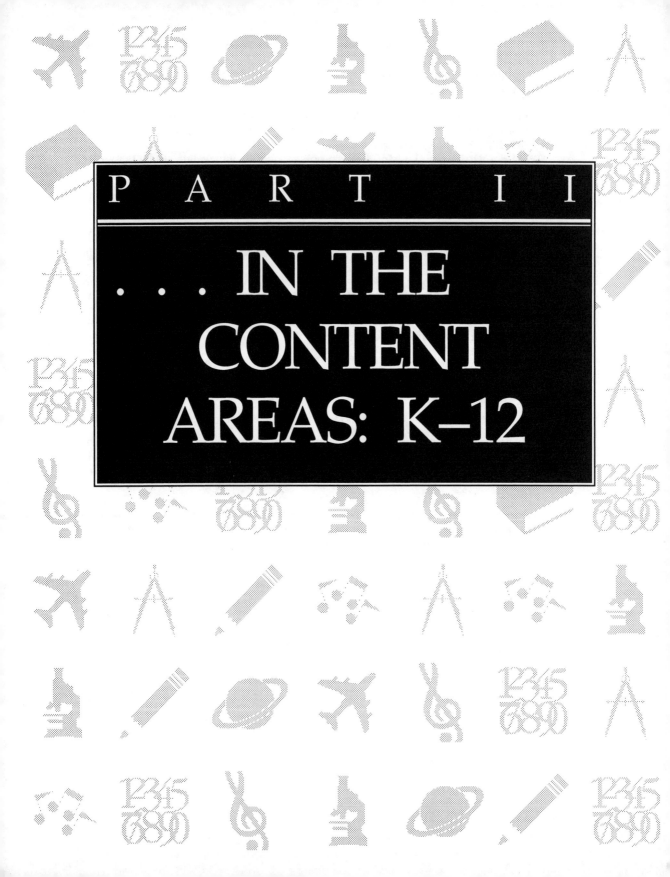

PART II

. . . IN THE CONTENT AREAS: K–12

P art II of this book illustrates how the principles and methods of instruction described in Part I can actually be implemented in the classroom. The information is presented in the form of a chronological narrative through fictional teachers' journals. This part of the book demonstrates how teachers might integrate the many aspects of reading and writing in the content areas throughout an entire school year. Part I compartmentalized information according to topics, but life in classrooms is not so orderly. Teachers must balance instruction in comprehension, vocabulary, literature, writing, study skills, and research within each day and across 180 days of school. Part II provides perspective on how teachers make this balance work.

In the next chapters you will meet four fictional teachers. Belle Lance teaches second grade. She is entrusted with the crucial task of getting youngsters off to a good start. Belle's students have only rudimentary content reading and writing skills, and she must launch them on the way to independence. Along the way, she must develop students' understanding of such subject matter as transportation, measurement of time, the five senses, and human wants versus needs. Connie Tent is a fifth-grade teacher. Her students are more sophisticated than Belle's, but they still have much to learn. Connie directs her students to information in the content areas and likewise furthers the development of her students' independence. Hugh Mann teaches the humanities in secondary school; he is assigned three sections of American history and two sections of sophomore English. Hugh is a second-year teacher who takes a little longer than Belle or Connie to teach as well as he would like. Do not be alarmed by how traditional and uninspired he is at the beginning of the year. We think it is important to show that a relatively inexperienced and conservative teacher can make real progress toward more balanced and effective content instruction. Finally, Annie Mull teaches high-school biology and consumer math. She must both deliver information and teach students to acquire information independently. In addition, she balances a process approach with a textbook approach to biology and must teach students to solve word problems in math.

You may want to read only one of the fictional accounts that follow if you are primarily interested in only one grade level. However, reading all the chapters will provide you with insight into how teachers develop students' thinking processes and literacy skills across the grades. Knowing what students have encountered earlier in school and what they will encounter in the future provides perspective on their present needs. Furthermore, instructional strategies for one grade level frequently are applicable at other grade levels.

As you read what follows, we hope you will learn how teachers engage students in meaningful instruction. We hope you will see how instruction builds and changes in one grade level and across grade levels. Perhaps most important, we hope you will evaluate the information presented here and apply what seems most sensible when you teach in your own classroom.

CHAPTER 9

Second Grade

A U G U S T

Every August I experience the same excitement that I did 33 years ago, when I first began school at age 5. Paul, my husband, laughs at me, saying, "Belle, you're as bad as the kids about wanting to get back to school!" I guess I am, but that is a much nicer feeling than the reluctance I see from some other teachers in our school district. I have heard about "teacher burnout," but my own theory is that burnout generally occurs when you are frustrated with your job and no longer feel you are accomplishing anything. Fortunately, I do feel successful, and I am grateful that I can work at something I truly love! Nevertheless, when I come back to school each August to ready my room for September, I have a mixture of feelings: apprehension about who I will be "living with" for the next nine months and excitement about teaching yet another group of youngsters to read and write easily and successfully.

This year I guess I am even more charged up than usual since I just completed my master's degree a couple of weeks ago, and I signed up to be one of our school's representatives for the school district's writing project! My thesis addressed the effects of using content area subjects to help improve children's reading skills. As a result of my findings, I am convinced that I need to integrate more reading and writing with the content of social studies and science in my classroom.

I've been sitting here for the past week, trying out one schedule after another, and it's not as easy as I had anticipated. I think I need to start this year as usual, with set times for science or social studies instruction every day, using textbooks as part of the reading material. If all goes well, I may come up with another plan for later in the year. I have sat here for a week surrounded by pieces of paper with lists of important elements to include in my classroom this year, and the problem has been trying to come up with a workable plan that will include them all.

Thinking Processes

First of all, there are nine thinking processes that I must systematically and frequently include in my lessons: call up, predict, organize, connect, form an image, monitor, generalize, evaluate, and apply. By incorporating each of the nine thinking processes on a regular basis, I will be teaching the content areas and developing skills that students can use in life as well as school.

Independence

Most importantly, I am going to emphasize student independence in learning. It really frosts my cookies to have someone I meet for the first time comment that they couldn't tolerate my profession because they wouldn't want to wipe noses and tie shoes all day. What an idea people must have of primary-grade students! Admittedly, these students cannot do what fifth-graders can, but we teachers can certainly expect that they be responsible for their learning to an ever-increasing degree. In fact, teachers who do not foster independence in learning are condemning their students to a "learning welfare" system that children will find hard to break out of later on. My battle cry for the year will be, "Get those kids off welfare!"

But, I ask myself, how can I meet these glorious goals of mine this year? I suppose the answer will unfold as the year progresses. What follows is my daily schedule, but I reserve the right to alter it should I find it necessary or appealing to do so!

Schedule

8:15–8:45	Attendance, news sharing, plan the day		Tuesday, Thursday
8:45–10:00	Reading groups		Writing groups and conferences—Friday
	Learning centers	12:30–1:00	Art—Monday
	Writing		P.E.—Tuesday, Thursday
10:00–10:15	Morning recess		Writing groups and conferences—Wednesday
10:15–10:30	Read to class or do storytelling		Music—Friday
10:30–11:15	Math groups	1:00–1:30	Language arts minilessons
	Learning centers		SSR
	Writing	1:30–2:15	Learning centers
11:15–11:45	Lunch		Independent work time
11:45–12:00	Read to students	2:15–2:40	Read to students
12:00–12:30	Science lessons—Monday, Wednesday		Review the day
	Social studies lessons—		Prepare to leave
		2:45	Dismissal

Learning Centers

I have designed many independent learning activities for the learning centers, where I will use tapes, picture directions, and color codes to help students who are not yet fluent readers. Students can turn on the tape recorder where I have recorded directions for certain activities, which frees me from having to explain everything in person. I also make use of rebus pictures, using pictures of scissors where they are to cut, and so forth. Each center is color-coded so that students can tell where to go for the different assignments given in their daily work folder. The math, science, and social studies centers contain materials that will help students learn more about the units of study we'll do this year. The eight centers I have placed around the perimeter of the room are a library corner, a language arts center, a math center, a tape and TV center, a computer center, an art center, a social studies center, and a science center. Occasionally I will create an extra center, such as one with cooking utensils for when we have classroom cooking.

In the morning, students will rotate among teacher-directed group work, learning centers, writing activities, and practice activities. In the afternoon, since I won't have reading or math groups then, I can circulate among those in the centers and those doing seatwork in order to do some over-the-shoulder teaching as children need questions answered. Each child's practice activities will include assignments to let everyone practice the skills already taught in reading group, as well as the concepts introduced in science and social studies units.

Literature Additionally, I plan to read to the children at least once every day, and I will give them a daily opportunity to read materials of their own choice. The reading and listening materials will be drawn from the finest of children's story books as well as from informational books. Such models of clear and interesting writing will demonstrate to my students how to organize their own writing. Storytelling and oral reports are two other regular features that I will use frequently to model oral composition techniques. By beginning the day with sharing of current events topics, they can develop better skills in content area reporting. In addition, they have a reason to pay attention to what is happening in the world around them.

I'm so pleased I got the tables that I asked for, rather than individual desks. All of my students' work materials will be kept in individual, brightly colored cardboard boxes stored around the edge of the room, but the tables will allow a lot more flexibility in grouping students for different activities.

This journal will focus on how I plan to incorporate reading and writing in the content areas. It certainly cannot represent everything that goes on each day in a classroom. Well, only a couple of more items to put up on the bulletin board in the back of the room and then I can call it quits until the children arrive. Oh! I am getting so excited!

S E P T E M B E R

And so September is over. Getting the children used to the routines took up an enormous amount of time; schooling is not innately understood. A good part of the month was spent just in helping them learn the appropriate behaviors to use in learning centers and at their seats.

Thematic Units So I could get to know all of them better, our first social studies unit was entitled All about Us. I participated, too, partly so they would learn who I am, partly so I could model what each step of the project required. Before going into the specifics of the unit, however, I want to record some of what I learned about them from the unit as well as from their school records.

Every year I think I have gotten the most unusual group ever, and this year is no exception. (Can this condition continue forever?) I have *two* sets of twins. Michael and Michelle are both supportive and independent, rather unusual for twins, so I suspect they will have no difficulty being in the same classroom. But I fear that Steven and Stephanie are another story: Stephanie functions at a much lower level than Steven does, and he constantly picks on her for missing questions, turning in sloppy or late work, and not reading as well as he does. I suggested to their parents that they need to be separated, for both their sakes, and the parents would not hear of it! They think that Stephanie needs Steven to challenge her. None of my arguments could con-

Special Learners

vince them otherwise, though they did agree to help try to tone down Steven. Other students who will be a challenge are Kazu and Mariane. Kazu has just come to the United States from Korea and speaks no English. Mariane is somewhat better off since her family came to this country from Brazil last year, though at home they spoke mainly Portuguese until she started kindergarten. I speak some Spanish, and since Portuguese and Spanish are very similar, we manage to communicate. For Kazu, however, I checked a Korean dictionary out of the public library. I've also met with his parents, who speak some English, to learn from them some common phrases I will need such as, "Do you understand?" "How do you say ___ in Korean?," and courtesy phrases such as "Please" and "Thank you." Carlos is another student who is not proficient in using English, though he understands much of what is said to him.

Dave and Jim, neighbors and friends from birth, are two students who did not have an easy first-grade year. They seem not too interested in school except for P.E., recess, and lunch. At the other extreme are those who came to second grade reading very well. John, David, Pat, and Sharon seem to enjoy everything we do, probably because they understand what is going on and why. I am glad that our school system doesn't provide gifted education for primary-grade students since I believe, based on my reading, that there are no special methods or materials for exceptionally bright students. Good classroom instruction should challenge all students to higher levels of functioning and thinking. That is certainly my goal. My other ten students seem "average" and are moving along well. It's not easy trying to plan lessons for so many levels of students. Even the "average" ones are so diverse that they certainly cannot all be treated alike.

Social Studies Thematic Unit

The All about Us unit took all of September since we worked on it only on Tuesdays and Thursdays. The unit is from our school's social studies curriculum, building from the individual to families to neighborhoods to the community at large to our state, nation, and world. The focus in our unit is on the uniqueness of each person as well as the many things all of us have in

Literature

common. Children learned about these two concepts in myriad ways. Many literature books, both old favorites and newer ones, address both concepts. For the whole month we have been reading books like *There's a Nightmare in My Closet; Leo the Late Bloomer; Frog and Toad Together; It's Me, Hippo!; Frederick; I Have a Sister—My Sister Is Deaf;* and *The Triplets.* In addition, I brought in such concept books as *A Snake Is Totally Tail; Is It Hard? Is It Easy?; Sugaring*

Time; Handtalk: An ABC of Finger Spelling and Sign Language; and *People.* I used those books both for this unit and for our science unit on the five senses—a nice compatible set of units to work on simultaneously. These books point out the similarities among people as well as provide information about those who, due to certain handicaps, must deal with life differently. The children had all expressed curiosity about Sharon's thick glasses, asking how she could see through them since they were unable to. Jakeitha's wheelchair also was a subject of study as students learned how many things she could do as well as they could without the use of her legs.

Thinking Processes

Meaning Vocabulary

Collaborative Groups

The All about Us unit was introduced by talking about *alike* and *different.* To start things off, students were asked to call up the names of types of transportation. Though the content seemed way off the topic, I wanted to use items that could be easily classified by children in a variety of ways. The various types, *boats, cars, trucks, trains, planes,* and so on, were listed on a chart. We talked about how all of the things on the chart were alike, with me listing, as students dictated, how the things were alike. Then students were assigned to groups and told to look for pictures or models of the different forms of transportation listed or of new ones that they discovered. In this scavenger hunt activity, I planned the groups so that each consisted both of very capable students and of those who needed more guidance. Students were able to use independent seatwork time for this activity on both Tuesday and Wednesday, as well as checking at home for pictures and models on Tuesday and Wednesday nights.

On Thursday, each group brought its pictures and models to school. I used the big bulletin board on the side of the classroom to pin up all the transportation pictures, with the models on a table underneath. I had cut apart all the names of the types of transportation from the chart, and we placed them by the appropriate pictures or models. Then I asked if they could organize or regroup them in any other way. Total silence met this question. But I waited it out. After ten seconds, Pat asked, "Do you mean by how many wheels they have?" We had quite a discussion about wheels and had to turn to several reference sources to settle the debates that arose. I find this a good way to model using references to answer questions that we have. That broke the dam, and the students realized that there were many possible ways to group the transportation pictures they had found. Next they grouped all the red pictures and models together, all the green ones, and so on, regardless of the number of wheels. Then they grouped all the forms of transportation by how many people they could carry—one, a few, or many. A fourth grouping consisted of sorting types by where they traveled—air, land, or water.

Social Studies Thematic Unit

So that they would apply their new understanding of grouping to our unit of study, I gave a list of each person's name in our class, including mine, to each group and asked them to think of at least two ways of organizing that could show how people are alike and at least two ways to show how they are different. On the following Tuesday they sorted us all into diverse groups by gender, hair color, and so on. They also put Jakeitha, Sharon, Michael, Michelle, and me into a group they labeled "black people." This activity helped them to organize their world, one of the essential thinking processes.

Writing   Along with organizing, we worked on writing activities. They each compiled a book of facts about themselves, as part of my content language experience lessons. I read a number of biographies and autobiographies to them. After reading several, I explained they were going to write autobiographies. They had to draw pictures of their family, home, pets, friends, favorite things to do, and so on. Under each picture, they had to tell about the picture.

After each person had completed his or her book, they all had to number each page and write in the numeral on the labeled table of contents page I had given them. They worked on this activity on the Wednesday and Thursday afternoons that I had set aside for writing conferences and groups. Within their small groups, they helped one another to copy over their sentences correctly and make sure that page numbers were in order and matched the table of contents page.

Interviewing   I also gave the children five questions to go home and ask their parents about, one at a time, over a three-week period. I have found that if you give children several questions at once, they frequently forget both the questions and the answers. However, if I give only one question on each day that we have social studies, students can generally remember to ask the questions. These five questions became the basis for the single paragraphs about each student, which they dictated and were then placed on the bulletin board along with their pictures. The five questions were as follows: When were you born? What was your parents' favorite thing about you when you were a baby? What did you like to do best when you were little? What was the funniest thing you did when you were little? What is the best thing about you now? Each question was turned into a statement using sentence stems again, such as "I was born . . ." and "When I was a baby. . . ." The com-

Writing   piled statements were then written right after one another to make the autobiographical paragraph. Not all the children could read their completed paragraphs, but they surely tried! And they loved having the paragraphs read to them. I used these paragraphs frequently during reading group time throughout the month since the paragraphs were planned to use much of the same vocabulary I was trying to teach and since they were intrinsically interesting.

Math   The number of mathematics tie-ins I could do was amazing! We had graphs all over that room—who was native to the state and who had moved from somewhere else, as well as such family facts as siblings, pets, number of family members, favorite family foods, and at-home chores. A few Venn diagrams allowed children to see how they could be part of several groupings simultaneously.

Special Learners   There are so many children representing various cultural groups that I have also been reading to them daily from folktales. For most of the children, I have had no problem finding folktales for their culture groups, and when I did find it difficult, I contacted parents for help. Two different parents came in to the class and told stories that had been told to them as children. It made those stories especially interesting to the class. One of the things we have noted as we discuss the stories is how themes are used over and over and how the characters experience the same feelings as we do. Children are learning to value differences as well as our shared humanity.

Science Thematic Unit

The science unit on the five senses was also interesting and fun. So many activities can help develop the nine thinking processes! We made charts as the children called up things they could hear. I wrote their responses on chart paper, allowing enough room for them to add illustrations. Another chart was used when I told them that I would be writing down words and they had to find the organization I was using and predict which label would be placed on it. For this activity, I wrote a word and asked them to predict another word to fit the category I was thinking of. If they guessed correctly, I wrote that word; if not, I said, "That is not an example." No one was to say the name of the category yet; I wanted to get many examples of each category so that nearly all the children would be in a frenzy claiming to know the category. The first thing I wrote was *ice cream*. The first discarded guess was *candy*. The second guess, *ice cube*, was added to the list. After several more guesses, both examples and nonexamples, we came up with a list that they all agreed could be labeled Things That Feel Cold, including ice cream, ice cube, snow, my dog's nose, rocks, and a glass of milk.

Thinking Processes

Writing

They also made books for this unit: a feeling book of textures, a seeing book of colors, and a hearing book of sounds. For each of these they had to call up possibilities and organize them (for example, putting all loud sounds together). They were constantly connecting what they already knew to new information they were gathering. They then applied that knowledge by creating books. As before, they took some of the group writing time to work on their books and to help one another evaluate how well they had accomplished the assignment. At the end of the month, I used the various books they had made for the science unit as reading material during reading group time.

Reading

O C T O B E R

Word Wall

Many of the children who come to school are able to count to ten or more in a rote fashion. But asking them to connect that knowledge to sentences with numbers in them is quite a leap for many students. Thus, I have made a Word Wall above the chalkboard just for math. Two other walls contain the list of commonly used and high-interest words that we use for writing. On the number Word Wall, I have the numerals 1 through 10 right beside the words and pictures of the corresponding number of objects. Other words, such as geometry terms, will be added as needed. I have also placed $+$, $-$, $<$, $>$, and $=$ up there with the corresponding definitions of each symbol. They love playing Be a Mind Reader, in which I try to get them to guess the math word or symbol I am thinking of. Following is an excerpted version of one such exercise:

Be a Mind Reader

ME: It's on the Word Wall. Write your guess on the first line.

Ray wrote "<."

ME: It's a numeral.

Ray wrote "6."

ME: It's more than one.

Ray wrote "6" again.

ME: It's less than six.

Ray wrote "5."

ME: You get this when you add two and three.

Ray excitedly wrote "5" again, waving his hand frantically in the air. He was among a group of three who had correctly read my mind before the final clue! He was proud.

Word Problems Since the math groups are doing addition, I decided to try yet another way to get them to understand symbols and number words better, as well as to use more writing. I had them convert the number sentences in their math series into small word problems. The first ones were very simple. Using **Writing** sentence stems, I gave them a formula for writing number sentences as word problems. For adding, I gave them the following sentences to fill in with numerals of their choice:

I have ____ books. I got ____ more.

Now I have ____ books.

For subtraction, they have this one:

I had ____ toys. I gave ____ away.

Now I have ____ toys.

Dave and Jim wanted me to exchange the nouns in the two problems; they would rather give away books than toys!

The children were told to make up their own word problems as the final step. They enjoy coming up with unusual items to add and subtract, challenging one another to further heights of ridiculousness, especially in this month of ghoulish happenings! Here is one of David's that made the rounds to great appreciation, invented spellings and all:

I have three vanshing vampiers. I got three more.

Now I have six vanshing vampiers. But how can I have six if they keep vanshing?

Twice a week, all the children bring to their math group a word problem that they have created. These are exchanged, and as a part of their independent work, the children must write each word problem as a number sentence and draw an illustration to demonstrate the word problem using sets. They may go to the person who did the original problem in order to discover what certain words mean. This is especially important for the children who cannot yet read more than a few words. They are allowed to use pictures in place of the words in their problems. Kazu, who understood David's word problem, was fascinated with the notion of vampires, even though David himself has only a fuzzy idea of what vampires are. I feel good about how much children are monitoring, evaluating, and applying when they do these exercises.

We also had great fun with an activity I found in *Books You Can Count On: Linking Mathematics and Literature*. As the authors of that book directed, I read the poem "Mice" by Rose Fyleman and had children work together on the worksheet shown in Figure 9.1. Reading their explanations of how they solved the problem gave me lots of interesting insights. One group started drawing mouse bodies and adding body parts while crossing them off the worksheet. Another group figured out that with four legs and two eyes to a mouse, they could group legs and eyes to see how many mice were possible. A third group started cutting up the worksheet and glued mouse parts to bodies they drew. I was very impressed with how they went about solving this problem and then explaining their solution.

Social Studies Thematic Unit   In order to help the children better understand their role in their families, our social studies unit pursued several different activities this month. First we had to discuss the definition of a family. Since there are so many families today which do not fit the traditional two-parent structure, we defined *family* as a group of related or unrelated people who live together because they care

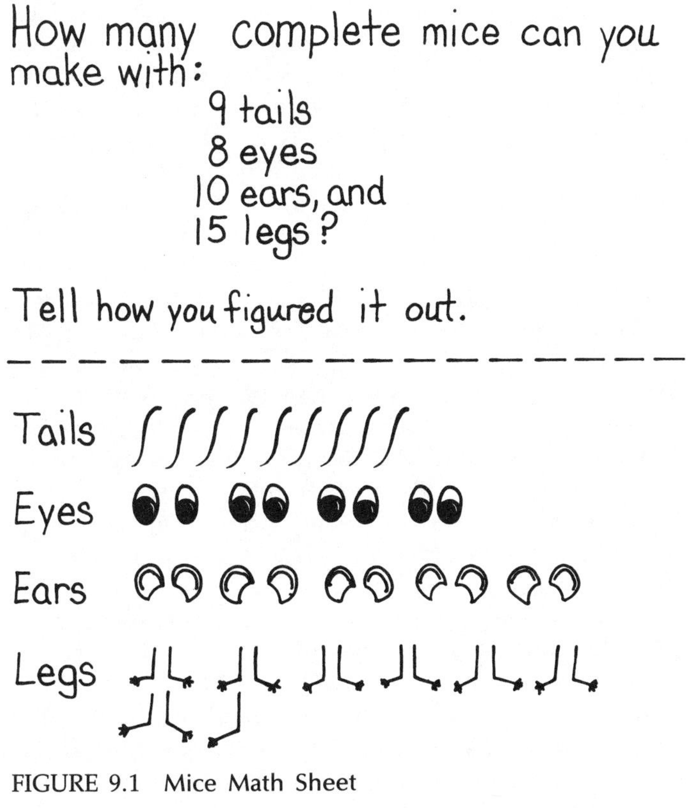

FIGURE 9.1 Mice Math Sheet

about one another and who try to help one another in a variety of ways. Families could consist of any number of adults and children. Each child then drew a picture of his or her family and wrote a few sentences telling how the members showed their care for one another.

Writing

Organizing Information

We took the information from last month's graphs (how many people in the family, chores, adults' jobs, and so on) and put them into a data chart with questions along the top and children's names down the left side.

Writing

Using the data chart entries, children wrote paragraphs about themselves and their families. No names were written on the paragraphs, and I read them aloud to the whole class during social studies time as we sat in front of the data chart, trying to predict with each new sentence who the person could be. They loved the puzzle aspect of this listening comprehension minilesson, which allowed them to review the questions asked and connect the answers with a name. Here is Dave's edited paragraph:

> Me and my dad, we live together. Dad, he drives a bus for the city. I have lots of stuff to do at home like take out the garbage and wash the dishes sometimes and dust the tables and stuff and help my dad wash clothes at the laundromat. I have always lived in this apartment even before my mom died. The most interesting thing about me and my dad is that we are going to win the lottery and go to Hawaii on a vacation for two weeks!

Science Thematic Unit

This month's science unit dealt with the calendar: How many hours in a day, days in a week, weeks in a month, days in a month, months in a year, and days in a year? Talk about some tough concepts! We do our daily calendar during the opening exercises each day. You know, the "Today is Monday. It is sunny" type of activity. A child, with help where needed, names the month, the day, and the year. Whenever a new month begins, together we count how many days there are in it and count other items like how many Mondays there are or how many birthdays there are in the month. Nevertheless, the concept of "what is a week" is still tough to communicate. To many of them, a week is five days; weekends don't count since there is no school! I've saved all the calendars for the current year from my husband Paul's bakery business, plus the ones the banks give away, and others I came across—it doesn't matter one whit that most of the months have been gone for some time now. The children dismantled the calendars and then organized the pages by putting all the Januarys together and so on. After the pages were all grouped by the twelve months, I assigned two children per month and told them to figure out how all the Januarys, Februarys, et cetera, were the same. They discovered to their delight that regardless of the picture on the calendar, all the Januarys had 31 days listed.

Meaning Vocabulary

Collaborative Groups

Organizing Information

The months were then grouped by cold ones and hot ones, fitting some, like October and April, in between. We also spent some time talking about events during the past year, birthdays, Christmas and Hanukkah, Thanksgiving, Fourth of July, and so on. What kind of weather were we having then? Did the event happen long ago or not so long ago? The relativity of some of these terms only added to their confusion. When they said Christmas happened during a cold time, we went to the cold months group and found

December. They always had trouble with the idea that all months don't have the same number of days. They'll begin to understand that concept a little better when they learn to divide 365 by 12! Their other concern was why all months don't start on Sunday (or Monday, if they still think of five-day weeks), but they are slowly beginning to understand. We made a continuous calendar for the bulletin board that shows the first day of each new month right beside the last day of the old one. So they are beginning to realize that each month is connected to the one before it.

Content Journals To help them understand days in the week better, I had them all keep journals for the month. During the school week, they wrote in their journals here, but each child took two pages home to write in over the weekend. I had dittoed off the journal pages, so that each one had the date already on it; all they had to do was fill in the day of the week and then write at least one sentence about something that happened to them, or that they saw, or about the weather. Naturally, Dave, Jim, and Ray consistently forgot their journals over the weekend and also forgot to bring back the sheets of paper on Mondays! I gave them extra sheets I had made, so that they could make up something for Saturday and Sunday during their Monday work time. At the end of the month, we stapled all the sheets together with a cover for each identifying it as the October journal. I know that many parents will prize these short anecdotes in years to come. And I do believe they are gaining some sense of what a week is compared to a month. Journal writing has been highly touted in this writing workshop I've been attending and does seem to work for kids.

N O V E M B E R

Despite the onslaught of the holiday season, which really begins right after Halloween, it has been a great month. The children are fairly well set in our routines now, so that they know what they are to do and when and, more **Independence** important, why. I make it a point to explain how the learning center materials will help them to learn. I have found it is worth it to take that little bit of extra time to help children understand why they are doing something.

SSR On my schedule of sustained silent reading (SSR) and read-aloud time, I am now taking ten minutes for reading aloud, with the children having up to five minutes of reading or examining books quietly on their own. I have found that since some of them are not actually reading during this time, they may need two books to "read" during SSR. They spend their time looking at the pictures and even matching some words they know with ones found in the books. "Sustained silent reading" is probably a misnomer with these second-graders, since there is a low roar of "mumble reading" going on. Young children find it nearly impossible to read silently, as do immature older readers and readers of materials too difficult for them. That's all right; at least everyone is engaged with books, even Jim and Dave!

Social Studies Thematic Unit Holidays are big events to children, associated as they are with changes in routines, presents, special happenings, and clothing. Therefore, as an ongoing miniunit in social studies this year, we are studying the various holidays associated with each month. Some months are chock full of holidays, while others are sparse. I have had to do some digging to come up with interesting holidays to study. However, October, November, and December are all full months. As part of our study of Thanksgiving, I brought in cookbooks like

The Taming of the C.A.N.D.Y Monster, Kids Are Natural Cooks, and *Kids in the Kitchen*. From these we adapted recipes to an easier form for children to follow, putting each recipe on a big sheet of chart paper back in the cooking center, so that we could do some classroom cooking for the dinner we shared with the kindergarten class. Even Kazu and Mariane were thrilled, although

Collaborative
Groups

Thanksgiving wasn't a holiday they had heard of before. Six groups each prepared a different food for the feast: cranberry relish, pumpkin muffins, turkey soup, popcorn, salad, and a fruit juice punch.

Using the cookbooks provided a real reading experience. To help them connect even more, we looked up information about all the foods in a variety

Research

of reference books, so that while we ate, each group told where its food came from and how it was prepared. I met with each group during social studies time to read them a little more about their foods, and they compiled

Research
Reports

a data chart of the information. The popcorn group told us about the Indians introducing the Pilgrims to popcorn and how kernels of corn were thrown around the edge of the fire rather than being cooked in a pot as we do now. They even told how people have gotten salt by collecting it from the sea or from natural salt deposits.

Meaning
Vocabulary

It made sense, therefore, to tie in the measurement unit from the math series with all the cooking activities. What better way to learn what a cup is than by having to measure out a cup of something for a recipe? That's really developing meaning vocabulary with "the real thing." I had the kids do a "water run-through" of their recipe before they tried it with the real ingredients. If a cup of flour was called for, they had to measure out and add 1 cup of water to the bowl. Cleanup was pretty easy, and the children got some idea of how much they could expect to have in their bowls when working with the real thing. Each cooking group had children from each of the three math groups so that I knew I had some very capable people in each group on whom I could count. Each group practiced its recipe three times with water run-throughs, so the days of the actual cooking went smoothly. My friends are always amazed at what children can create with an electric skillet

Thinking
Processes

and a crockpot! As for the thinking processes, the children certainly had ample opportunity to evaluate and apply their knowledge.

Social Studies
Thematic Unit

Before beginning the social studies unit on neighborhoods, I had the children call up their experiences with people, buildings, and activities in their neighborhoods. I then had them predict what they thought we would be

Organizing
Information

learning about in our unit. We made a big chart with their predictions of the most important people, buildings, and activities they thought would be included. They also predicted concepts we might learn, such as, "People help one another," which were likewise put on another chart. As the month went on, they found that they needed to add additional words and concepts to the charts.

<table>
</table>

Locating Information The sources of information we used included interviews with community helpers, films, speakers, and field trips, all liberally supplemented with books that I read to them which they located on their own. For "homework," they were encouraged to check out a book from our classroom collection— pulled together just for this unit—and take it home for someone to read to **Organizing Information** them. We put together feature matrices of the people, buildings, and neighborhood activities about which they were learning. Based on those feature matrices, they wrote paragraphs that formed the basis for the review materials at the end of the unit. Some children are already quite good at monitoring what more needs to be located. Pat looked at the feature matrix of **Writing** neighborhood buildings and noticed that we had left out houses! See Figure 9.2 for the feature matrix done on people in the neighborhood and some edited paragraphs written from it.

The neighborhood unit has been quite a busy one, but I think the children now have a much clearer idea about who provides services and goods for them. And, of course, by writing so frequently about the different aspects of **Content Journals** the unit, their composition abilities have been improving. In their journals this month I had them each choose several community helpers, services, and

	Wears uniform	Works with people	Works for people	Have to have
Police officer	X	X		X
Firefighter	X	X		X
Grocer			X	X
Mailcarrier	X		X	
Medical helpers	X	X		X
Utility workers			X	X
Gas attendant			X	

People in Our Neighborhood

There are many people who help us in our neighborhood. Some do jobs we couldn't do by ourselves. We need police officers and firefighters and medical helpers because they do jobs that we don't know how to do. We need grocers and utility workers because they bring us stuff we couldn't get if they didn't help us. We could get our own mail or pump gas into the car if we had to.

Some helpers wear uniforms like police officers, firefighters, mailcarriers, and medical helpers. That way you can tell real easy who they are when you need help. Some people just wear their own clothes to their jobs.

Police officers, firefighters, and medical helpers help save people. But some helpers just do jobs for us, like grocers, mailcarriers, utility workers, and gas attendants.

We need all of our community helpers because each one does a special job. That makes everybody's life easier because we don't all have to do everything.

FIGURE 9.2 Feature Matrix

buildings to draw pictures of and write about. I could even make out some of the words in Ray's invented spellings this time:

firfitres are god becus they hlep pepl ho is brn up i lick to liv with tem and go down tat bug po
(Firefighters are good because they help people who is burned up. I like to live with them and go down that big pole.)

D E C E M B E R

I, for one, am glad to have this break time. Not only do I plan to use my time on holiday and family obligations (my poor little girl, Vera, has hardly seen me this month), but I also find this an excellent time to regroup and plan for the next part of the year. I know that not even half the school year is over, but in second grade it seems that more than half the year has been covered by the time January rolls around. The children have come so far since September, reading and writing so many different things now.

Computers The children have been doing some very elementary kinds of word processing on the microcomputer. We have a school computer and printer in our room. Up until now the children have mostly just worked on keyboarding skills with cardboard templates and the computer keyboard and have played **Revising** with some of the software designed to teach beginning programming skills. This time, however, I introduced using the computer for revising writing. What a hit! Even Jim and Dave wrote more than they usually do and begged to write more! Children love to see their revised copy emerge tidily from the printer with very little effort. I'll bet I have trouble getting them to go back to revising on paper after this.

Social Studies Thematic Unit The continuing unit on holidays was very big with the children, of course, especially as they learned about how Christmas is celebrated around the world. They found it fascinating, if a bit disconcerting, that La Befana the witch (Italy) and little elves (Norway) deliver holiday presents in other countries. We also looked at Hanukkah and celebrations associated with the winter solstice. One strategy I have used somewhat successfully with this unit is **Comprehension Minilesson** Take Two. For each of the countries for which we studied the Christmas customs, I pulled four true statements from the passage I was going to read to the children. Here are the ones I selected from the passage on Italy:

1. Italian children have gifts brought by the witch La Befana.
2. Italian people eat eels for their Christmas feast.
3. La Befana was a witch who was too busy cleaning her house to go see the baby Jesus with the Three Wise Men.
4. Italian children open their gifts on January 6, the Feast of the Epiphany.

Two were main ideas from the passage and two were details. I read the four statements to the children in advance, pointing to the words of each numbered statement on the chart I had prepared earlier. I told them that all the statements were true, and that they were to listen as I read to determine which two were most important. After I read the passage, I asked each student to write down the numerals of the two true statements that contained the most important information. They love the secrecy of revealing their answers this way. All guesses were collected, and a group composed of Ray, Mariane, Sharon, and Dave compiled a tally for each of the statements.

Not surprisingly, the first time I tried Take Two, each of the four true statements got nearly equal votes. It was very clear to me that children who are only used to telling true and false are not able to detect what is the most important information. Luckily, the two main idea statements did receive a couple more votes than did the detail statements, so I built on that and helped students who had chosen the two main idea statements to explain why those two were most important. They are not very good at articulating reasons yet, so I can understand why some of my colleagues don't want to try higher-order thinking activities with young children. I still believe it's worthwhile, however. I tried to help children see that details occur just once in the text, whereas most important ideas are mentioned more than once. Also, details help give more information about important ideas. I used a web to show how we might organize information in the section read to them. Slowly, as the month went on and as we worked through the countries' holiday celebrations, most of the children began to see what was meant by "most important" information. They were getting so good that by the seventh country I introduced a twist on Take Two. After I read the four true statements to them, they predicted which two would be the most important. They listened to confirm or alter their guesses. I took a show of hands for the first guess and wrote the numeral beside each statement. The second guess was done in writing as before.

Science Thematic Unit

Organizing Information

Meaning Vocabulary

The science unit we worked on was solids, liquids, and gases. I began the unit by starting a big content web on the back bulletin board. In the center of the web were the words *Forms of Things*. Radiating out from the center were the terms *solids*, *liquids*, and *gases*. We met back by the bulletin board, and they started calling up "things." I wrote each of their contributions on separate cards to use later in a closed Word Sort, similar to what we had done with transportation earlier in the year. Of course, they at first named objects that were solids. I then started probing to get them to name liquids, asking what were some things they could drink, where they played in summer, and how they cleaned themselves. Then we used a Word Sort to separate all the items into like groups. As I showed them how to separate the cards into groups, I asked them to think how all the objects under each label were alike so that we could start to develop tentative definitions for solids, liquids, and gases. Not a single gas had been offered, so only liquids and solids had listings. With all the examples in front of them, we came up with some tentative definitions for solids and liquids. First they said you could feel both, so I wrote that on a card beside each label. Then they told me that solids stayed in a certain shape and liquids were the shape of the container they were in. Those two definitions were written on the board. Good start! After listening to books and watching films with information about solids, liquids, and gases, they should have even more to add to the chart.

It became immediately apparent that *gases* had no items listed under it. Jim suggested that we write *gas* on a card and place it underneath the term *gases*. Others said we couldn't do that because gas is a liquid. I must say, I ended the lesson with all of the children in a state of cognitive confusion! I gave them some homework to do. They were to talk with their parents, siblings, friends, bus driver, or anyone else to see if they could come to school with the name of at least one gas to add to the bulletin board.

Several children remembered to do this and came in with the name of a gas. Other children looked in science books for help. The problem with this unit is that the gaseous state children are most familiar with, air, is composed of several gases. I wrote the names of several gases, such as hydrogen, oxygen, and helium, on the web. We talked about ways gases were used in everyday life, such as in oxygen masks and balloons filled with helium. Even though the children will not be expected to know the names of these gases, they are fascinated by having such big words in their room!

Comprehension Minilesson

I decided to focus on causes and effects to help them see some relationships among the three forms of matter. For example, I asked them to listen as I read a section of a book to find out, "Why does a balloon have a shape if air (a gas) has no shape of its own?" and "What happens when an ice cube is left in a glass on the windowsill?" Then they were ready to try some experiments on their own.

Writing Minilesson

As we talked about each experiment, I made a content language experience chart for each, labeled with the number of the experiment we were performing. For the first experiment, I brought balloons to school. Here is what the chart looked like:

Air Is Something—Experiment One

Mrs. Lance gave us balloons. (Dave)

Nothing was in the balloons at first because we checked and they were flat. (Pat)

Mrs. Lance let us each blow up our balloon. (Steven)

It didn't look like anything was in our balloons, but they got big so something must have been inside and it was air! (David)

Mrs. Lance chewed an onion and then blew up a balloon. (Michelle)

She make balloon go boom. (Mariane)

We smelled what came out of the balloon and it smelled like onions. Yuk! (Jim)

Meaning Vocabulary

Other experiments and charts were made to demonstrate changing solids to liquids (by melting hard candy in the electric skillet) and turning liquids into solids by freezing or cooking. Evaporation was shown by putting ice cubes into the skillet and boiling them into nonexistence. Cause and effect statements were easily generated with all these experiments. For example, "Why did the solid suckers become liquid?" and "What happens when ice cubes are boiled?"

Content Journals   Students wrote steadily in their content journals about experiment results, hypotheses to explain results, and possible experiments to try. All the children are fascinated by the experiments, and the amount and quality of their writings confirm that.

It's been quite a month! I, for one, am ready for R&R.

J A N U A R Y

Content Journals   I have always enjoyed January so much because the children and I are both glad to be back to school and into a routine again. January is one of our more exciting months because I do try to provide many types of interesting activities. By the end of this month, I found it hard to believe that children were writing so much or so well in their journals. I guess it makes sense that if they regularly write and get reactions to their writing, their composition skills will improve. The children have been writing twice a week about the science unit on animals, which will continue through February. Here are excerpts from several journals:

We lerned that there are many kinds of animals. Some animals have hare and some have faethers. Some have scales. Sometimes babys are born from there mommys and sometimes they hach from eggs. (Pat)

All stuf is liveing or non-liveing. And anmals is part of the liveing ones. Anmals are liveing becuas they ned food and watre and air and they have babys. (Steven)

amnls have baby amnls they ned eet and dwink wotr. (Dave)

Clearly, the children have been learning about many new ideas while they are writing in their journals. Journals are a chance to get their ideas down. We can always work on editing the sentences when they turn entries from their journals into oral or written reports. So when I write a note by a journal entry, I react only to how accurate the information is, and I raise points that help elaborate their information: "Name some animals who are like this." "Why do animals need to eat and drink?" and "I would like to **Revising** know more about ____." Such queries cause them to think more about their entries. Occasionally I encourage them to rewrite entries to incorporate the points I suggested. The longer entries that result are *usually* more accurate!

I used to have children make booklets to go along with the units we were studying. But to do the booklets, I either wrote sentences on the board for them to copy or asked them to tell me some things to write about and then again had each child copy what I had written. I am happier with the journals since each child is challenged to write independently. Some write a whole **Assessments** page! I can see clearly how well each is able to apply what they have been learning rather than how well they can copy my ideas. Content journals require students to call up, organize, connect, form an image, monitor, generalize, evaluate, and apply. Not too bad for one little old strategy!

Collaborative Groups

I also put the students into heterogeneous groups every week or so and have them share what they have written in their journals with one another. I find that they all go away from those writing groups with more ideas to write about and with ideas, too, of ways to make their own entries better. As in all peer response groups, group members ask each other questions to elicit more information that will clarify the ideas stated. Some of the children have started keeping a journal for social studies, too. As you might guess, these are the children for whom writing is easier and more satisfying: Pat, David, Sharon, and John. Kazu and Mariane are also keeping their own journal for social studies so that they can improve their English language skills. Periodically they show me what they are writing, and I react to it just as I do to the science journals. I wonder if I should ask all of the students to write about social studies, too. I need to think about that one for a little while.

Independence

Each time the students form themselves into groups, it gets a little bit easier; they are really beginning to know what to do and how to do it. I am well on the way to my goal of independence with this kind of organization for writing.

Reports

I introduced the one-paragraph report to the kids this month, too. Each report begins with a topic sentence, explained to the children as the one sentence that tells the most important information, followed by supporting details. After all our experiences before the holiday break with Take Two, the children finally understand what I mean by "most important." We once

Comprehension Minilesson

constructed reports after viewing a film for our social studies unit, "Needs and Wants." I set the purpose, instructing the students to watch and listen to remember everything. After the film, children went to their heterogeneous groups (organized so that each group would have students who could model good thinking and language) and listed all they could remember. Then they sorted the statements into main ideas and supporting details. That way, they could select one main idea as their topic sentence for the one-paragraph essay and pick out several supporting details as well.

Group Writing

All groups then watched the film again to check the accuracy of their information. They made changes in their reports in their peer group sessions. Each group came out with a written report done on chart paper that was hung in the room, each group member's name listed on the paper. Children feel such pride in being part of a successful effort! Even though at this point Jim, Dave, and Ray would be unable to produce such a report independently, they can each be part of their various groups to complete the task.

To introduce the unit on wants and needs, I listed the two terms on separate pieces of chart paper and asked the students to talk about things they wanted and things they needed. We came up with an enormous number of frivolous and necessary items! For them, it seems that wanting and

Remember When?

needing are the same thing. We talked about the difference between the two terms through a Remember When activity in which I recalled things I needed as a child, how they were obtained, and why they were necessary. I then did a Remember When? with wants I had had as a child. After I was done (and

Meaning Vocabulary

did they listen attentively—children love to learn more about their teacher's personal life!), I asked them to tell me the difference between *want* and *need*.

Then they word-gathered wants and needs to put on the two charts. Sometimes we had to talk through where a word or phrase belonged because a child would insist it was both a want and a need. For example, Ray said pizza was both a want and a need. After discussion, it was decided that pizza belonged to the general category Food. So we made a heading that included many kinds of food for the need list. Chocolate cake went on the want list, since you could get along without that kind of nourishment (couldn't you?). Toys all went over to the want list. It took a couple of sessions to get everything down they wanted to list, but with my gentle guidance, we had examples of needs in each of the three categories: Food, Clothing, and Shelter.

I have been feeling so tired lately that I am having a hard time keeping up with all that's going on here! I must need to up my vitamin intake.

F E B R U A R Y

Content Journals

The wants and needs unit continued in social studies, as animals continued in science. I made one new addition: All the students now keep content journals for social studies, too. I have continued the holidays unit, which really picked up this month of presidents' birthdays and Valentine's Day.

Organizing Information

At the end of the month, the children constructed a web for animals that we placed on the back bulletin board. It was a great way to call up, organize, connect, form an image, and review information. I've put a sketch of it in my book so I'll remember it for future years (see Figure 9.3).

Reports

To apply what they had learned about animals in an art activity, each student was to take one of the seven groups we had studied and create a new animal with the characteristics of that group. Dr. Seuss has definitely had an influence on these kids; they were undaunted by either the creation or the naming of their critters. They all had to write short descriptions of what their animal looked like (hair, scales, feathers, and so on), how its young were born, and what it ate. They used the data charts we had made for each of the seven animal groups as their source of information. All animals were put on display in the form of pictures, clay models, papier mâché, and so on, with cards that each child had written describing the animal. We invited the principal, our upper-grade student helpers, and the parents in for a tour of this unusual zoo.

Meaning Vocabulary

Our major review activity for wants and needs consisted of review sentences that students constructed from the key words I had listed on the Word Wall throughout the unit. Since I now put reading, science, math, and social studies words on the same Word Wall, I find that it helps to use color coding. All the green words are for science, yellow is math, red is reading, and blue ones for social studies. To write review sentences for social studies, students first had to locate all the blue cards on the Word Wall. For some, that was a task in itself.

Collaborative Groups

In small groups the children listed each word on small pieces of paper. With all the words in front of them, they were told to think of two sentences

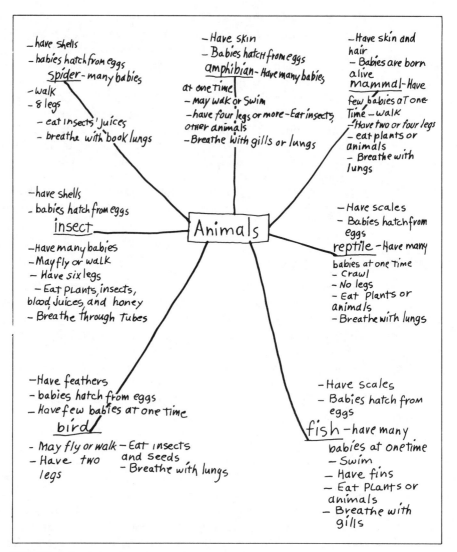

FIGURE 9.3 Animal Web

about what we had been learning, using at least two of the words in each sentence. After each group had had a chance to give one of their sentences, I asked if any other sentences had been developed that were not already listed. As they were given to me, I wrote the sentences and then circled the two words from the Word Wall. In this way, they could see which words had not yet been used and constructed additional sentences using quite a few of the leftover words! Here is their final review sentences chart on needs:

What We Need

We need and want many things. (Stephanie)

We need clean air and water or we would get sick and die. (David)

We need food so we don't starve. (Jim)

We need clothing, shelter, and warmth so we don't get too cold and die. (Jakeitha)

We need love and safety because people need more than just stuff to keep from dying because we need to not get hurt and to feel good about ourselves. (Pat)

Needs take care of how you live and how you feel about yourself. (Michael)

Math Unit The children are studying money in math, so the yellow cards on the Word Wall are the names of the coins and the symbols of dollars and cents. The children have been writing some pretty hard word problems for one another with these new words, asking for some addition and subtraction beyond their required level in the math series. What astounds me is that children who seemingly cannot add or subtract above ten can in fact make change and therefore can do difficult addition and subtraction when money is involved. Children today seem to have more money and to have handled it earlier than my generation did! I helped Jim to see that what he was able to do with making change from a quarter was harder than what he was having trouble with in math. He couldn't believe it! All those numerals were related to money? He has really gained confidence in his math ability as a result of this little insight. He now makes all of his addition and subtraction problems deal with money and then it seems to make sense to him.

Well, I had my own little insight at the beginning of this month about the reasons for my increasing fatigue, and the doctor confirmed it. Long about July, Vera is going to have a new little brother or sister! Just wait until I tell the children!

M A R C H

Near the end of the month, Kazu asked me if I was getting fatter! I thought it was a good time to break the news to the children, since I will get only fatter and fatter and I would rather they know why. They immediately wanted to pull out the webs and data charts we had put together for animals so that they could see where I fit. They had apparently forgotten that people are mammals, et cetera, et cetera. I pulled the charts out, and we all gathered around them on the floor to see if I met the characteristics. The children were fascinated. What did it really mean that the baby would be born alive? Was the baby alive now? They seemed to be in more of a mood for the animal unit now than when we originally did it.

Science Thematic Unit In response to their questions, I sent a note home to parents explaining my condition and the children's questions. Would they mind if I tastefully presented some basic information about how babies are created and develop? Some parents did object, of course, as is their right, and I arranged for those **Literature** children to engage in an art activity out of the room while I shared *How Babies Are Made* and *How You Were Born*, dealing with beginning sex education concepts. The children were fascinated and wanted to know if the same held true for other animals. Therefore, this month has included a review of the growth and development of baby animals in each of the seven categories. All of the children in the class found the information—presented in greater depth due to their increased questions—to be much more interesting the

Motivation second time around. It's amazing what motivation does for learning. And I thought I had done a good job with motivation earlier. Just goes to show you!

I am glad that I took the additional time to go back to the animal unit. I think we teachers are probably afraid to do that, since we feel the pressure to continue marching through all the assigned units. But in this case I saw clearly that our review was really time well spent for the students. A bit serendipitous, but isn't that what it's all about—seizing the teachable moment?

Science Thematic Unit Nevertheless, we did finally begin the science unit on plants. The children's first questions were about how baby plants were made! So that is where we began our data chart. But the children quickly lost interest when they discovered that plant reproduction was not nearly as interesting (to them) as was animal reproduction. The rest of the unit then continued pretty

The Real Thing much as I had planned it. We took field trips to the local plant nursery and the grocery store so they could see The Real Thing. Many of the parents who

Organizing Information had begun seedlings for their home gardens were willing to contribute seeds for our experiments. Using the outline shown in Figure 9.4, which I had first used when introducing animals, I was able to show the children how plants fit into the world around them. This outline is a little different because it shows one big idea broken down into successively smaller parts. The web we did on animals took that one section of the outline and developed it more; the same thing will be done with plants.

If plants are living things, I asked, what do plants need (to use a word from social studies!)? Children called up what they knew of plants and

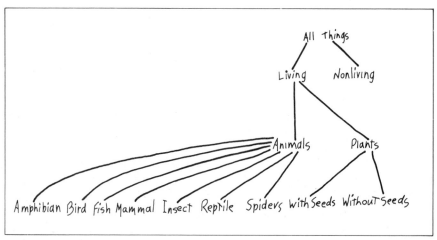

FIGURE 9.4 Living Things Web

Direct Experience

hypothesized about plant needs. We then constructed a series of experiments as we had done with solids, liquids, and gases. Each experiment concerned one of the plant's needs—air, light, water, or food. I had children predict what they thought might happen and listed the predictions on a content language experience chart. Here is the chart for one of the experiments:

Writing Minilesson

Experiment #3: Plants Need Water
Guesses: Both plants will grow if they have air and light.
One plant will not grow if it doesn't have water.

We put two pots in the window and they both had seeds and dirt and we didn't cover them up. (Ray)
I got to be in charge of one pot and I had to give it one tablespoon of water every day. (Jim)
I was in charge of one pot and I wasn't allowed to give it any water at all. (Michelle)
For long time it did not look like anything going to grow. (Kazu)
But, presto bingo! One day we saw something green in Ray's pot and a plant grew and nothing grew in Michelle's pot. (Sharon)
This must mean plants need water but how much is a very good question. (Steven)

A good question indeed, so we got some seedlings and experimented with the amount of water and discovered that too much water will kill plants as easily as too little. A good lesson for me with my house plants!

Math Unit

Fractions was the math unit of the month. I am glad that I have pulled out the units on measurement, time, money, and fractions for students to work on all at once. Even if some children cannot add or subtract very well, they may understand fractions, especially with all the cooking activities we have continued to do. "Interrupting the regularly scheduled program to bring them this important unit" is not only motivating but also a great pick me up, since math can seem to be only number-crunching for students at this level.

The Real Thing

Be a Mind Reader

They love doing The Real Thing with objects we cut into fractional parts and playing Be a Mind Reader with the fraction symbols and words on the Word Wall.

March has ended and I am feeling a tad more energetic these days. Thank goodness the school year will end before the tiredness returns! It's hard to believe we are on the countdown months!

A P R I L

Research

April has always been one of my favorite months. The world becomes colorful again, and the warmth is so welcome. We took some of our plants outside to see what might happen to healthy plants if they weren't kept warm enough. The black leaves on the tomato plants gave some indication, but students were puzzled about how the spinach had survived the same temperatures. That led into some research about when plants can be started outdoors and why. This has been a very interesting unit for the children, calling upon many research and writing skills.

Content Journals

The children wrote twice a week in their science journals about the various experiments we were doing. Some children even proposed additional experiments, which would have impressed the National Science Foundation with their complexity! The emphasis this month has been not so much on plant

Meaning Vocabulary

needs for survival as on the different kinds of plants and such terms as *root*, *stem*, and *leaves*. We looked at the functions of these plant parts and at food plants, sorting them by whether we ate their roots, stems, leaves, or several parts. Children were astounded to discover that we ate the part of the potato that grows underground. I used an old book that still has great information

Literature

(how much can carrots change, after all?), *What's Inside of Plants*. I also used a book on different food plants, *In My Garden*.

At the beginning of the school year I always wonder how I am going to fill up all the wall and bulletin board space in my classroom. By this point in the year I am wishing for more. It seems that every available space is covered with content language experience charts, illustrations, webs, and Word Sorts. There are also displays of books and magazines for our current units in the appropriate learning centers. Every week during the scheduled library time (though of course children may go to the library at other times as well), we find another piece of information to bring back to the displays. During these weekly trips, I have been modeling how to search for a key word to locate information in the card catalog. The children have also gotten to know the

Literature

names of some authors fairly well, too. "Oh, here's another book by Dr. Branley," someone may say as they locate another science book. Some of these authors are becoming as familiar to them as are story book authors Sendak, Lobel, Van Allsburg, Kellogg, Seuss, Steig, Mayer, and Marshall.

Organizing Information

We have been taking data charts to the library for a couple of months now, so that when we find out something new, we immediately add it to the chart along with the source. Filling in the data chart at the library has really

Thinking Processes

helped children learn to organize, connect, monitor, and generalize. As we fill out the charts, they monitor where we have little or no information so that we can search for more.

Identifying Questions

The children have discovered that some questions on the data chart are not as important as others. Thus we strike off some questions and write in substitutes. Students have also discovered that you cannot ask questions that are too specific ("Why is it colder at Aunt Ruth's house than it is here?") or too general ("What happens in January?"), as we have spent considerable time at the card catalog unable to find anything out about such questions. Then we talk about broadening or narrowing questions to make them more useful. For instance, we talked about where Aunt Ruth lives, posing such questions as, "Is the weather different in different places?" "What causes the weather to be different in other parts of the country?" "Which parts of the country usually have warm weather and which have a lot of cold weather?" I feel good about their developing research skills.

Social Studies Thematic Unit

The social studies unit this month was about rules and why they are necessary. I probably ought to start the year with this unit since discussing the reasons for rules has such an impact on their behavior. We began by talking about rules for different places, which are really sets of expected behaviors that allow all to do what they are supposed to with little interference from others. We had set some room rules together at the beginning of the school year, but they were just leftovers from expected behaviors in other situations. Children really had no idea why they should not talk too loudly in the room.

Direct Experience To show them the alternative, I bravely (foolishly?) abolished rules for one morning in the room, having warned our principal, Mr. Head, what was coming! Children crowded into the most popular centers and didn't go near others; children talked very loudly and missed being called to math group time; children didn't finish their work; children interrupted one another or got up and left groups before they normally would have been allowed to. Dave and Jim thought that this day was wonderful; most of the others, however, did not like being uncertain of what was expected of them and did not like the rudeness of some of the other children. We had a discussion during the next social studies period on the reasons for our rules and on what makes a good rule. We broadened this, of course, to playground and bus rules, home rules, and community rules.

I explained that long ago, before schools were available to all, most people could not read. People learned the rules for living together in the newly forming cities and towns of medieval Europe by listening to the tales told by storytellers. These storytellers would travel around from place to place telling tales that made the rules very clear to those listening. I reminded them of some familiar folktales, and we talked about how the characters behaved. We identified appropriate and inappropriate behaviors based on the story events and whether characters were rewarded in the end. I read a bunch of familiar and new folktales to the children, and we continued our analysis into societal rules and how they evolved. All the children came out of this experience with a greater appreciation for why societal rules developed. These discussions and brainstorming sessions were a prelude to each child making an oral

Oral Reports report about a rule. They had to state the rule and explain the reason for it. I find that they can plan such short oral reports by making a few notes on cards so that they are not just reading a written report.

Another busy month ends, and I find myself concerned about the nearness of the end of the school year with tons more left to accomplish! I have this same feeling every year—when will it end?

M A Y

Parent conferences early this month took up an enormous amount of my time, both for preparation and for the actual conferences. However, the parents and I gained a lot from the exchange of information. I always prepare the children for the conferences by telling them what I am going to tell their parents. Then I ask them to write down something they would like me to tell their parents that they are doing well. That's yet another way for them to monitor their learning, review what they know, and organize their thoughts.

Combined Math/Science Unit

In math the children were learning to tell time and in science they were studying what caused time to change, so we worked on the two units together. Time is such an abstraction. When you try to explain the passage of time, how the earth rotates around the sun while simultaneously turning on its axis, you are into heavy stuff. We showed how the earth moves (even though we can't feel it) by putting a stick outside and measuring the position and length of the shadow cast over time. This was a great way to apply their previous work with linear measurement to their new study of time. They began to predict what would happen as the day went on, predictions that I wrote on a chart so that they could test their hypotheses. Using the strategy A Picture Is Worth a Thousand Words, I chose films as the best way to help them grasp this unit. I also used such books as *What Makes a Shadow?* and *The Day We Saw the Sun Come Up*. We did a lot of one-paragraph essays to break the information into smaller bits for better understanding. Here is Kazu's first-draft paragraph on days:

A Picture Is Worth a Thousand Words

> A day is 24 hour long. Each day earth go around pretty fast so we have day and night. In 24 hour we have dark and light. Seven day make one week, and 365 day make a year. That mean earth turn around and around many time and make many day and night time.

Combined Social Studies/ Science Unit

A combined social studies and science unit dealt with simple machines and how they make work easier. Children first met as a whole class to talk briefly about the reason for having machines (to make work easier through pushing, pulling, and lifting) and then to hear about six types of simple machines. I had them call up jobs they had seen their parents doing or they had done themselves. Then I put them into small groups and asked them to go on a scavenger hunt to locate the machines used for each job or pictures of the machines. When students brought their findings in, we examined each one as best we could to see how simple machines were used to make more complex ones. For some this was easy to see. A crowbar was a lever, a wheelbarrow used wheels, and a pulley was the simple machine on which an elevator was based. However, dishwashers were tough. We asked Steven and Stephanie's father, an appliance repairer, to come in and talk to us about how some machines work. That helped some, but I'm afraid I didn't prepare him well enough about how basic he needed to be. The only thing they really understood was that gears were used. Good enough, I guess.

Scavenger Hunt

Organizing Information

We constructed a web on one bulletin board to list the simple machines we were studying: gear, lever, ramp, wheel, pulley, and screw, also showing examples of the tools that used them. We made a picture of each simple machine and outlined where the machine fit into pictures of tools. We also made a feature matrix listing each simple machine on the left and characteristics along the top. As we examined various simple machines, we filled in the feature matrix.

Content Journals

Children wrote in their journals about the simple machines they saw used around them and how they made the work easier. All in all, I think the

A Picture Is Worth a Thousand Words

children are beginning to understand the need for tools and how people's lives have been made easier with the development of tools. I showed a film about Native Americans who had lived in our state long before Europeans came to America. One part of the film dealt with the tools that Native Americans had used. Children were very surprised to find that the Native Americans had not discovered the wheel, since it is such an important part of many tools. They saw how Native Americans' transportation development was limited by this lack. I had them brainstorm what we would not be able to do if the wheel had not been invented. We then did the same for the pulley and the lever. Finally, children wrote descriptions in their journals of life without these machines.

Writing

During independent work time, the students had to create a new tool using one or more simple machines. During art, they made a model of this tool from clay or wood. Then they wrote a card describing their tool, listing its name, what it would be used for, and which simple machines it used. Those descriptions were refined during their peer group sessions and we were finally ready to invite guests to examine the products of our learning.

A tough month with such hard concepts to work on. We are now only days away from the end of this school year and I can hardly believe that the time is over.

J U N E

Assessment

As I looked back at my first entries about what I had intended to do this year, I was pleasantly surprised at how well I did. I discovered, for one thing, that I had been promoting many of the essential thinking skills with the units I had always taught and the methods I had always used. But I found myself getting rid of some activities that I realized were not helpful for developing thinking skills nor student independence and substituting in others that were. I guess that setting goals at the beginning of the year alerted me to be aware at all times of the value of each activity I used with the children. Certainly I can see great growth in both their content reading and writing abilities. Requiring them to write about the content areas from the beginning was a new idea for me, and it really worked. I gave up using my language arts textbook about January because the children were so far ahead of the second-grade skills we were expected to cover. Just through regular writing activity and responses from me and their peers, children's writing was more organized and better developed than I had ever seen for young children. Part of this is due, I'm sure, to the fact that they have learned about topic sentences and the need for supporting details. Additionally, the children this year wrote more total words; more different and varied words; and longer, more complex sentences than have my students in previous years.

The children are far more independent in their learning strategies than any group I have ever had. I guess all the modeling with gradual fading to student independence paid off. Not only did I "cover the content," but also I think that, for the first time, the majority of students learned it, too. There is no doubt in my mind that next year I will include even more strategies to help children learn to think as well as learn facts.

Helping the children organize information was a big part of my lessons, since children at this level need to bring some order to all the random facts they are acquiring. I used many webs, data charts, and one-paragraph essays, and did a lot of modeling followed by guided practice, allowing them to extend their learning with personalized inquiry. What a great year!

And now, off for the summer, which, with July looming, is going to be a pretty busy one for me. Maybe I can work on some more strategy development while I'm in the hospital!

REFERENCES

Andry, A. C., & Schepp, S. (1968). *How babies are made*. New York: Time-Life Books.

Barrett, J. (1983). *A snake is totally tail*. New York: Atheneum.

Bulla, C. R. (1962). *What makes a shadow*? New York: Crowell.

Charlip, R., & Miller, M. B. (1974). *Handtalk: An ABC of finger spelling and sign language*. New York: Four Winds.

Cole, J. (1984). *How you were born*. New York: Morrow.

Edge, N. (1975). *Kids in the kitchen*. Port Angeles, WA: Peninsula Publishing Co.

Goudey, A. E. (1961). *The day we saw the sun come up*. New York: Scribner.

Green, M. M. (1960). *Is it hard? Is it easy*? New York: Young Scott Books.

Griffiths, R., & Clyne, M. (1991). *Books you can count on! Linking mathematics and literature*. Portsmouth, NH: Heinemann.

Kraus, R. (1971). *Leo the late bloomer*. New York: Windmill Books.

Lansky, V. (1978). *The taming of the C.A.N.D.Y. monster*. Wayzata, MN: Meadowbrook Press.

Lasky, K. (1983). *Sugaring time*. New York: Macmillan.

Lionni, L. (1967). *Frederick*. New York: Pantheon.

Lobel, A. (1972). *Frog and Toad together*. New York: Harper & Row.

Mayer, M. (1968). *There's a nightmare in my closet*. New York: Dial.

Oeschli, H. (1985). *In my garden*. New York: Macmillan.

Parents' Nursery School. (1972). *Kids are natural cooks*. Boston: Houghton Mifflin.

Peterson, J. W. (1977). *I have a sister—my sister is deaf*. New York: Harper & Row.

Seuling, B. (1980). *The triplets*. Boston: Houghton Mifflin.

Shriberg, L. K., & Nicholas, C. (1980). *Kids in the kitchen*. New York: Wanderer Books.

Spier, P. (1979). *People*. New York: Doubleday.

Thaler, M. (1983). *It's me, Hippo!* New York: Harper & Row.

Zim, H. (1952). *What's inside of plants*. New York: William Morrow.

C H A P T E R   1 0

Fifth Grade

A U G U S T

Next week the students will arrive, and as always I am not ready and anticipate the year with my usual feelings of fear and excitement. Finding out last week that I would be teaching fifth grade rather than fourth was a shock and a disappointment at first. After two years in fourth grade, I was finally getting a good handle on what needed to be taught and had developed some good units. But when Ruby died so unexpectedly, Mr. Head asked me to move to fifth grade. "Connie," he explained, "Miss Stone was the Rock of Gibraltar and we need that kind of experience and stability in fifth grade. I know you are just starting your third year of teaching, but you are so stable and creative. I know you can fill the void left by Miss Stone's tragic death." I am not at all sure Connie Tent can even begin to replace Ruby Stone, but I am glad Mr. Head has such confidence in me! I will just have to learn some new content and develop some new units. Fifth-grade science content is interesting, and I know the kids and I will enjoy learning all about our country, Canada, and Latin America. I have traveled in most of the United States and some of Canada, so I should be able to help make that study real for them. Teaching health will be a problem. There is no curriculum guide to work from, and the textbook looks very hard. I will have to figure out how to make that material understandable and exciting when the time comes.

Schedule   I have a schedule and an overall plan for the year that I hope will result in a less choppy day, week, and curriculum. I was bothered both years I taught by the lack of time to study anything in depth and by the fact that we teach the skills of reading, writing, and computing but never relate these skills to learning about the world. It is so difficult to integrate reading, spelling, language, and math with the other subjects when each uses a separate textbook and an unrelated set of skills. I'm not comfortable just making up a whole curriculum and chucking all the texts (although that is tempting!). So, being a typical Libra, I have worked out a schedule that seems a good compromise. Monday through Thursday, I will divide the mornings up between the various skills subjects. We will begin with a forty-five-minute math period and then take the next two hours for reading and language arts.

We will go to physical education just before lunch. After lunch, the students will have fifteen minutes for SSR—sustained silent reading—in anything they choose to read. I, of course, will read during this time also to provide a good model and make sure I am not moving around the room distracting my students. Last year the students really came to look forward to this quiet interlude in our day, once they got used to it.

After our fifteen minutes of silent reading, I will read to them for ten or fifteen minutes. I have read to students my previous two years and my fourth-graders loved it. I hope my fifth-graders will, too. I am going to try to read books that are in a series or whose author has written several other books, because I know that will motivate students to read the other books. I am also going to read some of the good fiction, biographies, and informational books that complement our science, social studies, and health units.

We will then spend eighty to eighty-five minutes on a science, social studies, or health unit. I have decided to work on one unit at a time for several weeks, using large blocks of time to really focus on what we are learning. Nothing was more disorienting to me and my students last year than trying to do thirty minutes of science, thirty minutes of social studies, and then fit some health in. Just when we were getting into something, I had to say, "Now, put away your science book and take out your social studies book." I think this short time and these quick transitions were the main reasons the students and I did not get as interested in what we were studying as we could have. Still, I have tried to follow state guidelines about how much time to spend on each subject area. During each nine-week grading period, we will do two two-week science units, one one-week health unit, and one four-week social studies unit. Health is not really getting as much time as it needs, but several of the health units can be combined with our science unit on the human body. Then we can spend all day Friday learning about our current unit. Friday will be my integration day!

On Friday, we will not use any textbooks. Rather, we will spend the whole day reading, listening, writing, speaking, and computing problems relating to our unit. We will also do art and whenever possible will relate music and P.E. to what we are studying in science, social studies, or health. I am very excited about this plan. I hope that by taking all day Friday to do content area work, we will be more excited about our units, learn more, and better apply the skills we learn the other four days.

Thinking Processes In addition to my new schedule, I have established some new goals for myself and my students this year. At the top of my list is to help students develop their thinking skills. Of course we will focus on these as we learn the scientific processes of observing, predicting, experimenting, controlling variables, and so forth. But I also want to help students use their thinking processes as they read and write. To this end, I will try to assure that they are practicing nine thinking processes: call up, predict, organize, connect, form an image, monitor, generalize, evaluate, and apply. I have therefore developed a checklist to use each time I teach a comprehension or writing minilesson (see Figure 10.1).

Meaning Vocabulary
Another major goal is to emphasize meaning vocabulary. It is clear to me that the major reason students cannot read, write, or learn in their content subjects is that they lack appropriate meanings to link with the new words they must learn. I am going to have a Word Wall for each unit and will try to provide real and visual experience from which they can build new meanings. I will also help them connect their experiences to new concepts, using many analogies as I help them develop their own analogies.

Research
Helping students to become good writers and researchers is my third major goal. One of the major reasons for devoting Friday to integration is so that we have time to go to the library, locate resources, learn information, and organize and report on the data. You simply can't do this in thirty minutes, and I know I was never taught these important skills. I just had to figure them out as I went along. My students will get a better education than that.

Date	Call Up	Predict	Organize	Connect	Form an Image	Monitor	Generalize	Evaluate	Apply

Key: C = comprehension lesson; W = writing lesson.

FIGURE 10.1 Thinking Processes Checklist

Independence   Finally, I am going to work toward making my students independent learners. This will be hard: I tend to want to spoonfeed them information to be sure they all get it. But I know that they won't always have me there to do that. I shudder to think of how much those middle-school teachers will expect them to do and feel an obligation to do everything I can to prepare my students. This goal of independence is one I will work on all year, but I have dedicated March, April, and May specifically to this purpose. I even wrote it in big red letters on these months in my calendar.

Well, as always I have high hopes. I know I won't accomplish everything I want—but I will accomplish more with this schedule and with my four goals of developing thinking skills, meaning vocabulary, writing and researching skills, and independence clearly established. I just wish someone had shown me how to do this before I started to teach. I could have done so much better my first two years. Could it be that someone did try to teach me and I just wasn't ready to learn it?

S E P T E M B E R

I survived September! To anyone who hasn't taught, that may sound like an overstatement, but to teachers, September is the hardest month. You have to set up all the classroom routines and expectations and get to know a whole new group of students. This year, I also had to learn about fifth grade, get my new schedule working, and begin work on all my ambitious goals. Too ambitious, perhaps.

My new schedule does seem to be working. On Monday through Thursday, I like getting the math and language arts essentials accomplished first thing. Concentrating on just one of the content area subjects each afternoon really helps us focus. But Friday is clearly everyone's favorite day. I started off the year calling this Integration Day, but the children call it the Special Day, so I have started calling it that, too.

SSR   SSR is now running smoothly. It took a few weeks for the students to realize what Sustained Silent Reading meant. I had to be quite firm in making sure they all had a book—two if they thought they would need two for fifteen minutes—and that they sat right down to read. I then sat down too and set my timer for fifteen minutes. The first two weeks it took almost ten minutes to get everyone actually sitting down with a book. That meant I had less time to read aloud to them and our unit work started a little late. But now they walk in from lunch, pick up their book from our classroom library if they don't have one in their desk (which most do), and immediately begin reading. It just goes to show you what determination and routines will accomplish.

I did have a problem with Dave and Jim not reading the first day. We had all settled down with our books, and the next thing I knew they were laughing and talking with each other. I let them see how shocked I was. I walked right over to them, looked them straight in the eye, and delivered my lecture. "Perhaps you didn't understand," I began. "This is sustained silent reading time. It is the special fifteen minutes we take out of a busy schedule each day just to enjoy a good book. You have just interrupted me and everyone else. I don't expect to be interrupted again. You have your books. Open them and read them." I then returned to my seat facing the class and resumed reading. They were shocked enough to be quiet for the rest of the fifteen minutes. But the next day, they tried it again. This time I went one step further. I moved two chairs on either side of my chair and put Jim and Dave with their books into them. Dave was scarlet with embarrassment. Jim tried to look unconcerned, but I could tell he was embarrassed, too. The next day, without saying a word, I moved two chairs on either side of mine before we began SSR. I think Dave and Jim got the hint because they did not disturb us and the chairs remained vacant. I don't think Dave and Jim actually read during SSR. They are very poor readers, and I think they try to defy me by just sitting with their books open and not reading. But I ignore them as long as they are quiet. They have not interrupted us since (and neither has anyone else), and I noticed them actually turning pages recently. You may not be able to make a horse drink, but if you lead him to water regularly and don't allow him anything else to drink, the chances are pretty good that sooner or later, he will drink! So, SSR is now established, and I don't expect any more problems as long as I do it each day and read as the students read.

This is a most unusual group of kids. Bo says I say that every year. But, this year it is verifiable. I have not one but two sets of twins. Michelle and Michael are both delightful. They don't seem to compete with each other; indeed, they're quite supportive. Steven and Stephanie, on the other hand, should have been separated. Belle tells me that she wanted them separated way back in second grade, but the parents wouldn't hear of it. They want them together so that Steven can help Stephanie. *Help* is not the word I would use to describe what Steven does to Stephanie. Poor Stephanie is just a slow student, and Steven always picks on her when she does not catch on right away. I try to stop it but it is difficult since this appears to be a long-established pattern. I have already requested a conference with their parents.

Special Learners Then, there are Kazu and Che, both Korean. Kazu is a top student. Che came to our country only recently. He will be another top student once he learns English, but he is currently struggling. At least Kazu can help him. Hernando also knows very little English, and no one here speaks Spanish. I am learning a little and I have some Spanish books for him. I never realized when I was in school how many children I would teach who knew little English and how difficult it is to make adjustments for them.

I worry about Ray because he is so quiet. I can never get him to talk. He has little confidence and is always sure he will be wrong. Unfortunately, I think his perception is usually true! I am looking for some strength I can capitalize on but haven't found one yet. He is very uncoordinated, and the kids never want him on their sports teams. He appears to have no talent for art or music, either. Surely there must be *something* he does well!

The rest of the children seem quite average—although David, John, Sharon, and Pat seem to be unusually intelligent. I wonder if they need some kind of special gifted instruction. I will have to refer them and see. As always, I have a class full of the complete range of intelligence, motivation, and talent, and it will be a real challenge to see that all—both the brightest and the slowest—make some progress.

Social Studies Thematic Unit

We did a social studies unit on the geography of the United States, Canada, and Latin America this month. We made a Word Wall, which was hard to limit to only forty words since there are so many terms they need to understand. I had to decide on the basis of which words educated adults knew and so included words like *latitude, longitude, continent,* and *equator.* I used many films and filmstrips to provide visual experiences from which to build meaning. Of course, we became experts at maps and globes, constructing a variety of maps during the course of the unit. We did a listening comprehension minilesson in which I set the purpose by using a problem/solution format. The magazine article I read to them talked about problems that people living in North America must work together to solve. Before I began, I had them write down three major problems on one side of their notebook; as they listened, they filled in the proposed solutions on the other side. After I finished reading the article, they told me their proposed solutions. Then there were several disagreements, and I had to reread parts of the text. It appears that they can understand well if facts are stated explicitly but have difficulty when a concept requires them to make an inference. As I reread the parts of the text, I tried to explain how relating the text to prior knowledge allows you to make certain inferences, but I know not everyone understood. I will have to work on this.

Comprehension Minilesson

Writing

We have done some writing, and the results are not good. Most of my students don't like to write and don't write well, so my goal of making them good writers and researchers may be a little ambitious. But I am not going to give up trying to improve their writing. We probably just won't get as far as I had hoped. I plan to teach them to write paragraphs next month, since it appears that no one but Sharon and Pat has that skill. These students may indent from time to time, but where they "push it in" bears little relationship to where new ideas begin.

Thinking Processes

This month I am proudest of the progress I have made toward improving their thinking skills. My checklist for the nine thinking processes has many entries. I have found that it is quite natural to have students call up their past experience and make predictions based on it if you only remember to do so. It also seems to generate more interest to start from what they know and think. We have classified our Word Wall words and outlined several topics as a way of organizing information. I am also getting better at helping students connect the new things they are learning to what they already know. "Remember what we learned last Friday . . . " is becoming a normal part of my repertoire. Having students form images is also fairly normal, once you start to do it. "Now, close your eyes and picture yourselves on that mountain in western Canada. It is 6000 feet up and covered with snow. . . . " I find that the students like to form images of things both before and after they have learned about them from listening, reading, or viewing. Monitoring happens most frequently when students have had a breakdown in comprehension, and we must reread part of the text to clarify a point.

Generalizing also tends to occur quite naturally as I take the last few minutes of each lesson to try to bring closure on what we have learned. At the end of each lesson, I take a few minutes to ask them what they think are the most important things we have learned so far. If I have time, I have them each write down the three most important things they have learned and then share some of their responses. Sometimes they give me specific facts, but often their responses are generalizations or conclusions based on many facts. At the conclusion of our unit this month, Pat said that the most important thing she had learned was that all people couldn't live in exactly the same way because the places they lived were so different!—a truly high-level generalization about the relationship between geography and sociology!

Evaluate and apply are harder processes to teach, although I do try to remember to ask such evaluative questions as, "Do you think this is a good solution?" and "Would you like to live in this part of the continent? Why? Why not?" We did apply our knowledge when we made maps, and when we described various geographic features of different countries and had imaginary space invaders decide what they should pack if they were going to settle in that region. I must continue to think of ways to incorporate these two thinking skills on a daily basis. My checklist shows we are not practicing them nearly as often as we are the other seven.

Now that we are off and running, I expect to make great progress toward meeting my goals in October.

O C T O B E R

Science Thematic Units

Energy and Our Solar System were the two science units we did this month. The students loved the energy unit because we learned many of the basic concepts during P.E. We played soccer and related the energy source and energy receiver to the players. Transfer of energy was easy to understand once the students grasped that the food they ate gave them energy, which they then transferred to the ball when they kicked it.

The solar system was also fun to study. We led into it from our energy unit by beginning with the idea that all energy in our solar system originates from our Sun. The most important concepts that I wanted them to learn were the following: how our planets orbit our Sun, the various size and distance relationships in our solar system, and some of the distinguishing characteristics of each planet.

Before reading about planets in our science book, the students created two models of our solar system. We used reference books (*The Planets in Our Solar System, How Did We Find Out About the Universe?*) to find out each planet's size and distance from the Sun. One model showed the relative size of each planet, using assorted round objects to represent size. The students were amazed to see Mercury represented by a tiny marble and Jupiter by an enormous beachball. Another model showed the distance of each planet from the Sun. We had to use the hall to represent how far away Neptune and Pluto were. These two models helped the children image the size and distance represented by those huge and abstract numbers. It also helped generate interest in learning about the planets.

Comprehension Minilesson

When looking at the science chapter in our text, I realized that the way the various planets were described fit very well into a semantic feature matrix graphic organizer. I listed the planets down one side and their major features across the top and had everyone copy this pattern into his or her science notebook. See Figure 10.2 for the feature matrix they copied.

Based on what they already knew, I told the children to put a "+" or "−" to indicate whether a planet had a particular feature. If a child was unsure about a particular feature, the space was to be left blank. "If your mind is blank, leave the space blank," I explained. See Figure 10.3 for the feature matrix that Ray filled out before reading the text. As you can see, his mind was blank on many facts. I was particularly amazed to see that he was unsure whether Jupiter, Neptune, Pluto, Saturn, and Uranus orbit the Sun!

Next, the children read the science text section on planets. The children were clear about their purpose for reading: to confirm or change the pluses and minuses on their feature matrix and to fill in blank spaces. As the children read, erasers were used liberally and quiet cheers and groans indicated that the children were actively comprehending rather than passively getting through the pages. When the children had finished, we performed a group task: to correctly fill out our class feature matrix. For every space, I

	Closer to sun than Earth	Larger than Earth	Has moon	Has rings	Orbits the sun	Inner planet	Smallest	Largest	Has life as we know it
Earth									
Jupiter									
Mars									
Mercury									
Neptune									
Pluto									
Saturn									
Uranus									
Venus									

FIGURE 10.2 Planets in Our Solar System

	Closer to sun than Earth	Larger than Earth	Has moon	Has rings	Orbits the sun	Inner planet	Smallest	Largest	Has life as we know it
Earth	−	−	+	−	+	+	−	−	+
Jupiter	−	+	+	−		−			−
Mars	+	−	+	−	+	+		−	−
Mercury	+	−		−	+	+			−
Neptune	−	+		−		−	−		−
Pluto	−	+		−		−			−
Saturn	−	+		+		−			−
Uranus	−			−		−	−		−
Venus	+	−	+	−	+			−	

FIGURE 10.3   Ray's Feature Matrix: Planets in Our Solar System

had the children signal thumbs up if they had a plus and thumbs down if they had a minus. If I got a close to unanimous reply (a few are always too lazy to raise or lower their thumbs!), I put the plus or minus in the appropriate space. No response meant that we still did not know the answer, even after reading. For some spaces, there was still disagreement, so I had the children return to the text to argue their points and I again discovered the problem they have making inferences. Many children believed that the text did not say whether Pluto was larger or smaller than Earth, so I had David read the sentence stating that "Pluto is probably the size of Mercury." David explained that since we know that Mercury is smaller than Earth, we can infer that Pluto is, too. While the text did not directly state that there is no life as we know it on Jupiter, the text does state this: "There is no water on Jupiter." I had to explain to the children that since life as we know it requires water, and since there is no water on Jupiter, there cannot be life as we know it on Jupiter. This "since . . . therefore" reasoning is always required for comprehension, but for many of my students, if the text doesn't say something explicitly, they don't get it! At least with this lesson and task afterward, I could see where they were not making inferences and so could lead them back to the book and explain the reasoning.

Figure 10.4 shows the feature matrix as we finally completed it. As you can see, several spaces are still blank, even after reading. Pluto is so far away that we don't know if it has a moon or rings or if it might have life as we know it. We are also not sure about life on Uranus and Neptune. Jim was disturbed by these blanks and wanted to vote on what to put there. I don't know if he was serious or just putting me on, but I tried to explain that you can't make truth by voting on it!

	Closer to sun than Earth	Larger than Earth	Has moon	Has rings	Orbits the sun	Inner planet	Smallest	Largest	Has life as we know it
Earth	−	−	+	−	+	+	−	−	+
Jupiter	−	+	+	−	+	−	−	+	−
Mars	−	−	+	−	+	+	−	−	−
Mercury	+	−	−	−	+	+	+	−	−
Neptune	−	+	+	−	+	−	−	−	−
Pluto	−	−			+	−	−	−	
Saturn	−	+	+	+	+	−	−	−	−
Uranus	−	+	+	+	+	−	−	−	
Venus	+	−	−	−	+	+	−	−	−

FIGURE 10.4   Planets in Our Solar System

Research

Collaborative Groups

On Friday, we went to the library to do some more research on planets. I chose Venus and showed the students how I used the card catalog and other resources to find more information about Venus. I then divided them into groups for the other eight planets and helped them as they found information. Each group decided on three facts besides those we had read about in our text and one person in each group wrote these three facts on a chart to display in our room. Of course, I had showed them how I selected three facts about Venus and wrote these on my chart. They were very proud of their charts and of their burgeoning research skills—as was I!

Writing Minilesson

Finally, I used their interest in planets to do a writing minilesson on how to write a paragraph. Of course, I began by modeling for them as I wrote a paragraph on Venus. First, I reviewed what I knew about Venus from our feature matrix. Then I read the three additional facts from my chart. I told them that there were many different ways to construct paragraphs but that today we were going to write paragraphs with a topic sentence, three detail sentences, and a concluding sentence. I pointed to the title of our feature matrix, Planets in Our Solar System, and explained that their paragraphs' topic sentences should get the planet into its topic—which in a feature matrix is the title. The next three sentences should describe some details about the planet from the feature matrix or chart. The final sentence could do many things; often it gave a fascinating fact or an opinion. As the children watched, I talked through my construction of topic sentence and my selection and construction of detail and concluding sentences and wrote the following paragraph on the board:

Venus is one of the planets in our solar system. Venus and Earth are about the same size. Venus is hotter than Earth because it is closer to the Sun. Because there is no water on Venus, it can't maintain life as we know it. Venus is called the evening star and is the favorite planet of many people because it can often be seen on a clear night.

Having modeled how to write a paragraph, I had each child choose his or her favorite planet and write a paragraph about it. I reminded them to have their first sentence tell how their planet related to the larger topic of the feature matrix. Three sentences should then give specific information about their planet, based on the feature matrix, the charts, or any other information they knew. A final sentence should end the paragraph in an interesting way. "Remember, you can't include everything you know in just one paragraph. Just include what you believe is most important and interesting," I reminded them.

As the children wrote their paragraphs, the model paragraph, the feature matrix, and the charts were all available to them. When the paragraphs were written, I let several children read theirs to the class. I was amazed when Ray volunteered. His paragraph on Mars was a lot like mine in form, but it was all correct, and most important, he had volunteered to read! This was a most successful writing experience. The children actually seemed to enjoy it. I guess when you know the information, have the correctly spelled words in front of you, and have seen the form modeled, writing is not so arduous. In fact, I overheard Kazu comment, "The paragraph just wrote itself!"

Literature   I encouraged the students to read science fiction related to outer space this month. Among the most popular books were *Planet Out of the Past; The Deadly Hoax; The Doors of the Universe;* and *Another Heaven, Another Earth.*

N O V E M B E R

Health Unit   Our first health unit was a success. The topic was Your Emotions, the major idea being that we all experience a range of feelings, some happy and some not. In looking at the text, I thought the information was fairly trite and was unprepared for the response of my students. Many of them clearly thought that fear, anger, and inadequacy were emotions unique to them. They were amazed to read that we all feel these emotions—children and adults alike— and there are healthy and unhealthy ways to deal with them. We did many

Collaborative Groups   skits and a lot of talking. I put them into small groups, gave them a description of some events in a child's life, and had them decide which emotions that child would probably feel and how best to deal with them. They worked well in their groups, better than I had expected. I think their concentration and the strength of their discussion stemmed from the immediacy of the topic to their own lives. I had a time limit for the groups and had each group prepare a summary of their discussion. I think this structure also helped to keep them on task.

Literature   In the weeks before our unit, I had read them *Bridge to Terabithia* and *Ramona Forever.* I was able to refer to these characters and their emotions as we worked in our unit. Finally, I assigned each student to find a book in which the character experiences some strong emotions and to prepare a short report listing the emotions, the reasons for them, and the way they were handled. They all did a good job with these reports—even Dave read *The Flunking of Joshua T. Bates* and reported on it. I know the unit was a success because I have heard the children use the terminology in talking among themselves. I think they now have more empathy with each other when they are experiencing strong emotions. They also seem to have a better idea of how to handle emotions. I heard Jim say to Bob, "I'm angry at myself right now, so you and me will both be better off if you just stay clear for a while." I think before our unit, Jim might have just hauled off and hit Bob. Next year, I think I will start the year with this health unit.

Scavenger Hunt

Our social studies unit took most of the month. We learned about the European settlement and expansion of the United States and did our first scavenger hunt. To prepare for the scavenger hunt, I read through the materials I wanted the students to read or listen to and wrote down all the interesting things that students might find either an object or a picture for. Here is the list:

prairie	Rocky Mountains	wagon train	gold
canal	mission	textile	immigrant
pioneer	cotton gin	trains	Indians
totem pole	sod house	lantern	spinning wheel
basin	grub hoe	broad ax	iron skillet

Collaborative Groups

We did the scavenger hunt during the week that we worked on our health unit. I had hoped that by the time we actually started the settlement and expansion unit, the students would have been motivated by the search. Before I started the children on the scavenger hunt, I asked them to call up their experiences with scavenger hunts. Many had been on them and explained how you had a limited time to find a bunch of things. I helped them to see that no group usually found everything but that the group that found the most was the winner. I then divided the class into six groups of four and gave each group the list. I appointed a leader and recorder for each group. We read over the twenty items on the list and discussed what they were. If the group was unsure about something, I suggested they would have to find out for sure if they were to find the correct object or picture. To my question "Where can you find out more about what these words mean?" they responded, "Dictionaries, encyclopedias, and other library books." "Right," I said, "and I will let each group go to the media center for fifteen minutes this afternoon to look up the things you are unsure about." I then explained that real objects or models counted two points, while pictures—photographs, magazine pictures, tracings, or drawings—counted one point. I warned the students that I would not count any "thrown-together" drawings or models. They would have one week to find and make what they could. I also asked them not to bring anything to class that they could not hide in their desks until the appointed day—next Friday. "You don't want the other groups to see what you have," I chided. Finally, I told them that just as in real scavenger hunts, I was sure that no group would be able to find an object or even a picture for each word. The knowing glances that passed from Sharon to Pat and from Dave to Jim let me know that my challenge was going to be met.

I let the groups meet several times for just a few minutes during the next week. I emphasized whispering and secrecy, and the children soon got into the mood of the hunt. I gave them tracing and drawing paper as needed and granted their requests to go to the media center alone. I knew my effort to get them interested in our unit was working when I ran into my old friend, Lib Booker, a librarian at our public library. She remarked on how many fifth-graders suddenly wanted books on our country's discovery and expansion!

On Friday morning, there was much excitement. I let each group display what they had scavenged and then had each group tally their score—two points for each object, one for each picture. Most of the groups had pictures of almost everything and objects for common things, such as gold and the lantern. After the groups had done their own tallies, I double-checked the points of the winning group: Sharon, Michelle, Bob, and Ray. They had made a papier mâché model of the Rocky Mountains, a small wooden totem pole, and a sod house out of mud. They also had a miniature wagon train. The others were amazed. I can tell that there will be a lot of models constructed for the next scavenger hunt.

As their prize, I let Sharon, Michelle, Bob, and Ray have the rest of the morning off to put up their bulletin board. Sharon very neatly lettered cards for each word, and they all arranged and stapled the pictures collage style. They put the labeled objects on a table that they pushed under the bulletin board. A title and credits, The Settlement and Expansion of the United States by the Scavenger Hunt Winners—Sharon, Michelle, Bob, and Ray, completed the display that would serve as a springboard for our study. This first scavenger hunt was a success, but I believe the next one will be even better now that the children understand what to do. I already heard some groans and comments like, "We could have made those things, too."

Research We finished this unit with a research day. During our unit, we had developed a list of explorers. I added a few names to this list and then assigned each child a partner. The partners picked one explorer that they wanted to learn more about. Then we made a list of WH Questions to which we might seek answers. Here are the questions the students came up with:

What did the explorer explore?

When did the explorer explore?

Where did the explorer explore?

How did the explorer get here?

Why did the explorer come here?

Who was in the explorer's family?

Who did the explorer find while exploring?

How were the explorers treated by the people they found?

How did the explorers get the money to explore?

To model for them how to locate and organize information, I picked an explorer that no one else had picked and showed students both how to locate sources and how to find information within those sources. I read aloud from the information I had found, with the students stopping me when I read the information that answered one of our questions. I recorded each answer next to its question. When we found some fascinating information that didn't answer any of our questions, David had the idea of adding P.S. at the bottom for miscellaneous facts. The children then worked in pairs under my direction. I had paired the better and the weaker students so there was a lot of one-to-one teaching going on. I have decided that only one teacher cannot possibly teach twenty-four individuals, so I must maximize partner and group work for my students to teach one another. I no longer feel guilty about these pairings since Belle told me that research shows that the child tutor often learns more than does the tutee!

D E C E M B E R

Meaning Vocabulary

To me, December, not February, is the shortest month of the year! Between doing holiday things with the children here and preparing for the holidays myself, I find it very hard to accomplish any of my normal academic tasks. I did unexpectedly add another Word Wall to our room. Of course we have one on the side bulletin board that changes as our unit changes. But when I discovered recently that many of my students did not really understand many of the words in their math books or its symbols and abbreviation, I turned the space above the front chalkboard into another Word Wall for math items. Since I began it so late, I added five terms each day this month until I got them all up. We spent a good part of our math period learning these symbols and attaching appropriate meanings to them. From now on, I will add new terms gradually as we begin a new chapter in math. I select the terms from the fifth-grade textbook, but there is much overlap for my group working in the fourth-grade book, and I know it will help them next year to have learned the essential fifth-grade math vocabulary. Here is the math wall as it currently looks. As you can see, I have translated the symbols and abbreviations.

hundreds	cent (¢)	ray (→)	degree (°)
billions	angle (←)	tens	millions
right angle (L)	thousands	prime number	acute angle
sum	average	digit	addends
kilometer (km)	obtuse angle	estimate	meter (m)
round off	regroup	centimeter (cm)	difference
common	ones	factors	multiples
multiples	product	even numbers	odd numbers
greatest	quotient	remainder	common divisor
common	divisor	less than (<)	greater than (>)
denominator	dollar ($)	percent (%)	line (↔)

Each day at the beginning of our math time, I have the students number a sheet of paper from 1 to 5 as I call out the definition of five terms or write something on the board to express them. The students write the word for each term and then we check. Here are some meaning cues I gave them, followed by the answers in parentheses:

1. 2, 4, 6, 10, and 106 are examples of this. 1, 3, 5, 107, and 409 are not. (even numbers)
2. The symbol for ray ($\rightarrow$)
3. The abbreviation for kilometer (km)
4. When I do this problem ($64 \times 35 = 2{,}240$), the numbers 64 and 35 (multiples)
5. For the same problem, the number 2,240 (product)

Be a Mind Reader

I also use a game called Be a Mind Reader that students particularly enjoy and that helps us review the meanings for these terms. Again, students number their paper from 1 to 5, but this time I think of only one term and give five clues for it. The first clue is always the same, "It is one of the words, symbols, or abbreviations on our math wall." The children always moan, but I tell them to try to read my mind and guess what I am thinking of. They write their guess on the first line. The remaining four clues narrow down the problem until by the fifth clue, only one answer is possible. As I give successive clues, the children continue to write the same one unless my clue tells them that theirs can't be right. Here is one set of clues I used:

1. It's one of the words, symbols, or abbreviations on the math wall.
2. It is a symbol.
3. It is not "<" or ">."
4. This symbol refers to money.
5. This symbol means dollar.

Jim guessed this one on the first clue! He was so proud! "How did you do that?" everyone asked. "He read my mind," I responded. Jim beamed and I was delighted he was getting some positive attention. Some children need a little luck to shine, and Be a Mind Reader allows the chance for that lucky guess.

I wish I had started the year with work on these math terms, but it just didn't occur to me until recently that not understanding what the book said was a part of my students' problem with math. It is clear from their improved work that this vocabulary work is helping. Next year, I'll start a math wall the first week of school!

Science Thematic Unit

We did manage to complete a science unit on the ocean this month. Many children had not been to the ocean, and it is a hard concept to explain to someone who has never experienced it. I relied a great deal on visuals. I got from the state department media center two good films that helped the children to see the ocean's enormous size and to build concepts for terms like *low tide* and *high tide*. I did a prediction activity to set the purpose for a viewing lesson on a filmstrip that showed the various parts of the ocean bottom. I gave the students the following list and asked them to guess which things we would find on the ocean bottom:

Comprehension Minilesson

mountains
shelf
roads
floor
treasure boxes
ridges
slope
fences
cracks
oceanographers
plains
continents

Of course, many of the students didn't know the ocean bottom is called the *floor* or that there is a continental shelf there. They accused me of tricking them, and I protested, "You know I would never do such a thing!" We talked about the different meanings of *floor* and *shelf*. I also had to allow that although our filmstrip hadn't shown a treasure box, you might indeed find one on the ocean's floor.

Prediction

Prediction has been quite a successful way to help the children have clear purposes. Sometimes I use prediction in an open-ended way. I might have said, for example, "Name some things that you think our filmstrip will show at the bottom of the ocean." Other times, I give them a list of things or of true or false statements; have them make guesses about them; and then they read, listen, or view to confirm their predictions. It is amazing how much more actively they read after making that small investment of guessing or predicting. They attend very carefully when they want to find out how they did! I guess this is a normal part of human nature, and I am glad I can capitalize on it to help them become more active learners.

I suppose the high point of the whole unit was when Bo brought in his scuba diving equipment and some things he has collected in and near the ocean. The children seemed to hang on his every word. Bo has never had much experience with children and had been a little nervous about coming. He really got into it and even expressed regret that we couldn't take the whole crew with us when we go to the shore for the holidays. I must admit that I am attached to my children—but not that attached!

J A N U A R Y

Combined Health and Science Unit

We spent this entire month on a combined health and science unit on the human body. The four chapters of the health book and the one in the science book covered much of the same information. I borrowed some bones and a lot of models from Annie Mull, who teaches at the high school. I had an X-ray technician and a pediatrician come in and talk to us. We have become more health-conscious since we began our study. We kept charts of the food we ate and the exercise we've had, and we evaluated how well we were nourishing and exercising our bones and muscles. (The children were amazed to learn that I go to a health spa several times a week. I brought my sweat suit and my tape one day and taught them a few aerobics routines. They loved it!)

Math has once again been the focus of much of my creativity. The math wall vocabulary activities have definitely helped, but I noticed the children **Word Problems** are still having a great deal of difficulty with word problems. I know that computation is not their main problem because I set up the computations for some word problems that many of them had missed and the children breezed right through them. Their difficulty seems rather to be a lack of understanding of what they are trying to find out and an inability to figure out which operations to perform. I have been taking them through a set of steps that I hope will improve their ability to think through word problems. I have listed these steps on a chart, and each morning we work through several problems following these steps:

1. Decide what question the problem asks you to answer.
2. Decide what facts are given.
3. Estimate your answer.
4. Decide which operations to do in which order.
5. Do these operations to get your answer.
6. Compare your answer to your estimate.

Coming up with the steps and writing them on the chart was the easy part. The hard part is teaching the students to follow the steps! As with everything, I began by modeling what to do. I made up a word problem related to members of the class. (They are always more motivated and attend better when the problems are about them.)

Sharon, Pat, and Sarah all want to make cheerleading outfits. It will take 3½ yards of cloth for each, and the cloth costs $4.99 per yard. How much money do they need to buy enough cloth for all three outfits?

I wrote this problem on the board as I read it to the class. I then modeled how to go through the five steps. (Modeling is just a fancy term for thinking aloud as you do something, so the kids can figure out what you're doing and why you're doing it.) "Well," I began, "I have to figure out what the question is and it is a little tricky. The question is not how much cloth they need, although I will have to figure that out, too. The question is how much money they need in all." I then wrote, "How much money in all?" next to step one. Next to step two, facts, I wrote, "3½ yards for each outfit; 3 outfits; $4.99 per yard."

"Estimating is important," I mused aloud, "so that I can tell if my answer makes sense or if I misplaced a decimal point or did something else dumb like that." (The children tittered at the idea of their teacher making dumb mistakes.) "If the material costs $4.99 per yard, that is close to $5.00. There are three of them, so if it only took one yard each, that would be $15.00, but it takes 3½ yards each. Three times $15.00 is $45.00. The answer will be a little more than $45.00." I then wrote "$45.00" next to step three.

For step four, I reasoned that since I knew how much one yard cost and wanted to know how much 3½ yards cost, I would have to multiply. I would then know how much it would cost for one girl, and since there were three girls, I would have to multiply again. I wrote, "Multiply $4.99 × 3½; multiply that times 3" next to step four. Finally, I did the calculation, compared $52.40 to $45.00, and decided my answer was indeed "in the ballpark."

After modeling the whole procedure for the students, I took them through several other problems and let them help me decide what to write and why. Then I had them turn to a set of word problems in their books (those working in fourth-grade math used their book) and had each student write down only the question he or she was trying to answer. I went around and gave help as they worked. It became very clear that deciding on the question was not easy or automatic for many of them.

On the following day, we worked together on just that step—deciding the question. I gave them many problems that used their names and we decided what questions were being asked. I then assigned them a page of word problems they had already worked on (not very successfully) and had them write the question for each one. We continued to work on determining the question for a few days and then went on to step two, determining the facts. This was easier for them. Step three, however, estimating the answer, continues to be a problem. Many of them still can't come up with a reasonable estimate. This worries me, because the people who are good in math always have an estimate to provide them feedback. I hope that if we continue to work on this skill all year, they will get better at estimating.

Step four, deciding which computations to do in which order, is also difficult, but we are continuing to work on it. The last step, when we finally get to it, will be easy. If computation were all there was to word problems, my students would be home free! At least the children and I now have a systematic way of attacking these problems and I understand how much complex thinking goes into them. Bo has heard me talk all month about word problems, and he says the steps I am teaching—determining the problem, gathering facts, considering a reasonable solution, deciding what to do in what order, and then actually solving the problem and seeing if your solution works—is how we solve not just word problems, but life problems. Perhaps the process I am teaching my students has a wider application than I realized!

I am also emphasizing using these steps to solve the word problems I give them on Friday. All year, I have integrated some real-world math applications with our study of whatever topic we were exploring. We have done lots of measuring and graphing. Now, I am going to make sure that I give them some written word problems to solve about each topic. Next month, we will be taking an imaginary voyage to Canada, and I have some great word problems ready for them to think about and solve. Each morning I plan to put on the board two problems that will require them to use their research and math skills. I will give them until lunch to find the needed information and correctly solve the problem. They will get a bonus point on their math grade for each one they correctly solve. I think this will really motivate some of my brightest students. Here are the two I plan to give them for the first day:

How much larger (in square miles) is Canada than the United States?

How much higher (or lower) is Canada's highest mountain peak than our highest mountain peak?

F E B R U A R Y

Social Studies Thematic Unit — Canada was our social studies adventure this month. We pretended all month that we were actually there to explore this vast and diverse land. Several of the children had been to Canada, and they became our guides. Pat's grandmother had emigrated from Canada, and Pat shared the stories she had heard. We learned a little French and a lot more geography. This was also a month to do a lot of writing. Developing good writers has been one of my goals all year, but I have not given it as much time as I think it deserves. For this unit, I decided we would write every day. One way I **Writing Content Journals** accomplished this was to have the students keep journals. This fit in with our idea that we were not just learning about Canada but actually imagining ourselves there. We kept journals—my boys would object to their being called diaries—of the major things we had seen and what we had learned. Each day, at the end of our social studies time, we had five minutes to write in our journals. Just as for SSR, I stuck firmly to the idea that this five minutes is sustained time for silent writing and I wrote, too. At first, the children were unsure about what to write, but I assured them that they were recording personal remembrances, impressions, and questions, with no particular form or content that they needed to include. They were their own audience, and the only restriction was to relate their writing to our study of Canada. As the month went on, the children became used to this time and, as with SSR, they seemed to enjoy it. I did not grade what they wrote, but I did check to see that there was an entry for each day and that the entry related to Canada. The daily points they got for recording their thoughts accounted for a small portion of their grade.

Grading System/Assessment — Grading their work has been a problem all year. In skills subjects like math, spelling, language, and reading, it is fairly easy to give a grade. The children are working on their own levels. Once I have modeled and provided guided practice with the skills, I feel comfortable testing their ability to perform them independently.

Grading their work on the units, however, is much more difficult. I believe that a grading system should motivate all students to work hard. This is easy to say and not nearly so easy to do. Many of my students—Dave, Jim, Hernando, Che, and Ray, most particularly—have very limited prior knowledge of the subjects we are studying. They are also limited by lower reading ability and, for Hernando and Che, limited command of English. If I simply taught the fifth-grade content and then gave them a comprehensive test, they would fail. Some teachers think they should fail if they can't do "fifth-grade" work, but I know that children come with different abilities. Just because they are all in fifth grade does not mean they all have fifth-grade ability.

Special Learners

Then, there are those on the other end of the spectrum, specifically Sharon, Pat, David, John, and Kazu. These children bring huge stores of prior knowledge, motivation, and intelligence to our units. They probably already know most of what we are supposed to learn in fifth grade. My grading system must motivate them, too. I can't let them think that they don't have to study but can just slide by on what they are fortunate enough to know.

The problem is complex, and I am not totally happy with the solution I have worked out. For each unit, I set up several parts that count toward total grade points. I give points for daily assignments, such as the journals and homework, which I never grade but simply check to see that "a good effort was made." Of course, a good effort from Hernando is not of the quality I expect from David, but I can determine this fairly easily. By now, all the kids know what it means to see, "You just threw this together—no way!" on their assignments. Knowing that life is not perfect and that no one can complete all assignments every day, I always have more assignments than can be counted for points. For the Canada unit, for example, I had thirty-five assignments, short daily and homework activities including the daily journal entries. The children could get up to thirty points out of the thirty-five. Thus anyone who was there every day with the first thirty assignments did not have to do the last five! The children loved this and tried to get all the first ones done so they could "lay back" later. I had already planned to make the last five assignments less crucial than the others because I knew that many of the children would not need to complete them.

The second part of the grade comes from the unit tests. We had three tests on Canada that were all worth ten points, plus two bonus points. The ten points part of the test was taken by everyone and included the most important information, which we had learned in class and reviewed. The other two points was based on any other information intended to challenge my really top students. Only children who chose to took the bonus part of the test.

Projects

Finally, I gave my students credit for up to three projects. These projects ranged from library research projects to reading additional books on Canada (*Canada's Kids* and *Take a Trip to Canada,* among others) to creating models, maps, visuals, or realia. For the most part, students did these projects out of school, although we did have some time to work on them on Fridays. These projects were each worth ten points if they were done well. Again, "well" differed for different children, but all children knew I didn't accept sloppy work.

Thus for the Canada unit you could get thirty points for daily assignments, and anyone who was making a good effort should have gotten these. The test on the most important concepts accounted for another thirty points, which again everyone should have gotten. The bonus tests and projects were there to motivate my top students, although most children did at least one project per unit. For Canada, two of the slower students—Che and Bob—did three good projects.

For the most part, I am happy with this grading system because it does seem to motivate my slow students to work with me and learn the most important information, and my top students to do projects and bonus test points. Of course, not everyone is happy with this system. John's mother complained about her son's C in social studies. I had to show her that he just hadn't put out much effort. He had not attempted any bonus test points and had done only one project. "He must learn that he must earn his A's," I explained. She agreed to see to it that he made a greater effort during our next unit.

Writing In addition to our journals, we did other writing activities this month. I have been saving the free postcards I get at motels, and the children learned the postcard form, which they enjoyed. We also wrote pen-pal letters to children in a fifth-grade class in Canada. I had met Kay Beck at a meeting I attended last May and when I realized I would be teaching fifth-graders about Canada, I wrote to set up this pen-pal arrangement with her. The children love having real friends in another country, and we will continue our letter writing for the rest of the year. Who knows? Some of them may remain pen pals for the rest of their lives!

M A R C H

Independence It's a good thing I wrote the word *Independence* in big red letters on my March, April, and May calendar months way back in August, or the year might have ended before I realized that I needed to move my children (I must stop thinking of them as children—they will be big middle-schoolers in **Meaning** five months!) toward becoming more independent learners. This month, I **Vocabulary** have tried to show them how they can independently learn new word meanings. Instead of me previewing the unit on plants and selecting the key words, I had the students look through the science chapters and write down words that seemed important to them of whose meanings they were not totally sure. I gave them about five minutes for this, then I made a list of all their words. I chose those I considered most important and least known, and we pronounced them and talked about what they might mean. Of course, some students knew some words. But no one could tell me the meanings of words such as *monocot*, *dicot*, and *photosynthesis*. I told students that as we studied plants, I would help them see how they could use their texts, our dictionaries and other reference books, and their own common sense to learn meanings without my telling them or showing them. Some of my students looked a little skeptical and so was I, but I knew that I must attempt to move them toward independence since they were sure to meet some "sink or swim" teachers in the coming years.

Fortunately, most of the words that the students had identified were also the words that I had deemed most important for them to learn. I added two words—*vascular* and *nonvascular*—and left the rest of the list as they had written it. That meant we had more words than I usually allot, twenty for a two-week unit. But they had chosen some words that I thought most of them knew and others that were so obscure, I didn't intend to focus on them much. So I left their list intact. That night, I divided their list into words for which I thought they had no meaning and words for which they had experienced the meaning but did not know the technical term. Fortunately, there were only four words for which I thought they might have little or no experience—*chlorophyll, photosynthesis, carbon dioxide,* and *stomata.* All the other words, though unfamiliar to the children, represented something they had experienced. They had all seen ferns, but did not know the leaves were called fronds. They had all seen vascular plants—trees, tulips, and carrots—as well as nonvascular plants—mosses. Likewise, they knew some plants lived only one year—annuals—and others lived a long, long time—perennials.

Science Thematic Unit I then looked through the chapters in their science book to find pictures from which students could build or call up their experience and to see what context clues were provided by the words. Finally, I looked at the list to see what morphemic clues the new words contained. For all the words for which the students had meaning, I found that the pictures, words, and morphemes would help the students call up their experience and connect it to the new words. The problem came, of course, with the process of photosynthesis and its related words, *chlorophyll, carbon dioxide,* and *stomata.* I knew that the text explanation of this process would make no sense; even though the children could read the words, they would not understand what was actually meant by them. I decided to follow the suggestion in the teacher's guide providing for direct experience through an experiment: we would deprive some plants of light, others of water, and others of air, by smearing petroleum jelly on both sides of the leaves. Still other plants would be given light and water and not smeared. Over the two weeks of our science unit, we watched the deprived plants grow. I helped them connect this experience with photosynthesis by explaining that light, water, and air, from which plants get carbon dioxide, are all required for plants to make their own food. I further explained that all green plants got their green coloring from a chemical called chlorophyll and that the air enters the leaf through stomata, the tiny openings that we had clogged when we smeared petroleum jelly on the leaves. The plants that died had chlorophyll, as we knew from their green color, but because we had deprived them of light, water, or carbon dioxide, they could not make food and died. This process of making food, I explained, can be done by all green plants, and it is called a big word—*photosynthesis.*

The experience I provided for the children allowed them to build meaning to associate with photosynthesis and the related words. I used pictures, context, and morphemic clues to help them call up and link their experience with the unfamiliar words. I have been using these clues all year, but this month I focused more on the pictures and context in the textbook and tried to get the children to discover the morphemic clues themselves.

Meaning Vocabulary

To begin my lesson, I circled the words *vascular, nonvascular, botanist, biennials, conifers, monocots, dicots,* and *life cycle* on the chart of words the students and I had selected to learn. I then had each child write a definition for three words of his or her choice. By now, the children know that they can write whatever they think, even a silly definition or something the word sounds like, and that we then compare these guesses made without context to our more probable guesses made from context. I let the children share a few of these guesses, and the class hams always have a good time. Dave said that *vascular* was what you had left after the vase had shattered. Jim suggested that a *botanist* was a scientist who studied bottles. Sharon said that *life cycle* was a new kind of bike you didn't have to pedal. The children enjoy their silly guesses, but the guessing serves a serious function, too. When we read a word in context or see a picture, sometimes we think we knew all along what the word meant. The guessing focuses the children's attention on the words and lets them see that they don't really know what they mean. After guessing, they are curious to find out the real meanings and see clearly how much the context and pictures help.

I directed the children's attention to certain sentences and pictures in their books and asked them to explain the words' meanings based on what they read and saw. In previous units, I had written context sentences on the board or provided pictures from magazines, books, or filmstrips. But now I wanted them to utilize the resource in which they were most apt to encounter unfamiliar words, their textbook. As the children explained their meanings based on the text, I probed to get them to explain their reasoning, since often the book doesn't come right out and say, "This means that." I also helped the children to connect their own experiences to the words. "Can you name some vascular plants you see on the way to school?" I asked. "Some nonvascular plants?" I let a few children look up some of the words in our encyclopedia to give us other examples of the meaning. Finally, I had each child write the words on a page in their science notebook along with our class definition, an example, and, if they liked, an illustration.

To help children use morphemic clues, I directed their attention to the word *conifer* and asked them if there was anything about the word that would help them remember that conifers are plants that produce seeds in cones. With my help, they noticed the *cone-conifer* relationship. I then asked them what word we could use to describe someone with courage? To describe something associated with danger? I wrote their responses on the board next to the root word (*courage, courageous; danger, dangerous*). I then wrote *conifer* and *coniferous*, and the children saw that *coniferous* was a word used to describe conifers. In a similar way, I helped them to see that bicycles have two wheels, to bisect is to cut in two parts, and biennials are plants that live two years. I also pointed out that many words that start with *bi-* have nothing to do with two, reminding them about *biographies*. Morphemic clues are helpful, but in English, they can mislead you. I try to remind my students to check morphemic clues against the other information in context and pictures.

Research

We did many other activities in our unit on plants. We created a class horticultural guide to which each child contributed by researching and writing a one-page illustrated report on a selected plant. The books *Being a Plant* and *Plants Up Close* were most helpful. We took on a beautification project, planting some lovely shrubs donated by Hernando's dad and some pachysandra and ajuga that we dug up at my house.

Writing Minilesson

We even wrote some poetry: plant cinquains. Cinquains are poems for nonpoets. There are many different ways to create these five-line poems. In this unit we brainstormed ideas for each line as a group. Then each child selected from the brainstormed list or came up with more ideas of his or her own. We wrote cinquains about monocots, dicots, conifers, annuals, and perennials as a way to review their important characteristics. The first and last line of the cinquain were the same for everyone—the topic of our cinquain. For the second line, we brainstormed a list of *-ing* words that described the topic. For the third line, we brainstormed examples of the topic. For the fourth line, we brainstormed four-word phrases and sentences that summed up the topic. Each child then chose or made up two *-ing* words, three examples, one four-word phrase or sentence, and created his or her own unique cinquains. Here is Ray's cinquain for dicots. I am so proud of him!

Dicots
Blooming, growing
Pines, roses, beans
Two seed leaves each
Dicots

A   P   R   I   L

Social Studies Thematic Unit

Well, April was Latin America month! I feel like I have been on one of those "see six countries in four days" tours. I am sure that we could have studied Latin America all year and still had more we wanted to learn. There is just never enough time! At least, I think we accomplished the major goal of the unit: to give our youngsters some understanding of the similarities and differences between us and our southern neighbors.

Comprehension Minilesson

Independence

I have tried to use more graphic organizers in my comprehension minilessons this month in my continuing crusade to move my students toward independence. In earlier units, they completed many partial outlines, feature matrices, webs, and time lines that I set up for them. This month, I had them make outlines, webs, feature matrices, or time lines from their reading assignments, but I did not give them the headings or categories or tell them how many boxes or slots to fill in. This was hard for all of them, and Hernando, Dave, Jim, and Stephanie did not write much down after reading. We had to spend far more time following up the reading and constructing the outline, feature matrix, web, or time line. But most students did get better by the end of the month and if I can teach them to preview text and decide on a note-taking structure—which is really what outlines, features matrices, webs, and time lines are—they will be able to determine and note the most important information by themselves.

Research We have also continued to work toward becoming independent writers and researchers. This month, we created a travel book, and I had each child type the final copy as a way of getting them to use the word processing skills they have been learning during our weekly computer lab time. My artistic children did some wonderful illustrations, and we duplicated the book so that everyone could take a copy home and take his or her family on an imaginary journey to Latin America. I must admit that the children worked as hard as I did, and they were very proud of their creation, as was I. I have tried all year to give them real audiences and purposes to write for, but this was my most successful attempt. Creating a real book to share knowledge about Latin America with their families was indeed a real purpose for a real audience.

We spent the first week with maps, globes, and other resources studying the geographic, cultural, and political boundaries of Latin America. The children were amazed that there are over thirty countries to the south of us, ranging from tiny Trinidad to huge Brazil. During the next week, we did an in-depth study of Mexico, which I used to model the research and writing process we would use to create our book. First, I had them generate questions about Mexico. Then we tried to organize them. We decided that there were questions about people (How many people live in Mexico? Why do people from Mexico come to the United States? Where did the people in Mexico come from?), customs (What do they like to eat? Do they go to school in summer? Do they have Christmas, too?), government (Who is their president? Do they have a good government?), and the economy (Where do people work? Why are so many people poor?). We put two questions into our all-important miscellaneous category.

I put each category of questions on a transparency, and we trooped off to the library to locate sources likely to contain the answers. Using the card catalog, *The Readers' Guide to Periodical Literature*, and indices of reference books, we collected quite a few. We found seven books devoted entirely to Mexico! How could we find our answers without reading everything? Of course, we brainstormed some key words to find the information more efficiently. For some questions, it was easy to come up with a useful key word. *Food* helped us find information about what people eat. For other questions, it was more difficult. To answer the question about why people come to the United States, I had to suggest that we look under *emigration* and *economy*.

As we were finding our answers, we also found other information, so we added some categories. Our question about where people came from led us to information about Mexico's early history, creating an early history category. We also decided that since we were writing a travel book, we needed information about recreation and good places to visit—another category. Eventually, we had transparencies with information about the people; early history; the government; the economy; customs; things to do and places to visit; and, of course, miscellaneous. The children wanted to write down everything they had found, but I tried to show them that in our one travel book we could not duplicate the information in many books devoted solely to Mexico, especially since we wanted to cover all of Latin America. I modeled for them how I decided what seemed most important, but when they got started on their own work, it was clear that setting priorities and limiting your notes is a skill they won't master this year!

During the third week, the students researched their chosen country. Previously, I have had them do this research in small groups or pairs but, keeping my independence goal in mind, I decided they should try it on their own. I did assign smaller countries, which have much less information to plow through, to my slower children. I don't think anyone noticed this, and it made the task more manageable for everyone. Each child had one sheet of paper for each category, with some questions and key words. With the help of our librarian, we located sources for everyone and helped students to find

Special Learners the information within. Of course, Dave, Jim, Hernando, Stephanie, and Ray required the most help, but even they put out a good effort and found some information. Much of what they found was very hard for them to read, so I read a little to them and helped them write down the important facts. It is at times like this that I wish the pupil-teacher ratio were about five to one! Fortunately, some of my better students finished their research and helped the slower ones to make workable notes.

Writing Minilesson Finally, we got ready to write the reports. We decided to use a standard form with one paragraph for each subtopic. I pulled out my transparencies on Mexico and showed the children how to combine the information into paragraphs on the people, early history, and so forth. By now, most of the children have a good idea about how to construct a good paragraph. The fact that the notes were organized on separate sheets of paper around subtopics helped them keep their paragraphs on track. We used miscellaneous information in our concluding paragraph if appropriate. We had to make some return trips to the library for missing information or to check contradictory facts. I had shown the children how to write the source for the information in the margin in case they needed to find that information again, but I think most of them forgot this little detail! In some cases, we simply could not find the source so we found another one or deleted the information.

Revising Once the first drafts of the reports were written, I paired the children to read theirs to each other. They were to listen for information only at this point, to help the writer make the piece clearer or more interesting. I myself sat down with Dave, Jim, Hernando, Che, and Ray and helped them finish sentences and clarify what they meant as much as I could. Once the children had revised for content, we began the editing process. Again, I had them work with their partners first. This time I had the partner read the piece aloud as the writer looked on. I have been having them edit like this all year and it is most helpful to the writer. Writers cannot generally proof their own writing since they read what they meant to write, not what they actually wrote. Bob wrote, "Were did the erly peoples of trinidad come from." When Kazu read this, he noticed the misspelling of *where,* the unnecessary *s* on *peoples,* and the need for a capital *T* on *Trinidad.* Once Kazu pointed these out, Bob saw them too and fixed them. They both missed the fact that early was misspelled and that the sentence should have ended with a question mark, but three out of five is better than none.

Once the partners had worked together to edit the papers, I did a final editing and then each child typed his or her paper. It took awhile but they helped each other and they were so proud of the professional look of their travel books.

M A Y

Science Thematic Units

This month, we finished our final two science units: Matter and Animals. The children already had a tremendous amount of prior knowledge about animals; from what I can tell, it is part of the science curriculum at every grade level. I know I taught an animals unit in fourth grade and Belle teaches one in second. Matter, on the other hand, was another matter! Jim even showed his language prowess when I got frustrated with their inability to keep mass and weight distinctions straight: He asked, "But Miss Tent, what does it really matter?"

Meaning Vocabulary

We continued our push for independence and they are actually acting more like middle-schoolers. Once again I let them preview their textbook for vocabulary words and tried to focus their attention on picture, context, and morphemic clues as well as show them how our dictionaries and reference books could help them develop meanings for unknown words. As I mentioned, we had a great deal of difficulty making the mass/weight distinction. Of course, children think of weight as how many pounds they are, which is in fact their mass. Weight, or the amount of pull between objects, is a concept many of them never did understand. It helped to have them view films of astronauts and to realize that the astronauts still had the same mass but were weightless because of lack of gravity. We used a balance scale to measure mass and made a simple pulley scale to measure weight. I do believe my more able students understood the difference by the time we finished.

Research

The conceptual difficulty of the unit on matter was balanced by the ease with which my students approached the unit on animals. Even my slower students knew most of the information in our textbook, so we read it quickly to remind ourselves of what we knew and reestablish the terminology. Then we spent our time researching various animals and their habits. I divided the class into five groups, each to become experts about one class of animals. One group learned about invertebrates. Another group studied both amphibians and fish, because there are so few amphibians. The other three groups studied reptiles, birds, and mammals. We decided that each group would

Collaborative Groups

create an "encyclopedia" for their class of animals and that we would donate these to our school library as this fifth grade's graduation present to the school. The encyclopedia would include a general introduction giving characteristics of the animal class and illustrated pages for as many different animals as we had time to do.

Of course, we brainstormed a list of questions about each animal, classified the questions, and decided on key words to help us locate information. We then set up a data chart with the questions along the top and room to list the various animals down the side. I also had the children keep a list of sources, each of which they numbered as they added it to their list. They then put the number and page number next to the various pieces of information they found. This was not perfect but they did note more source information than they had last month.

In addition to everyone's main function of finding and recording specific information, I gave each child an official duty. In each group, one child was the leader, keeping all the group's information and making sure everything got done. I tried to put good organizers in every group and appoint them leaders. Another child in each group was appointed reference librarian, taking primary responsibility for locating sources and keeping information accurate. I appointed an art director for each group, although all the children could do art, and I provided tracing paper for the less artistic. The art director was to oversee the production of the art, however. I also had an editor, who looked at each article before it came to the editor in chief (me!). Finally, each group had a production manager whose job it was to put the finished pieces into the book and see to pagination, binding, cover design, index, and so forth.

It is hard for me to believe even now how hard all my children worked. They took their individual responsibilities very seriously and were determined that their group's encyclopedia would be the best. Parents told me stories of weekend trips to the public library and of hours their children spent reading, drawing, checking off what was there and what was needed, designing covers, and editing. We did not type the books this time but let the children write the pages in their neatest handwriting. I had no idea some of them could write so well.

The idea of giving every child some special responsibility worked out much better than I had anticipated. It used the strengths of all and made each child feel that his or her contribution was critical. The groups—which contained bright and slow, industrious and lazy, impulsive and reflective children—all worked well and developed a strong sense of cohesion. Next year I shall have to find more ways to assign groups in which each has a special responsibility.

J U N E

Why is it you think the year will never end and then it ends before you are ready? This year's students are grown-up middle-schoolers now, and I am looking forward to a super fifth-grade year next year, knowing so much more than I did when I began this year.

We did our final health unit in the final week of school. This was a required unit on drug abuse. I still contend that fifth-graders are too young to be considering this sophisticated topic. I was surprised, however, at how much some of them knew. Jim suggested we have a scavenger hunt, but I demurred.

Thinking Processes In looking back over the year, particularly at my ambitious goals, I am "cautiously optimistic"! My checklist demonstrates that, for the first time in my illustrious teaching career, I paid more than lip service to helping students learn the thinking skills that seem to be the foundation for all other learning. The two I always found hardest were, of course, the highest-level ones, evaluating and applying. But as the year went on I did learn how to phrase questions so that students would have to evaluate and apply what they were learning to new situations. And I finally got in the habit of saying, "This question requires a lot of brain power. You will have to think and decide what your answer will be. I don't want to see any hands until I have counted slowly to five." This five seconds of wait time was crucial to the students' ability to develop thoughtful answers and, as research suggests, improved the quality of their answers dramatically. I also tried to assign projects that required evaluation and application.

Meaning Vocabulary Meaning vocabulary was probably the area in which I felt most satisfied with the progress we made toward our goals. I was particularly excited to see that students could select their own words to learn, and could independently apply the strategies I taught them to learn the appropriate meanings.

Writing/Research My students made tremendous progress in writing and researching, but they are still a long way from where I would like to have had them when they went off to middle school. I guess these are such complex processes that they take a very long time to develop. Some children, Sharon and Pat particularly, are indeed independent writers and researchers. My slower ones made some progress and seemed to learn a lot of content as they engaged in writing and researching, but their skills are still very rudimentary. Many of my average children also made progress in learning how to write and do research, but they continue to need a lot of guidance. I always wonder how much real teaching they get once they leave elementary school. My friends who are high-school teachers are always ribbing me about my "misguided" beliefs that the only real instruction goes on at elementary school. I hope in this case that they are right because, even with good elementary instruction, these kids still have much content to learn as well as independent learning strategies.

Next year I plan to use the same schedule as this year, with one exception. I am going to use both Monday and Friday for integration. By the end of the year, I found all kinds of opportunities to integrate math, reading, and writing into the units. I also found that there are always art, music, and drama possibilities. I even found some ways to integrate physical education activities and games into what we were studying. There just wasn't enough time to do all the integration I wanted to on just one day. In addition, I could tell that the children were much more motivated and involved on our integrated days. Their excitement convinced me that one day a week is just not enough. I chose Monday and Friday so that we can have a big kickoff and then a grand finale. I think it will also help all of us to get over the "Monday blahs" to know that Monday is going to be a "Special Day."

Mr. Head, who was skeptical about my Friday integration at the beginning of the year, was actually very pleased with what he saw on Fridays and sent other teachers to observe. He even suggested I might want to consider two days of integration. I didn't tell him I had already decided to do so!

All in all, a quite successful year! Now, if I can just stay at the fifth-grade level another year or two, I think I could get quite good at this. This summer, I plan to become proficient in Italian and French as Bo and I take our railpasses through Europe!

REFERENCES

Asimov, I. (1983). *How did we find out about the universe?* New York: Walker & Co.

Branley, F. M. (1981). *The planets in our solar system.* New York: Crowell.

Cleary, B. (1984). *Ramona forever.* New York: Morrow.

Collier, J. (1983). *Planet out of the past.* New York: Macmillan.

Corbett, S. (1981). *The deadly hoax.* New York: Dutton.

Engdahl, S. L. (1981). *The doors of the universe.* New York: Atheneum.

Holbrook, S. (1983). *Canada's kids.* New York: Atheneum.

Hoover, H. M. (1981). *Another heaven, another earth.* New York: Viking.

Lyle, K. (1983). *Take a trip to Canada.* New York: Franklin Watts.

Paterson, K. (1977). *Bridge to Terabithia.* New York: Crowell.

Pringle, L. (1983). *Being a plant.* New York: Crowell.

Rahn, J. E. (1981). *Plants up close.* Boston: Houghton Mifflin.

Shreve, S. (1984). *The flunking of Joshua T. Bates.* New York: Knopf.

C H A P T E R   1 1
Social Studies and English

A U G U S T

My name is Hugh Mann, and this is my second year of teaching. I've been hired primarily to teach social studies and some English; I'm also the head varsity baseball coach. Sports and books have always been a part of my life. I even read for fun in high school, when most of my friends barely touched a book—unless it had especially interesting pictures.

This year's teaching assignment is the same as last year's. I have two sections of American history and three sections of English II. Both courses are intended for sophomores. My department head said that he typically assigns first- and second-year people just two different courses, but that the load will go to three or even four preparations as experience is gained. I appreciate the relatively light load because I'm still getting a handle on how to teach effectively. My student teaching and my first year of teaching were largely matters of staying alive. The students and I got along well, and they seemed to learn something, but I frequently was at a loss while planning lessons. I've given some thought to my teaching over the summer and intend to try some new things this year. One of the guys I played baseball with this summer teaches also, and he gave me some tips I intend to try out.

My reaction to the curriculum guides for my courses still is near panic: "How can I ever cover all this stuff?" The history curriculum guide contains twelve units, which consist of three to five topics each. The topics are broad and just filled with issues and facts! There are two curriculum guides for English, literature, and language arts, which presents mechanics such as grammar, spelling, and writing conventions.

My other big concern is managing approximately 130 students each day. Maintaining discipline and keeping students interested in the subject can be big problems, as I remember from my own high-school days and from my teaching experience to date. Stay tuned, and as I report my teaching adventures each month in this journal, we'll find out how I do.

S E P T E M B E R

Study Strategies

One of my first activities in American history was to take my classes through a "tour" of the textbook. I pointed out the table of contents, the glossary, and the index. Within each chapter I directed the students' attention to the introductions, conclusions, boldfaced headings, footnotes, illustrations, maps, graphs, and review sections. I wanted to accustom the students to the text so they could better predict, organize, and review while moving through it. When I recommended reading the end-of-chapter questions before reading the chapter, several students spoke up. One student, Ken, thought my recommendation sounded like cheating; Judy informed me that she did it all the time because her honors English teacher in junior high had suggested it; and Lonnie sullenly announced that if they had to answer the questions, then it only made sense to go to them first, find the answers, and be done with it. I responded that the special features of a textbook were intended to help people learn and that I did not plan to have students merely copy down answers to sets of questions. "I want to develop your abilities to think, not to regurgitate," I rather pompously declared. "Use the special features of the book in order to learn what is presented. We'll spend most of our class time discussing what you've read."

Discussion

Well, we discussed our way through the first unit of the American history text, Early Years in America, and, frankly, the discussions weren't very productive. The unit consisted of about 100 pages with chapters on Native American culture before Columbus's arrival, the European age of discovery, and England in the New World. Our discussion of the first chapter typifies how the other discussions went.

The students came in on Monday, having been told to read the chapter on early Native Americans over the weekend. I was ready to go. "What did you think of the chapter?" I asked. When nobody responded right away, I called on Ken. "There sure were a lot of tribes," he answered. Nobody else had anything to say. I could see some of the students in the back begin to put their heads down for a nap or whisper to each other, so I immediately asked another question, "What did you learn about the tribes?" Judy piped up that they played different ball games. "Mr. Mann, the Eskimos played some kind of kickball, and I think the book said the Algonquins invented lacrosse."

Rod, this year's football quarterback, wanted to know how lacrosse was played. I told what I knew, and the discussion picked up as comparisons were made between lacrosse and the various other sports the students knew. I chimed in to explain in some detail how catching and throwing a ball with a lacrosse stick differed from catching a baseball and either hitting it with a bat or throwing it. Before I knew, the hour was over and our discussion of the chapter had ended. I felt uneasy about what had been accomplished, but the next class came in and I didn't have time to sort out where I had gone wrong.

Meaning Vocabulary

In order to help develop vocabulary, I reproduced word puzzles from the teacher's resource book. The puzzles consisted of words with their spelling scrambled accompanied by definitions. For instance, *UTRIPSAN* was next to "Fundamental religious group that established a colony under the auspices of the Massachusetts Bay Company." When I passed out the first set of scrambled words, Judy completed it in about ten minutes and asked if she could make up her own for the class to do. At the other extreme, Ambrose never turned his in. I asked him about it, and he reported that he never was good with "them kind of things." In general, the classes worked busily completing the worksheets; the sharper students got all the items correct, and the duller students missed some. I wonder if the puzzles are producing any new insights into the words and their meanings?

Content Area Literature

Sophomore English began about the same as American history. One assignment dealt with book reports. Since our anthology kept everyone on the same track, I wanted to give students a chance to branch out on their own. There are terrific books written specifically for teenagers, and some of my sophomores could easily handle materials intended for adults. Thus, the assignment was for each student to read at least one book per month and turn in a written summary as well as a statement about whether they would recommend the book to a friend. I heard some grumblings like, "We've been doing book reports since third grade," but when I reassured the class that they could choose any book they wanted, they seemed to accept the idea.

Language arts probably should be called "language skills" because it covers such topics as parts of speech, sentence construction, and report writing. There is very little about the artistic, creative side of language in the text. I decided to cover language skills Monday through Wednesday and do literature on Thursday and Friday. Language skill work mostly consisted of me explaining various rules and definitions ("Proper nouns name particular persons, places, or things") followed by exercises in locating the item that had just been defined ("Underline the proper nouns in the following sentences"). I usually also have the students make up sentences containing the items being studied.

Thinking Processes— Generalize

The literature anthology unit focused on theme. The passages are pretty interesting, so most of the students read them. After reading each passage, we discussed its theme.

All in all, I'm not really satisfied with how my classes went this past month. My routines are functioning smoothly enough, but my students seem like automatons going through the motions. They don't seem to be thinking very deeply. I'm going to have to do something about this.

O C T O B E R

Discussion Our discussions in both classes of American history moved this month from very loose to very structured. I was getting concerned about the students coming in unprepared and leading me off on tangents, so I resolved to hold the class closer to the text. This month's unit was on the American Revolution. One day we were talking about the early events in Boston. After dealing with the Stamp Act, the Quartering Act, and the Boston Massacre, we got to the Boston Tea Party. Lonnie wanted to know why it was called a "party." After I stated that some words have several different meanings, Rod interjected that the Boston Garden, home of the Celtics basketball team, really wasn't a vegetable or flower garden. "Who are the Celtics?" Ambrose wanted to know. Well, Ken eagerly began explaining the past triumphs of Larry Bird, Bill Russell, and Bob Cousy when I interrupted forcefully, "No more talk about words with multiple meanings! What did Lord North and King George do after the tea was dumped into the harbor?" As soon as I got the answer that I wanted ("passed the Intolerable Acts"), I asked, "What did the Intolerable Acts consist of?" After Judy finally supplied the correct answer, I continued with questions such as, "When did the First Continental Congress meet?" "What actions did it take?" "Why did General Gage order a march on Concord?" and "Where did the Second Continental Congress meet?" Answering these questions kept all my students on their toes, and we moved efficiently through the textbook chapters, although I must confess that I began feeling like a prosecuting attorney. I also began to wonder if I were promoting only rote memory in my students.

Content Area Literature A high point this past month was the arrival of the first edition of the weekly magazine we'll be receiving during the year. The magazine is quite appealing! It has many visuals, lots of color, timely articles, and features that the students really like. I pass the magazines out each Friday, and the students either read them on their own or complete assignments that are due by the end of the following week. I hope this is the best way to use the magazines.

The scrambled word puzzles began losing their appeal by the end of September, so I began setting aside about thirty minutes a week for vocabulary work using the dictionary or the textbook. I wrote a list of important **Meaning Vocabulary** words on the board, and the students copied the words and looked up their definitions. This started off about as well as the puzzles because everybody kept busy and almost everybody turned in completed papers. The students worked with such abstract terms as *sovereignty, loyalist, representation, inalienable right*, and *confederation*; the list also included names such as *Lafayette, Greene, Adams, Hamilton*, and *Jefferson*.

American history still doesn't seem to be engaging my students' thinking the way I want it to. As in September, we're moving through the material, but the students don't seem to be connecting anything they're learning with their present lives. Something else is going to have to happen!

Collaborative Learning

In English I implemented a rather successful grouping system to help with our boring study of the parts of speech. I introduced the grouping system by explaining the value of collaboration. I read some excerpts from business leaders' reports calling for today's students to learn how to work in groups and described the changes in the work force that called for group interaction. Next, I explained that each student would be responsible for his or her own learning as well as that of their teammates. "Individual and group scores will be maintained," I pronounced. Other guidelines were that I would assign group membership, productive group interaction would be emphasized as much as academic learning, the groups would last for one month before forming new ones, and they would always meet in the same spot during group work time.

Before turning the students loose, a group of five came up and demonstrated particular roles individuals played (mayor, scribe, timekeeper) and a few important interactions (praising others, summarizing, taking turns talking). This simulation was to identify key features of group work for the students to emphasize when they were in their groups.

Then I explained the day's assignment, which was conducive to group work. Following the contents of the language arts text on pronouns, I presented specific elements, such as personal, relative, and demonstrative pronouns, then distributed handouts calling for appropriate pronouns to be inserted in sentences ("Those who hurt others hurt ____."). I established a time limit, so that groups who didn't finish in class had to do so on their own. When time was up, I collected the papers and then went over them with the class. To be sure, analyzing the types of pronouns was a bit of a drag—I wonder what effect knowing which pronoun is which has on anything?—but I must say that the group work stirred the class in a rather positive way. Even Lonnie got involved with his two friends and actually turned something in.

Assessment

Holding students accountable for daily language arts work posed a problem until I decided to work with points. If a paper met criteria that I established, then I accepted it and gave it one point. Unacceptable papers were returned for another attempt. For instance, one assignment might consist of twenty unfinished sentences to be filled in and five original sentences to be written using a certain part of speech. If my criterion was 80 percent accuracy, those papers with at least twenty items correct received one point. I have posted the points, not grades, permanently on a bulletin board so group members know where they stand individually and as a group. The posting also helped solve the problem of coping with students' absences, showing students who missed a day how to keep track of what was due. Posting points took a good deal of time, but luckily I had two seniors assigned to me as teacher assistants. Once I showed them the system, they took full responsibility for keeping it updated.

The testing procedures that I began in English worked out rather well. The tests that I gave matched what I had been teaching as closely as possible. If in class I'd had the students write essays, then my tests also included essay writing. If the students made up their own sentences, then they did likewise on the test. Thus, all who had consistently worked with me in class had a good chance to succeed. However, I also tested students on some material that I had assigned for work at home. This allowed my high-ability students to show what they could do. During the month I made sure to demonstrate such test-taking strategies as returning to difficult multiple-choice items and generating key words before writing essay answers. When it came time to report midterm grades, I included points earned in groups, test scores, and the great intangible, class participation.

As I think about October, I believe my instruction picked up in English but didn't do well in American history. The group work in English is allowing some good interaction among the students as they deal with the rather mundane mechanics of language. I'm still bound to the texts in my courses, however; I'm having difficulty getting them to come alive.

N O V E M B E R

Our study of The New Nation in American history this month leveled off at a new plateau. My procedure of assigning certain pages and then discussing them just wasn't succeeding. The discussions either ranged far from the topic, or I ended up conducting an interrogation that emphasized isolated facts. This month I got tired of discussions and spent most of the time lecturing and showing movies. I began the lectures and movies when we came to the section of the text about the Bill of Rights. We had slogged our way through federalism and checks and balances, and I was getting no response to my questions about the first ten amendments to the Constitution. As a result, I just began talking. There were few interruptions, so I continued. Occasionally someone wanted to know, "Is this going to be on the test?" to which I answered, "Maybe." The next day I showed a surprisingly interesting movie that detailed the contents and implications of the Bill of Rights. Basic liberties such as freedom of speech, protection from unreasonable search and seizure, and due process of law were made somewhat real by the situations enacted in the film. Most of the class actually watched the movie, there were no discipline problems, and my preparation time was practically zero. I'll probably continue with this lecture-and-film procedure a little longer.

Meaning Vocabulary
Vocabulary instruction took an upswing this month. The word puzzles and searches for definitions had kept everybody well occupied, but little learning seemed to go on. The students rarely remembered the definitions and were at a total loss to explain the terms in their own words. So one day I decided

to explain each term by analogizing, that is, by connecting new concepts and terms to something I thought the students had already experienced. For example, *strict construction* and *loose construction* were two high-sounding terms with somewhat vague meanings that came up during our study of the Constitution. "Let's say that you get grounded at home for doing something against the rules," I explained, "and a school club or team that you belong to is going somewhere after school the next day. Would you be able to go?" Judy volunteered the fact that she had never been grounded, but, if she were, her parents probably would make her come home right after classes. On the other hand, Allison contemptuously reported, "They wouldn't dare try to keep me in the house every afternoon and evening." Ken reported that it probably would depend on the mood his parents were in each day, and Rod was sure that he could practice with his team but would then need to be home soon afterward. I pointed out that some families seemed to interpret the "grounding" punishment strictly while others saw it loosely. Thus distinguishing *strict* and *loose constructions* of grounding, I explained how Jefferson's and Hamilton's debate over a federal bank was based on the conflict between strict and loose constructions of the Constitution. This explanation seemed to take hold and I made a mental note to connect more terms with students' lives in that way.

Two words, *party* (as in Federalist party) and *cabinet,* came up in this unit and deserved special attention. These multiple-meaning words can be really confusing for some students, so I explained their meanings in American history as clearly as possible, pointing out how those meanings differed from general uses of the terms. I reminded the class about the Boston Tea *Party* and compared that use of the term with its uses in Federalist *party*, being a *party* to a crime, and weekend *party*. As I explained each term, the students took notes. This way of developing vocabulary definitely makes the students depend on me for information, but there is a lot to learn and sometimes my explanations are the best way to get that information across. In fact, my lectures seem to be getting the students' attention, but I wonder if this is the best way to teach.

The group work during language skills exercises in English continued nicely this month. Allison brought in some soft rock albums from home, so we play background music during this time. Terry, perhaps the hardest-working student in school, really gets involved with these worksheets; whereas Allison more than once questioned the value of knowing the difference between an action verb and an auxiliary verb. "Mr. Mann," she would say, "sometimes I just get tired of answering your paper questions." During our literature study, Allison does a little better. We're into characterization now, having finished theme, plot, and setting, and she contributes to those discussions.

Comprehension Minilesson

One teaching strategy that I tried with characterization worked especially well. I called my strategy an Adjective Checklist. Before having the students read a short story in the anthology, I listed five adjectives on the board: *shrewd, brusque, honest, witty,* and *helpful.* The students and I spent a little time going over those terms by describing behaviors that exemplified each of the five. I then read aloud a brief poem by Shel Silverstein and explained why I thought *helpful* best described the main character in the poem. Lonnie disagreed, saying that *shrewd* was better, but he couldn't support his argument when I pressed him. "What part of the poem supports the fact that he was shrewd?" I asked. Allison stepped in and gave quite a convincing argument for *shrewd* that would never have occurred to me. I accepted her argument and complimented her on her insight into the poem. Only then did I give the assignment, "Read the story on pages 38 to 45 in the anthology and decide which adjective best describes Mr. Steiner, the main character."

The next day we had a lively discussion about whether "witty" or "brusque" best described Mr. Steiner. Students who argued for either adjective came up with some logical reasons for their choices. Finally, Ambrose spoke up. "What's the answer, Mr. Mann?" I knew I was in a dilemma. Giving my answer would limit future discussions because students simply would be trying to anticipate what I would say; on the other hand, not giving an answer seemed unfair because students like to get closure on a problem. Additionally, I must admit that I was becoming used to playing the role of the all-knowing teacher, so not giving the "correct" answer was **Writing** difficult. My solution was to have students write their choices and justify them on notebook paper. This allowed students to get some closure in their minds, and it allowed me to evaluate their rationales rather than their actual choices.

The adjective checklist continued to work well throughout our study of characterization. It let us cover the traditional aspects of characterization study (physical appearances, motivations, effects on others) while providing a way to analyze characters in real life. The students learned some new vocabulary and they obtained good insights into the stories. Additionally, our discussions stayed on track without me asking a thousand picky questions. Whenever a student would choose an adjective, I would ask something like, "What makes you think that?" or "What leads you to that conclusion?" Comprehension was directed, and the students' writing consisted of more than completing unfinished sentences or taking notes.

Collaborative Learning The adjective checklist also worked well with the groups. I brought in several stories written at different levels of difficulty and had each group choose two. Including materials of different levels provided appropriate challenges for my good as well as poor readers. The task was to decide as a group which adjectives from a list of eight gave the best and worst descriptions of the characters I designated. I went from group to group and had them justify their choices to me. Time was short for me to get to all the **Assessment** groups, but I made it. My follow-up test consisted of six adjectives and a two-page story, which I read aloud while the class followed along. The task was to choose the best description and justify it. The clear insight of practically every student's response indicated that the group interactions had been valuable.

In English our discussions were productive, group members interacted well and completed their tasks, and my grading system was holding up. The students seemed quite alert throughout the class periods. Vocabulary study in American history also picked up this month, thanks to analogizing. But I'm still looking for a way to deal with comprehension of the text.

D E C E M B E R

The success we had in English with the adjective checklist made me think twice about the book projects I had assigned. Some good books were being read. Students were picking up old favorites such as *Watership Down*, *The Pigman*, and *Kon-Tiki*, as well as new titles such as *Everything Is Not Enough*, *Adrift*, and *Shoeless Joe*, from the school and public libraries, from each other, and from bookstores. I recommended some titles and provided class time for the students to recommend others. However, the reports weren't very compelling. The summaries were mostly adequate, but the brief evaluative statements that I required were on a pretty low level. Students typically stated either that a book was interesting or that it was boring.

Book Projects   So I changed the assignment. Students still needed to read novels out of class, but they had choices of ways to respond to the novels. I divided the assignment among the "big four" literary elements—plot, setting, character, and theme—and provided alternatives for considering those elements. For instance, students could consider setting by diagramming a stage for a scene to be dramatized or by drawing a map depicting locations in the story. Students analyzed characterization by completing an adjective checklist or by justifying their choices of popular actors and actresses to portray the main characters. Once I got to thinking about it, I saw many options for eliciting responses to stories. Some examples that emerged included the following: select a piece of representative dialogue, choose the book's most important word, describe a change that occurred in a character, explain how a situation you've been in is similar to one in the book, convince a movie producer that your book should be made into a movie, write the book's epilogue. I tried to provide a mix between strongly academic options (What was the theme of the story?) and more artistic ones (Create a mobile that represents the story).

Thinking Processes   The students seemed to appreciate this new freedom, and more thinking processes seemed to be in evidence with the new system. Some of the images produced when students dealt with setting and character were outstanding; the connections students drew between their lives and the characters' were sharply drawn; and the hypothetical sales pitches to movie producers were organized well. Moreover, students seemed to like the combination of clear expectations plus some freedom of choice.

A major change begun in English this month was to integrate what I was teaching. I had felt uncomfortable with the diversity of doing worksheets on superlative degree, collecting projects on whatever book each student chose, and studying the genre of adventure and one or two literary elements in the literature anthology. This fragmented way of doing things was relatively easy to manage, but it lacked the coherence that I thought an English class should have. Science fiction was the next genre in our anthology, so I decided to extend that topic to language arts and the book projects.

Literature   Making the extension to the book projects was not too difficult. I met with the school librarian and the English department head to learn what science fiction books were available. We turned up individual copies of numerous books and found a class set of *Flowers for Algernon*. I then announced to my sophomores that December's book projects were to follow the response format that I had begun and were to be based on science-fiction novels. Judy reacted to my news in a surprisingly negative way, "Science fiction, yucch! Why do we have to read that stuff?" I explained the value of the topic and informed the class that tying the novels in with the short stories made all kinds of sense—at least in terms of deepening insights into a topic. "Besides," I said, "there are some great science-fiction books. *The Postman, Moonwind,* and *Singularity* are great new books, and the *The Martian Chronicles, 20,000 Leagues under the Sea,* and *2001: A Space Odyssey* are classics. You'll love them! Trust me."

Teacher Read Alouds   One way to get students such as Judy into science fiction was for me to read some stories to them. When I told the class my plan, I sensed a "wait-and-see" attitude. I don't think too many male secondary-school teachers had read to these students. The story I chose was punchy and reasonably short, I reviewed it the night before I presented it, and I read it with as much force as possible. I told myself that I was at a speech contest, the students were the judges, and I intended to impress them. Well, the group attended to every word. It was a great experience! I think they were amazed at how much fun it was to form their own images while listening rather than have a filmmaker form the images for them.

Writing Minilesson   Extending the language skills work to science fiction took more planning on my part, but it seems to have paid off. Writing informal letters and business letters was the unit in our language arts text, so I tied letter writing into science fiction by having students compose letters that were related to situations in the stories. For instance, as a group we read a great Ray Bradbury story about a hunter who went back in time to shoot dinosaurs. "OK, group," I said, "we're going to write a letter to a close friend describing the trip." After detailing the topic, audience, role, and form of the assignment a bit more, I projected an overhead transparency of a model letter. I pointed out aspects such as where the date went, how to address the letter, how to sign off, and how to develop the composition. My model letter was brief, but it did have an introduction, a chronological description of the trip (which I pointed out as only one way to go), and a summarizing statement at the end. The students then went to their groups for ten minutes to brainstorm and organize what they intended to say. Finally, twenty minutes of class time was devoted to individuals writing their letters. Rather than grade the letters themselves, I gave one point to each letter written according to the form I'd presented. Students who didn't follow the form were given another chance.

The same basic procedure was followed with business letters. I assigned a business letter to a government agency requesting a permit to take hunters back in time. Possible governmental objections posed by the story were to be countered in the letter. Again I explained the task, modeled the writing of a business letter, allowed the students to generate and organize information before writing, and then let them write. As with the lesson on informal letters, I took the skill from our language text and applied it to our current topic. I still assigned one or two of the skill book exercises as practice in letter writing, but the skill had already been tied into the content of our study. I don't know why I didn't do this earlier.

And finally, thank goodness for the holiday season! Teaching is hard work, and I was ready for a break. My social life took a dip during the past four months, so I've been trying to revive it during this time. Some college friends came into town, so we had some catching up to do. I invited Kay Bella, a first-year Spanish teacher at school, to one of our parties, and she handled herself well with my rowdy friends. She and I talked shop for a few hours, but that's what we had most in common. I told her how I integrated what I taught in English, how the group assignments and book projects worked, and how frustrated I was with American history. She said she had some control problems with her classes, but that basically she was getting along fine. She briefly described how she supported students' reading comprehension. It was fun comparing observations about teaching with her.

J A N U A R Y

Well, I made some major changes in American history this month. At the beginning of the month, students were coming late to my class and some were even skipping. This upset me because I had thought at least I had kept things moving. I spent a good amount of time preparing my lectures, I always included some humor, and I was familiar with the quirks of every movie projector in the school because I showed so many films. Allison was the one who helped me see the light. She came into class one day muttering about another session of brain death. "Allison, what are you talking about?" I asked. She looked me straight in the eye and replied, "When do we get to *do* something in here? All we do is listen to you or some electronic voice." I didn't confront her, but I did think about what she said. Maybe she was right. Perhaps I overreacted to the unsatisfying discussions we had at the beginning of the year. I thought about our discussions in English with the adjective checklist and about what Kay had said about supporting comprehension, and I decided to try something similar in American history.

Comprehension Minilesson

We were finishing the Civil War and Reconstruction when I first attempted to guide comprehension of part of the text. My planning consisted of several steps. First, I decided what portion of the book my students would read. In September I had everybody read every page of the text. That was unreasonable because the text simply contained too much information; after all, I, too, was learning new material. Thus, I decided to show a film about the major Civil War battles and to have students concentrate their reading on the aftermath of the war. Once I decided to have students read only about Reconstruction, I further pared down the points I wanted them to understand. The text provided more than enough information, so I decided that it would be good for my students to read in order to find out why Reconstruction had ended. Why would a seemingly good thing stop?

Then I had to figure out what my sophomores needed to know in order to get the desired information from the text. I decided to spend some time explaining the reasons for Reconstruction as well as the terms *carpetbagger, freedman, sharecropper, scalawag,* and *Ku Klux Klan*. The first three terms could be presented by pointing out that they were compound words and then explaining the background of the parts of the words. For instance, *free* and *man* gave awfully good clues about the meaning of that word; I just needed to develop them a bit. I found some pictures representing all five of the terms, too. In order to explain the reason for Reconstruction, I decided to present an analogy between reconstructing the South and making up after a family fight. I intended to point out how the winner actually comes out even further ahead if the loser is welcomed back and the wounds are healed. This analogy was meant to develop students' background knowledge and motivate them to read. All of this planning took about an hour. One hour seemed like a lot of time at first, but it occurred to me that if it worked, my life in the classroom would be much more pleasant.

I began the lesson at center stage once again. I informed the class that they needed to know important concepts in order to understand Reconstruction. I then went through my analogy of a family fight, presented the pictures, and pointed out the parts of the compound words. Next, I had them open their books to the pages on Reconstruction in order to survey the information for one minute. Then I set a specific purpose: "I would like you to read these five pages in order to find out why Reconstruction ended. If healing the wounds of a family fight is so important, then why did the healing process stop?" This purpose for reading seemed especially useful because the students couldn't just scan the pages to find a specific fact, nor could they answer my question based on what they knew already. They needed to read the whole passage, and they needed to read between the lines.

As the students were reading, I sat at my desk and read also. This was to model the behavior I wanted them to follow, and it allowed me one more opportunity to brush up on the information. After almost everybody had finished reading, I repeated my original question, "Why did Reconstruction end?" The discussion that followed stayed right on target. Rod didn't interject any comments related to sports, and Ken didn't go off on any tangents. Even Terry, who rarely spoke up in class, contributed some thoughts. After a while, I imposed some organization by saying, "OK, let's see if we can list the major reasons on the board." We then listed four major reasons: corruption, incompetence, economics, and changes in leadership. Next I said, "Take another few minutes, reread the text, see if we've listed all the major reasons, and see if these four are correct." Nobody came up with any substantial changes, so the list was left for the class to copy into their notes.

This strategy had many similarities with the adjective checklist. Perhaps the biggest similarity was that students knew in general what they were looking for when they were reading. Before, even Judy had seemed to have difficulty separating important from trivial information. That's not surprising when you look carefully at textbooks; they seem to consist of just one darn fact after another. It's also not surprising when you consider the questions I had asked after reading; students needed to memorize the whole passage because they never knew what I might ask about. Setting purposes before reading seemed to help considerably.

My comprehension minilessons worked well, but I was concerned that my students might come to depend on me totally for direction. What would happen when I wasn't around to tell them what to learn? I liked providing clear, specific direction, but I wanted my students to provide some direction on their own. Because of this concern, I implemented my second big change of the month. I began fading my instruction.

Fading to Independence

Fading myself out of center stage and my students in will take place over a long period of time, but this was the month I began to bring my students in on the act of setting purposes for comprehension. After a few weeks of me setting the purposes, I began by having the students set their own. "OK, group, what is the first thing you should do when getting ready to read in order to learn?" I asked. Judy responded that looking over the material in order to gain an impression of what was coming should be done first. Allison spoke up, "Once you know generally what to expect, you should establish some goals about what you intend to learn." When I was reasonably sure that the group knew the strategies for approaching a text, I had them apply those strategies to what we were reading in American history. Rod spoke up, saying he thought they should read in order to determine five key terms from the passage. The group agreed that was a good enough reason for reading, so they got into their books. After reading, I said, "You know that you should follow up to see if you got the information that you set out to get, so let's do it." Students reviewed the information they gathered by listing key terms on the board and eventually selected five key terms.

My supporting comprehension of assigned readings, as well as my fading of that support, made a big difference in the general tone of the class. Students seemed more involved in the content, and I felt as though I were providing some skills that students could take with them to eleventh grade and beyond.

F E B R U A R Y

Literature

February in sophomore English class was spent on the skill of persuasive writing and on the general topic of relationships, both among family members and among members of racial groups. Some fine novels deal with both types of relationships, so I recommended such older books as *Black Boy*,

Roots, I Know Why the Caged Bird Sings, and *Cry, the Beloved Country,* as well as such newer books as *The Moves Make the Man* and *Going Home.* You never know, some assignments really stimulate some students, while leaving others cold. Requiring book projects seems to have worked well for Theresa, my student who rarely spoke. Theresa read *Roll of Thunder, Hear My Cry* and astounded me with a series of pen-and-ink sketches of scenes from the book. She showed fine technical skill producing the sketches, and her selection of scenes depicting Cassie's encounters with prejudice was just incredible. I showed the drawings to Kay, over in Foreign Languages, who informed me that Theresa always did superior, creative work in her class when they emphasized the cultural aspects of Spanish-speaking countries. You never know exactly how things are going to work.

SSR Fridays were set aside for free reading because I was getting so many complaints from the students about not having time to read after school. I told them that as long as they actually read they could have Fridays to do so, but that I would go back to regular work if they didn't. The time we spent reading—I always had a book going, too—was quite pleasant, so I hope it works out.

Writing Minilesson Perhaps the most effective lesson in persuasive writing dealt with magazine and newspaper advertising. The language arts book presented the major appeals advertisers use—such as bandwagon, testimonial, name calling, and glittering generality. In order to teach these to my classes, I had my teaching assistants go through some magazines and newspapers I had gathered to find examples of each. I listed the appeals on the board and passed around examples of each so the students could experience them directly. Then I gave the following assignment: "We're going to collect advertisements and display them in brochures for a fifth-grade class at our elementary school. Locate at least two ads that exemplify each appeal. Write a brief definition under each example and mount it for display." We devoted three days to completing the brochures, and I delivered the acceptable ones to Connie Tent, a very nice fifth-grade teacher in our district whom I had met at a party.

The next step in my lesson on advertising was to have the students compose their own ads exemplifying the various appeals. "Take one short story or novel you've read that deals with relationships and create three different advertisements for it. Pick any three of the appeals that we've studied and use each appeal to sell the same product. For instance, you might use a testimonial, a bandwagon, and a family approach for *Roots.* The audience for your ad consists of other tenth-grade students." Having studied the ads already, the students seemed to have a fairly good idea about how to start. Ken got very enthused and produced ads illustrating all the appeals. Allison pointed out that her one ad incorporated all three appeals.

Collaborative Learning After everyone had produced three ads, I had the students prepare to work in groups to revise their first efforts. "As you know, no composition is ever perfect after the first attempt, but with a little help from your friends, you might approach perfection on the next attempt or two." I demonstrated how I wanted the group members to work as peer response teams in order to polish each other's work. I displayed an ad for *Cry, the Beloved Country* that I had created for this demonstration and made the following comments: "The most effective aspect of this ad, I think, is its layout. The pictures and lettering are well balanced. The ad is eye-catching. The one thing I would like to know more about is the general topic of the book. The terms *riveting* and *sensational* don't provide much insight into the content of the story. I would like to know more about what is especially riveting and sensational." After commenting this way, I paused and then explained what I had done. My students were aware that I had first commented on positive features, then on the negative. I made it clear that my negative comments were couched as a request for information ("I would like to know more about . . .") rather than as a direct criticism ("The weakest part of this writing is . . .").

Following this demonstration, I presented a few more ads and had students comment on what they liked and what they wanted to know more about. I then gave the final assignment: "All right, now please get into your groups and do to each other's ads what we just did to mine. However, instead of saying your comments aloud, please write them on a separate sheet of paper. When you get everybody's comments, then redo your ads as you see fit. You are to turn in to me your first drafts, the comments, and your second drafts for each of the three ads."

Most of the groups functioned well with this somewhat dangerous assignment. I was afraid that the comments would either be so snide and hurtful or so gushy and congratulatory that they wouldn't be useful. Lonnie and Allison started insulting each other's work—in a good-natured way, I think—but they stopped when I reminded them that their comments were to be written.

Once the ads were finished, I posted some of the better ones, with the authors' names concealed, on the bulletin board. I hid the authors' names because peer pressure is intense with this age group and displaying work might leave someone open to hurtful comments. On the other hand, I wanted to display some ads in order to model exemplary ones, increase interest in the topic, provide a focus for what we were doing, and just plain dress up the room. Some of the high-school classrooms I've been in look more like waiting rooms to contain people for an hour than like places to stimulate learning.

Comprehension Minilesson My comprehension minilessons in American history have resulted in some effective discussions. My setting a clear purpose before reading provides a great stabilizer for keeping us on track. One day Kay suggested that I have students predict what they will learn from the passage and then read to see how their predictions come out. She thought the predictions might help students assume more control for their own learning, which is my goal in fading instruction. I tried predictions the very next day.

We were studying the Progressives of the early 1900s, and I wanted students to learn about some of the changes legislated by the federal government under Theodore Roosevelt. So after introducing some essential concepts, I asked the class, "What reforms do you think were implemented during Roosevelt's two terms?" I believe in wait time, but sixty seconds was a long time even for me. "Come on, I know you don't know, but what's your best guess?" I prodded. Judy then volunteered that the Pure Food and Drug Act, the Hepburn Act to control freight transportation rates, and the conservation of natural resources might be some of Roosevelt's reforms. Needless to say, her "prediction" was right out of the book, which she confessed to having read the night before as part of her ongoing quest to earn straight A's. As Kay and I left school that afternoon, I belittled her suggestion about predictions. "Hugh," she replied, "next time have Judy write on the board what the other students predict. You might also use passages from your classroom magazine because nobody will have a chance to read ahead in them. Why don't you use those magazines for more than a way to keep your students busy?"

Kay really knows how to get my attention! Well, to make a long story short, I had students predict the contents of a current events article in response to my question, "What might the administration do in order to calm this latest international disturbance?" If someone accurately predicted one of the plans, I just said "Uh-huh, maybe" and proceeded nonchalantly along. At one point, Ambrose called out, "All right, so what are the administration's plans?" And somebody chimed in with, "Give us the article!" It was then that I realized the motivational impact of predictions. I passed out the magazines, and the students read the current events article as intently as they had read anything all year.

M A R C H

March is over. In history we finished studying the Great Depression, the New Deal, and World War II, so we are pretty much on target with regard to covering the content. At the beginning of the year I was concerned about getting through everything, but my decision to direct students' comprehension to the most important information, assign the reading of less important information, and ignore the least important information was a lifesaver. I use the textbook selectively; I am no longer a slave to it. I escaped total reliance on the text by introducing book projects in American history, using an American history magazine and good videos.

Book Project A big difference between the American history book projects and the English II book projects concerned the type of book that was appropriate. My English classes had to read only literary materials, that is, novels. But the history classes could choose either a literary or an expository book. Topical books, biographies, and fiction were fair game for this assignment. I figured that students could learn as much, if not more, from *Johnny Got His Gun* as from some factual treatise on the horrors of war. The only stipulation I set was that I had to approve the book before students began reading it. I granted these approvals before and after class as students brought their books to me for a quick check. My criteria for approval were rather loose; I just didn't want an able student working with an elementary-level picture book or a less able student saddled with some graduate-level scholarly tome.

Another difference between the English and the history projects was the format. In English I emphasized such literary elements as plot and setting, but those were not useful for history. In history students had first to summarize their books' contents. I showed them examples of summaries, so I felt reasonably confident that they were familiar with what I expected. Additionally, students were to produce a "creative" response to their book. I passed out a list of possible responses, including visuals, realia, dramatizations, and written or oral compositions. Students might produce a time line or a collage; they might bring in representative artifacts; they might stage a brief play; or they might write a special dictionary for their book.

The American history book projects are meant to deepen students' understanding of specific aspects of history while allowing me to press on through the different eras. The projects allow both good and poor readers to tackle materials that present appropriate challenges. The projects also allow attention to historical themes rather than just a particular era. For instance, World War II was one of our topics this month, so I promoted *Hiroshima* along with other eras' war-related books, such as *The Red Badge of Courage, All Quiet on the Western Front*, and *Warday*. Students who reported on these books invariably commented on the power of their themes.

Meaning
Vocabulary Vocabulary still is being emphasized in history. I frequently present new words and their meanings during the comprehension minilessons, and I also spend time focusing on vocabulary whenever a new term is used. Analogies and pictures are used most often when presenting the meanings for the words, and we've put on a few skits to help develop concepts. Rod and Judy presented a well-received skit this past month related to deficit spending. They played a newlywed couple with limited finances wanting to buy a state-of-the-art stereo system. After much debate, they resorted to using a department store credit account and then having to come up with the money later. Rod and Judy then stopped the skit and explained how a married couple using a credit card to buy a stereo is similar to a government agency using deficit spending to pay for such items as freeways and defense hardware.

Whenever possible, I tried to make things real when presenting concepts. To make some of the New Deal legislation come alive, I asked if any student's grandparents had worked in a CCC or WPA project. Terry brought in his grandfather, and I conducted an interview with him. Mr. Donahue related some fascinating stories about why he joined the CCC in the 1930s, what the camps were like, and how some of the jobs were completed. I referred to the presentation as "oral history," which seemed to make it more acceptable than "grandpa telling stories."

Class time also was spent with the "alphabet soup" of New Deal innovations so that students would become more aware of abbreviations and acronyms. CCC, WPA, NRA, TVA, and AAA were some of the abbreviations that I presented. Students also came up with contemporary abbreviations such as FBI and CIA as well as acronyms such as SCUBA and MADD

(Mothers Against Drunk Driving). Another vocabulary tactic I used was to highlight common parts of derived words. Many social studies terms contain morphemes that are helpful in figuring out the meanings of new words as well as retrieving the meanings of old ones. During one week with the New Deal, *conservative, unconstitutional, intrastate,* and *progressive* were the key vocabulary terms containing morphemes. I knew I should point out the root word in *conservative* because it is related to several words: *conserve, conservation, conservationist,* and *conservatory.* I listed the five words in a column, aligning the shared part, and asked what the words had in common. It was obvious that all five words contained *conserv,* so the discussion then was directed to its meaning. "Keep the same," "preserve," and "traditional" were associated with *conserve.* I closed this five-minute lesson by drawing attention to the fact that looking for morphemes in words was helpful but occasionally misleading: "Remember, folks, *undone* means 'not done,' but *uncle* does not mean 'not cle.' "

Fading to Independence

Writing

In English we continued our study of relationships, and worked on the language skill of reading and writing plays. I must say, most of the students are becoming quite independent with their writing. They are well aware that every composition has a topic, audience, role, and form, and they now seem to determine those three aspects automatically before writing. They also generate and organize information on their own before writing. Their revising is becoming automatic, although I do occasionally need to remind them about it. As part of the unit on relationships, we read *West Side Story* in class and I showed a movie of *Romeo and Juliet.* "Hey, Mr. Mann," Ken called out, "why don't you let us write our own play?" "Why not?" I said. "I'll be here to help, but now you all know what you need to do in order to compose a play, so go to it." This was an extremely loose assignment, but I wanted to see just how independent this class was.

To my great satisfaction, the plays turned out quite well! I gave some class time to play production, but some time also was spent outside of school. Some students worked in groups, and others worked individually. Some wrote for young children, some for a teenage audience, and some for adults. They all used the same basic form, with stage directions and characters' lines presented as in *West Side Story.* Each group who wanted to present their play to the class practiced it in a conference room in the library, which turned out to be a great stimulus for revision. I didn't pressure all the groups to present their plays because time simply wouldn't allow it. Having some plays presented orally and some only in written form worked out fine. As with other group assignments, points were awarded for acceptable work, although in this case a play was worth five points.

A P R I L

Research

The major emphasis this month in history was on conducting library research. We had done brief projects throughout the year, looking up information about famous people and places and sharing it orally in class, but April was the month for large-scale researching and reporting. I figured students would be reasonably interested in studying the American history unit A Decade of Change: 1960–1969, so I launched research projects on that era. One of my first steps was to help students ask researchable questions. First, I told the students about the general nature of the research they would be conducting, then I had them skim the chapter of the text that dealt with the 1960s. I wrote 1960–1970 at the top of the chalkboard and the words *Cuba, equal rights, Berlin, space exploration, John F. Kennedy,* and *Great Society* at the head of columns. "What do you know about these topics?" I asked the class. As information was presented, I placed key words under the headings. *Ted Kennedy; Martin Luther King, Jr.; Bay of Pigs; Cuban Missile Crisis; Peace Corps;* and *Lee Harvey Oswald* were some of the terms that were listed. I then took one of the words and asked, "What do you know and what don't you know about this term?" I again listed the information and questions that were presented. Following this class brainstorming, students brainstormed in groups. The lists they made of what they didn't know pointed out the need for research.

Students Asking Researchable Questions

The next day I spent more time helping students formulate researchable questions. I reminded the sophomores that questions typically began with a *wh* word (who, what, when, where, and why) and that while *why* could give the most trouble, it could also lead to the most interesting research. Following this brief introduction, I moved into a question-asking exercise. "Meet with one other person about one of the topics you are interested in researching," I directed. "Write down all *WH* Questions about the topic that you can think of. For instance, if you took *Peace Corps,* you might ask, 'Where do Peace Corps volunteers work?' 'When did the Peace Corps begin?' 'Why was it begun?' and so on." The two-person teams were given exactly five minutes for brainstorming questions about one topic before I directed them to move to the other person's topic for five minutes. Following this exercise, many of the students had the beginnings of a research project.

Locating Information

Locating information in order to answer questions and generate new questions was the next step. I assumed that everybody had been introduced to aids such as indexes, encyclopedias, and the library card catalog, so I designed a scavenger hunt as a quick and dirty refresher. I came up with questions such as, "What page of our history textbook contains information about the Lusitania?" and "How many books does the library hold on the topic of nuclear energy?" We spent a day scrounging around the library to locate the appropriate information. I reviewed students' answers in class and probed to see whether everyone was comfortable locating information in the traditional sources.

Thinking that the *Readers' Guide to Periodical Literature* was new to my sophomores, I asked our librarian to present it to my classes. As for all aids for locating information, the role of key words in using it well became apparent. The students saw that a few key terms were essential for research. For instance, Lonnie wanted to investigate "flower power," which he had heard was a mass movement of the 1960s. He was having trouble getting started, so I suggested looking under *youth movement, counterculture, protest,* and *hippie.*

Along with printed materials, I wanted each student to interview at least one person. I had already demonstrated interviews when Terry's grandfather came to class. The students had seen how I covered the questions I had prepared beforehand, how at certain times I simply said, "Can you tell me more?", and how I explained the presence of my tape recorder. A few students had difficulty locating someone who knew much about their topic (Ambrose was ready to quit after his parents told him they didn't know anything about Cesar Chavez), so I had to be resourceful at times (I suggested that Ambrose interview Kay).

Organizing Information

As students began locating information about their topics and refining their questions, the hardest part began—organizing the information I had been teaching periodically about taking notes from text, so my classes had a bit of a head start on this aspect of organization. One of my more frequent generic purposes for comprehending had been, "Read in order to choose the three most important words from this section." After reading, students would explain why the three words they selected were most important; then I would explain my choices. At first Allison, Judy, and Ken were the only ones to volunteer their most important words, but more students began to open up as they became comfortable with the lesson. In fact, the students and I eventually began producing the same three words for the same reasons, indicating that we were beginning to organize text information in the same way.

Webbing

Taking good notes from a passage is only the first step in organizing information; putting the notes into a logical framework is the other step. Constructing webs was my answer to organizing the mass of notes that students acquired. When I first introduced webs in class as part of my comprehension minilessons, I got the "Aha, I understand" response from several of my low-achieving students. It seemed that for the first time they understood the logic of organizing information on paper. Because we had constructed several webs in class, my suggestion that individuals construct their own webs was readily accepted. Terry created a web that I used as a model. He had taken a large sheet of drafting paper and neatly written his topic, Beginning the Vietnam War, in the middle, surrounded by his subtopics, French withdrawal, Ho Chi Minh, Ngo Dinh Diem, and Gulf of Tonkin Resolution. He had then written key terms underneath each subtopic. Terry's paper demonstrated how to impose order on the mass of facts and ideas that researchers invariably uncover. He admitted that he probably would need to change his organization as he continued locating information, perhaps adding Viet Cong, but he was proud of the initial framework he had produced.

As we moved through the steps of asking questions, locating information, and organizing information, I had the students show me their work so I could help monitor their progress. Staying in touch systematically during these beginning steps seemed valuable as I was able to defuse many potential problems. For instance, Rod had decided to investigate the Soviet Union during the 1960s. "What do you want to know about the Soviet Union?" I asked. He replied that he would figure that out after doing some reading. A few days later I had the students turn in statements of their topic and research questions, and Rod still was unsure of what he wanted to do. I met with him briefly the next day, and together we decided that a study of U.S.-Soviet relations on nuclear testing would be interesting and feasible. Helping out during the research process was far more helpful than simply reacting to the finished product.

I also checked on students' webs before giving them the go-ahead to begin writing, a time-consuming but worthwhile procedure. Each student turned in a web that showed the order of presentation of the subtopics, along with the primary information associated with each subtopic. The webs were difficult to interpret because they were only outlines, but I could form impressions about who had a sense of direction and who was floundering. I wrote specific suggestions when I could, and set up brief meetings with those who required more complete overhauls.

Writing Once the webs were approved, students went to work on their written reports. I presented models of reports that my department head had on file so that the class had an idea of what their reports should look like. I required both a first and a second draft. A student of the author's choice and I both reacted to the first draft. The two questions that were to guide the first-draft readers were, "What was the most interesting aspect of this paper?" and "What do I want to know more about?" The students had experience reacting to others' work, so things went smoothly.

After responding to the comments about their first drafts, students wrote second drafts and again submitted their papers to another student for a check on the mechanics of spelling, punctuation, and capitalization. The final, polished version then was turned in to me. One thing I learned for next year was to stagger the times that the reports were due. I had two classes working on reports, and the paperwork I faced when all the papers came in at once was staggering.

M A Y

Good old May, my favorite month! Spring was here in full force and so was baseball season. The baseball practices and games after school added to my responsibilities and decreased my time for lesson planning. It's a good thing my students had become quite independent.

Content Area Literature We moved away from the text more and more throughout the school year. The students increasingly relied on library books, brochures, and articles for their reading material. I would describe the available materials, and the stu-

Collaborative Learning dents, working in their collaborative groups, would select the one or two titles they wanted to pursue. For instance, we were studying the United States during the 1980s, so *The Bonfire of the Vanities* was one of the reading choices. One group selected this novel, individuals took the role of various characters, and they presented selected portions through readers theater. The group members—not I—decided how they would respond to the book.

Fading to Independence

Portions of the history text still were required reading, but I didn't pre-teach as many concepts or set purposes as much as I used to. The students did that for themselves. When I established the fact that the portion of the text on President Reagan's terms of office was to be read, I asked the class, "What do you need to do?" Terry answered, "Look it over, think about what we already know about the topic, and decide what we should read carefully for," which indeed captured the essence of reading for a purpose. "Then go to it," was my directive. After a while, we decided that a time line was called for, so after reading, one was created on the board, separating the trivial from the noteworthy information.

Study Strategies

Vocabulary was handled much the same way as comprehension. Students identified the key terms and proposed ways to handle them. They pointed out the acronym in *laser* (light amplification by stimulated emission of radiation); identified the root word in *miniaturization*; and connected the changes in lifestyles begun by the computer age with the changes that had occurred at the beginning of the industrial age. My role was simply to keep the class on track as I continually asked, "What terms do you need to know? What can you do to understand and remember each term?" I was comfortable posing such a question because throughout the year I had demonstrated ways to learn vocabulary. Of course, my help still was needed. *Reaganomics* was a term that the students easily separated into *Reagan* and *economics*, but that didn't do much to explain the underlying concept. I had to step in and explain the plan of cutting personal taxes as well as federal spending in order to reduce inflation. Analyzing the morphemes and reading the book simply didn't go far enough for gaining insight into that term.

Content Journals

A practice that I began hesitantly in April but pursued much more confidently in May was journal writing. Most of the writing I had students do consisted of brief entries, taking notes, or producing one- or two-paragraph essays. The research projects involved a good deal of writing, but they occurred too infrequently. The idea of having students informally record their impressions of historical topics really appealed to me. The classes were accustomed to free reading time, so time set aside for free writing was easily accepted. Once journals were started, I occasionally made a specific assignment, such as, "The average life expectancy has increased from about 47 in 1900 to 74 at present. Write a letter to our mayor informing him what the city needs to do in order to handle the increasing numbers of elderly people."

Assessment

Grading the journals was bound to be a problem, especially with students like Lonnie who rarely do anything if it's not for a grade, so I modified the point system I had used for group work. A certain number of pages needed to be filled with some evidence of independent thought in order to deserve one point. At the end of a month, twenty points were possible, so students with eighteen, nineteen, or twenty points (that is, those with 90 percent or more of the possible points) earned an A; those with 80 to 89 percent of the possible points earned a B, and so on. Most students produced the required amounts of writing and got a good grade for their journals. But more importantly, journal writing allowed students the opportunity to think through topics presented in class. It also seems to have promoted independent writing abilities; the most notable difference between the first entries and the later ones was the amount of writing that was produced.

Book Project   A good deal of writing was being produced independently in my English classes. In fact, this month's book projects consisted of some exceptional pieces of writing. This month's topic in literature was sports, so books such as *The Amateurs* and *Jackie Robinson* were candidates for book projects. Rod read about George Plimpton, the writer who assumed the role of different professional athletes; he then wrote a poem about Plimpton that paralleled "Casey at the Bat." Allison read a biography of Ingrid Kristiansen, the distance runner, talked informally with some of her friends, and produced several insights into why individuals might devote themselves to competitive distance running.

J U N E

School is out, baseball season is over (we had a winning season, taking second place in our conference!), and the students have gone to their various summer adventures. As I think back over the year, I realize that class sessions definitely picked up once I provided better direction and when I allowed students more choices in their learning activities. During comprehension minilessons, the students seemed to appreciate being prepared for the passage and knowing what to look for when they read. As I began fading my instruction, it was heartwarming to see the class take responsibility for their learning. I also feel good about some of the creative and insightful responses some of the students produced when they decided on their own learning.

Once I integrated skill work with literature topics in English, I felt much better about my writing instruction. Working on sentence structure in the context of meaningful passages, rather than with worksheets, made a lot more sense to me as well as to the students. I seem to have faded my writing instruction more completely than my comprehension instruction. The students could all independently plan, draft, and revise a composition rather well, or at least they all knew the steps to follow! I'm still not sure that they preview a passage, read it, and review it the way I would like. Next year I need to fade my comprehension instruction better.

Developing the students' vocabularies seemed to progress well. Rather than simply have the class copy dictionary definitions, I made every effort to present new terms in meaningful, memorable ways. Analogies, pictures, skits, webs, and morphemes seemed to help. I plan to spend more time next year helping students develop their vocabularies independently. For instance, once I show the class how to form analogies, I will gradually shift that thinking process over to the students.

The book projects, group work, and research projects all went smoothly and students seemed to benefit from them. These projects involved both good and poor readers and writers in activities at appropriate levels of difficulty. I'm convinced that one of secondary-school teachers' biggest challenges is accommodating the wide range of individual differences that each class presents. The projects and my grading system seemed to go far toward meeting those differences.

This last journal entry summarizes the parts of my teaching that I intend to keep and the parts I intend to change. In August I'm going to reread this whole journal, paying special attention to these closing comments. I fully intend to keep refining my instruction. At the end of ten years, I want to be able to say that I had ten years of experience—not one year of experience ten times.

REFERENCES

Adams, R. (1975). *Watership down.* Riverside, NJ: Macmillan.

Allen, M. (1987). *Jackie Robinson.* New York: Watts.

Angelou, M. (1970). *I know why the caged bird sings.* New York: Random House.

Asher, S. (1987). *Everything is not enough.* New York: Delacorte.

Bradbury, R. (1970). *The Martian chronicles.* Garden City, NY: Doubleday.

Brin, D. (1985). *The postman.* New York: Bantam.

Brooks, B. (1986). *The moves make the man.* New York: Harper.

Callahan, S. (1986). *Adrift: Seventy-six days lost at sea.* Boston: Houghton Mifflin.

Clarke, A. C. (1968). *2001: A space odyssey.* New York: New American Library.

Crane, S. (1944). *The red badge of courage.* New York: Heritage.

Halberstam, D. (1985). *The amateurs.* New York: Morrow.

Haley, A. (1976). *Roots.* Garden City, NY: Doubleday.

Hersey, J. (1946). *Hiroshima.* New York: Knopf.

Heyerdahl, T. (1950). *Kon-Tiki: Across the Pacific by raft.* Chicago: Rand McNally.

Keyes, D. (1966). *Flowers for Algernon.* New York: Harcourt, Brace & World.

Kinsella, W. P. (1982). *Shoeless Joe.* New York: Ballantine.

Laurents, A. (1958). *West side story.* New York: Random House.

Lawrence, L. (1986). *Moonwind.* New York: Harper.

Mohr, N. (1986). *Going home.* New York: Dial.

Paton, A. (1948). *Cry, the beloved country.* New York: Scribner's.

Remarque, E. M. (1938). *All quiet on the Western front.* New York: Buccaneer.

Sleator, W. (1985). *Singularity.* New York: Dutton.

Strieber, W., & Kunetka, J. (1984). *Warday.* New York: Warner Books.

Taylor, M. (1978). *Roll of thunder, hear my cry.* New York: Bantam.

Trumbo, D. (1939). *Johnny got his gun.* New York: Lippincott.

Verne, J. (1925). *20,000 leagues under the sea.* New York: Scribner's.

Wolfe, T. (1987). *The bonfire of the vanities.* New York: Farrar, Straus & Giroux.

Wright, R. (1945). *Black boy.* New York: Harper & Row.

Zindel, P. (1968). *The pigman.* New York: Harper & Row.

CHAPTER 12

Science and Mathematics

I feel a little strange keeping a journal. I used to keep a diary when I was ten. I wonder if I am regressing. Dr. Knowles, who taught the content area reading and writing course I took in my senior year, suggested that keeping journals allows teachers to do something they seldom have time for—to pause and reflect. He also said that a journal allows you to look back across the year and be reminded of the little triumphs that are frequently overshadowed by the daily problems teachers face. I have decided to keep this journal on just two of my classes this year, one of my regular biology classes and my consumer math class. When Dr. Knowles talked about keeping journals, he suggested we focus on our most challenging classes. From the look of the names on my preliminary rolls, the two classes I've picked should certainly be that!

In the six years I've been teaching, I have vacillated between a textbook approach and a process approach to teaching biology. When I first started, I was strongly influenced by the methods used by my supervising teacher during student teaching. I made a great deal of use of the textbook, supplemented with lectures. Of course we had our lab periods, but these tended to be isolated from the content we were learning. This approach kept the students busy and was obviously what they expected. Soon, however, I found that most students were not learning very much. My below-average students seemed bewildered much of the time. My average and above-average students did satisfactory or even excellent work, but when I referred to something we had studied only a few weeks before, almost all looked blank. Nor were the students very interested in biology. One student said to me that very first year, "Miss Mull, this stuff is as dry as a bone!" Can you imagine how I responded to him? I am ashamed to admit that, out of my frustration, I said sharply, "Well then, why don't you moisten it with a little sweat from your brow!"

It became obvious that to almost all my students, "Mull's bio class" was either a boring frustration or a dull obstacle course. My hopes of making biology, the study of life, an inspiring and edifying experience seemed no more than a naïve dream. I sought advice from the principal, assistant principal, science supervisor, and other teachers, all of whom generally agreed that I was "too idealistic" and should realize that there is a limited amount that can be accomplished with "today's kids." So I continued teaching biology the same way for the next three years until I had become quite adept at assigning the textbook, lecturing, and giving tests. I never became any more satisfied with this way of teaching, however. The summer after my third year of teaching, I had a crisis. I finally made up my mind that I could no longer stand what I was doing. A radical change was in order, and I made it. I swung to the pure process approach that my undergraduate science methods courses had so strongly advocated. Everything we did was hands-on. I brought living things into the classroom, and we dissected several plants and animals. We used the microscopes regularly. The students did become more interested, but I soon discovered that while they remembered the hands-on experiences, they could not organize their thinking along more global and abstract general principles. In other words, they could not relate the hands-on experiences to a "big picture."

As you can imagine, I gradually began to get frustrated and even cynical. During this time, there was increased pressure in my school system to raise test scores, making me feel that I had to cover everything in the biology curriculum whether my students had time to learn it or not. Trying to cover a lot of curricular ground using demonstrations, experiments, and field trips can really strain a person's system!

This year, when I first walked into my classroom, I found that I had burned out. I couldn't face teaching again. Biology was my major in college and I had always liked it. However, biology is the most often failed high-school subject in my state, and it is also the most failed subject in the school where I teach. Students often dread it before they take it, hate it while they take it, and criticize it as they look back on it.

The beginning of school this year was a time of real introspection for me. The more I thought, the more I realized that I had been lying to myself, kidding myself along for at least the previous year. Now I could fool myself no longer. I wanted to do anything but teach. I wanted to be anywhere but walking down those halls into that classroom. I carefully considered my options. I was not tied down with a husband or children. I was only twenty-seven years old. I had a little money saved and my car was relatively new. I was free to resign my job to go wherever I wanted to, change careers completely if I wanted to. I thought of going to work for a biological supply company near where my parents live. On the other hand, I thought that I might like to begin a career in retail sales, selling women's clothes or shoes.

But another force within me pulled strongly in the other direction. I really believe in education as a positive factor in influencing young people. I looked back fondly on the teachers across my school years who had taken an interest in me and taught me things that I needed to know or enjoyed learning. How had they avoided burnout? Or had they? Perhaps they had just hidden it from us. Finally, one night that first week of school, I called one of my teachers whom I remembered particularly fondly and who lives only twenty-five miles away. She had been my life science teacher in seventh grade. She graciously invited me to her home although I had not seen her in over ten years.

The next evening I arrived at Mrs. Plante's house a little after five o'clock, and she welcomed me in. It was so good to see her. Though she was noticeably older than I had remembered, her face brought back so many sweet memories to me. We hugged each other and began to catch up on news about my old classmates and my other middle-high teachers. Time passed quickly. Before I knew it, it was time for me to go and I had not even broached the subject I had really come to talk about.

"Oh, Mrs. Plante," I exclaimed, "I'm miserable in my job. That's why I really needed to talk with you. How have you stood it all these years?"

"So that's it, Annie," she sighed into her coffee. "Has it been this bad for—how many years have you taught?"

"Five, not counting this one. No, I was pretty happy my first year because I thought I would get better. And I did, but so many students aren't learning very much and they don't particularly like biology or think it's worth much. I just don't think I can stand to do this any more."

"Annie," she asked, "why do you think you became a biology teacher?"

"I always loved the sciences, and biology in particular. I also love kids, especially teenagers. I thought teaching high-school biology would be the perfect marriage of those two loves."

"You don't think you're good at teaching, do you?"

"Mrs. Plante, it's strange that you should ask that. I get good evaluations, and everyone seems reasonably pleased with what I'm doing. But I still feel like a failure almost all the time."

Professionalism   "People who see themselves as professionals are always interested in finding out what needs doing so they can do it. Other people's evaluations aren't good enough for a professional."

"Up to a point, you're right, Mrs. Plante. I'm not satisfied with what I'm accomplishing in my classes even if everyone else is. If this is the best it gets, I want out. Let somebody else mind the mental morgue!"

"Do you think this is the best it gets, Annie?"

"I suppose I'm beginning to think so. Actually, I'm pretty arrogant down inside. I used the traditional method and got pretty good at it. Then I used the vanguard method and got pretty good at that, too. But neither method produced a high-level understanding or appreciation of biology except in one or two students who already knew a lot and were interested when they started."

Suddenly, Mrs. Plante looked very old. "I don't know what to tell you, Annie. Maybe you are too idealistic. Maybe it is too much to expect most students to grasp the big picture of biology and to like it as well."

"That means I have to resign and do something else. Thanks, Mrs. Plante, for helping me see what I must do."

We talked longer, but nothing else substantive was said. I had made up my mind and Mrs. Plante seemed to agree with me. I drove home, sat down at the computer to type my letter of resignation, and went to bed.

That night, I had a dream that was to change my life. In the dream, I was led kicking and screaming to a post and tied there. Then a firing squad of two soldiers came and took aim at me. Just as they were about to fire, I realized that one was Dr. Bass, the professor who had taught my science methods class in college, and the other was Mr. DeBoer, my supervising teacher during student teaching. I called out that I had done my best, but they continued to point their rifles at me, frowning. Suddenly, Dr. Knowles, the professor of my content-area reading and writing course, appeared from nowhere and untied me. I grabbed a gun from somewhere to shoot my two executioners, but Dr. Knowles took the gun from me and said, "No, you'll need them both." He walked over to disarm them as well, forcing them to shake hands with each other in spite of their resistance. As their hands finally clasped, he turned to me and asked, "Do you see?" All I could say was, "See what? Tell me what I'm supposed to see!" I said that over and over to no avail until I woke up in a sweat.

My first reaction was to try to forget my dream, but I couldn't get it out of my mind. During breakfast and in the shower, it vividly came back to me, and each time it did, my mind seemed almost ready to understand what Dr. Knowles had meant.

As I drove to school, I suddenly remembered something I had once read or heard, "If two intelligent people totally disagree about something, you can be reasonably sure that they are both partly right and partly wrong." In an instant, I saw everything clearly. Textbooks and lectures aren't wrong if properly used, but they can't provide concrete experiences; demonstrations, experiments, and field trips aren't wrong if properly used, but they can't ensure high-level thinking. What I needed was a way to integrate the two, to use the strengths of each to compensate for the weaknesses of the other. Dr. Knowles had taught us how to use direct experiences to build the basis for understanding abstract concepts. He had also taught us that you can't just assign a textbook; you have to be sure that students know their purposes for reading. Writing can also be used to help students organize and integrate information. I remembered with regret how I had yawned through his class, resenting instruction in reading and writing when I wanted to teach biology. I drove right home and dug out my notebook and text from his course.

Then I tore up my letter of resignation. I'll give it a year, I said to myself with determination. If it works, fine. If not, well, I gave it every chance.

S E P T E M B E R

Dr. Knowles taught us that main ideas and generalizations are important aids to learning: First, these key concepts are themselves the most important content to be learned; second, knowing the main ideas helps us to learn the less important ideas. As a result, I decided to start out this year by giving my students a firm grasp of the overall structure of biology. Neither the textbook nor the lab manual provided students such a structure, so I had to construct the structure for myself out of both of these sources, my own knowledge, and various other references.

Web

After spending a couple of classes introducing the students to the laboratory, the textbook, and the lab manual, I placed the diagram shown in Figure 12.1 on the bulletin board.

To introduce my students to the structure of biology, I only had to teach them to understand the diagram. First, we discussed the term *biology* itself. What would we study in biology class and what was not included in that discipline? I allowed the students to name all the things they could think of that we would and would not study, and I told them whether they were right or not. Some things they named were not even in the domain of science, though most were. Many of their items fell under other branches of science, such as astronomy, geology, chemistry, or physics. In only one class did they have a good sense of the meaning of biology. Then we spent some time on the terms *zoology* and *botany*. Again, I allowed the students to name a large number of examples and nonexamples of each, on which I commented.

At this point, as always, I taught my students the proper handling and use of a microscope. It takes time, but an once of prevention saves the school

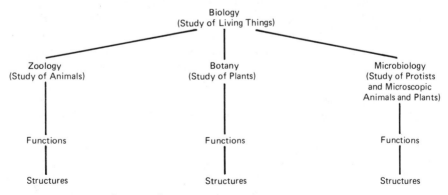

FIGURE 12.1 Biology Web

Direct
Experience

Meaning
Vocabulary

money! I then brought out the microscopes. The students took turns at their tables viewing some prepared slides of common organic and inorganic substances such as hair and dust. When I was sure they understood the term *microscopic,* I introduced them to what I thought would be a new domain of life for them: protists. At this point, I defined protists only as "all living things that are neither plants nor animals." Most of them had trouble believing that there could be life that was neither plant nor animal, but I was able to get them to suspend judgment. Based on these understandings, I then led

Web

them through a discussion of microbiology and what we would cover under that heading on the course diagram. Finally, they understood that virtually all life that can be seen with the naked eye is either plant or animal, but that microscopic life includes plants, animals, and protists.

Meaning
Vocabulary

I knew that they might have some difficulty understanding what was meant by *functions* and *structures* on the diagram and I moved to the chalkboard for those lessons. I wrote Functions at the top of the board, underlined it, and wrote Structures at the top of the board on the other side, underlining it as well. Under Functions I wrote, "walking," "talking," and "smelling"; under the word "structures" I wrote, "legs," "mouth," and "nose." I then asked for volunteers to explain the difference between functions and structures. In each case, I told them where they were correct and where they still lacked some insight. After a while, they appeared to have a good grasp of the difference, so I wrote "tasting" in the middle of the board. I required each student to take a piece of notebook paper and tear it in half. On one half they were to write a large dark *f* and on the other, an *s.* They were given a few seconds to examine the examples still listed on the board; then I had them classify "tasting" by raising the appropriate piece of paper. I did not allow students to show their papers before or after I gave them a signal, but only at that one moment. Then we discussed the correct classification and the reasons for it. I continued to put words in the middle of the board for them to classify until they became automatic at getting them right. Eventually, they were able to classify correctly terms like *heart, stem, imagine,* and *transpire.*

Web

We then returned to the course diagram on the bulletin board. I asked them to predict what we would study this year in biology. After some discussion, they came to understand that we were going to study the three kinds of living things, animals and plants (both microscopic and not), and protists, and that we would study them by learning the functions that they perform and the structures that enable them to do so. I fielded questions about specific issues, using the diagram whenever possible to show where their question fit into the overall structure of biology. I left the bulletin board up so that students could see at a glance "the big picture" of our year of studying biology.

Meaning
Vocabulary &
Background
Knowledge
Building

This process took a lot of time. At first, it was difficult for me not to be impatient, for I remembered that in the past I had spent no more than a few minutes on each of the six terms in the diagram. I had merely defined them, the students had written down these definitions, and we had gone on to other things.

Now that I had decided to teach each of these terms and their interrelationships until the students understood them clearly and could apply them, I was shocked at how long it took. Why, no wonder no one has learned very much biology in my other classes—I've thrown out major concepts as if they were minor facts that needed only to be memorized!

Once the class had a grasp of the diagram, it was assigned to read the portions of the text that pertained to the overall structure of biology, and to how that structure has gradually developed as biology has grown as a science. It's not enough to expose students to a concept; I must continue to work with them on that concept until I am sure that they truly understand it.

Oops! I have been so intent on carrying out my new approach to teaching biology that I have just let my consumer math class ride. Well, they're about to ride me out of town on a rail! I must do something different from what I am doing there, too. The course is supposed to be a practical study of consumer arithmetic for students who are not outstanding in mathematics. So why is the first chapter of the textbook filled with discussions of "interpolating and extrapolating data," and exercises with nothing but confusing word problems to solve? Help!

O C T O B E R

Word Problems I began the month in my consumer math class by trying to help my students with word problems. I never realized how much of consumer math consisted of word problems! Word problems present a major difficulty to almost all groups of math students. Fortunately, I came across some research by H. Ballew and J. Cunningham that showed me how to diagnose my students, determining what areas of word problem solving were holding them back. Because we had not yet begun Chapter 2, I picked out the word problems from that chapter and randomly assigned them to one of three testing conditions as Ballew and Cunningham had done. For test A, I set the word problems up in pure computational form, "the computation test." For test B, I simply wrote down all the numbers from each problem in the order they appeared in the problem. I called this "the problem interpretation test." For test C, I presented the problems exactly as they were in the book (oh, the miracle of copying machines!). Each test had fourteen items.

On successive days, I gave the three tests to the class. Test A was merely handed out and taken up after a reasonable time, and I simply graded each problem for the correct answer. When I gave test B, I handed out the mimeographed pages with the numbers on them and read aloud each problem to the students as they followed along, looking at the numbers. By this method I eliminated the need for them to be able to read the problem in order to interpret it. I graded each problem not for correct answers *per se*, but for whether the problem was correctly set up or not—that is, whether they would have gotten the right answer if they had done the computation properly. When I graded test C, I gave the students two scores, one based on how many problems they had set up correctly (the reading and problem interpretation score) and one based on the number of correct answers (word problem solving score). I came up with the following averages for my class on the four scores generated from the three tests of fourteen problems each:

Computation Average Score	Problem Interpretation Average Score	Reading and Problem Interpretation Average Score	Word Problem Solving Average Score
11.7	11.5	9.2	7.4

I was shocked that my students averaged only 7.4 out of 14 word problems correct when they had to do everything independently. Yet, their average score on the computation test shows that they can do the arithmetic that the word problems require; their average score on the problem interpretation test shows that they can generally figure out what computation to do and in what order. Their major difficulty seems to be reading! They did far worse on problem interpretation when they had to read the problems than when I read the problems to them. They also seemed to have difficulty with what Ballew and Cunningham call "integration," the ability to perform arithmetic, problem interpretation, and reading simultaneously, as indicated by the fact that their word problem solving score was lower than any of the other three. For this class, then, I must design activities to improve ability to read word problems and to integrate skills in solving word problems.

Comprehension Minilesson

Meanwhile, I have been doing a unit on reading and understanding advertisements. My students are so gullible! I have had the hardest time getting them to see past the hype to consider the facts. Finally I decided to require them to rewrite a number of newspaper, magazine, and radio ads, eliminating everything that is not factual information. Then, we talked about making purchasing decisions solely on the factual version of the ad. Most of the time, they realized that they were no longer interested in making the purchase. But some seem to resent their new understanding. Ken and Allison both said that it was more fun to be convinced to buy something than to be so analytical! Maybe when they're earning their own money, they'll feel differently.

Direct Experience

Our first major biology unit has been The Cell. When the students came into the room on the first day of that unit, they found the seven lab tables prepared for seven groups of students. At each table was a scalpel, some forceps, an onion, several glass slides, two eyedroppers, some toothpicks, staining solution, and a microscope. The students followed the directions I had passed out to them, a dittoed sheet that told them to look at a layer of onion tissue and some scrapings from the inside of their cheeks under the microscope. In each case, they looked at the materials both before and after staining them. I explained to them that they were seeing cells—the basic unit of all living things except viruses. Their lab manual contained a drawing of a cheek cell and an onion cell and they were required to find the various parts of these drawn and labeled cells in the real cells they were viewing. I then distributed a set of questions that led them to compare the cells in the onion layer with those from inside their cheeks. Thus I focused their attention on some differences between plant and animal cells.

Writing   Students were also assigned the part of the textbook that described the development of cell theory by various scientists. Their purpose for reading was to write a one-paragraph summary of the major contribution of each scientist. The next day, I selected names at random and had those students read paragraphs they had written about various scientists.

I then reminded them of the difference between functions and structures and explained that the chapter they were going to read next described the functions and structures of the cell. I showed them the graphic organizer in Figure 12.2.

Their purpose for reading then was to fill in the graphic organizer on paper while they read. The text described functions and structures in a clear and literal fashion, but to understand the particular links between functions and structures required careful reading. I was convinced that this assignment would require students to process more deeply the concepts I considered most important than just telling them to read the chapter would do.

The next day, the students came in and I took up their completed diagrams. With their books closed, they then suggested how to fill in the diagram I had on the board. I did not correct any of their suggestions, just kept them on task and facilitated consensus when they got bogged down. When they had achieved consensus on a completed diagram, we opened our books and made corrections together. Finally, we ended up with a correct diagram.

For the remainder of this unit, I will use a combination of lectures, experiments and demonstrations, and content comprehension minilessons like the one in Figure 12.2 to teach the students about various types of cells. We are making extensive use of the microscopes with both preprepared slides and

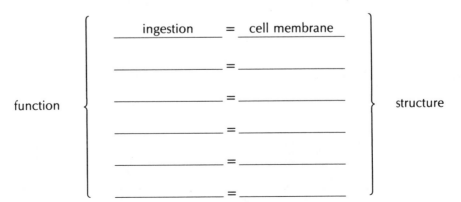

FIGURE 12.2   Graphic Organizer

Direct
Experience
slides that we prepare ourselves. We are also making a detailed study of the structures and subfunctions that permit each function of the cell. And we are examining the similarities and differences among plant cells, animal cells, and protists.

N O V E M B E R

Assessment
In biology, we finished our unit on the cell during the first part of the month. By the end of the unit, most students could label the various structures in a drawing of a cell and could write a brief explanation of the function of that structure in various types of cells. The difference between the most and the least successful students was in their understanding of the cell's more complex structures and functions. The range between my top and bottom students is as great as it has been in the past, but the amount learned by the bottom students is far ahead of any year I've ever taught. These methods seem to be working well. My emphasis on main ideas seems

Web
to facilitate the learning of facts and details. The quality of student questions is higher than ever before and they appear much more interested in biology, perhaps because they can always relate what they're learning to the basic structure of the discipline.

Graphic
Organizer
Following the unit on the cell, I created a new bulletin board with a new diagram (see Figure 12.3). I explained to the students that they were now ready to study the structures and functions of the various kinds of plants,

Animals	Plants	Protists
Invertebrates		
Sponges	Algae	Diatoms
Coelenterates	Fungi	Protozoans
Worms	Mosses and liverworts	Bacteria
Echinoderms	Ferns	Viruses
Mollusks	Cone-bearing plants	
Crustaceans	Flowering plants	
Arachnids		
Myriapods		
Insects		
Vertebrates		
Fish		
Amphibians		
Reptiles		
Birds		
Mammals		
Nonhumans		
Humans		

FIGURE 12.3 Living Things

animals, and protists. I showed them the diagram and told them the order in which we would investigate these various forms of life during the rest of the year.

Research   I have decided that I want my students to be able to do library research in biology—a basic skill that all biologists certainly need. Moreover, anyone with questions needs to know how to find accurate answers to them efficiently. Consequently, I developed an approach that requires library research and does not allow mere copying from sources. I gave students a mimeographed copy of the following list:

Fields Related to Biology

Anatomy	Eugenics	Microbiology
Bacteriology	Exobiology	Molecular biology
Biochemistry	Genetics	Morphology
Biophysics	Gnotobiotics	Paleontology
Botany	Heredity	Pathology
Crybiology	Histology	Phenology
Cytology	Limnology	Physiology
Ecology	Marine biology	Taxidermy
Embryology	Medicine	Zoology

Writing Minilesson   I then wrote the words *compare* and *contrast* on the board and asked them about those words. They generally manifested a good understanding of the two terms. I told them that we as a class were going to write a short composition on the board, "comparing and contrasting botany and zoology." They were given three minutes to try to write the first sentence and to list any details they thought should be included individually. When this brief planning time ended, I took the chalk and stood at the board. "Who has a particularly good first sentence for our composition?"

Allison volunteered that first sentence and I wrote it down as it was dictated to me: "Botany and zoology are both fields of biology."

I then led them to give me sentences comparing what they knew about botany and zoology with what we had already learned. Thus we gradually completed our group composition. My role was only to require consensus and to remind them of the task as often as necessary. Through creating a group composition, every student came to understand what a compare and contrast paper is. I reminded them of the list I had given them and told them to select two fields on which to write a compare and contrast composition based on library research. One week later, after some preliminary library research, they submitted their pairs of fields to me for my approval. The compare and contrast papers themselves were due one week after that.

Concept Development   Since I recently read C. Santa and D. Alvermann's *Science Learning: Processes and Applications*, I have also become more aware of several problems with my students' reading of our biology textbook. This book stresses the difficulty of getting students to read (or listen) for conceptual change in science. Apparently, most students in science are just trying to get the assignment completed satisfactorily rather than really trying to learn what is being taught. This leads to the persistence of misconceptions even after reading or hearing information that should have cleared them up!

Chapter 6 in this book, by K. Roth, used the illustration of how students' misconceptions of photosynthesis continued even after their study of that process was completed. Since we were studying photosynthesis this month anyway, I decided to see if my students were like the ones Roth had examined. Boy, were they!

When I asked my students on the test to write an essay on how plants get their food, almost all of them mentioned from the soil or the air or both, even though the book stated clearly that plants manufacture their own food through the process of photosynthesis. This was so, even for most of the students who otherwise correctly defined terms and completed short-answer questions. It became obvious to me that the students were often just memorizing information rather than using that information to revise their knowledge and understanding. They had come to the study of biology with their own theory of how plants get food, and they seemed destined to leave biology with some additional terms and facts but the same incorrect theory intact.

Comprehension Minilesson

I developed a simple and straightforward approach to helping students realize that their preconceived notions may be incorrect. I asked them the same questions in advance of reading that I wanted them to be able to answer after reading. They answered them individually in writing both times. I then led them through the book-based answers to the questions by showing them in the book exactly how the answers were presented. I then had them compare their postreading answers with both their prereading answers and the book-based answers. It was a revelation to many of them. "Why, I just answered the questions the same way both times!" admitted Sarah. "I thought that was what the book was saying, too, but it wasn't."

Thinking Processes— Evaluate

Ambrose angrily asked me if I was trying to brainwash them! His insolent but important question helped me realize that critical reading is also required when reading or listening for conceptual change. We certainly don't want to disregard everything we think just because a book contradicts it. I explained to Ambrose and the class that I would require them to know what the book was saying, not that they agree with it.

Comprehension Minilesson

This process of comparing their own ideas before reading with the ideas of the text in an objective fashion has really helped my students' comprehension of the text. Only a few students still persist in reading their own notions into the text, and they are making some progress.

Word Problems

In consumer math this month, I have really worked hard on helping my students with word problems. I have consistently used two approaches to improve students' ability to read the problems. First, I have tried to get them to transfer their ability to interpret word problems that they hear to their own reading, as I alternate between having them hear a problem and having them read one. I read the first problem to them and give them time to solve it. All pencils are put down and then a student who I see has it right goes to the board and works that problem. We briefly discuss why it was worked that way. Then students read the next problem to themselves and work it. Again I choose a student to work it correctly on the board. We discuss why that problem was worked that way. The method seems simple, but students do better on the third or fourth independent problem than they did on the first. I believe they will continue to improve.

I also use an overhead projector so that I can uncover a word problem one clause at a time as we try to solve it as a group. The goal is to solve the problem by seeing as little of the problem as possible. Everyone has to explain any suggestion he or she makes. The students are getting good at using all the information in each word in the problem.

The major factor in integrating skills to solve word problems seems to be lots of successful practice. Unfortunately, that means that only those students for whom word problem solving is already easy can learn to do it well (the rich get richer!). So I have employed two means for providing students with successful practice. First, I have procured math textbooks and workbooks from grades four through eight and have selected consumer-oriented word problems from them. I duplicated these problems on mimeographed copies

Homework to give out to my students. They make perfect homework assignments because the students can work them successfully and are therefore less likely to "practice their ignorance." I made the mistake of telling Mr. Burr that I was doing this. (He teaches all the other sections of consumer math.) He told me that the students wouldn't do their homework unless it was challenging for them. Rather than arguing with him, I just tried my idea. The proportion of students doing their homework has actually increased since I initiated this practice. I do not understand why we think our top students should perform tasks that they can do well while our bottom students must be given tasks that are nearly impossible for them.

The second thing I did was periodically to assign students to work five

Word Problems problems in class that they have previously solved. This time, however, I place them under a tight time limit. They must both get the answer right and show all their work to get credit for a problem. I determine their daily grade based on the time they take:

Daily
Grade *Time*
A = 2 minutes
B = 3 minutes
C = 4 minutes

Missing even one problem because of a careless mistake results in a daily grade of D, regardless of time spent. At the end of each amount of time, students who are finished put down their pencils and turn their papers over. I spend the next minute walking around and writing the number of minutes on the back of each turned-over paper.

This system has really cut down on carelessness, a major problem these students have with word problems. And I am seeing an overall improvement in both their success and their attitude toward word problems. At least now when they miss a word problem, it is usually because of their computation or problem interpretation rather than their reading or integration.

D E C E M B E R

Biology is supposed to be the study of life. This month, I thought it was the study of words! My efforts this year to combine the process and the traditional approach have been largely successful, but I have still been concerned about how little some students were learning. Students like Lonnie, Theresa, and Ambrose failed the first nine weeks in spite of all my efforts.

Professional Growth

Right after Thanksgiving, I went to an all-day content area reading workshop sponsored by the regional education center. These things are usually a waste of time but I had heard that Dr. Wurdz, the presenter, was quite practical, so I decided to give it a whirl. Am I glad I did! He spent all day

Meaning Vocabulary

convincing us that it is the onslaught of new vocabulary that hurts most students in content areas and he targeted the sciences as being particularly at fault. He gave us several passages to read from high-level statistics and management textbooks, and none of us could understand a thing we read. It became perfectly clear to me that if you don't have immediate access to the meanings of important words, comprehension of a passage is downright impossible!

Dr. Wurdz also showed us that there are two kinds of vocabulary words: the easy ones to teach and the toughies. The easy words are those for which kids already know the meaning but not the word that represents the meaning. His example was the word *obstreperous*. Many students don't know what the word means, but every one of them can practice the concept! The toughies are words for which students lack both the word and the meaning. Of course, of all the disciplines, science is the most plagued by terms with which students have absolutely no experience.

During the workshop, we had to look at a chapter in our textbook to divide the new words into those for which students probably lacked only the word and those for which they probably lacked both word and meaning. The list for one chapter in my text had thirty-two words—of which twenty-four were the tough kind! Then he told us that research showed you can effectively teach only ten tough words per week! Ten! Most of my chapters have twenty-five to thirty-five words, and I certainly can't spend three or four weeks on every chapter. Fortunately, he gave us some rules for getting our list down to the sacred number ten. First, he said, eliminate words for which students already have enough meaning. I didn't think the book would list vocabulary to be taught if most students would know it, but I found that my book had many such words. What tenth-grader doesn't know what a blade or a leaflet is? (I wonder who decides on these vocabulary lists? Have they ever seen a tenth-grader?) Next, he said, eliminate very technical terms that most educated adults don't know and that even teachers have to review before the lesson. (How did he know I sometimes had to do that?) These technical terms are defined enough in context for students who can read well to understand them for the moment, and in any case they are not words that anyone remembers. That made sense, although it is hard not to feel guilty about not teaching all these terms. Finally, he said that we needed to read the chapter again to see if any important words had been left off the text's vocabulary list. Once again, he was right. My textbook's list had left out the words *broad-leafed, narrow-leafed,* and *needle-leafed.* Understanding these words was what the chapter was all about!

By following these new guidelines, I am now able to get my list of vocabulary words down to about ten per week. I still don't feel quite right about this, but if my students really learn 360 new biology words in one year, words that they really know and can use, I guess that is not a bad accomplishment. And I realize that my students must have a good command of these words if they are to understand what they read and what I present to them.

Following is the vocabulary list from our textbook's most recent chapter with the additions and deletions I have made based on these new guidelines. Words marked "x" I have totally eliminated from consideration: we won't discuss it, there won't be activities that use it, and it won't be mentioned on any test I give. Bracketed words at the end are those I added to the list. For example, I eliminated *fibrovascular bundle* while adding its more common name, *vein.* Then I marked with an asterisk each word that I planned to emphasize in both teaching and testing, leaving the other words to be learned by students on their own. A common word, *leaf,* remained in the list because of the precision of its definition in the chapter.

* abscission	* [broad-leafed plant]	* [compound leaf]
sheath	* [narrow-leafed plant]	* [simple leaf]
cuticle	* [needle-leafed plant]	x bundle
x fibrovascular bundle	blade	* epidermis
x insectivorous plant	epidermal hair	x guttation
* mesophyll	guard cell	leaflet
petiole	leaf	palmate leaf
fiber	palisade mesophyll	x sclerenchyma
sessile leaf	pinnate leaf	spongy
mesophyll	x spine	x succulent leaf
stipule	stoma	* venation
x tendril	x transpiration	* [vein]

Direct Experience   Once I have selected the words I am going to teach, I must be sure to focus on those words. Students have no concept for many of these words. Fortunately, the laboratory part of our course provides them with the real thing on a regular basis. I see now that one reason my dual-emphasis program is effective is that the laboratory part provides the direct experiences for many new terms. If I don't have the resources or time to develop a concept adequately through direct laboratory experience, I make sure to provide some visual experience for it. This is not too difficult since we have some good films, videos, film loops, and slides in our media center, with more available from our regional education center.

I have also been using the visuals in our textbook more systematically. Dr. Wurdz suggested that many students simply ignore all photographs, charts, and diagrams in their textbooks. He challenged us to assign some in-class reading and watch what the students did with their eyes as they came to the visuals. Sure enough, many of my poorest students read the text, glanced at a wonderful half-page diagram and continued reading. I could not stand the thought that the students who most needed to build the concepts provided by the visuals in the text were largely ignoring these visuals. I now do a quick, five-minute, visuals-only introduction to each chapter. I give the students exactly five minutes to look at the visuals and any captions under them and to write down everything they can learn from the visuals only. At the end of the five minutes, we go around the room and each person gives me one thing to write on the board until all the information is exhausted (as am I!). I then direct their attention to the information on the board that I consider crucial and ask, "Where in the text did you get this piece of information?" We all look at that visual and discuss it. It is amazing to me how naive my students are in understanding diagrams and charts. After all these years in school, I just assumed they had picked up this skill, but many just don't know how to learn from a visual. They will by the time they leave my class!

I have had the students begin a vocabulary notebook. This is a bit old-fashioned, but I wanted to be sure to focus my attention as well as the students' on the vocabulary, and with so much to do, I was afraid I might lose track of this component. Whenever I begin a new chapter, I put the ten or so selected words on the small bulletin board in the corner and have the students write them in a notebook reserved for vocabulary. The notebook is divided with five pages for each letter of the alphabet and the words are usually entered four words to each page. We enter only the words on the first day of each unit, then fill in the meanings as we do the activities that build meaning for the words. Eventually, for every word, we have written a personal example and a sentence that defines the word. I do not allow them to copy dictionary definitions but sometimes we look up the word to help us formulate our own examples and sentences. We may add whatever we need to make the word clear and easy to remember. If the word is hard to pronounce, we put a phonetic pronunciation next to it. If the word can be illustrated or diagrammed, we do so. If the word has a common morpheme, we highlight it and note its meaning. So far, we have been doing these vocabulary entries together, but once the students learn what I expect, I plan to assign the actual writing as homework after I have provided the in-class experience to build meaning. Here are some entries for a few of our words from this month:

> **abscission** (ab si shun)—Example: When a leaf falls off a tree in the fall. *Sentence*: Abscission occurs when any leaf falls off of any plant at any time of the year for any reason.

venation—Example: The hard little tubes you can feel with your fingers when you hold a leaf.

Sentence: Venation is the arrangement of veins in leaves and is used to identify from which plant a leaf has come.

Root word: Vein

Assessment   I give a weekly vocabulary test on these words, making the test cumulative across all words entered in the notebook so far. This is tough on the kids, but we often do some quickie review activities during the last few minutes of each period. Some students are finding that if they study, they can do very well on these tests, which helps their grade since the average vocabulary grade equals one big test grade each quarter. Even Ambrose did well on my last vocabulary test.

Meaning Vocabulary   Having become so attuned to vocabulary problems in biology, I couldn't help but notice that my consumer math class's comprehension was also hampered by a lack of technical vocabulary. We are studying taxes (yuk!), and I discovered that students were not clear about the meaning of words like *exemptions* and *withholding*. Some students didn't get back money due to them because they couldn't figure out all that gobbledegook on the tax form. I have made a list of crucial tax words and we are working through some realistic student-job tax situations so that they understand what these terms mean. Imagine letting the government keep your money because you couldn't understand the silly form!

J A N U A R Y

Well, we are halfway through the year, and while far from satisfied with everything, I am more content than I have ever been with my teaching. Semester grades were better, too. I have a new grading system that gives stu-

Assessment   dents points for effort on their in-class and homework assignments, which I don't grade but simply initial if they appear to demonstrate a good effort. Students must also fix anything that was not right after we go over the work in class, and I require them to turn in their notebook with these initialed and self-corrected assignments. I take a quick glance to see that everything was fixed and again give points toward the final grade. Students also get points for good effort on their laboratory work.

Of course, I have grades from our weekly vocabulary tests—which have gotten better each week—as well as chapter and unit test grades. About 80 percent of these test questions are concerned with the most important information, which we have gone over in class and everyone should have learned. The other 20 percent comes from reading assignments, which are not completely covered in class.

I had only three D's in this biology section and only one in consumer math! I believe that all my students are making more of an effort because they see

Research   that their effort pays off. This coming semester, I am going to assign some projects whereby students can extend their knowledge beyond what we are learning in class. It worries me that while students seem less frustrated and a little more motivated, they are not exactly turned on to my subject. I realize that I used to read a lot of books and magazines about biology and famous biologists and I think that is how I became so engrossed in this topic. So I plan to have my students research famous biologists next month and then we will find some way (entertaining, I hope) of sharing what they learn.

I am continuing to stress meaning vocabulary and to teach comprehension minilessons on textbook material. This month I did several comprehension minilessons using a feature matrix to guide student reading. This seems to work particularly well in biology, where so much material is a description of different members of a classification and the features that make each distinct. The students enjoy predicting, before they read, where the pluses and minuses will go and their comprehension seems to be much better when they have something specific to look for. Usually, I have them copy the feature matrix from my transparency and fill in their guesses in class; then they read the chapter to fill in and correct their matrix for homework. When they come to class, they take out their matrix and I quickly initial those that show a good effort. Then together we fill in my matrix on the transparency, as they show thumbs up for a plus and thumbs down for a minus. As long as there is consensus, we move right through it. When some thumbs are up and some are down, I know that comprehension has broken down and leave that space blank. We then reread the part of the textbook that discusses the point and resolve our disagreement. The students keep the corrected feature matrices in their notebooks and even claim to study them before my tests! This is a very efficient way of organizing a lot of information and helps students who are not good notetakers to keep their information in an organized fashion. See Figure 12.4 for one of the feature matrices I used this month.

Comprehension Minilesson

Review

I have used a new review strategy this month that works quite well. It is called Three to a Customer. You ask the students to write down three things they remember about your topic, limiting them to two minutes. Then you call on different students to tell just one thing each. The goal is to see how many different things the class as a whole can remember. We keep score on a little chart and the competition seems to appeal to them. The first time we did it, they remembered a total of eighteen items, which I recorded. The next time, they remembered twenty-five. This Monday I said, "Let's make sure your brains have not totally atrophied over the weekend. Take out a sheet of paper. You have two minutes to write three things you remember about arthropods." And I heard Rod say, "Twenty-five is the number to beat!" Sure enough, they had a total of twenty-seven different things written down. Now they try hard to remember something unusual or trivial in order to accumulate a large total. A little friendly competition with themselves seems to add to their motivation!

Thinking Processes— Apply

We even had fun in consumer math this month. I am a *Consumer Reports* devotee and as I was looking through their ratings of microwave ovens I realized this was a perfect periodical for my math kids. I found the annual car issue and after leading my kids in a general discussion of which cars they

Feature Matrix

Features/ Examples	Crustaceans	Myriapods	Arachnids	Insects
Jointed Legs	+	+	+	+
Segmented Bodies	+	+	+	+
Hard Exoskeleton	+	+	+	+
Gills	+	−	−	−
Three pairs of legs	−	−	−	+
Four pairs of legs	−	−	+	−
Antennae	+	+	−	+
Trachae	−	+	+	+
Crabs	+	−	−	−
Centipedes	−	+	−	−
Spiders	−	−	+	+
Termites	−	−	−	+
Shrimp	+	−	−	−
Grasshoppers	−	−	−	+
Millipedes	−	+	−	−
Ticks	−	−	+	−

FIGURE 12.4 Arthropods

loved and wanted to own (a very hot topic for tenth-graders), I pulled out *Consumer Reports*. I asked them to write down their dream car, how much they thought it would cost, how much they would have to pay for it each month if they borrowed 90 percent at 12 percent interest for four years, and what its mile-per-gallon rating, repair record, and crash test ratings were. Then I paired them up with copies of the article and had them work out the real figures! Such a bunch of shocked, disheartened kids you have never seen. Even Ken was momentarily taken aback, until finally he said, "Well, I'll just have to make my first million faster!"

Only Allison was unconcerned. "My father is buying me a Jaguar on my next birthday," she smirked.

F E B R U A R Y

Content Area Literature

February was famous biologist month! When I was a teenager, I loved biology, and it has always bothered me that *loved* is hardly the correct verb to describe my teens' reactions to the subject. As I was considering how I came to love biology, I remembered that I got a junior science set for my tenth birthday and that I was always collecting plant and insect specimens and performing various experiments on them. We got *National Geographic* and

Smithsonian magazines, and they often had fascinating articles on various plant and animal life forms. Mr. Lively, who lived three doors down from us, was a biomedical engineer, and while I wasn't quite sure what a biomedical engineer did, it sure sounded fascinating. In addition, I became interested in biographies, particularly biographies of famous scientists. I read every one I could get my hands on and discovered that these scientists had led very interesting lives. In addition to their important discoveries, many of them were adventurous, courageous people. After reflecting on the development of my love affair with biology, I realized that it had much to do with real things and real people and little to do with biology textbooks and lab reports! I decided to try three ways to develop in my students the fascination I felt when I was their age. The first was the study of famous biologists that we did this month. In the coming months, I have planned to have them design and carry out a real experiment of their own, and to deal with some of the career options available to people with training in biology.

Research   I decided that each student would research a famous biologist. I came up with a list of thirty and wrote their names on index cards. Each student would draw a card for his or her assignment. I knew the kids would rather pick their own, but with the exception of Charles Darwin, Louis Pasteur, and Rachel Carson, most students would not have heard of any of these scientists. I did tell the kids they could try to get someone to swap with them.

Deciding how to have the students share what they learned was a difficult task. I remembered the term papers I had to write, and the oral reports I had to stand up and give with my knees knocking and my voice breaking. Somehow I knew that these traditional methods of reporting did nothing to promote attitudes of excitement! I worried for several days and then found the answer in the letter announcing my tenth-year high-school reunion. "At least I won't get any prizes," I chuckled, as I remembered the awards for "parent of the most kids" and "traveled farthest" that are usual at these affairs. Then I realized that I might just have found the gimmick to get my kids excited about their biologists.

After I explained to their skeptical looks that each person was to become an expert on one biologist, I told them that we would give prizes for these biologists' various accomplishments. I asked them to help me think of some awards we could give and suggested that we include demographic data, such as who had lived the longest, as well as more subjective data, such as who had made the biological discovery of greatest importance. I wrote these two things on the board and asked them to brainstorm other possible awards. They were slow to start but once they got started, you couldn't stop them. Here is the list we finally made from the students' brainstorming:

Most Ancient (one born longest ago)

Most Recent

Oldest

Youngest

Most Married (Most husbands or wives!) [Lonnie suggested this one]

Most Blessed (Most children) [Ken was serious; I tried not to laugh]

Tallest

Shortest

Heaviest

Richest

Most Degrees Earned

Most Important Biological Discovery

Most Adventurous Life

Most Interesting Life

Most Tragic Life

Best Biologist (Life-long contribution)

Once the list was made, I turned the awards into questions. I put these on dittos and left room for the students to write their answers. For the subjective awards, the questions were worded as follows: "What did your scientist do that qualifies him or her for the Most Adventurous Life award?" Students were asked to write answers to all demographic questions, plus a sentence or two for any nominations they wanted to make. Ambrose asked if that meant they didn't have to write anything if they didn't want to nominate their scientist for any of the subjective awards. "You must nominate for at least one," was my exasperated response. I asked them to use three or more sources of research to list and number these sources, and to attach this list to the dittoed sheets. Then they only needed to write down the number of the source next to each question they answered. If the information was found in more than one source, they only needed to list one source but could include more.

Students had two weeks to complete their library research. I asked them to keep secret what they found out so that the awards would be a surprise for everyone. They were not very enthusiastic to begin with, but as awards day grew closer, I heard people saying things like, "I've got the Most Adventurous Life sewed up!"

For the demographic awards, we went down the list and each student who thought his or her scientist was in contention gave the data required. These awards were granted automatically. For the more subjective awards, students had one minute to nominate their candidate and to argue that he or she deserved the award. All the students then voted. In some cases, I believe they were voting for the popularity of the student researcher rather than for the merit of the biologist but, all in all, they enjoyed it. Most importantly, they learned that biologists are real people, many of whom lead fascinating lives. Mission accomplished.

Study Strategies   In consumer math, I have been using an idea that I gained from M. Birken. I have students use 3-inch by 5-inch index cards to develop a deck of review cards for a math test. For each different type of homework problem, the student generates one card. On the front of the card is a sample problem. On the back, the student writes the name of that type of problem and a step-by-step procedure for solving it. I require them to add to the deck each day by having them hold up the new cards until I see them all. At test time, the deck can be used as flash cards for studying. I required my students to use them in an in-class study session we had to get them in the habit. It has been very successful for several of the students who were having trouble remembering algorithms. I have also had particular students develop cards for types of problems they should already know how to work from previous years in school but don't.

I shared this strategy with some of my fellow math teachers. Hiram Hath, who teaches Algebra II, told me he has insisted that his students who are struggling use it and it is helping them.

M A R C H

Fading to Independence

My two greatest accomplishments this month were both in the cause of independence. I am pleased with how much better my students are learning and with their improved motivation, but I do feel that I am spoon-feeding them a bit too much. I decided to try to equip them with some strategies they could use to become more independent learners. I told them that they would not always have good old Miss Mull to identify vocabulary and help them summarize and review their work. (I didn't tell them that if they took Chemistry next year, they would have good old Mrs. "Some got it and some don't" Hardy!)

Meaning Vocabulary

For vocabulary, I first showed them how I selected the ten words. (Don't tell Dr. Wurdz, but sometimes I just have to have eleven or twelve. This is compensated for by the one time I had only nine!) We took the list for the last chapter and I showed them how I first eliminate those words they already know. (Judy made a disparaging remark about the people who made that vocabulary list not knowing anything about how much tenth-graders knew. I ignored it but thought, "Smart kid!") Then I showed them how I eliminated very technical terms. This was hard for my students because all the words looked technical to them, but we decided that if a term only occurred once or twice, was defined by the context, and was a very picky detail, it could be eliminated. Getting them to see that there were some words they needed to add was harder. "Aren't there enough already?" Ambrose asked. I had them read the introduction and summary for each chapter, however, to find the chapter's key words. Most saw that these words had to be added to the list. Once we did this, we still often had more than ten or twelve, so we eliminated a few more picky terms—those used in only one small part of the chapter—and got the final list.

I had shown them all this for last week's chapter. This week I paired them up with their lab partners and had them go through it all again for this week's chapter. I gave them ten minutes to work and then put the words suggested by the pairs on the board. There was general agreement on most words (Thank goodness!) and of course some overlap on the close calls. All in all, I thought they did a good job of deciding what the important vocabulary was. I then had them write these words on the appropriate vocabulary notebook pages as we have since December, and I led them to complete these entries with personal examples, sentence definitions, and whatever else was helpful.

After three weeks of having the students pick the words, I decided it was time for them to decide on their own vocabulary entries. After the words were picked, I assigned each pair of students one word (two pairs overlapped) and had them decide what to write for that vocabulary entry. I encouraged them to use their textbook and classroom reference books. I instructed them to provide their own personal examples to serve as models for everyone else, and a definitional sentence that gave the crucial information. I reminded them that we included phonetic spelling when the word had a tricky pronunciation, illustrations or diagrams when possible, and morphemic information when helpful. I then gave each pair a transparency on which to write the notebook entry they thought everyone should use. They did a very good job, and I intend to continue this paired working during April. In May, I will have the students come up with notebook entries on their own.

Writing   The other strategy for promoting independence is five-minute summary writing. At the end of class a couple of times a week, I reserve five minutes for them to summarize in their notebooks the major things they learned that day. We did a few of these as group summaries so that they would get the idea, then I turned them loose. At the beginning of the next class, I picked two students to read their summaries as a review of what we have learned. The students are not exactly wild about this writing, but they are getting better at it. I intend to suggest that they take five minutes to write summaries at the end of other classes even when it is not assigned so that they will have something to review. There is usually some dead time at the end of most classes—but not mine! I wonder how many will write summaries if not forced to. Oh well, if only two or three learn to use this strategy, that is two or three more than would have if I hadn't taught them!

A   P   R   I   L

Content Journals   I have benefited so much from keeping this journal! It occurred to me that my students might also benefit from keeping one. I knew it was risky, so I decided to do it with just one class for the rest of this year to see how it goes. My consumer math students were elected. They have been keeping their content journals now for only a month, but it seems to be catching on. All I require is for them to write a minimum amount each day about what they think of what we are studying and how well they think they are understanding it. At first, they groaned, and I had to discipline them into cooperating. Now the groaning has almost completely subsided. I get more and better questions from them. Reading them has helped me plan better activities and assignments also. I take six or seven home every night and read them *without* a pen in my hand. It's like reading that many letters. I just write a personal response of two or three sentences at the end of each one after I finish it. I'm finding out where confusion remains and where I should move on because they have it and are getting bored. I'm going to start reading them less often and see if they will continue to write as much.

While my students continued to learn new content in biology this month (we were just beginning our study of human biology), I also emphasized application of the content they had already learned. In April I tried to move them into seeing themselves as potential biological scientists. Most of our experiments and demonstrations have been more or less prescribed. While the hands-on biology we did certainly improved learning and attitudes, the students have rarely participated in actually designing experiments to investigate hypotheses that interest them. They had been studying biology without learning how to be biologists!

Knowing how difficult this assignment would be, I began April by telling the students to conduct and report on an original experiment investigating a particular hypothesis. Then I began the process of teaching them how to do the assignment.

First, they needed to understand what a hypothesis is and where one comes from. After a brief discussion, I saw why scientists like Edison have always emphasized "perspiration" over "inspiration" when explaining their achievements. My students certainly attributed much to scientific inspiration. Most seemed to think that ideas just "popped into biologists' heads." I told them that scientists are no different than other curious and observant people. Imagine, I explained, that a person was watering some house plants some years ago and a child asked why plants have to be watered. The adult could simply have said, "Because they will die if they are not watered."

Children being persistent, however, the child might have asked, "Why will they die without water?"

Then the adult might have explained to the child why he or she needs water and that plants need water for similar reasons. So far the adult is answering the child's questions based on the adult's general knowledge. But what if the child than asked, "After I drink water, it goes out when I use the bathroom. What do plants do with the water after they drink it?"

The adult, after thinking a moment, might have said, "I don't know. That is a very good question. Let's find out."

Imagine, then, that the adult looked in various books to find the answer and discovered that the answer was not available. Let's say that the adult thought and thought about what might happen to the water and finally guessed that the water might be given off into the air from the leaves, like sweating. Then let's say that the adult designed an experiment to see if leaves give off water into the air and found out that they do.

After this explanation, I asked them to help me to use it as an illustration. Any curious and observant person, even a child, has questions about living things and how they function, I explained. Then I tried to convince them that all scientific investigation begins with a question about something.

[margin note: Thinking Processes— Apply]

[margin note: Research]

Furthermore, I explained that adults are different from children only because, by going to school, they have learned the answers to certain common questions that curious and observant people have. They do not have to be constantly confused by the world in which they live, but instead can look around them and realize that they have a certain degree of understanding of their environment. This, I said, is the major reason that everyone is required to study science in school.

At this point, I explained why it is important that people learn how to use libraries and other sources of information so that they can learn answers to questions that they do not remember or never learned. So far, so good.

But, I asked them, what happens when you ask a question whose answer you cannot find? You must try to develop your own answer by thinking about what you know. The answer you come up with is called a *hypothesis*.

At this point, I wrote on the board:

hypothesis—A possible answer to a previously unanswered question.

I gave the students the opportunity to come up with hypotheses that some scientist had once developed about the same material we had studied in biology up to that point. We discussed each one, focusing the question and finding the precise wording for a possible answer. Each of these possible answers we labeled as having once been a hypothesis.

Ambrose raised an important question during these discussions, "How do you know which questions have already been answered?"

I referred him back to our previous discussion of the adult and child and showed him that there are only two ways: Either know an area of biology so well that you know what is known and what is not or go to the library and do research until you are convinced that you are now aware of what is and isn't known.

"So that's why biologists have to go to graduate school!" remarked Terry. I strongly supported that comment.

"But we haven't been to graduate school yet!" said Ambrose in his "I'm just-about-to-give-up" voice.

"No," I agreed, "but actually that will make it easier for you. You see, we really won't be able to answer questions that haven't yet been answered about biology. You don't and even I don't have the knowledge or equipment necessary to do new research in biology. You do have a lot of questions, however, that *you* don't have answers to. You've been asking me such questions all year! It is those questions for which you will develop first hypotheses, then experiments. Besides, even famous scientists replicate experiments in order to check results."

Students Asking Researchable Questions

I had gone through the units we had studied and chosen those that could be investigated by the students. I reminded them of a unit and asked them to think of important questions they still had. We listed these on the board. Through a process of brainstorming and selection, we developed quite a list of questions across the several units I had chosen. Each student then picked a question for which he or she had to think of a possible answer (hypothesis) that could be investigated by a simple experiment.

We then went back to the story of the adult and child. As a group, we planned an experiment to determine whether plant leaves give off the water that the plant has taken in. I insisted that they design the experiment themselves. I kept them on task only by making them vote on decisions instead of endlessly arguing about them. They had to see any weaknesses themselves and try to repair them. Once they had the basic design of the experiment, I then gave my suggestions for improvements. I am very proud of them. They were able to figure out that they had to have some way to water the plant without getting water into the air at the same time. They had also determined that the air around the plant would have to be contained so that water could not get in from any other source. Finally, they figured out that they had to have a control, a space just like that occupied by the plant, but without a plant in it.

Direct Experience   So we obtained large plastic containers, put water in two of them, and covered them with wax paper. Then we cut a hole in one of the pieces of wax paper and inserted a small plant so that the roots went in the water in the container and the top stuck out above the wax paper. We used petroleum jelly to seal around the base of the plant so that no water could get out of the bottom container. We covered the two bottom containers with two top containers, turned them upside down, and sealed around where they joined with more petroleum jelly. Naturally, it wasn't long before the inside of the top container with the plant in it began to fog up with moisture, but the container without the plant remained dry just as the hypothesis would lead one to predict.

Writing Minilesson   Once we had completed our class investigation, I modeled how to write up the report on a sheet I had made up for this purpose. I also had several students find books that described similar investigations, including results against which we could check our own results.

They then started on their individual investigations. I required them to get an approval from me at each of three points. I had to approve of the question each chose to prevent unnecessary duplication and to make sure that it was not too broad. Then I had to approve of the hypothesis that each one developed. I wanted to make sure it was their own hypothesis and not one they had copied from somewhere. And I wanted the hypothesis to be one they could design an experiment to investigate. Whether it was the correct answer to their question or not made no difference to me. Finally, I had to approve the design of their experiments. Here was where I did most of my teaching this month. Reasoning with them and holding conferences about their experiments took a lot of time, but I believe they learned a lot from designing them. They met in small groups to get feedback from one another while I met with individuals. After I approved the design of an experiment, I assigned a day for that student to set up the experiment in the lab. After everything was completed, I required them to report the results of their investigations on a sheet with the following entries:

Writing   Question:
Hypothesis:

Experiment:

Data:

Interpretation:

These reports were shared with their lab partners first and revised based on those comments. I read them to make comments, and they revised them again. Finally, we published these research reports in a class book called "Our Biology Experiments," which we shared with everyone who was interested and some who were not. Our librarian even put a copy in the science section of our library! We ended the month with quite a sense of accomplishment and admiration for biological scientists.

M A Y

Research

May is probably the best month for teaching biology, not just because it is almost the end of the year, but because new life is everywhere and it is impossible not to be excited about life—and its science this month. We have had many things to do this month, so I didn't begin anything new except for their research on careers in biology. This was part of my plan to get them excited about biology. Since the famous biologists' awards had worked so well, I decided to use the same format. I wrote various careers biologists could pursue (nutritionist, teacher, animal husbandry specialist, and microbiologist) on index cards and let each student pick one. We then brainstormed a list of questions in the form of awards. The list again included objective features (highest paid, most job mobility) as well as subjective features (most prestigious, most dangerous). When we had the brainstormed list completed on the board, someone suggested that we have "booby prizes," too. We ended up deciding to try to find out about both the high and the low end for each of the career features.

The students researched the career they had picked (or "gotten stuck with," as Lonnie put it), filling in the information on a dittoed sheet. They noted sources as they had done for the famous biologists project. They had more trouble finding information this time and Paige Turner, the librarian, and I had to help them. We also made some calls to our state employment office and interviewed some people in biological careers.

When the data was compiled, we gave awards and booby prizes in each category. What category of career do you think came up with the lowest pay and was voted to have the lowest prestige? *Teacher* won these two booby prizes hands down, naturally! I was not surprised that teaching was at the bottom, but I was reminded of the enormous salaries many biologists make. It's a good thing that I didn't do this last year when I was at such a low point in my job satisfaction! Rod was very worried about my low salary and prestige, but Allison told him not to worry because I had "chosen" to do this and had my summers completely free!

Writing

After the awards were given, I had each student write a one-paragraph essay indicating which career they would choose if they were to pursue work in biology. They had to state the career choice and at least three reasons why. We made a tally of the various careers chosen and there was a great deal of diversity. Several students told me that they had no idea there were so many interesting and well-paying jobs for biologists and were seriously considering pursuing the career they had selected!

Meaning Vocabulary

Study Strategies

This month, I had students select independently the vocabulary words they thought we needed to learn and write those entries in their notebooks. Most did quite well but I wonder if they will make the effort to do this next year when they are not required to. They have also gotten very good at writing a five-minute summary of the important information learned; I think many of them will continue to do this because they see how useful it is when it comes time to study for a test. They even tell me that writing the summary helps them to sort out what is important and to organize the information. I have certainly found that writing this journal this year has helped me to organize my own thoughts and to reflect upon what is most important.

Meaning Vocabulary

I have continued to work on vocabulary with my consumer math class. I am constantly amazed at how little they understand such common terms as *interest*, *dividends*, and *balance*. I think next year if I teach a section of consumer math, I will start a vocabulary notebook with them at the beginning of the year. I will also use *Consumer Reports* earlier and more frequently. Their interest always piques when I use real-life newspapers and magazines to let them see how crucial is their ability to compute what things cost and where money comes from and goes.

Direct Experience

I did do one new thing in consumer math over the past two months. I had each student study stocks and then select some stock to buy with an imaginary $500. We checked stock prices regularly and charted the growth or decline of our stocks. The students got very excited, almost as if they were actually making or losing that money. Although their money investment wasn't real, the investment of time and energy in choosing and following the stock was, and their motivation to learn about the world of money grew. I just wish I had had five hundred real dollars and had invested them in Rod's stock. The boy is uncannily lucky. His stock split, so he almost doubled his money. My imaginary stock, on the other hand, is now behind $46.40!

J U N E

Well, as Allison said, "She gets the whole summer off!" And thank goodness for that! Even with a good year like this one, I am ready for the change of pace in June. This summer will be a real change of pace. I am once again playing the role of student—complaining about "meaningless assignments" and "boring textbooks."

Professional Growth

I had been toying all spring with the idea of going back to school to pursue graduate work in science education. Once I knew that I found teaching fulfilling and that you could teach even below-average students to understand and appreciate biology, I began to wonder why everyone who taught biology didn't feel this way. I concluded that we ourselves hadn't been taught well, and hadn't been taught how to teach well. Suddenly I wanted to run out and gather up teachers and teachers-to-be and teach them everything that was such a struggle for me to learn. I might never have gotten past the mulling-it-over stage had I not run into Dr. Knowles at a political rally. I was so shocked to see him there—he looked just like he did when I had him for content area reading and writing in my senior year! He even remembered my name and seemed pleased to see someone he knew since he had just moved into town. "I got tired of living in such a small university community," he explained. "I have always liked this little town and have decided that a thirty-minute commute is worth it to live where real people live."

We talked for almost an hour after the meeting. I told him my life history, or at least my teaching history. He was fascinated with how I had realized that I had to provide the students with real experiences with science while simultaneously providing activities in reading, listening, and helping them think the material through. I almost told him about the dream in which he forced me to deal with the two components, but I wasn't quite sure enough of him to share that. I did tell him that I had started keeping a journal as he had suggested and how much it had helped me to reflect upon what I was doing.

After standing and talking on the steps for almost an hour, he began to look impatient. I realized I had been babbling on and that he had probably just been polite. I apologized but he only laughed and said, "I'm not bored—just famished. I came straight from the university to this meeting." We went to my favorite Italian restaurant and I told him even more. (Well, he is such an enthusiastic listener and asked question after question!) Finally, I told him about my frustrations with how teachers were taught. He said, "I know just how you feel and there is only one thing to do about that!" So now I am enrolled in a graduate program—though if I only take courses in summers or in the evenings, I will be old and decrepit before I finish! Some days I commute in with Jer (that's Dr. Knowles's nickname, short for Jerry, and he insists he can't spend an hour in the car with someone who calls him "Dr."!) and that is usually the hour in which I learn the most. He has so many good ideas—I don't remember him being so fascinating when I was in his class. Next year, he is going to come and watch me teach. Horrors! He is even talking about designing an experiment to see if students are learning more content and—as important to both of us—if their attitudes toward biology are improving. It is going to be such a super summer and next year should be even better than last. I must call Mrs. Plante and catch her up on my life. She would love Jer. I think I will invite her and Jer for dinner.

REFERENCES

Ballew, H., & Cunningham, J. W. (1982). Diagnosing strengths and weaknesses of sixth-grade students in solving word problems. *Journal for Research in Mathematics Education, 13,* 202–210.

Birken, M. (1986). Teaching students how to study mathematics. *Mathematics Teacher, 79,* 410–413.

Santa, C. M., & Alvermann, D. E. (Eds.). (1991). *Science learning: Processes and applications.* Newark, DE: International Reading Association.

ADDITIONAL READINGS

The following readings are reports of actual experiences in schools. These accounts cover teachers' and students' experiences with all aspects of the school day; the accounts are not restricted to reading and writing in the content areas. We include these because we believe that you need to know about the realities of working with administrators, other teachers, and groups of students. The following books describe those realities clearly. Although the accounts frequently are critical of public schooling, they are quite informative about the pleasures and the pressures of teaching.

The following description of teaching during the mid-1800s points out how far some aspects of the teaching profession have progressed; it graphically portrays the primitive conditions early American teachers endured:

Woody, T. (1954). Country schoolmaster of long ago. *History of Education Journal, 5,* 41–53.

The following books deal specifically with modern secondary schools. The author of the first book was a university-level researcher who became the confidante of several high school students while attending classes with them. The second book is an edited collection of real teachers' journal entries. Its title comes from the hard-bitten advice sometimes offered to beginning teachers.

Cusick, P. (1973). *Inside high school.* New York: Holt, Rinehart & Winston.

Ryan, K. (Ed.). (1980). *Don't smile until Christmas.* Chicago: University of Chicago Press.

These last books are based on elementary-school experiences. The first is an inspiring account by one teacher of her experiences instructing disadvantaged children through an integrated reading and writing approach. The other two are more jaundiced reports of teachers' concerns about issues such as classroom control and the status of teachers in the community and the school.

Ashton-Warner, S. (1963). *Teacher.* New York: Simon & Schuster.

Eddy, E. M. (1969). *Becoming a teacher.* New York: Teachers College Press.

McPherson, G. (1972). *Small town teacher.* Cambridge, MA: Harvard University Press.

I N D E X